Mel Brooks—Seriously!

ALSO OF INTEREST
AND FROM MCFARLAND

The Good, the Bad and the Ancient: Essays on the Greco-Roman Influence in Westerns (edited by Sue Matheson, 2022)

A Fistful of Icons: Essays on Frontier Fixtures of the American Western (edited by Sue Matheson, 2017)

Mel Brooks—Seriously!

Essays on the Films, Television Shows and Standup

Edited by SUE MATHESON

Afterword by Jeremy Dauber

McFarland & Company, Inc., Publishers
Jefferson, North Carolina

This book has undergone peer review.

LIBRARY OF CONGRESS CATALOGING-IN-PUBLICATION DATA

Names: Matheson, Sue editor | Dauber, Jeremy, 1973– contributor
Title: Mel Brooks--seriously! : essays on the films, television shows and standup / edited by Sue Matheson ; afterword by Jeremy Dauber.
Description: Jefferson : McFarland & Company, Inc., Publishers, 2025. | Includes bibliographical references and index.
Identifiers: LCCN 2025026210 | ISBN 9781476690032 paperback ♾ ISBN 9781476655819 ebook
Subjects: LCSH: Brooks, Mel, 1926—Criticism and interpretation | BISAC: PERFORMING ARTS / Television / Genres / Comedy | PERFORMING ARTS / Film / Genres / Comedy
Classification: LCC PN1998.3.B7596 M45 2025 | DDC 791.4302/33092—dc23/eng/20250611
LC record available at https://lccn.loc.gov/2025026210

ISBN (print) 978-1-4766-9003-2
ISBN (ebook) 978-1-4766-5581-9

© 2025 Sue Matheson. All rights reserved

No part of this book may be reproduced or transmitted in any form or by any means, electronic or mechanical, including photocopying or recording, or by any information storage and retrieval system, without permission in writing from the publisher.

Front cover image: Mel Brooks, circa 1965 (Photofest); *background* © Yarrrrrbright/Shutterstock.

Printed in the United States of America

McFarland & Company, Inc., Publishers
  Box 611, Jefferson, North Carolina 28640
    www.mcfarlandpub.com

In honor of Cyril Harold Goulden and Flora Matheson Goulden

~

For Cindee Laverge

Acknowledgments

I would like to thank Virginia Goulet, Ray Merlock, Kathy Jackson, Cindee Laverge, Heather Smith, Lynette Plett, Harvey Briggs, and Kim Laycock for their encouragement and outstanding support of this project. I must especially thank my editor Layla Milholen for her patience and guidance while I was working on this collection. I am particularly grateful to all the contributors whose enthusiasm, dedication, and hard work brought this collection to life. Most of all, I would like to thank my son Stuart for standing by me while I worked, herding our sheep and training our foster dogs as my work was completed. Like Brooks', his sense of humor was invaluable.

Table of Contents

Acknowledgments   vi

Introduction: Mel Brooks, Tailor Retailored
   Sue Matheson   1

יסודות Foundations

"Totally Crazy" Cabaret: Drag Shows, Song-and-Dance, Parody, and Dark Jewish Humor in the Films of Mel Brooks
   Peter Scott Lederer   18

"He shoulda been called *Yitzhak*": Mel Brooks and the Pleasures of Parody
   Terry Lindvall *and* Chris Lindvall   38

אויסגעקליבן ווערק Selected Works (1965–1991)

Got Smart: Mel Brooks, Ambivalent Parody, and the Cultural Politics of Foolishness
   Kerry Soper   56

Springtime for Strangelove! The Holocaust, Nazism, and Jewishness in the Films of Mel Brooks and Stanley Kubrick
   Nathan Abrams *and* Michael Lipiner   72

Around a Proscenium: Representation and Distance in *The Producers*
   Murray Pomerance   87

Between the *Mensch* and the *Pícaro*: Greed, Deceit, and Friendship in Mel Brooks' *The Twelve Chairs* (1970)
   Ralph Beliveau   96

Brooks, Gogol, and Dali: Surrealism, Simulacra,
   and Simulation in *Blazing Saddles* (1974)
   SUE MATHESON — 108

Parody, Pastiche, and Intertextuality in Mel Brooks'
   Young Frankenstein (1974)
   FRANCES PHEASANT-KELLY — 131

Comedic Film Criticism, Filmed: Mel Brooks' Love of Cinema
   in *Silent Movie* (1976) and *The Critic* (1963)
   MATTHEW CIPA — 146

"The Hitchcock picture to end all Hitchcock pictures":
   Mel Brooks' *High Anxiety* (1977)
   THOMAS GROCHOWSKI — 159

Hitchcock, Brooks, and Pure Cinema
   DOUGLAS C. MACLEOD, JR. — 178

The Court Jester's Tale: *History of the World, Part I* (1981)
   as Epic, Parody, and Epic Parody
   A. BOWDOIN VAN RIPER — 194

Mel Brooks, THE Producer: David Lynch's *The Elephant
   Man* (1980) and David Cronenberg's *The Fly* (1986)
   JONATHAN WINCHELL — 209

A Jewish Future: The Diverse Diasporic Universe
   of *Spaceballs* (1987)
   DAVID L. REZNIK — 224

The Rich Get Richer: *Life Stinks* (1991)
   CYNTHIA J. MILLER — 239

Afterword
   JEREMY DAUBER — 252

A Bibliography on Mel Brooks
   CAMILLE MCCUTCHEON — 253

About the Contributors — 261

Index — 265

Introduction

Mel Brooks, Tailor Retailored

Sue Matheson

In *All About Me!*, Mel Brooks begins with anecdotes about his mother, Kate (née Brookman) Kaminsky—her love for her sons, her love for her family, and her remarkable work ethic. "My mother was a true heroine," he says, "losing her husband when she was only thirty, and then having four little kids to raise without a father. She was busy from morning to night: getting breakfast, washing dishes, doing laundry, scrubbing floors, cooking dinner and finally getting her children to sleep." Brooks' Aunt Sadie, a "floor lady" in a clothing factory on Seventh Avenue, in New York's Garment District, supported her sister's family, giving Kate about a third of her income each week and providing her with the opportunity to earn extra dollars by bringing home some work from her factory. At a very young age, Brooks found what he thought were little diamonds sitting in front his mother on their kitchen table. They were rhinestones which she was attaching to "little tin stars with a hoop on the back so they could be sewn together" (10).

Fast forward to February 1975—on *The Tonight Show*, Brooks is a star in Hollywood, proof of his mother's hard work, an embodiment of America's possibilities, and the hero of his own story. In a superbly tailored, three-piece suit, he is, as Johnny Carson, *The Tonight Show*'s host, says, the most popular man in America, appearing "on the cover of everything." "*Newsweek* magazine, *Time* magazine ... he has a whole interview in *Playboy* magazine," Carson says; "How are you, you mad genius? That's what they call you." Brooks immediately signals he and Carson are performing. "The guts," he says. "You have such guts.... The suit. Everything you wear is so crazy." In a loud checkered jacket, Carson proceeds to support Brook's rags-to-riches story. "You're making a fortune," he protests good-naturedly. "People are queued up all over the country." Immediately,

2 Introduction

Brooks breaks the fourth wall, stopping the show to rib its piano player. "Why don't you wear a tie?" he asks the musician. "You've got people out there!"

Raised in Brooklyn's Garment District, Mel Brooks knows *vestis virum facit*.[1] Born Melvin James Brooks Kaminsky (מעלווין קאמינסקי), he *tumeled* to poolside audiences during the 1930s in Borscht Belt resorts dressed in "a black derby and a big black-alpaca overcoat" (in Darrach). In 1950, he had become a "well-trained maniac": wearing a "white duster and a straw hat," he crashed "a big conference in the RCA Building [interrupting all] the big shots. General Sarnoff, the chairman of the board of RCA; Pat Weaver, the president of NBC; Max Liebman and Sid [Caesar]."[2] Brooks wanted to know "would there be a new show? Should I buy a new car?" He jumped on the boardroom's table, yelled, "Hurray! Hurray! Lindy has landed at Le Bourget," skimmed his hat out the window, and "burst into the Marseillais" (in Darrach). Fast forward to February 1984. As the founder of Brooksfilm and a Hollywood mogul, Brooks, tastefully dressed, is being interviewed by Sir Terry Wogan for BBC1. Brooks takes control of their conversation while he and Wogan spar on camera. He upends Wogan's authority, commenting, "I'm not crazy about your tie. I can tell you that right now.… Solid ties have been in for six years now. You know that." When asked what he will do next, Brooks alludes to Diogenes Teufelsdröckh's refashioning of German idealism in Thomas Carlyle's *Sartor Resartus* (1831). "Sartor Resartus" is generally translated as *The Tailor Re-tailored*. Channeling Teufelsdröckh, he tells Wogan, "I'm gonna tailor. I'm gonna get pins and needles, I'm gonna get cloth, and I'm going to cut suits to fit the perfect man." Wogan ignores the reference and offers himself as an ideal model for this project. Point, set, and match went to Brooks.

Brooks, of course, had the advantage during his interview with Wogan. A superb satirist, he had spent his career ridiculing American idealism and Americans' vices, follies, abuses, and shortcomings. His Jewish humor caught Sid Caesar's attention in the Borscht Belt in the 1930s. After the Second World War, Caesar asked him to contribute to the *Admiral Broadway Revue* (NBC and Dumont, January 28 to June 3, 1949), and Brooks obliged, shifting from standup to sketch comedy. He became a writer for *Your Show of Shows* (NBC, 1950–1954), his delivery of type characters re-tailored for Caesar's mainstream audience.

Broadly speaking, Brooks' *métier* has always been social satire, his mode, comedy of manners. Reminiscing in 2004, he reminded BBC1's interviewer Michael Parkinson that the Borscht Belt "was dangerous" for its upwardly mobile customers who were chasing the American Dream. Vacationing at sumptuous resorts in the Catskills, "the Jews would eat a lot of chopped vegetables smothered in sour cream," he said. "They'd eat a lot of it, and then they'd slather heels of pumpernickel with two inches of sweet butter. And they'd eat all that, but that didn't kill them. It didn't hurt them." "They died, but not of that," Brooks told his host. "Then they would sit on the porch after that meal of sour cream, and they'd rock. What killed them was singing 'Dancing in the Dark' in the wrong key." While Parkinson collapsed laughing, Brooks explained, "'Dancing in the Dark' is a very rangy song, and if you sing it like Bing Crosby in 1936, you won't be in trouble. The Jews didn't know this." Demonstrating the hotel guests' demise, Brooks rocked and sang "Dancing in the Dark" in an impossibly high key. "Stroke! Death!" he shouted after hitting the highest note. He observed "there would be this nice, big Gentile kid who would come and take them off the porch" ("Mel Brooks").

For *Your Show of Shows*, Brooks also wrote parodies of "the great foreign films" (in Darrach). In his 1975 interview with Brad Darrach from *Playboy*, he notes it was the arrival of "Rossellini's *Open City*, De Sica's *The Bicycle Thief*, films by Fellini, Bergman, Kurosawa, [and] the French New Wave" that prompted him to make his first two films, *The Producers* (1967) and *The Twelve Chairs* (1970), both outlets for his ethnic humor (in Darrach).[3] In New York, Brooks "hated, hated, *hated* Hollywood" (McGilligan 104) and knew the Dream Factory controlled national identity in "the face of ethnic diversity, class tensions, and the global spread of American culture" (DeCherney 2). He knew "[i]f you were a Jewish intellectual, whose parents had immigrated from Russia, you could like my pictures, but there were hardly any of those in Amarillo, Texas, where you gotta play in one of their three or four theatres or else you're outa luck?" "You gotta break into one of the John Wayne houses," he said, "or you ain't ever gonna break out" (McGilligan 300).

In Hollywood, Brooks merged his talents, parodying films and producing social satire. Laughing at the Hollywood Western, he overturned the American film industry's codified system of middle-class values and sensibilities, deconstructing "institutionalized notions of America's national culture and the idea of American identity" (DeCherney 2). Released on February 7, 1974, *Blazing Saddles* was, as Brooks says, "breakthrough comedy. It carried the audience into territory that film comedy had never entered before" (in Darrach), upending the Hollywood ideal (and the Hollywood Western) by juxtaposing it with America's social and political realities. Gutsy counterculture "designed as an esoteric little picture" (in Darrach), *Blazing Saddles* (1974) was also his first hit. "We wrote it for two weirdos in the balcony. For radicals, film nuts, guys who draw on the washroom wall—my kind of people," Brooks said. "I had no idea middle America would see it. What would a guy who talks about white bread, white Ford station wagons and vanilla milkshakes on Friday night see in that *meshugaas?*"⁴ (in Darrach). But in the 1970s, the American mainstream was full of "weirdos in the balcony"—Gentiles, raised on television variety shows, serial Westerns, and Hollywood classics. Radicalized by the Vietnam War and the Watergate scandal, they knew the Real from the Ideal and understood *Blazing Saddles'* associative logic. *Blazing Saddles* was so popular, Warner Bros. re-released it right after its first run.⁵ Brooks' parody of James Whale's Hollywood classic was also a blockbuster. Released on December 15, 1974, *Young Frankenstein* (1974) grossed $86,273,333 million ("Young Frankenstein"), as Frederick "Fronken-steen" (Gene Wilder) and his Monster (Peter Boyle) burlesqued Fred Astaire, dressed like Gary Cooper in top hats and tails and puttin' on the Ritz.

Attributing his success in Hollywood⁶ to the crossover comedy he wrote for television, Brooks says, "[I]f there was no Sid Caesar, there never would have been a Mel Brooks" (118). According to Brooks, his "finest hour was writing for Sid Caesar as a young comedy writer."⁷ Wide-ranging, the 90-minute *Your Show of Shows* demanded Brooks broaden his skill set. It usually featured a guest host (who played a minor role), at least two production numbers, sketches between Caesar and Coca, the showcase parody of a popular film (for example, "Aggravation Boulevarde" and "From Here to Obscurity"), more sketches (as many as ten per show), Caesar in monologue or pantomime (for instance, being an expectant father in the waiting room or performing the autobiography of a gum-ball machine), and the entire company in a production number. As Larry Gelbart points out in *Caesar's Writers*, television audiences of the 1950s were smarter than those which followed them—in part, because television sets were more expensive when the industry began. "Only the more affluent people bought sets," Gelbart said, "and most of them were better educated." Caesar's audiences recognized and understood the ironies that were sketch staples. Speaking of the comedy and sitcoms that followed, Gelbart remarked the audience was "dumbed down to a great degree" and "the comedy too, so they'll get it" ("Caesar's Writers").

Brooks also wrote for *Caesar's Hour,* which replaced *Your Show of Shows* on NBC in 1954. After *Caesar's Hour* was canceled in 1957, he continued to earn his living by writing for television, film, and Broadway. It was in 1965 that he began to experiment with sustained parody. David Melnick of Talent Associates commissioned Brooks and Buck Henry to co-write *Get Smart*, a sitcom that spoofed the spy drama of the 1960s. Capitalizing on the popularity of James Bond and Inspector Clouseau, Brooks and Henry created a bumbling anti-hero. In an October 15, 1965, *Times* interview, Brooks said, "I was sick of looking at all those nice, sensible situation comedies," he said. "They were such distortions of life. If a maid ever took over my house like *Hazel*, I'd set her hair on fire. I wanted to do a crazy, unreal, comic-strip kind of thing about something besides a family. No one had ever done a show about an idiot before. I decided to be the first" ("Smart Money").[8]

Then the unexpected happened. *Get Smart* was canceled in September 1970. To make matters worse, *The Twelve Chairs*, budgeted at $1.5 million, flopped at the box office. "[T]he roof fell in," Brooks told Darrach. "There I am, strolling around in silk shirts and thinking, I'm cut out for greatness. Television's too small for me. How am I going to get out of this lousy racket? And suddenly I am out of it. The show is off the air. One day it's $5,000 a week, the next day it's zilch. I couldn't get a job anywhere! Comedy shows went out of style and the next five years I averaged $85 a week. Five thousand a week to $85 a week! It was a terrifying nosedive." Brooks knew he needed to recapture mainstream audiences, but this was easier said than done. By 1972, all of his projects, based in New York, had evaporated. He "was practically missing meals and skipping auto payments" (McGilligan 307) when David Begelman, his agent, offered him the opportunity to develop a script called "Tex X" that Warner Bros. had taken an option on—"a Wild West comedy about a hip, militant black sheriff who is hired to uphold the law in a prejudiced frontier town" (McGilligan 308).

Accepting Begelman's offer, Brooks re-tailored his career to become the most unlikely of Hollywood's auteurs. On the crest of the American New Wave, he told Kenneth Tynan, "I can walk into any studio—any one in town—and just say my name and the president will fly out from behind his desk" (McGilligan 359). A new King of Comedy, he was housed "in a big corner office on the third floor of the 20th Century–Fox executive building which he stocked with a black lacquer piano, a large portrait of Leo Tolstoy, and a blow-up label of a 1929 Chateau Lâtour" (McGilligan 359). Continuing the strategy that made *Get Smart* an Emmy-winning hit, Brooks went on, using the studio system to deconstruct the silent movie, Hitchcock classics, Hollywood historical drama, and the Hollywood action picture by doing "what they did except just stretch[ing] it half an inch" (Smith).

Talking to *Playboy*'s Brad Darrach, Brooks also attributes his success to his comedy's vulgarity. Brooks' use of vulgarity has always been controversial—in some cases making, and in others breaking, his career. Reviewing for *Esquire*, John Simon was so offended by the infamous farting scene in *Blazing Saddles*, he wrote, "If this is what makes audiences happiest, all future for the cinema is gone with the wind" (145). In 1974, Roger Ebert also noted that "[a]t its best, [Brooks'] comedy operates in areas so far removed from taste that (to coin his own expression) it rises below vulgarity" ("Blazing Saddles"). Then, a year later, Ebert retracted his opinion, judging *The Producers* and *Blazing Saddles* (the latter he termed "a total mess" a year before) "rare comic anarchy." Reviewing *Young Frankenstein*, Ebert thought Brooks' comedies "weren't just funny, they were aggressive and subversive, making us laugh even when we really should have been offended"; *Young Frankenstein*, he said, demonstrated "artistic growth and a more sure-handed control of the material by a director who once seemed willing to do literally anything for a laugh" ("Young Frankenstein"). Brooks' acceptance in film's critical mainstream continued to grow. In 1974, Andrew Sarris compared Brooks' "intuitive" filmmaking with Woody Allen's "cerebral" approach, finding Brooks "in a strange way … more likeable than Allen": Sarris found Brooks' work, even at its most cynical, spilling over with "emotional generosity … reckless abandon and careless rapture" (in Tynan). In 1978, Kenneth Tynan reported hearing from another of Brooks' former colleagues that Woody Allen had "become a professional, whereas Mel is still a brilliant amateur," he said. "*Amateurs* are people putting on parties with multimillion-dollar budgets." Now, it is impossible to think of Brooks as a vulgar amateur. He is an EGOT, one of the few winners of an Emmy, a Grammy, an Oscar, and a Tony. Curiously, his use of vulgarity has become his trademark.

Of course, Brooks himself is not a vulgarian. Recently, Maureen Dowd of *The New York Times* has pointed out that Brooks is "a sophisticated guy who appreciates and drops references to Nikolai Gogol's 'Dead Souls.'" Dowd adds Brooks "was married for 40 years to that epitome of elegance, Anne Bancroft," and he was "a favorite lunch companion of Cary Grant, the suavest man who ever lived." Then, after furthering his gentility, she notes, "In the new Hulu show '*History of the World, Part II*,' you can still find all the Mel Brooks signature comedy stylings: penis jokes, puke jokes and fart jokes." Adept at marketing, Brooks likes "fart jokes." Zooming with Dowd from his tastefully decorated home in Santa Monica, California, he adds irony to bait his audience and attract his viewers' attention. "It adds some *je ne sais quoi* to the comedy," he remarks, "a touch of sophistication for the smarter people helps move the show along." Heightening the buzz his interviews create, Brooks also revels in playing practical jokes to promote his work. His Hollywood star, for example, has one six-fingered hand. "I did it with a plaster mold just so that somebody from Idaho would scream, 'Henry, come over here! Look at this. Mel Brooks has six fingers,'" he said. Moving to California, Brooks learned, lived, and, on occasion, still reminds us what Sid Caesar's career epitomized—"satire pays the rent" (McGilligan 364).

Paradoxically, mainstream filmmaking has also supported Brooks' social and artistic values. "I don't want to make just another movie," he said, continuing to brand himself an arthouse director when *Young Frankenstein* was in production. "I want to make trouble. I want to say in comic terms, 'J'accuse.' We dealt with bigotry in *Saddles* and with neo–Fascism in *Producers*. Underneath the comedy in *Frankenstein*, the doctor is undertaking the quest to defeat death—to challenge God" (Parish 205). In *Silent Movie*, Brooks tackled the evils of corporate capitalism. "We came up with a great engine," he said. "Money versus Art. Big commercial companies that had nothing to do with the art of entertainment but were loaded with money were gobbling up old traditional movie studios just for their financial value. I pointed out that Coca-Cola was buying Columbia Pictures, Transamerica now owned United Artists, and Gulf + Western had 'engulfed and devoured' Paramount. The bottom line was that they had no regard for what kind of movie they were making as long as they brought in money" (*All About Me!* 257).

According to Rosalie L. Colie, paradoxy formally observes the decorum of its content while mocking formal limitations and insists on continuity between thought and experience (21). Brooks' paradoxy, its social incompatibilities, anomalies, and intellectual contradictions, offer viewers a privileged, diplopic position, being at once "creation and re-creation … invention and imitation" (Colie xiii). "I had taken the Western apart in *Blazing Saddles*, and in *Young Frankenstein* I had a party with black-and-white horror films," Brooks said. "I was satirizing specific genres, but I was also paying tribute to them at the same time" (255).

As Jeremy Dauber remarks, Brooks, like other Jewish American success stories, constrained himself within the system in which he found himself instead of working outside it (2). Here it is important to note that as a product of New York's cultural milieu, Brooks personally appreciates the workings of paradoxy. His life and career have been shaped by New York City's cultural and artistic tensions. Brooklyn's ethnic enclaves housed Jewish, Puerto Rican, Greek, Italian, Russian, and Ukrainian communities. Williamsburg, where Brooks was raised, "was more polyglot and fluid than Brownsville, Brooklyn's most religious Orthodox Old World" (McGilligan 9). As a child, Brooks believed "Christians were a minority," because his neighborhood was predominantly Jewish.[9] Part and parcel of the Big Apple's European character, Brooks, the son of Russian-Jewish and German-Jewish parents, understood New York's ethnic fluidity intimately. "Everybody assumed my mother had a Yiddish or Jewish accent," he remarked, "probably because of my being the 2000-year-old man with Carl Reiner, which I performed with a decidedly Jewish accent." Correcting this misperception, he said, "Actually, strangely enough if my mother had any accent at all it was Irish. As a little kid she went to public school in New York city on the Lower East Side and practically all the teachers in the city at that time were Irish. So when she learned how to speak English, she spoke it with a bit of an Irish brogue. Instead of Thirty-third Street' she'd say, 'Tirdy-tird Street.' And instead of 'Flush the toilet!' she'd say, 'Flush the terlet!'" (*All About Me!* 7–8). Clearly, Brooks' New York was *not* the American melting pot described in Ernest Duvergier de Hauranne's *A Frenchman in Lincoln's America*, a place in which new immigrants wore "the clothes of their new country," and spoke its language, ensuring their children would no longer "even remember the mother country" (240).[10]

New York's early cinema was also culturally specific, playing in a variety of venues, from art houses to ethnic enclaves, to niche audiences. The Hungarian-American film producer Adolph Zukor opened Astoria Studios in 1920 after merging his Famous Players Film Company to form Famous Players-Lasky and later into Paramount Pictures, one of the Big Five studios that later dominated the movie market. Astoria Studios' proximity to the Broadway theater district attracted a diverse workforce that produced over 100 films throughout the 1920s (Caballo). Another Jewish film mogul, William Fox moved his studio from New York City to Los Angeles in 1915 and named it Fox Film Corporation there. The Universal Film Manufacturing Company, destined to become Universal Pictures, was incorporated in New York City. Its president, Carl Laemmle, was a German Jew from Laupheim, Germany. Harry and Jack Cohn and Joe Brandt were Jews from New York City who founded Columbia Pictures.

An *Amerikaner-gebroyen* from Brooklyn, Brooks followed the path to Hollywood blazed by Zukor, Fox, Laemmle, Cohn, and Brandt. Faithful to his beginnings. Brooks insists his comedy belongs to the East Coast. "It's really New York humor," he said. "It has a certain rhythm. It has a certain intensity and a certain pulse. Lenny Bruce, Rodney Dangerfield, Jackie Mason, and stand-up comedians like me were not simply Jewish. They were New York—there is a big difference" (*All About Me!* 36). Jewish comedy is softer and sweeter, Brooks says. "New York comedy [is] tougher and more explosive" (Shulman). As he reminds Johnny Carson on *The Tonight Show*, in New York, his humor thrives on its victims. According to Brooks, "God made pigeons, he made little doves and he made Howie Morris. And he said, 'They shall be called prey.' And then he made wolves and foxes and tigers. And he said they shall be called Melvin. The minute I saw Howie after *The Show of Shows* I went for his neck. I couldn't help it. You have to go for him.'" His earlier send-ups of popular films on *Your Show of Shows* stood him in good stead as he shifted his cinematic sights in California. Popular film audiences, in particular, appreciated his remarkable ludic combination of styles, tones, and genres. Making "it funny by making it Jewish" (Dauber 1), Brooks critiqued mainstream American culture, roasting and re-tailoring *goyishe* norms and forms of proper behavior and citizenship, blending pastiche and genre parody.

As Alex Belth observes, Mel Brooks is an American Rabelais, a master of *via negativa*. Like Rabelais' Gargantua and Pantagruel, the protagonists of Brooks' movies are larger than life—his grotesques, be they Jewish or Gentile, are at once sympathetic and repugnant, driven by voracious, and, at times, operatic appetites. Impoverished, charming, and Jewish, *The Producers*' sleazy Bialystock (Zero Mostel) and neurotic Bloom (Gene Wilder) take advantage of rich, gullible, elderly widows. Appealing and equally disgusting, *The Twelve Chairs*' highly-strung treasure hunters, Father Fyodor (Dom DeLuise) and Vorobyaninov (Ron Moody), are as poor, greedy, and unscrupulous as Bialystock and Bloom. Brooks' mainstream standouts include Dom DeLuise's gluttonous Nero in *History of the World: Part I*, Daphne Zuniga's caricature of a Jewish American princess and Rick Moranis' geeky burlesque of *Star Wars*' Darth Vader in *Spaceballs*, and Richard Lewis' neurotic King John in *Robin Hood: Men in Tights*. Embedded in parodic patterns of the world turned upside down, their stories also imply a strict correspondence of opposites that juxtaposes the low and the high, balancing vice with virtue. Like Rabelais, Brooks upends society's balanced binaries. Challenging orthodoxy, relative (and often competing) value systems collide: there are hilarious anachronisms, incompatibilities, and impossibilities in his films that create Menippean turnovers of incidents, characters, styles, and genres.

To date, several excellent pioneering studies of Brooks' works have been published. Among them are Robert Alan Crick's *The Big Screen Comedies of Mel Brooks* (McFarland, 2002), Alex Symons' *Mel Brooks in the Cultural Industries: Survival and Prolonged Adaptation* (Edinburgh University Press, 2012), Samuel Boerboom and Beth E. Bonstetter's *The Political Mel Brooks* (Lexington, 2019), and Jeremy Dauber's *Mel Brooks: Disobedient Jew* (Yale UP, 2023).

No collection of scholarship, however, has been devoted to examining Brooks' range (and development) as a cabaret performer, television comedy writer, writer and director of alternate film comedy, and writer, director, and producer of mainstream cinema. Consisting of fifteen essays, a selected bibliography, and an afterword, this ground-breaking volume offers a variety of approaches by Jewish film and popular culture scholars from the United States, Canada, Britain, and Australia on selected topics that explore Brooks' incredible comic range. Responding to the diversity of Brooks' canon, many of its essays are clearly academic in nature; others adjust this academic approach, being more personal and reflective, drawing heavily on their authors' own experiences and reactions to Brooks' work. They contain valuable information about Jewish creators/representations, Hollywood history, who influenced Brooks and whom he in turn influenced, auteurism, film/media adaptation, capitalism in film, comedy studies, and film performance.

10 Introduction

Mel Brooks—Seriously! is divided into two parts. "יסודות / Foundations" introduces its readers to important cultural and aesthetic intersections grounding Mel Brooks' canon in his uses of Jewish humor, Biblical text, parody and pastiche. " ווערק / Selected Works: 1965–1991" houses readings of selected works that span Brooks' career. These essays offer a variety of vantage points, providing increased insights into and understandings of his Jewish humor, crossover comedy, and comic diversity.

"יסודות / Foundations" begins with Peter Scott Lederer's "'Totally Crazy' Cabaret: Drag Shows, Song-and-Dance, Parody, and Dark Jewish Humor in the Films of Mel Brooks." Pointing out that Brooks' canon belongs more to the tradition of the European cabaret than the Broadway musical, Lederer examines Brooks' association of Jewish identity formation with discrimination in terms of his stand-up experiences and use of camp, modifying Jewish comedy for diverse film audiences, subverting normalcy and racialism, and resisting violence by making stories his own. Terry Lindvall and Chris Lindvall's "'He shoulda been called *Yitzhak*': Mel Brooks and the Pleasures of Parody" follows. This essay introduces Brooks as a 2,000-year-old Man, an old man of the Jewish Bible who explicitly points back to the roots of his comedy in Jewish tradition. Examining Brooks' works as *Peshat*, Terry and Chris uncover a wonderfully vulgar incarnation of a Divine comedy.

"ווערק / Selected Works (1965–1991)" contains deep dives into Brooks' works and is arranged chronologically to celebrate the development of Brooks' canon (and its parody and satire). In it, thirteen essays examine his output (in television and film and on Broadway) beginning with Kerry Soper's discussion of the hit series *Get Smart* (NBC 1965–69; CBS 1969–70) and ending with Cynthia J. Miller's reading of *Life Stinks* (1991). Arguing that the mainstream success of *Get Smart* (NBC, 1965–69, CBS, 1969–70) prevented critics from recognizing its genuinely subversive qualities or celebrating it like *Blazing Saddles* or *Young Frankenstein*, Soper's "Got Smart: Mel Brooks, Ambivalent Parody and the Cultural Politics of Foolishness" finds Brooks' use of the James Bond franchise and auteur sensibility simultaneously crowd-pleasing and counter discursive. *Get Smart*, Soper concludes, is a genuinely popular parody that offered its fans psychological relief from—and ideological alternatives to—its Hollywood genre's inflated and sometimes oppressive ideals. Nathan Abrams and Michael Lipiner's "Springtime for Strangelove! The Holocaust, Nazism, and Jewishness in the Films of Mel Brooks and Stanley Kubrick" follows. Abrams and Lipiner trace the extent of Stanley Kubrick's influence on Mel Brooks' *The Producers* (1967) and demonstrate how Brooks' films, in turn, reveal an ongoing-on screen conversation and relationship with this cinematic master. Deepening our understanding of Brooks' films and how his

Introduction (Matheson) 11

critique pushes past Kubrick's, Abrams and Lipiner examine Kubrick and Brooks' views about war and the Holocaust and their use of black comedy, satire, and cultural stereotypes. Abrams and Lipiner also consider instances in which Kubrick and Brooks broke free from comedy to broach serious issues about persecution and genocide by providing a realistic look at war and drawing on Golem folklore. Murray Pomerance's "Around a Proscenium: Representation and Distance in *The Producers* (1967)" then considers the functions of critical laughter and on-screen reactions to *Springtime for Hitler* before examining our own responses to *The Producers*. Ralph Beliveau's "Between the *Mensch* and the *Pícaro*: Greed, Deceit, and Friendship in Mel Brooks' *The Twelve Chairs* (1970)" follows. Beliveau discusses the *picaresque* in Brooks' favorite and most under-appreciated movie before examining his remediation of the art film in Ernest Pintoff's Academy Award–winning short, *The Critic* (1963).

Moving from Brooks' work in television and alternative cinema to his Hollywood movies, my essay "Brooks, Gogol, and Dali: Surrealism, Simulacra, and Simulation in *Blazing Saddles*" (1974) considers this film's aesthetic and social issues that continue to call for critical attention. I conclude that Brooks draws on the grotesque to critique the greed and racism of Manifest Destiny's nation-building activities, finding *Blazing Saddles'* surreality speaks to America's anxieties about its epic intent and actual condition. Next, Frances Pheasant-Kelly's "Parody, Pastiche, and Intertextuality in Mel Brooks's *Young Frankenstein* (1974)" examines elements of parody and intertextuality as well as frequent examples of slapstick humor and innuendo in *Young Frankenstein* and interrogates the film's close following of aesthetic details in James Whale's classic films, notably the inclusion of the original Strickfaden laboratory, early cinematographic techniques, and lighting effects, expressionist tropes, characterization and *mise-en-scène*. She concludes that *Young Frankenstein*'s primary purpose is homage, making it a secondary text that valorizes Whale's films, taking its classic status and the idea of film classics seriously. Matthew Cipa's "Comedic Film Criticism, Filmed: Mel Brooks's Love of Cinema in *Silent Movie* (1976) and *The Critic* (1963)" investigates the ways in which *Silent Movie* and an animated short, *The Critic* (dir. Ernest Pintoff), in which Brooks voices a disgruntled spectator, function as works of criticism in and of themselves. Brook's treatment of absorption and theatricality, two concepts drawn from the work of art historian Michael Fried, is also considered.

Next, Thomas Grochowski's "The Hitchcock picture to end all Hitchcock pictures: Mel Brooks' *High Anxiety* (1977)" finds Brooks' narrative and stylistic borrowings engage in parodic tourism while repurposing of Hitchcock's canon, reminding viewers what the master filmmaker accomplished in his half-century of filmmaking. Douglas C. MacLeod, Jr.'s, "Hitchcock, Brooks, and Pure Cinema" follows. MacLeod finds in *High Anxiety* a pastiche that successfully houses takeoffs of Hitchcock's unforgettable moments, parodying scenes from *Spellbound* (1945), *Strangers on a Train* (1951), *Rear Window* (1954), *Vertigo* (1958), *North by Northwest* (1959), *Psycho* (1960), and *The Birds* (1963) in the terms established by the master filmmaker's pure cinema, particularly his use of subjective camera, montage, and the MacGuffin.

Then A. Bowdoin Van Riper's "The Court Jester's Tale: *History of the World, Part I* (1981) as Epic, Parody, and Epic Parody" argues *History of the World, Part I* is very much part of Brooks' ongoing experiment with cinematic parody: one that lampoons the historical-epic film while taking satirical swipes at narrative conventions that run through nearly *all* popular history. Jonathan Winchell's "Mel Brooks, THE Producer: David Lynch's *The Elephant Man* (1980) and David Cronenberg's *The Fly* (1986)" follows. Addressing Brooks' often overlooked work as a producer, Winchell identifies Brooks as a *cineaste* and traces the trajectory of Brooksfilms while discussing the production histories of two of the most notable films Brooks produced in the 1980s, David Lynch's *The Elephant Man* and David Cronenberg's *The Fly*.

David L. Reznik's "A Jewish Future: The Diverse Diasporic Universe of *Spaceballs* (1987)" follows. According to Reznik, *Spaceballs* is unique in both the range of its Jewish representations and, just as importantly, the temporality of its narrative, because Brooks constructs a vision of the future in which Jews are neither non-existent nor peripheral, but rather one in which Jewishness is at the center of an entire human universe. Finally, Cynthia J. Miller's "The Rich Get Richer: *Life Stinks* (1991)" addresses another side of Brooks—one that is sentimental, philosophical, and reflective. According to Miller, it was this side of Brooks that gave rise to *Life Stinks*, a comedy about a billionaire who experiences homelessness and life on the streets that delivers the message that, for some, life really does stink.

Mel Brooks—Seriously! does not claim to be a comprehensive work about the nature and development of Brooks' bountiful career and diverse canon. Critical work that remains to be done in these areas could easily fill volume after volume. For example, essays dealing with his work as a teenage *tumler*,[11] his humor in the Army and Second World War experiences, and his adventures in New York's early television are not housed in this collection. Essays about his contributions to *Your Show of Shows* and *Caesar's Hour* and about *The 2000-Year-Old Man* could create several collections of their own. Brooks' song writing, script doctoring, and contributions to Broadway productions as well as his own Broadway productions also call for critical attention and offer new areas of discovery for researchers—as do all his films which I believe are still underappreciated. Camille McCutcheon's "A Bibliography on Mel Brooks," concludes the book, listing books, book chapters, journal articles, magazine and newspaper articles, interviews on *YouTube*, reviews of Brooks' autobiography and biographies, reviews of television series and films, and reviews of films directed by Mel Brooks. It is hoped that these excellent resources will encourage further viewing of his films, inspire more reading about them and Brooks' career, and produce more scholarship in these areas.

Because Brooks' comedy has been, and continues to be, an important marker of the American Experience, it is my hope that readers interested in American comedy's cornerstones will appreciate Brooks' willingness to cause what he called "trouble" in the television shows and movies that have helped form our characters and influence our lives. I look forward to the conversations that *Mel Brooks—Seriously!* will generate and anticipate that opportunities for further study of his humor will continue as long as his films are shown.

Here, I must end by welcoming the hero of this critical collection. It would not be complete and cannot begin without the comic who put us in stitches for so many years first taking a bow. He has been waiting patiently in the margins with his pins and needles (and his cloth) to cut more suits to fit the perfect man (and woman). Please join me in celebrating his work. Without his tailoring, America would be in a much darker, more somber place. Let's welcome the amazing Mel Brooks into our hearts. Can you hear the drumroll?

> Here I am, I'm Melvin Brooks!
> I've come to stop the show.
> Just a ham who's minus looks
> But in your heart I'll grow!
> I'll tell you gags, I'll sing you songs
> (Just happy little snappy songs that roll along)
> Out of my mind. Won't you be kind?
> And please love Melvin Brooks! [McGilligan 46].

Notes

1. Erasmus coined the term *vestis virum facit*, the clothes make the man.
2. Isaac Sidney Caesar (September 8, 1922–February 12, 2014) is best known for two pioneering 1950s live television series: *Your Show of Shows* (NBC, 1950–1954), which was a 90-minute weekly show watched by 60 million people, and its successor, *Caesar's Hour* (NBC, 1954–1957). *Your Show of Shows* was particularly significant for the evolution of the variety genre by incorporating situation comedies such as the running sketch "The Hickenloopers," adding a narrative element to the traditional multi-act structure.

14   Introduction

3. In the 1960s, Brooks was also known as a promising art house director who specialized in Jewish and alternative humor. He received an Oscar for his voice-over work in Ernest Pintoff's *The Critic* (1963). *The Producers* (1967) garnered him an Academy Award for Best Story and Screenplay Written for Screen and the Writers Guild of America Award for Best Written American Original Screenplay. An adaptation of Ilf and Petrov's 1928 Russian novel, *The Twelve Chairs* (1970) was nominated by the Writers Guild of America for Best Comedy Adapted from Another Medium. Frank Langella who played the part of Ostap Bender also won the National Board of Review Award for Best Supporting Actor.

4. Yiddish, *meshugaas* is a slang term for madness, craziness, nonsense, or foolishness.

5. *Blazing Saddles* has grossed $119,616,663. For more box office information see "Blazing Saddles (1974)" at *Box Office Mojo*, https://www.boxofficemojo.com/title/tt0071230/.

6. In the 1970s, Brooks was one of the most successful film directors in Hollywood. Many of his films were among the top 10 moneymakers of the year they were released. His best-known films include *The Producers* (1967), *The Twelve Chairs* (1970), *Blazing Saddles* (1974), *Young Frankenstein* (1974), *Silent Movie* (1976), *High Anxiety* (1977), *History of the World, Part I* (1981), and *Spaceballs* (1987). A musical adaptation of his first film, *The Producers*, ran on Broadway from 2001 to 2007. He received a Kennedy Center Honor in 2009, a Hollywood Walk of Fame star in 2010, the 41st AFI Life Achievement Award in June 2013, a British Film Institute Fellowship in March 2015, a National Medal of Arts in September 2016, and a BAFTA Fellowship in February 2017. In 2023, he received the Academy Honor Award, celebrating significant achievement in the Hollywood film industry. Three of his films ranked in the American Film Institute's list of the top 100 comedy films of the past 100 years (1900–2000) are ranked in the top 15: *Blazing Saddles* at number 6; *The Producers* at number 11, and *Young Frankenstein* at number 13.

7. Sid Caesar encouraged Brooks to contribute uncredited material to him for the *Admiral Broadway Revue* (NBC and Dumont, January 28–June 3, 1949). After Caesar's *Your Show of Shows* premiered on February 25, 1950, Brooks' name was included on *Your Show of Shows*' credits. Working with Neil Simon, Danny Simon, Lucille Kallen, Selma Diamond, Joseph Stein, Michael Stewart, Tony Webster, Woody Allen, Larry Gelbart, Mel Tolkin, and Carl Reiner, he became a senior member of the writers' room. An enormous hit, *Your Show of Shows* won the Emmy Award for best variety program in 1952 and 1953.

8. *Get Smart* premiered on NBC on September 18, 1965, and was broadcast to September 13, 1969. The series moved to the CBS network for its final season, running from September 26, 1969, to September 11, 1970, with 138 total episodes produced. During its five-season run, *Get Smart* broke the Nielsen Top 30 twice, won seven Emmy Awards, and was nominated for another 14 Emmys and two Golden Globe Awards. It was ranked at number 12 during its first season, and at number 22 during its second season, before falling out of the top 30 for its last three seasons.

9. As Dauber points out, Brownsville was estimated to be 75 percent Jewish the year Brooks was born (7).

10. *De Hauranne's* speaker adds, "America is the melting pot in which all the nations of the world come to be fused into a single mass and cast in a uniform mold" (241).

11. In the Jewish-American lexicon, a *tumler* is someone who makes a lot of noise without accomplishing anything, someone who is the life of a party, or someone who is a paid social director at resorts in the Borscht Belt.

Works Cited

Belth, Alex. "BGS: The Playboy Interview: Mel Brooks." *Alex Belth's Bronx Banter*. December 20, 2013. http://www.bronxbanterblog.com/2013/12/20/bgs-the-playboy-interview-mel-brooks/.

Boerboom, Samuel, and Beth E. Bonstetter, editors. *The Political Mel Brooks*. Lexington Books, 2019.

Brooks, Mel. *All About Me: My Remarkable Life in Show Business*. Ballantine, 2021.
Caballo, Marian. "Hollywood at Home: Cinema History in Queens, New York City." *TheScience Society*, April 27, 2022. https://thesciencesurvey.com/arts-entertainment/2022/04/27/hollywood-at-home-cinema-history-in-queens-new-york-city/.
"Caesar's Writers." [Video]. *YouTube*, June 16, 2021. Original airdate January 26, 1996. https://www.youtube.com/watch?v=kjgcjPB1qlI.
Carlyle, Thomas. *Sartor Resartus*, edited by Kerry McSweeny and Peter Sabor. Oxford University Press, 1987.
Carson, Johnny. Interview with Mel Brooks. [Video]. *YouTube*. Original airdate February 13, 1975. https://www.youtube.com/watch?v=WYuv-8SjjPg.
Colie, Rosalie L. *Paradoxia Epidemica: The Renaissance Tradition of Paradox*. Princeton UP, 1966.
"Commentary." *Blazing Saddles: 30th Anniversary Special Edition*. Dir. Mel Brooks. Crossbow Productions, 1974. DVD. Warner, 2004.
Crick, Robert Alan. *The Big Screen Comedies of Mel Brooks*. McFarland, 2002.
Darrach, Brad. "Mel Brooks: The Playboy Interview." *Playboy*, February 1975. *The Stacks-Reader*, http://www.thestacksreader.com/mel-brooks-the-playboy-interview/.
Dauber, Jeremy. *Mel Brooks: Disobedient Jew*. Yale UP, 2023.
de Hauranne, Ernest Duvergier. *A Frenchman in Lincoln's America*. Volume 1, Lakeside Press, 1974.
Dowd, Maureen. "Mel Brooks Isn't Done Punching Up the History of the World." *The New York Times*, March 11, 2023. Updated March 15, 2023. https://www.nytimes.com/2023/03/11/style/mel-brooks-comedian.html.
Ebert, Roger. "Blazing Saddles." *RogerEbert.com*, February 7, 1974. https://www.rogerebert.com/reviews/blazing-saddles-1974. Cited parenthetically as "Blazing Saddles."
———. "Young Frankenstein." *RogerEbert.com*, January 1, 1974. https://www.rogerebert.com/reviews/young-frankenstein-1974. Cited parenthetically as "Young Frankenstein."
McGilligan, Patrick. *Funny Man*. Harper, 2019.
"Mel Brooks · Interview (The Producers/Borscht Belt/Anne Bancroft) · 2004 [RITYArchive]." [Video]. *YouTube*, November 6, 2004. https://www.youtube.com/watch?v=3v3a1suYmrY. Cited parenthetically as "Mel Brooks."
Shulman, Michael. "Mel Brooks Writes It All Down." *The New Yorker*, November 28, 2021. https://www.newyorker.com/culture/the-new-yorker-interview/mel-brooks-writes-it-all-down.
Simon, John. "The Lower Shallows." *Reverse Angle: A Decade of American Films*. Clarkson N. Potter, 1982, pp. 140–45.
"Smart Money." *Time*, October 15, 1965. https://content.time.com/time/subscriber/article/0,33009,834525,00.html.
Smith, Kyle. "How Maxwell Smart and His Shoe-Phone Changed TV. *The Wall Street Journal Online*, March 21, 2008. https://web.archive.org/web/20081123105044/http://online.wsj.com/public/article_print/SB120606471734053849.html.
Symons, Alex. *Mel Brooks in the Cultural Industries: Survival and Prolonged Adaptation*. Edinburgh University Press, 2012.
"The Twelve Chairs." *AFI Catalog*, 2019. https://catalog.afi.com/Catalog/moviedetails/23558#:~:text=A%20box%2Doffice%20chart%20in.
Tynan, Kenneth. "Frolics and Detours of a Short Hebrew Man." *The New Yorker*, October 22, 1978. https://www.newyorker.com/magazine/1978/10/30/mel-brooks-frolics-and-detours-of-a-short-hebrew-man.
Wogan, Terry. Interview with Mel Brooks. [Video]. *YouTube*. Original airdate February 18, 1984. https://www.youtube.com/watch?v=WuzAm70xLJ8.
"Young Frankenstein." Box Office Mojo by IMDbPro. https://www.boxofficemojo.com/title/tt0072431/credits/. Cited parenthetically as "Young Frankenstein."

יסודות
Foundations

Ippolit Vorobyaninov: [*trying to remember his lines*] I am cousin Michael from Kiev. All the Vorobyaninovs are dead. [*He knocks on the door*]

Worker at Old Ladies Home: [*answering the door*] Yes?

Ippolit Vorobyaninov: I am cousin Kiev from Vorobyaninov. All the Michaels are dead.

—*The Twelve Chairs* (1970)

"Totally Crazy" Cabaret

Drag Shows, Song-and-Dance, Parody, and Dark Jewish Humor in the Films of Mel Brooks

PETER SCOTT LEDERER

Introduction

Mel Brooks was part of the American cinematic revolution of the 1960s and 1970s. His films' dark humor, I suggest, emerged from the cultural disruption caused by Jewish nightclub comedians and their projection of anti–Semitism and Nazi spectacle onto American culture in order to critique it. It was not simply that cultural and aesthetic innovation "articulated a strong opposition to the prevailing rules, morality, and aesthetic standards of the time" (Sobral 3) or that the "culture/counterculture divide was facilitated by the prosperity of post-war America" (Gair 4). The Jewish stereotypes developed within underground cabarets initiated an unconventional aesthetic that challenged the mainstream tyranny of Hollywood and Gentile institutions of assimilation in their different manifestations. Using a "New Cabaret," Brooks relives the climate of the Old-World cabaret and borrows from it. His re-engagement with cabaret principles and a mixed multitude encourages multi-ethnic dissent within mainstream institutions. Reflective of underground Weimar entertainment amorality, Brooks subverted normalcy and racialism while attracting diverse audiences. Weimar cabaret culture was one of "attitude," created out of "a sense of anxiety, fear, a rising sense of doom" (Farina 8). Although it was a "creation of outsiders," it enjoyed mass appeal among crowds for whom the stand-up comedy was "edgy" and "sophisticated" (8, 84). Unlike the Nazis, who were incapable of laughing at themselves, and even Orthodox Jews, who detested decadent performances (85), these Old-World performers were admirable because their themes were "boundless and unpredictable rather than narrowly restricted to any single or small group of topics. For enthusiastic audiences, cabaret's overriding mantra was one of surprise and delight" (9). Whereas many film heroes allow audiences to forget their misery, Brooks' protagonists do not. Instead, his characters replicate the intimacy of Jewish stage comedians who unabashedly expose their misery, increasing an insecurity of Otherness to master a sense of control over their audiences and Jewish and Gentile cultures. They are freighted with dialogue and imagery that may seem controversial and "self-hating." However, Brooks' use of specific stereotypes in his repertoire reveal some of the ways he re-appropriates and adapts anti–Semitic stereotypes. He reveals an association between Jewish identity formation and discrimination and a commitment to ridicule as the most palatable form of subversion.

Desser and Friedman point out that "Jewish filmmakers had no direct tradition, no previous examples or models, to draw upon in creating a visual art filtered through their Jewish consciousness" (3). However, Brooks' experience as a stage comedian made him an adept regarding the modification of Jewish comedy for diverse film audiences. The performance venue of the comedy club requires consideration as the catalyst for the cultural expressions of subversion and innovation achieved in New Hollywood, because the political radicalism of the period did not impact the critique of cultural assimilation crucial and specific to these films as much as the comedy backgrounds and dissenting nightclub subculture of their directors. Throughout the 1930s, subversive Jewish comedy undermined the "superior" aesthetics of Nazi Germany. Fleeing club owners and entertainers renewed such comedy in the United States in venues like The Blue Angel, The Den in the Duane, the Bon Soir, and Café Society, popular among African Americans, Jews, and others who wanted to escape post-war troubles (Gavin 2, 3, 48, 72).

William Farina argues that the cabaret style should not be defined "too narrowly," although Josef von Sternberg's *Der blaue Engel* (*The Blue Angel*) (1930) and Kurt Weill and Bertolt Brecht's *The Threepenny Opera* (1928) are its usual examples (5). This entertainment was developed in the cabarets of Europe that gave eccentric performers a platform. They may be defined as small venues with small stages and intimate contact with audiences where performances included song-and-dance, comic monologues, pantomimes, satiric skits, and films, as well as "parody on sex, commerce, culture, or politics" (Farina 5). The nightclub acts in these venues came in contact with diverse groups: gay and lesbian communities, and Black clientele and jazz musicians, among others. This cabaret style resurfaced in America when Jewish impresarios like Herbert Jacoby opened nightclubs on America's East Coast in 1937 (Gavin 21). The fact that this cabaret style is resistant to a specific definition makes it a form suitable for the Jewish comedians who performed in them. One of cabaret's "distinctive associations [was] its perceived (and very real) Jewish ethnicity" (7). Within these venues, performers critiqued "reality by contrasting it with a norm or ideal to usually humorous effect" (Lareau 2). Indeed, if performance always has a way of "knowingly or unknowingly impos[ing] the cultural values of one group upon the members of another" (Reinelt and Roach 13–14), then dark Jewish comedy attempts to derail that intention through an amalgamation of narratives. Moreover, the Jewish nightclubs were less concerned with memberships and were less homogeneous than non–Jewish clubs (Gavin 2). The "anti-club" atmosphere of these venues was one that contested membership literally and figuratively, permitting Jews and other minorities. Jewish comedians within this industry likewise (to borrow Terry Eagleton's description of postmodern culture) turned their

> distaste for fixed boundaries and categories on the traditional distinction between "high" and "popular" art, deconstructing the borderline between them by producing artifacts which [were] self-consciously populist or vernacular, or which [offered] themselves as commodities for pleasurable consumption [202].

They sought to "dismantle the intimidating aura of high-modernist culture with a more demotic, user-friendly art, suspecting all hierarchies of value as privileged and elitist. There [was] no better or worse, just different" (202).

In *The New Jew in Film*, Abrams identifies Brooks' films as "black comedies" (7). Critics have also applied the label "low-brow" to Brooks' comedy. Jamie Moshin dismisses Brooks' humor as common and lacking any profoundness (33). Indeed, *The Producers* was condemned by critics for its lack of sophistication. Pauline Kael called it "amateurishly crude," noting how it revealed "show-business Jewish humor" and the self-exploitation of Jewish "television comedians" who suddenly saw "themselves as stereotypes" (140). Gregg Rickman denigrates Brooks, a former television writer, by saying that he will be remembered for "'putting on a show' [...] rather than as a satirist or performer" or even as "a showman capable of amazing spectacle" (302). Rickman's greatest criticism of *The Producers* is that it has too many "irrelevant gags" (298). These criticisms fail to appreciate the usefulness of Brooks' dark, low-brow humor in exploring how "in modern memory ... people and events are remembered" (298).

The Catskills has also been, although not incorrectly, credited as a source of Brooks' humor and described as "an authentically American Jewish source" (Sandrow 25). As Irving Howe observes, the Borscht Belt served as a place where young comedians could hone their skills (559).¹ "Apart from such old-fashioned ethnic enclaves," Albert Goldman argues, "there was no room in America for Jewish humor, which was regarded as a dangerous and embarrassing commodity: something the *goyim* ['Gentiles'] could never understand; something the Jews themselves—the successful, highly assimilated Jews—would be embarrassed to acknowledge" (81). The audiences were mostly Jewish, and this posed a problem for comedians who needed to redefine their acts to appeal to a larger market, especially if those entertainers wanted to go to Hollywood. If Catskills comedians performing "material of the Jews, for the Jews and, most important of all, *in* 'Jewish'" were considered "dirty" (Lewis 94; emphasis in original), then how would non-Jewish audiences respond? Brooks discovered the answer to this question when he took his product to the American film market.

The Films: The Producers *(1967),* The Twelve Chairs *(1970),* Blazing Saddles *(1974),* Young Frankenstein *(1974),* History of the World, Part I *(1981),* To Be or Not to Be *(1983), and* The Producers *(2005)*

In order to understand how dark Jewish cabaret informs Brooks' work, it is important to first look at *The Producers*. *The Producers'* Max Bialystock (Zero Mostel) is an amoral comic fool, but one conscious of the complexities of contemporary Jewish identity. One moment in the film stands out not only for Mostel's masterful delivery of a line soberly and sincerely, but also for its poignant statement about the absurdity of life and the tragedy of his circumstances. After having searched hundreds of scripts for the worst and coming across Franz Kafka's *The Metamorphosis* (1915), Bialystock realizes that the isolation of the anti-hero, Gregor Samsa (who is coded as being Jewish), is too close to the reality for Jews: "It's too good!" (*The Producers* 25:23–25:33). *Lakhn mit yascherkes* ("laughter through tears") is appropriated by the producers, and they exploit the Holocaust. Bialystock endeavors to use the traumatic memory of the Third Reich to secure financial success: the musical he proposes should be such a failure at the box office that he will have no profits to reimburse his financiers. This comical portrayal of amoral and fraudulent behavior echoes the spirit of the subversive cabaret in its progressive message of anti-authoritarianism.

The Producers follows Bialystock and his hysterical accountant, Leo Bloom (Gene Wilder), as they plot to put on a failing play and keep the financiers' investments. On the surface, Brooks is perpetuating the old "pejorative tales and jokes" Sarah Blacher Cohen describes in *Jewish Wry: Essays on Jewish Humor* (1987) as too often depicting "Jews as avaricious, cunning Shylocks" in an attempt to prevent them from "polluting the mainstream" (6). Paul McDonald also describes the protagonists as a continuation of Hollywood's "corrupting values": "Max is an unscrupulous gigolo," and "the movies have made Leo a criminal and a purveyor of tasteless and distorted narratives; worse, they have turned him from being an unassuming Jewish accountant into someone willing to collaborate with a Nazi" (25). Both Andrew Sarris (47) and Stanley Kauffmann (24), in their 1968 reviews, call the plot unbelievable, especially since, as Kauffmann notes, "the Nazi is oblivious to the Jewishness of his producers" (24). Moira Walsh expressed her disapproval for anyone laughing at the play within the film *Springtime for Hitler* (451). Brooks also received a multitude of letters from Jews in protest, as he explains in his interview with *Der Spiegel* (21). These letters from moviegoers rejected the film, not because it had dared to use Hitler as an object of ridicule, but because Brooks' Jewish protagonists made light of the Holocaust.

An awareness of the problems of Jewish identity is apparent throughout *The Producers*. Like Kafka, whose writings permit the Jew to "see himself in an ironic light, recognizing the essential absurdity of his situation even in the most dangerous or tragic circumstances" (Beck 29), the cabaret style employed satire and gallows humor in ways that influenced Brooks. From comic theater and nightclubs, like The Compass and The Blue Angel, to Hollywood, Brooks' despair and rage are played out through a sense of the bizarre. The filmmaker's memories of Nazi Germany and the atrocities committed contribute significantly to his comedy. His post-war Jewish-American environment fostered a cynicism and outsiderness that evolved into a dark humor that used Jewish film identity to contest all forms of authoritarianism. Like Brooks, Bialystock and Bloom remain uncomfortably stuck, straddling two worlds.

In his 1980 interview with Jerry Bauer, Mel Brooks acknowledges the role of hostility and an "inability to deal with the realities of the world" in his comedy (12). Brooks has explained at length how he interprets his work as a memorialization of the unthinkable atrocities: "[t]he great Holocaust by the Nazis is probably the great outrage of the Twentieth Century. There is nothing to compare with it. So what can I do about it? If I get on the soapbox and wax eloquently, it'll be blown away in the wind, but if I do *Springtime for Hitler* it'll never be forgotten" (Fleishman 2). For Brooks, "every contemporary movie has its antecedents in films of the twenties and thirties" (12). However, these films also find their forebearers in Weimar cabaret. Not only does Brooks use dark humor effectively, but Zero Mostel also uses cabaret performance to further augment it.

Jelavich describes the cabaret in Berlin as a show consisting of short episodes of song, dance, witty dialogue, and comic monologue, often dealing with "topical issues," such as sex, politics, and cultural fads in a "satirical or parodistic manner" (2). The subversive style of Brooks' comedies is revealed by returning to this predecessor, in which performers used dialogue and skits that incorporated musical numbers:

> Despite the growing attendance of the cabaret by a general public, its personnel and creators continued to be drawn from peripheral groups whose viewpoint remained ironic. The proliferation of cabarets allowed minority concerns to infiltrate popular entertainment. [...] [A]lthough there were only a few exclusively Jewish cabarets, comedy and political commentary were permeated with Yiddish rhythms, attitudes, and words [Senelick xiii].

There are many parallels between Weimar entertainment and New Hollywood. Alan Lareau explains, "The end of censorship after the fall of the monarchy in 1918 promised to pave the way to a new openness on the stage, as performers would finally be able to take a stand on contemporary issues and address the daily concerns of the audience" (13). In Weimar Germany,

> cabaret survived longer than other art forms in providing a platform which vocal opposition to the régime could reach an eager public; its several forms varied from subtle innuendoes, addressed to a sophisticated audience in the capital, to more down-to-earth and often crude jokes to listeners in a Bavarian beer-cellar-cum-stage [Hillenbrand 112].

Sexual themes were heavily explored, and the conservative romanticism of more mainstream entertainment was openly satirized (Jelavich 5). Not everyone, of course, interpreted this artistic movement as one of liberation. Some called it "a flood of obscenity and nudity" and "smut" (13, 14). At its best, left-wing cabaret contested totalitarianism by means of clever dialogue and entertaining song-and-dance (Senelick xii).

In this European context, cabaret and many of its writers and performers who were Jewish were targeted by the National Socialist Government. From 1933 onwards, a wave of migration from Germany brought performers to American cities (Jelavich 9). Among such performers were Marlene Dietrich, Elisabeth Bergner, Peter Lorre, Grete Mosheim, Oskar Homolka, and Conrad Veidt, as well as directors Josef von Sternberg and Fritz Lang (Grunberger 478). Joseph Goebbels saw it as his responsibility to end the form of entertainment that ran counter to "the demands of good public taste" (Senelick 281). Jewish cabaret entertainers, given the "artists' license to be fools," delivered mocking performances that were especially threatening (280). Jews told jokes about Jews, Gentiles, and even Hitler "to audiences that were primarily Gentile" (Jelavich 6). In Nazi political propaganda, Jews became associated with the agitprop of the Communist party and Blacks (3). Brooks' *Blazing Saddles* (1974) draws parallels between the discrimination and persecution affecting Black and Jewish populations. One of Brooks' characters, a Native-American chief, comes across a Black family on a wagon. At first he is shocked, but then he is sympathetic and allows them to pass unharmed: "*Shvartzes* ['Blacks']? [...] They're darker than us!" (38:18–51). For this reason, Jews in these stories are presented as darker than the Gentile antagonists—not only to draw attention to their being out of place, but also to highlight their unique qualities.

Brooks' time in Berlin as a soldier and his deep family ties to the region pervade his films. The dangers of being a Jewish performer in Nazi Germany are integrated into Brooks' work. Before the rise of the Nazi government, Berlin had been "a city of enlightenment," where a *de facto* policy of religious tolerance attracted many immigrants, particularly Jews (Colerick 67). It was in Berlin that Brooks first saw *The Threepenny Opera*, and he credits his being "totally crazy" about musical theater to this musical play that premiered on 31 August 1928 (Colerick 2). Starring the German-Jewish actor Kurt Gerron as Jackie "Tiger" Brown, the play ran successfully until 1933 when the Nazis banned it (Colerick 81). The humor of the opera, which Colerick calls "the anarchic spirit" that makes the musical "appear a characteristic expression of 1920s' dissidence" (81), is reshaped in *The Producers*.

Brooks' mother's family suffered through the pogroms in Ukraine (Fleishman 22) and his father was forced to flee Danzig (Belth 12). In "The Making of *The Producers*" (2002), Brooks explains that many relatives perished in the Holocaust (45:10). The influence of Mel Brooks' Polish-Jewish ancestry is even more readily apparent in *To Be or Not to Be* (1983), in which he and his wife, Anne Bancroft, play a song-and-dance duo that displays their Polish fluency in the opening musical number. Brooks parodies the classic Hollywood musical form through an exaggerated dance, undermining the glamorous performance of Bancroft in her silver gown.

Many scholars have proposed that Brooks' fraught relationship with the past is evident in these films. Yacowar suggests that although Brooks participated in the fight against the Nazis, because he was not directly involved in battle, he carries "some subconscious frustration as a result" (17). Desser and Friedman also argue that Brooks' "failure to engage the hated Huns directly apparently left him with a permanently thwarted sense of duty" (118). The protagonist's name in *The Producers*, Max Bialystock, supports such claims. The Polish city of Białystok was the site of a pogrom in 1906 (Bender 14). Under Nazi rule, the city turned into a ghetto and was the location of the second largest uprising against the Nazis (103). Brooks' father was also named "Max," adding importance to the name.

In his interview with *Der Spiegel* (2006), Brooks argues that "by using the medium of comedy, we can try to rob Hitler of his posthumous power and myths," and *The Producers* does just that to undermine and ridicule "the holy seriousness that always surrounded [Hitler] and protected him like a cordon" (12). There are reasons Brooks uses humor for serious situations. Alan Dundes and Thomas Hauschild explain the basic assertion of gallows humor as "[n]othing is so sacred, so taboo, or so disgusting that it cannot be the subject of humor" (56). They also note that "gallows humor generally refers to jokes made about and by the *victims* of oppression. They are jokes told by those supposedly about to be hanged, not by the hangmen" (56; emphasis in original). One example of a joke in this tradition is credited to Weiß Ferdl, a popular anti–Nazi compère in Munich: "Good evening! I'm sorry I'm so late. I've just come back from a little excursion to—Dachau! Well, you ought to see the place! Barbed-wire fence, electrified, machine-guns; another barbed-wire fence, more machine guns—but I can tell you, I managed to get in all the same!" (112). This joke, told by a victim "often imprisoned" at Dachau (112), also relies on the element of absurdity that Brooks insists is integral to comedy: "The more serious the situation, the funnier the comedy can be. The greatest comedy plays against the greatest tragedy" (Yacowar viii). Brooks also explores the absurd in *The Twelve Chairs* (1970), in which a choir sings "Hope for the Best (Expect the Worst)," at one point with heavy Yiddish inflection: "Live while you're alive. / No one will survive. / Life is funny. / Save your worries, spend your money. / Live while you're alive. / No one will survive. / There's no guarantee" (7:53–58).

Brooks' films also continue the cabaret tradition of Hitler caricatures, where underground comics developed a "contemporaneous satire about Hitler" that concentrated on "his background, appearance, path to power, personal traits, 'universal genius' and his decline" (Hillenbrand 8). After World War II, comedians continued to mock Hitler. Yacowar mentions Will Jordan's routine "about show-biz moguls casting a replacement for Hitler" as a possible inspiration for *The Producers* (83). Jordan himself accuses Brooks of outright theft (Nachman 38). Lenny Bruce's routine "Hitler and the MCA" appears on his 1959 comedy album, *The Sick Humor of Lenny Bruce*. Bruce was a good friend of Jordan's and "lifted the skit" (Holtzman 231). Bruce's version is about two agents casting auditions for the perfect dictator. In it, they suddenly discover a possible candidate painting a wall:

> First Agent: Oh ya.... Zis is really veirdo! Look at dot fink mit dot mustache! Hey, you! Frenchy! Put down dot painting. You, ya, mit da hair jazz there. Put down dot painting und step around in front. Yes, you! Ve vonna look at you. Right? Ya. Alright.... Look at zis face! Is zis an album cover? Hey, vat is your name, my friend?

PAINTER: Adolf Schicklgruber.
FIRST AGENT: You're putting us on.
PAINTER: Hey, come on, don jerk me around, you guys. I got tree garages to paint in Prague today. I gotta finish dem up.
FIRST AGENT: No von is jerking you around, dere. You ever did any show business bits?
PAINTER: Vell, I did a Chaplin impression at a party once [222].

In Brooks' version, the Nazi author of *Springtime for Hitler*, Franz Liebkind ("dear child"), praises the Führer's work ethic: "Hitler—there was a painter. He could paint an entire apartment in one afternoon—two coats!" (31:07–13).

In *The Producers*, Bialystock and Bloom cast Lorenzo Saint DuBois (LSD; played by Dick Shawn) after his outrageous performance as Hitler during the auditions. LSD is an earring-wearing hippie with the personality of a spoiled, narcissistic adolescent prone to bursting into tantrums (1:01:40–59). He takes himself as seriously as the historical Hitler. Like the Weimar cabaret crowd, for whom the real Hitler is the butt of a joke, the *Springtime for Hitler* audience finds LSD comical. They also laugh when the dictator is revealed as a volatile and pretentious upstart seeking to prove his masculinity. Although LSD has some of the characteristics of a hippie, such as the "flower power" mantra, his manner of speaking belongs more to Lenny Bruce's underground club subculture. His jazz-inspired inflection, for example, is closer to the jive of the post-war hipster, which Torquemada (Brooks) also uses in "The Spanish Inquisition" in *History of the World, Part I* (1981).

For these reasons, Brooks' work belongs more to the tradition of the European cabaret than the Broadway musical. Even when Brooks does draw from the Busby Berkeley musical, his treatment of the material at hand is more risqué. Take, for example, the reference to *Gold Diggers of 1933* (1933) in the overhead shot of the choreography in *The Producers*. Whereas the Berkeley Hollywood musical is inoffensive and tame, Brooks' treatment (1:26:05) ridicules and undermines the communal experience of mass demonstrations. Brooks was able to put his spin on the Berkeley musical to parody the demonstrativeness of the National Socialists, who also relied on such spectacle during their torchlight parades (0:24). The Nazis suppressed subversive ideas in entertainment, instead favoring the musical, which was full of "dance and spectacle" (Colerick 74). The Nazi rallies sought to intimidate by asserting strength of force, glamorizing the military, and aggrandizing the dictatorship. The rallies "are often remembered more for the visual spectacle of totalitarian coordination they present than for the content of the speeches from the podium" (Herf 41). Wide shots are used to show off the numbers and strength of the party. The smaller staged choreography of *Springtime for Hitler* counters this while also demonstrating the intimacy of cabaret performance. Brooks' tiny human swastika formed by the dancers pokes the satirical knife into the pompousness of Nazi theatrics (1:00:27). Brooks also mocks Nazi spectacle by using chorus showgirls in beer and pretzel bustiers, a performance of which any anti–Nazi cabaret entertainer would be proud. Brooks' musical numbers not only appear to be "camp," they also reveal the Nazi parade to be preposterously camp as well.

"Camp has long been a central component of American musical theater," where "race and ethnicity," as well as their divisions, "matter tremendously" (Knapp 5). Sanford Pinsker uses the term "Jewish camp" to describe Brooks' humor (249). In "Notes on 'Camp'" Susan Sontag argues that "Jews and homosexuals are the outstanding creative minorities in contemporary urban culture" (291–92). Brooks' version of the form makes it dangerously subversive, akin to African American jazz in the Berlin cabaret. His works deny that "Jewish victimization hardly seems the appropriate source for laughter" (Erens 390).

Brooks' campy gallows humor is present again in "The Spanish Inquisition" musical number from *History of the World, Part I* (1981). Whereas in *Springtime for Hitler* Brooks focuses on the persecutors, fellow Borscht Belt comedian Jackie Mason's performance in "The Spanish Inquisition" focuses on the persecuted after a bound rabbi sees the torture of other Jews at the hands of monks. Mason's character places the agony of the *auto-da-fé* in a fun rhyme: "I'm sitting flicking chickens and I'm looking through the pickin's / And suddenly these *goys* break down my walls. / I didn't even know them, and they grabbed me by the scrotum / And started playing ping pong with my balls. / Oy, the agony, / Ooh, the shame, / To make my privates public for a game" (53:47–54:04). The beginning of the rhyme makes light of systematic torture by drawing a benign image of a rabbi performing kapparot, the Jewish ritual of atonement that is practiced by waving a chicken over a person and then slaughtering it. The juxtaposition is artful because Brooks explores the role of ritual in the two faiths. Brooks ends the sequence with another parody of Busby Berkeley—using synchronized swimming nuns—mimicking *Million Dollar Mermaid* (1952), reminding viewers of the film's relationship to its forebearer, *The Producers*. The nuns, like the Nazi chorus line in *The Producers*, more importantly, recall the chorus lines, cancan dancers, and showgirls of the cabaret.

The drag show is another popular cabaret art form that Brooks reinterprets. Cabaret offered a context in which the long-oppressed male homosexual could caricature himself (Gavin 44). Jewish comedians and drag queens alike turn the joke on themselves before their aggressors can, thereby exposing the prejudices entrenched in old stereotypes. In *The Producers*, Bialystock solicits drag queen director Roger De Bris (Christopher Hewett)—whose equally flamboyant assistant Carmen Ghia (Andreas Voutsinas) dons his own eccentric outfit—to stage *Springtime for Hitler*. De Bris is chosen because, like his name suggests, he is discarded trash; he is an unsuccessful director known for creating rubbish. He is the antithesis of everything tasteful and mainstream. "Bris" is also similar to the Yiddish word *bris*, referencing the Hebrew *brit milah* ("covenant of circumcision"), indicating both the emasculation and Jewishness of the character. Excessively eccentric, he fits right in with the bohemian club crowd.

Even though Andrew Sarris criticizes the filmmaker for his "thoroughly vile and inept" direction (qtd. in Yacowar 84), Brooks' direction is simplistic in order to undermine homophobic Nazism and other hypermasculine, heterosexual myths (47:06). Brooks uses three-point, balanced lighting to show off the stage performers' garish environment; the tacky décor—wallpaper with a metallic flower design and a closet of outdated costume dresses—demonstrates these cabaret artists' gauche taste. Likewise, Nazi transvestism in Bob Fosse's *Cabaret* (1972) reinforces cabaret's critique of idealistic Gentile spectacle and showcases a preference for anti-membership. Fantastic colors and tilted and distorted shots underline cabaret's "degenerate" influence. Fosse's low-key lighting and the choreography during the "Tiller Girls" number indicate how the Jew is out-of-step and clearly an imposter (1:27:51). Both Brooks' *Young Frankenstein* (1974) and Jim Sharman's *The Rocky Horror Picture Show* (1975) later share in this transformation of narrative. The cabaret-esque performances of Gene Wilder (Dr. Frankenstein) and Peter Boyle (The Monster) singing "Puttin' on the Ritz," and Tim Curry's as the "sweet transvestite from Transsexual, Transylvania," parody Mary Shelley's story while emulating the interrogation of gender and group membership. In both instances, cabaret takes the form of imperfect cultural miming to alter social constructs. Like these later films' critiques of culture, *The Producers* offers more than "the grotesque images of heterosexuality" and "kinky instances of homosexuality" that Yacowar finds (76).

Rickman contends that it is specifically the "flamboyant gay" and the "mock hippie" stereotypes that undermine Brooks' critique (299), and Desser and Friedman call Brooks' use of homosexuality "unfortunate" (154). These critics, however, have failed to note how performances in Brooks' work play a part in what many admit is the filmmaker's greatest strength: the critique of "traditional American myths" and the "cultural hegemony dominated by a white, middle-class, masculine, and decidedly gentile worldview" (111–12). Rather than what Robert Hatch calls a "mean" treatment of homosexuals (486), Brooks' characters should be interpreted as participating in a tradition of shock and unconventionality as perfected by the underground cabaret performer. Albert Vorspan argues that on the Broadway stage "Jewish themes" competed with "homosexuality and race for dominion" (viii). But Brooks' work is less about such competition and more about cooperation. African Americans, Jews, homosexuals, and many other multi-ethnic dissidents entertained in the cabaret; many clubs like The Blue Angel had a policy of non-discrimination (Gavin 69). Brooks references the club in *The Producers* when Bialystock goes to "The Blue Gypsy" to meet one of his elderly donors. Brooks also stresses the importance of discriminated groups bonding together in *To Be or Not to Be* (1983) when Bronski (Brooks) states "without Jews, gypsies, and fags, there is no theater" (42:47–52).

Since cabaret performances like those found in *The Threepenny Opera* (1928) and *Der blaue Engel* (1930) heavily inform Brooks' comedic choices, it is no coincidence that one finds them throughout Brooks' repertoire. He parodies *Der blaue Engel* in *Blazing Saddles* (1974). In the film, Madeline Kahn's character, based on Dietrich, is renamed Lili von Shtupp. *Shtup* in Yiddish means "push" or "shove" and is also a vulgarism for sexual intercourse ("Shtup" def. 1). These scenes also allude to Dietrich's cabaret

An icon of Weimar cabaret culture, Marlene Dietrich straddles a chair as Lola Lola in *Der blaue Engel* (1930).

30   יסודות / Foundations

Highly sexual, Lili von Shtupp (Madeline Kahn) straddles a chair like Lola Lola in *Der blaue Engel* (1930). Her Prussian chorus line is also an object of Brooks' derision in *Blazing Saddles* (1974).

performance in *Destry Rides Again* (1939). Brooks' work employs stereotypes of all kinds, here specifically that of the Gentile woman as highly sexual or "easy," to ridicule the oppressor. In *Blazing Saddles*, the Prussian military, representative of German authoritarianism, is the object of Brooks' derision. Brooks explains his attitude towards the Germans:

> Why should I not like the Germans? Just because they're arrogant and have fat necks and do anything they're told so long as it's cruel, and killed millions of Jews in concentration camps and made soap out of their bodies and lamp shades out of their skins? Is that any reason to hate their fucking guts? [qtd. in Yacowar 17].

Here it should be noted that cabaret performers were effective at insulting Nazi officials and Jewish cabaret was everything antithetical to the romanticized visions of Nazi aesthetics propagated in Leni Riefenstahl's documentaries. The crude caricatures of Weimar art and cabaret were insulting to the myth of superior Teutonic taste. Hitler's idealism contrasted greatly with the "degenerate" Jewish cabaret lifestyle. For example, the exciting fringe climate of the nightclub conflicted with the grandeur and unrealistic aspirations of the Nazi fantasy perpetuated in Riefenstahl's *Triumph des Willens* (1935) and *Olympia* (1938). The volume, cost, and spectacle of Riefenstahl's work demonstrate Nazi indulgence. Grandiosity in these films is justification for aesthetic and racial superiority. The contrast of the image of the Jew as a rat and a dirty street hustler in *Der ewige Jude* (1940) reminded German audiences that Jews were curious objects at which to be gazed. Whereas Riefenstahl focuses in *Olympia* on singular bodies to highlight the strong Aryan man as an individual, *Der ewige Jude* relies on depicting Jews as a unit or tribe to show them as scoundrels and subversives who should be viewed as subhuman. Crude images of unattractive clusters of Jews underline the narrator's argument that they "prolong all conditions of sickness" (12:44).

Brooks is very conscious of both "Jewish" and "Gentile" art and this anti–Semitic imagery. Thus, he does not exploit Jewish victimhood. Instead, his films satirize and critique both authority and stereotypes to find humor in even the darkest of moments. In *The Producers*, Bialystock and Bloom create a play that ends up undermining the tyranny and horrors of Nazi Germany and ridicules violence and hate. Dark humor is presented as a resistance disguised within victimhood and "exercised within the symbolic space of performance" (7). Bialystock and Bloom also encourage performance as a response to imprisonment. The protagonists sing "Prisoners of Love" for their fellow inmates, refusing to let their dire situation dissuade them from laughing and enjoying their clumsy performance; it recalls not only the degenerate art of Weimar cabaret that was driven by protest and dissidence but also concentration-camp cabaret in which entertainers relied on their misery for performance (1:23:16). In prison, Brooks' characters continue to celebrate performance as a form of self-defense.

Understanding the Jewish cabaret, one can uncover what *The Producers* achieves with its New Cabaret style, especially what Mostel's performance adds. Samuel Joel "Zero" Mostel was born in Brooklyn, New York, on 28 February 1915. His father, Israel, was raised in an Orthodox Jewish family in Eastern Europe. His mother, Cina, was born in Poland but raised in Vienna (Brown 1). Mostel's family's Orthodox upbringing had an effect on the comic actor's future ambitions. As he would recall, "being an entertainer of that kind came under the heading of making fun of human beings, which is objectionable in the orthodox Jewish religion"—"could you imagine my father, a Jew in a black hat with a long beard, sitting in a night club?" (qtd. in Brown 4). Mostel had no interest in Judaism, although his mother and father wanted him to be a rabbi (6–7). Instead of standing before a congregation reading sacred texts, he stood before an audience doing impressions of Jimmy Durante, Charles Boyer, and Adolf Hitler (25).

Mostel was an intellectual and a clown. He had years of experience in nightclubs, where he perfected an "aggressive, larger-than-life, highly energetic performance style [...] whereby passionate outbursts were frequently intermingled (or alternated) with songs, dances, and jokes" (Brown 30). His acts combined "pantomime," "general silliness," and "political satire," to a level of "ferocious intensity" that some found dangerous (25). The intense, over-the-top nature of both Bialystock and Bloom makes them "caricature Jewish figures" (King 153) and part of a strategy "in comedy of a distinctive racial or ethnic slant" (152). King explains how "exaggeration to the point of absurdity of negative stereotypes" can be an act of subversion (152). Mostel, nevertheless, was apprehensive about playing such a character. He was uneasy both about the Jewish protagonist's attitudes towards women and his avariciousness. After playing the self-righteous and anti-assimilationist Tevye in *Fiddler on the Roof* (1964), this new character was very different. He saw the part of Bialystock going in the opposite direction. He associated the role with the negativity of the Jewish stereotype of avariciousness that has long existed (Brown 264). Max Bialystock's taking advantage of women and exploiting the suffering of others was a stark contrast to the considerate Tevye. This stereotype, according to Abraham H. Foxman, is one of the three pillars of anti–Semitism, along with the identification of Jews as dedicated anti-assimilationists and "murderers" of Jesus (43). There was a problem with presenting such openly "Jewish" types ingrained in the minds of anti–Semites, which Jewish critics found offensive (Desser and Friedman 147). Desser and Friedman describe Bialystock as the seductive, "boisterous conniver" (147). Associations with the wolfish stereotype are apparent from Bialystock's first appearance on camera with a large "B" embroidered on the red smoking jacket he wears (3:34). It marks him as the type that Desser and Friedman accuse Brooks of frequently abusing: "the cunning Jew who unscrupulously fleeces others, the money-hungry Jew who sacrifices morality on the altar of immediate riches, the manipulative Jew who trades on the finer emotions of others for his own gain, the garish Jew who flaunts his wealth at the least opportunity" (147, 149). This avaricious Jewish figure also has a long history, dating back to at least 17th-century European culture. This stereotype appeared "on stage and elsewhere as completely unscrupulous and untrustworthy, a fiend-like agent who would sell his very soul for financial gain […]. All these aspects of the stereotype combined to portray a pariah" (Felsenstein 34–35). Mostel, though, was successful in this role.

Mostel, as a live performer, is stylistically built for the stage. Brooks' simplistic set design and medium level of framing provide the actor with ample space to move about, allowing the star to make full use of the bravado that made him successful. Mostel's casting is an essential part of why typage works in the film; in other words, his physique and facial features, in combination with the gauche décor and high-key lighting, reveal the authenticity of the character and the credibility of his performance. When contrasted with the steadfast and devout Tevye, it is clear that *The Producers* makes light of the exaggerated nature of stereotypes more than it promotes them.

It is useful to compare the 1968 version of *The Producers* with the 2005 remake in order to see how Brooks updated the cabaret humor of the film.

The 2005 version was co-written with Thomas Meehan and directed by Susan Stroman, a Broadway choreographer. The Jewish characters drew less reaction from critics (Fermaglich 77), and Fermaglich argues that Brooks "transferred his anxieties from the emergence of a proto-fascist subculture of hippies and college radicals in the 1960s to the rapidly expanding visibility and power of gay men and women in American culture" (72). Bialystock is played by Nathan Lane, who had been a likely candidate to play Bialystock in Brooks' 2001 Broadway production of *The Producers*.

The American LGBT community's position in the mainstream is explored in the new version of *The Producers*. The musical number "Keep It Gay" summarizes both the philosophy of the drag queen director, Roger De Bris (Gary Beach), and Brooks himself: "No matter what you do / On the stage / Keep it light, keep it bright, / Keep it gay. / Whether it's murder, / Mayhem or rage, / Don't complain, it's a pain, / Keep it gay" (47:40–53). De Bris' assistant, Carmen Ghia (Roger Bart), then continues the song: "People want laughter when they see a show. / The last thing they're after is / A litany of woe" (47:55–48:01). De Bris' production team comes down the stairs: the set designer (a gay biker), the costume designer (an Elton John lookalike), a wild choreographer dressed in tight purple velvet pants, a lesbian lighting designer, and a group of Village People impersonators (48:38–49:32). This flamboyant entrance prepares viewers for what is to come in *Springtime for Hitler*: Roger has to play Hitler after Franz (Will Ferrell) breaks his leg. Carmen Ghia gives his approval to the gay director: "You're going out there a silly, hysterical, screaming queen, but you're coming back a great big, passing-for-straight, Broadway star" (1:26:07–17). Indeed, here "passing-for-straight" is still looked upon as superior to one's being different. Even if the LGBT community has worked hard to develop and maintain the arts and entertainment, like Jewish actors and producers have, it still falls short of complete acceptance in the dominant society. Here, Brooks acknowledges how mainstream culture still fails in replicating the attitudes and ethics of the cabaret, which operate and thrive in an environment in which non-membership will always be more important.

Brooks parodies several Broadway plays in the final scenes of the 2005 remake. Titles of Bialystock and Bloom productions appear in lights: *A Streetcar Named Murray*, *She Shtupps to Conquer*, *High Button Jews*, and *Katz*. The marquees demonstrate Brooks' commitment to making his comedy Jewish through their use of Yiddish puns. They also show the nostalgia for Broadway and the great narratives that helped to build it. These closing parodic titles finally remind the viewer that they have just heard Brooks' swan song. Other than voice work, the now-ninety-nine-year-old filmmaker has not directed or produced a film since.

The success of *The Producers* was important because it set the stage for Brooks' other "Holocaust comedies." Hitler is also an object of derision in *History of the World, Part I* (1981) when "Hitler on Ice" sums up in one visual the egotism, ethnocentrism, and tyranny of anti–Semitic Europe in a twirling, figure-skating dictator (1:23:36). Here, Brooks not only again ridicules Nazi spectacle with a long shot that reduces Hitler in stature, making him appear like a miniature figurine, he also mocks an arguably popular form of Gentile entertainment: the Ice Capades. Furthermore, in *To Be or Not to Be* (1983), the musical number "Naughty Nazis" is halted by Polish bureaucrats worried it might be "construed as a direct insult to Chancellor Hitler" (10:58–11:00).

Conclusion

To respond to an important question critics raise—"what role did humor play in Jewish survival?" (Ziv and Zajdman xviii)—one answer is that it helped, and still helps, the community cope with suffering and persecution. Mel Brooks does not minimize or ridicule human suffering; he offers creative ways to resist the violence by making the story one's own. Even if his films are described as "tasteless," "despicable," and "dangerous" (Fermaglich 60), they are part of the darker comedy from Jews who were altering stereotypes to create a new Jewishness—a New Cabaret—on screen.

Note

1. The list of Borscht Belt comics is impressive: Sid Caesar (Isaac Sidney Caesar), Jerry Lewis (Jerome Levitch), Danny Kaye (David Daniel Kaminsky, no relation to Brooks), Red Buttons (Aaron Chwatt), Milton Berle (Mendel Berlinger), Don Rickles (Donald Jay Rickles), Jack Benny (Benjamin Kubelsky), Joan Rivers (Joan Alexandra Molinsky), Jackie Mason (Yacov Moshe Maza), Buddy Hackett (Leonard Hacker), Phyllis Diller (Phyllis Ada Driver), Shecky Greene (Fred Sheldon Greenfield), Henny Youngman (Henry Yungman), Lenny Bruce (Leonard Alfred Schneider), Zero Mostel (Samuel Joel Mostel), and, of course, Mike Nichols (Mikhail Igor Peschkowsky), Mel Brooks (Melvin Kaminsky), Elaine May (Elaine Iva Berlin), and Woody Allen (Allan Stewart Konigsberg).

Filmography

Der blaue Engel. Dir. Josef von Sternberg. UFA, 1930. DVD. Kino, 2001.
Blazing Saddles. Dir. Mel Brooks. Warner Bros., 1974. DVD. Warner Bros. Home Video, 2004.
Cabaret. Dir. Bob Fosse. Allied Artists, 1972. DVD. Fremantle, 2002.

Der ewige Jude. Dir. Fritz Hippler. Terra, 1940. *YouTube.* 1 Aug. 2016.
Fiddler on the Roof. Dir. Norman Jewison. United Artists, 1971. DVD. Two Discs. MGM Home Entertainment, 2004.
Gold Diggers of 1933. Dir. Mervyn Leroy. Numbers creat. and dir. by Busby Berkeley. Warner Bros., 1933. DVD. Warner Home Video, 2006.
History of the World, Part I. Dir. Mel Brooks. Twentieth Century Fox, 1981. DVD. Twentieth Century Fox Home Entertainment, 2006.
"The Making of *The Producers.*" *The Producers.* DVD. Optimum, 2008.
Million Dollar Mermaid. Dir. Mervyn LeRoy. Numbers creat. and dir. by Busby Berkeley. MGM, 1952. DVD. MGM, 2002.
Olympia. Dir. Leni Riefenstahl. Universum Film AG, 1938. DVD. Demand, 2008.
The Producers. Dir. Mel Brooks. Embassy, 1968. DVD. Optimum, 2008.
The Producers. Dir. Susan Stroman. Columbia Pictures, 2005. DVD. Sony Pictures Home Entertainment, 2006.
The Rocky Horror Picture Show. Dir. Jim Sharman. Twentieth Century Fox, 1976. DVD. Twentieth Century Fox, 2019.
To Be or Not to Be. Dir. Ernst Lubitsch. United Artists, 1942.
To Be or Not to Be. Dir. Mel Brooks. Twentieth Century Fox, 1983. DVD. Twentieth Century Fox Home Entertainment, 2006.
Triumph des Willens. Dir. Leni Riefenstahl. Universum Film AG, 1935. DVD. Demand, 2008.
Young Frankenstein. Dir. Mel Brooks. Twentieth Century Fox, 1974. DVD. Twentieth Century Fox Home Entertainment, 2006.

Works Cited

Abrams, Nathan. *The New Jew in Film: Exploring Jewishness and Judaism in Contemporary Cinema.* Rutgers UP, 2012.
_____. "'My religion is American': A Midrash on Judaism in American Films, 1990 to the Present." In *Religion in the United States,* edited by Jeanne Corriel, Kornelia Freitag, Christine Gerhardt and Michael Walla, Winter Verlag, 2011, pp. 209–25.
Beck, Evelyn Torton. *Kafka and the Yiddish Theater: Its Impact on His Work.* U of Wisconsin P, 1971.
Belth, Alex. "Mel Brooks Is Always Funny and Often Wise in This 1975 Playboy Interview." *Daily Beast,* 16 February 2014. *TheDailyBeast.com,* 7 December 2016. https://www.thedailybeast.com/mel-brooks-is-always-funny-and-often-wise-in-this-1975-playboy-interview.
Bender, Sara. *The Jews of Białystok During World War II and the Holocaust.* Trans. Yaffa Murciano. Brandeis UP, 2008.
Brooks, Mel. "Interview with Jerry Bauer." *Adelina,* February 1980. 20 September 2016. www.brookslyn.com/print/Adelina1980/Adelina1980.php.
_____. "With Comedy, We Can Rob Hitler of His Posthumous Power." Interview with *Der Spiegel. Spiegel,* 16 March 2006. https://www.spiegel.de/international/spiegel/spiegel-interview-with-mel-brooks-with-comedy-we-can-rob-hitler-of-his-posthumous-power-a-406268.html.
Brown, Jared. *Zero Mostel: A Biography.* Antheneum, 1989.
Bruce, Lenny. *The Essential Lenny Bruce: His Original Unexpurgated Satirical Routines.* Edited by John Cohen. Panther, 1975.
Cohen, Sarah Blacher, ed. *From Hester Street to Hollywood: The Jewish-American Stage and Screen.* Indiana UP, 1983.
_____, ed. *Jewish Wry: Essays on Jewish Humor.* Wayne State UP, 1987.
Colerick, George. *From* The Italian Girl *to* Cabaret: *Musical Humor, Parody and Burlesque.* Juventus, 1998. https://www.jstor.org/stable/466522?seq=1#page_scan_tab_contents.

Desser, David, and Lester Friedman. *American-Jewish Filmmakers: Traditions and Trends.* U of Illinois P, 1993.
Dundes, Alan, editor. *The Blood Libel Legend: A Casebook in Anti-Semitic Folklore.* U of Wisconsin P, 1991.
———, and Thomas Hauschild. "Auschwitz Jokes." *Humor and Society: Resistance and Control*, edited by Chris Powell and George E.C. Paton, Palgrave Macmillan, 1988, pp. 56–66.
Eagleton, Terry. *Literary Theory: An Introduction.* U of Minnesota P, 1983.
Erens, Patricia. *The Jew in American Cinema.* U of Indiana P, 1984.
Farina, William. *The German Cabaret Legacy in American Popular Music.* McFarland, 2013.
Felsenstein, Frank. *Anti-Semitic Stereotypes: A Paradigm of Otherness in English Popular Culture, 1660–1830.* Johns Hopkins UP, 1995.
Fermaglich, Kirsten. "Mel Brooks's *The Producers*: Tracing American Jewish Culture through Comedy, 1967–2007." *American Studies*, vol. 48, no. 4, Winter 2007, pp. 59–87.
Fleishman, Philip. "Interview with Mel Brooks." *Maclean's*, 17 April 1979.
Foxman, Abraham H. *Jews and Money: The Story of a Stereotype.* Palgrave Macmillan, 2010.
Gair, Christopher. *The American Counterculture, 1945–1975.* Edinburgh UP, 2007.
Gavin, James. *Intimate Nights: The Golden Age of New York Cabaret.* Backstage Books, 2006.
Goldman, Albert. "Laughtermakers." *Jewish Wry: Essays on Jewish Humor*, edited by Sarah Blacher Cohen, Wayne State UP, 1987, pp. 80–88.
Grunberger, Richard. *A Social History of the Third Reich.* Phoenix, 1983.
Hatch, Robert. "Films." *The Nation*, 8 April 1968, p. 486.
Herf, Jeffrey. *The Jewish Enemy: Nazi Propaganda during World War II and the Holocaust.* Harvard UP, 2006.
Hillenbrand, F.K.M. *Underground Humor in Nazi Germany, 1933–1945.* Routledge, 1995.
Holtzman, William. *Seesaw: A Dual Biography of Anne Bancroft and Mel Brooks.* Doubleday, 1979. Google Books, 16 February 2018. https://archive.org/details/seesawdualbiogra00holt.
Howe, Irving. *The Immigrant Jews of New York: 1881 to the Present.* Routledge & Kegan Paul, 1976.
Jelavich, Peter. *Berlin Cabaret.* Harvard UP, 1997.
Kael, Pauline. "O, Pioneer!" *The New Yorker*, 23 March 1968. *Newyorker.com*, 23 November 2016. https://www.newyorker.com/magazine/1968/03/23/o-pioneer.
Kauffmann, Stanley. "Zero and Others." *New Republic*, 13 April 1968.
Kesselman, Jonathan. E-mail to Peter Lederer. 22 May 2019.
King, Geoff. *Film Comedy.* Wallflower P, 2002.
Knapp, Raymond. *The American Musical and the Formation of National Identity.* Princeton UP, 2005.
Lareau, Alan. *The Wild Stage: Literary Cabarets of the Weimar Republic.* Camden, 1995.
Lewis, Anthony. "The Jew in Stand-up Comedy." *From Hester Street to Hollywood: The Jewish-American Stage and Screen*, edited by Sarah Blacher Cohen, Indiana UP, 1983, pp. 58–70.
McDonald, Paul. "'They're Trying to Kill Me': Jewish American Humor and the War Against Pop Culture." *Studies in Popular Culture*, vol. 28, no. 3, April 2006, 19–33. *JSTOR*, 16 Nov. 2016. https://www.jstor.org/stable/23416169?seq=1#page_scan_tab_contents.
Moshin, Jamie. "On the Big Screen, but Stuck in the Closet: What Mel Brooks's *The Producers* Says about Modern American Jewish Identity and Communicating the Holocaust." *Journal of the Northwest Communication Association*, vol. 35, 2006, pp. 22–45.
Nachman, Gerald. *Seriously Funny: The Rebel Comedians of the 1950s and 1960s.* Knopf Doubleday, 2009.
Pinsker, Sanford. "Mel Brooks and the Cinema of Exhaustion." *From Hester Street to Hollywood: The Jewish-American Stage and Screen*, edited by Sarah Blacher Cohen. Indiana UP, 1983, pp. 245–256.
Reinelt, Janelle G., and Joseph R. Roach, eds. *Critical Theory and Performance.* U of Michigan P, 1992.

Rickman, Gregg, editor. *The Film Comedy Reader*. Limelight Editions, 2001.
Sandrow, Nahma. "Yiddish Theater and American Theater." *From Hester Street to Hollywood: The Jewish-American Stage and Screen*, edited by Sarah Blacher Cohen, Indiana UP, 1983, pp. 18–28.
Sarris, Andrew. "Films." *Village Voice*, 28 March 1968, p. 47.
Senelick, Laurence. *Cabaret Performance: Volume II: Europe 1920–1940: Sketches, Songs, Monologues, Memoirs*. Trans. Laurence Senelick. Johns Hopkins UP, 1993.
"Shtup." *A Dictionary of Yiddish Slang and Idioms*. Citadel P, 1995.
Sobral, Ana. *Opting Out: Deviance and Generational Identities in American Post-War Cult Fiction*. Rodopi, 2012.
Sontag, Susan. *Against Interpretation*. Anchor, 1990.
Vorspan, Albert. *My Rabbi Doesn't Make House Calls*. Doubleday, 1969.
Walsh, Moira. "The Producers." *America*, 6 April 1968.
Yacowar, Maurice. *Method in Madness: The Comic Art of Mel Brooks*. St. Martin's P, 1981.
Ziv, Avner, and Anat Zajdman, eds. *Semites and Stereotypes: Characteristics of Jewish Humor*. Greenwood Press, 1993.

"He shoulda been called *Yitzhak*"
Mel Brooks and the Pleasures of Parody
Terry Lindvall *and* Chris Lindvall

Even as a secular filmmaker, Mel Brooks (né Melvin James Kamisky) is an old man of the Jewish Bible. His film comedies follow the paradigm of a Jewish patriarch, one who stumbles through the wilderness, questioning and kvetching with the Divine, mocking the pretensions of religious hypocrisy, and wrestling with questions of existence with his tongue firmly planted in his cheek. He takes down cinematic idols to expose a common humanity. The 2000-year-old Brooks may deny a faith in the Almighty (although always ready to thank Him for giving him his wife, Anne Bancroft), but his film parodies present a glimpse into the nature of God through his curious creatures. He offers a unique pleasure highlighting a mirror of humanity through the lens of laughter, bequeathing hints of hope in the humor of a most fallible human nature. Brooks does not mask the deep connections between his Jewish identity and his comic work. He explicitly points back to the roots of his comedy in the Jewish tradition, from where distinctive motifs and patterns bounced forth. He has playfully alluded to himself as "your obedient Jew," a phrase that scholar David Desser calls "squeaking with mock obsequiousness while affirming his outsider status." His awareness of anger, a percolating animosity towards all things German, and his own impoverished origins connect his comedy to the suffering of his cultural heritage and Jewish history. This little loud man with the wide grin and boisterous energy sprouted from the soil of Job. His life philosophy adopted words from that early biblical schlimazel, whose suspect comforters suggested, "at destruction and famine you shall laugh" (5:22). Brooks' early tragic trajectory sprang from growing up in the rough Williamsburg section of Brooklyn. His father died when he was two, and his mother kept her family of four boys together by working in the garment industry. Brooks' comic voice is a pastiche of everyone around him, from his Uncle Joe to his grandmother, all connected with "five thousand years of Jews pouring through me." He told late night television host Steve Allen, "So, for every ten Jews beating their breasts, God designated one to be crazy and amuse the breast beaters. By the time I was five, I knew I was that one. You want to know where my comedy comes from? It comes from not being kissed by a girl until you're 16. It comes from the feeling that, as a Jew and as a person, you don't fit into the mainstream of American society. It comes from the realization that even though you're better and smarter, you'll never belong" (Allen 59).

A Hebrew patriarch of 20th-century American comedy, Brooks, at times, has been brash and obnoxious, but celebrating his "wild amalgam of chutzpah (guts) and mazel (luck)" (Parish 185), he has not given up on his gift of laughter to the human race. As Bildad the Shuhite promised the beleaguered soul of Job, "God will yet fill your mouth with laughter and your lips with shouts of joy" (8:21). Brooks has defined his laughter as *a "defense against the universe"* between these two poles in the Hebrew text (Kennedy Center). Against centuries of suffering, he has reaffirmed a common core of humanity and shared it with millions. Examining Brooks' comic art as *Peshat*, this close-textual reading of his *oeuvre* finds a wonderfully vulgar incarnation of a Divine comedy.

In *Old Men of the Bible*, religious studies professor Craig Wansink investigates key biblical characters at the ends of their lives, observing that the old patriarchs were not progressively getting better; they were only getting older. Mel Brooks echoes this condition. When asked if stand-up comics "get funnier as they get older," he responded, "Not necessarily. They tend to drool more, that I know" (Atlas). Brooks' comic art stems from his role as a modern patriarch of parody, a prophet of its vulgar pleasures, and a jester of religious tropes. In Shakespeare's plays, the upstart fool calls ordinary people back to reality. In *As You like It*, Touchstone mutters, "The fool doth think he is wise, but the wise man knows himself to be a fool" (Shakespeare, *As You like It*). A New York jester, Brooks, with method in his unabashed *meshugaas*, proves another of Shakespeare's quips true. In *King Lear*, "jesters oft do prophets prove" (Shakespeare, *King Lear*). Brooks does not fit the usual portrait of a prophet like Isaiah, Jeremiah, Hosea, or Amos. They use wit to satirize the idolatry of their enemies and fellow Jews, but their rhetorical flourishes rarely raise a smile. Though Isaiah and the Roman poet Horace both mock those who made idols out of wood that they had just used to cook their food, and then worship the artificial constructions that can neither see nor hear, it is the fool who exposes bigotry, racism, idolatry, and all manner of stupidity. Sometimes, however, the medium, or the messenger, is the message, and this seems to be true of Brooks.

Brooks' personal life, however, is not a case in point. After his first marriage broke up, he met the illustrious and talented actress Anne Bancroft. Their famous long-lasting and happy marriage of more than 40 years shaped him into a good husband and father (he did humbly attribute their son Maximillan's good qualities to his wife). The two got married in 1964, during Mel's lunch break, the Jewish comic and the Italian Roman Catholic star wed by a Presbyterian minister in a civil ceremony. Ironically, as a patriarch, in contrast to his aggressive and boisterous personality in show business, he relinquished control on the home front. In fact, he acknowledged, "She was a very hard woman to dominate if you wanted to be Mr. Male. But I wasn't interested in dominating" (in Darrach). If a man were the head of a household, it was only as a figurehead. Bancroft, whom Brooks confessedly acknowledged he could never bamboozle, worked her miracle by humanizing the short upstart. She even negotiated to get their son Max baptized as well as being initiated into his bar mitzvah ceremony.

For Brooks the path to patriarchy was also paved with menial tasks. He worked as a clerk in the Brooklyn Navy Yard and then advanced to the lowly labors of being a bus boy. At the Borscht Belt resorts in the Mountains, he stumbled into becoming a *tumler*, keeping entertainment alive with musical and comic bits. The Catskills offered opportunities for the young jazz drummer to make friends and experiment with comedy. As an ersatz social director at the Grossinger's Hotel, he met saxophone player Sid Caesar. His breakthrough occurred in 1950 when Caesar collared one of the most talented gangs of gag-writers for his variety television production *Your Show of Shows*. At the outset, Brooks was an outlier, continually rejected by producer Max Liebman. His chutzpah enabled him to imitate everything "from a rabbinical student to the white whale of Moby Dick thrashing about on the floor with six harpoons sticking in his back" (Sennett 25). Irritated with the little man who made "loud noises," Liebman would often throw lighted cigar ends at him. Once, however, he exploded at Brooks, screaming, "You are nothing!" Mel retorted, "If I am nothing then you are king of nothing," one of the best rejoinders of a juvenile to a superior that could be had (Parish 73).

In this brilliant coterie of writers, Brooks met Carl Reiner, Woody Allen, Neil Simon, Larry Gelbart, and other rising wits and humorists. He excelled at writing movie burlesques for the shabby and indomitably ignorant "Professor" Sid, an expert on mountain climbing, nutrition, or insomnia (frequently interviewed by baffled "reporter" Carl Reiner). As Dr. Ludwig von Pablum, the self-proclaimed expert, Caesar waxed ridiculously on his book, *Children Are People, Only Smaller*, who, in describing the psychological make-up of small boys, opined that they were made of "snakes and snails and puppy dog tails. That's what little boys are made of" (Sennett 54). The soil of Mel's parodies came out of his passion for classic and foreign movie films. Burlesque sketches like *From Here to Obscurity*, *A Trolleycar Named Desire*, and the Western *Strange* spoofed movie conventions, fertilizing the earth for Mel's future harvest.

The legendary 1960 creation of "The 2000-Year-Old Man" character with Reiner (again as an interviewer) soared into becoming a best-selling album. Steve Allen urged the pair to record it, suggesting a more apt name for his unique and hysterically comic character would have been "The Wandering Jew." He jauntily caricatured Jesus as "a thin lad, always worse sandals. Hung around with 12 other guys" and he would come into the store but never buy anything. He would just ask for water. Episcopalian Robin Williams extended Brooks' caricature by arguing that Jesus was Jewish: "Some people say Jesus wasn't Jewish. Yes, of course he was Jewish: 30 years old, single, lives with his parents, come on! He takes his father's business; his mom thought he was God's gift. He's Jewish; give it up!" However, Brooks' Old Man mostly complains about his own problems, namely that while he had 42,000 children, "not one comes to visit me."

With Buck Henry, Mel sketched out his first real spoof, the *Get Smart* television series from 1965 to 1970, parodying the spy craze of Ian Fleming's James Bond. In the midst of this creative output, *The Producers* (1967) won the Academy Award for Best Original Screenplay. Its precise inside-jokes regarding the bottom line of the entertainment industry, from prostituting and pimping oneself for a flop, knocked out cynicism with a sweet smell of fallible producers with their own fetishes. All of this was a preamble to Brooks' emergence as the patriarch of parody, with his discovery of a calling to lampoon the cinematic arts.

The Parody Recipe

"When you parody something, you move the truth sideways" (207), Brooks writes in his autobiography, *All About Me!* Various characteristics mark parody as a unique and gratifying film genre. The most foundational criteria include the requisite conditions of imitating a recognizable form with deep affection and being funny.

The early 20th-century French comic theorist Henri Bergson has quipped, "transpose the solemn into the familiar and the result is parody" (Bergson 140). Accordingly, film parody offers an original narrative imitating a familiar work or text. It usually incorporates a multiplicity of targets (such as Mel Brook's subtexts on Germans and prayers in his films) and includes gags, stunts, and what are known as anomalous surprises, namely unpredicted violations of audience expectation (for example, Igor not realizing he has a hump).

The first rule of an effective parody, according to scholars Wes Gehring, Michael Tueth, and Dennis Bounds, is that the work must grow out of a familiar genre like the musical, while tinkering and toying with its conventions and tropes. The Greek etymology of *parody* reaches back to the prefix *para* (alongside, opposite) and the noun *ode* (song, lyric poem) suggesting an imitation of a familiar and established artistic form. In fact, Brooks' love of music and his inventive musical compositions burst forth from his desire to do Broadway musicals. His own songs became classics, from Frankenstein's monster (Peter Boyle) singing "Puttin' on the Ritz" as a vaudeville number in *Young Frankenstein* to Mel Brooks' character in *High Anxiety* channeling the crooning of Frank Sinatra in a Las Vegas hotel.

Even his Western Soap Opera parody *Blazing Saddles* opens with a musical number featuring legendary Western singer Frankie Laine who croons out the theme with all the sincerity of his previous classic works. Brooks confided that in a performance that was remarkably "so sweet and so sad," Laine did not realize he was singing for a movie comedy. "With tears in his eyes, he said to me, 'This is a beautiful song.'" In his philosophy of comedy Brooks aims at playing the "absurd as if it's normal," and Laine's rendition helped him to do just that.

Familiar film classics of the early 1930s, Busby Berkeley Warner Bros. musicals and Josef von Sternberg's *Der blaue Engel* (1930) receive musical burlesques in the raunchy Western. Brooks auditioned Madeline Kahn to play a cabaret type singer like Marlene Dietrich ("See What the Boys in the Back Room Will Have" from *Destry Rides Again* [1939]). He wanted her to sing a slightly off-key, sultry *Sprechstimme* (talk-sing style of the 1920s of Bertolt Brech and Kurt Weill) composition of "I'm Tired." Entreating Kahn to be a saloon chanteuse Lili von Shtupp, he needed her to straddle a chair like Lola Lola (Marlene Dietrich) in *Der blaue Engel*. Entreating Kahn to be a saloon chanteuse Lili von Shtupp, he needed her to straddle a chair like Lola Lola (Marlene Dietrich) in *Der bleue Engel*. Brooks asked her to raise her skirt so he could see her legs. "What the hell is this, a 1930 Broadway musical?" barked Kahn. "Who are you, Warner Baxter in *42nd Street*?" She had the legs and got the world-weary role as the seductress-for-hire. Like Dietrich, Kahn wearily moans, "Who can satisfy their lustful habits? I am not a rabbit! I need some rest. I'm tired," and ends up singing the crude lyrics, "I've been with thousands of men / again and again / they promise the moon / they're always coming and going and going and coming … and always too soon…. Right, girls?"

The outrageousness of Brooks' parody in exaggerating a familiar text (reaching its apex, or nadir, with "Springtime for Hitler") also illuminates the difference between entertainment elites and the common spectator. A preview of *Blazing Saddles* for Hollywood executives almost led to a shelving of the film until a lower class of viewers embraced its vulgarity. Its vulgar moments have been attributed to Brooks' meticulous attention to "familiar" details. For example, he had watched numerous Roy Rogers and Gene Autry westerns as a child. He noticed that the cowboys

> would be sitting around the campfire playing the guitar, and you could see these tin plates and beans. And I always wondered: How many beans could you eat and how much black coffee could you drink out of those tin cups without letting one go? I don't know if *Blazing Saddles* was the first movie to have a fart in it. But when I went to work on it, I said: "Let's tell the truth of the campfire. So we got a bunch of guys around a microphone, soaped up our armpits and Brooks recognized how parodies easily capture and tweak movie conventions: 'I realized all one really had to do was just observe. Observe and slightly exaggerate and you had comedy'" [Tynan].

The second, and more important, criteria for parodies is that they be funny, even to the uninitiated. If it ain't funny, it ain't good for the makings of a good parody. One must be able to sit in the easy chair of Rabelais or the tavern of Chaucer and laugh one's head off. *Blazing Saddles*, *Young Frankenstein*, and *High Anxiety* stand on top of the pantheon of film Westerns, horror films, and Hitchcock parodies. Lampooning genre codes and conventions, Brooks impishly distorts old forms and punctures expectations with the unexpected, just for the laughs. For Brooks, the primary fruit of his sowing and reaping is the precious commodity of laughter. When one of the many Johnsons (Howard, Olson, Van, and Dr. Samuel) in *Blazing Saddles* bellows against parking a horse, Mongo "hits" the equine actor and knocks him flat. One laughs at the outrageous slapstick of the action. Brooks believes that spectators laugh more at physical comedy and slapstick action than at clever dialogue. And the more outrageous the better. Once asked if he was afraid of losing his audience by being too offensive, he answered, that the goal of his writing is "to please myself. If it makes me laugh, then I think it's good" (Atlas, 54).

The process of eliciting laughter includes "anomalous gags," unexpected and surprising interruptions of the narrative, what Tom Gunning calls the "pies" within the narrative. Brooks breaks the fourth wall with an anomalous gag in *Blazing Saddles* when cowboys smash through a studio wall to discover a sound stage with a musical production going on. He explained that "what I did when the gunfight spilled over onto the Busby Berkeley set with fifty dances was what Picasso did when he painted the two eyes on the same side of the head." Less sophisticated, but funnier, anomalous jokes appear in *Young Frankenstein*, with Igor's (Marty Feldman) shifting hump or the whinnying and stamping of terrified off-screen horses whenever the name of Frau Blucher (Cloris Leachman) is mentioned. Charles Champlin of the *Los Angeles Times* has extolled the movie for being faithful to "the spirit of old times ... [even with] Vaudeville jokes that may well be older than Mary Wollstonecraft Shelley herself" (Brooks 251). Even Brooks' snappy dialogue is aimed at chuckles. In *Blazing Saddles*, (the foreboding defensive tackle Alex Karras) ironically laments, "Mongo only pawn in game of life."

As the French philosopher Pascal observes, "two faces which resemble each other make us laugh, when together, by their resemblance, though neither of them by itself makes us laugh" (Pascal 196). The faces of Brooks' cast (e.g., Marty Feldman looking in a mirror at himself in *Young Frankenstein* and Cloris Leachman declaring that Viktor Frankenstein was her "boy—friend") evoke laughter because of their familiarity and strangeness. At the base of this laughter lies the incongruity of human nature, with the individual pitted not only against a mechanistic and a natural world but also the entire human race. Brooks capitalized on producing incongruities of difference when writing *Blazing Saddles* by hiring Richard Pryor to write the Jewish jokes while "the Jews wrote the black jokes." He saw the rich possibilities of exploiting a topsy-turvy world, of inverting or reversing a familiar trope. In an interview with Brad Darrach, he offered to sell his T-shirt to his interlocutor: "See this little alligator on the pocket? I understand that in the Everglades, there are alligators with little Jews on their shirt pockets" (in Darrach).

Otherness, of course, becomes comic in the contrast of its

Anomalous gags abound in Mel Brooks' *Young Frankenstein* **(1974), with Igor (Marty Feldman, left) asking Dr. Frederick Frankenstein (Gene Wilder), "What hump?"**

incongruities. Difference, not deficit, creates laughter. For Brooks, two physical characteristics were humanly hilarious: shortness and fatness. He said, "I had a lot of uncles who thought they were funny. But you know, the funniest thing about them is that they were incredibly short" (Fussman 78). Asked what makes him laugh by Gene Shalit of *The Today Show*, he responded. "Fat people, a fat person, really. I'm talking about four hundred, four-forty, fat. I love very stout people [but they don't appear in my movies because] they take up too much screen room" (Tynan). According to Brooks, "'Out of the suffering of Jews, the need to laugh is critical for the survival of the race.' But we didn't become comics out of misery. We became comics because there are a lot of laughs in Jewish households. There's always some wise-guy making cracks about how fat Aunt Sadie is, and it's a need for that joy to continue that was the engine for all of us to become comics" (Freeman 1). It is worth noting that even the sound of a word provokes laughter for Brooks. Chortling over the word, "chicken," he says, "The ch, the I, ... the k. Put it together, you've got the funniest word in the English language: Chicken." Add the word rubber, and one evokes a boffo laugh, what James Agee defines as the laugh that kills.

Brooks' brazen comedy spares neither Jew nor Gentile. In *History of the World: Part I*, as Torquemada, the Grand Inquisitor, he sings, "The Inquisition, let's begin; The Inquisition, look out sin / We have mission to convert the Jews / We're gonna teach them wrong from right / We're gonna help them see the light / And make an offer they can't refuse," leading his audience to a parody of an MGM Esther Williams production of beautiful dancers in bathing suits diving into the water and rising onto a giant menorah. His greatest *schtick*, however, impersonates Moses delivering the Law from Sinai: "The Lord, the Lord Jehovah, has given you these Fifteen...." Abruptly, Brooks as Moses drops one of three stone tablets, and improvises, saying "...Ten! Ten Commandments!" As Comicus, a stand-up philosopher and Jewish waiter at the Last Supper, Brooks asks the disciples (sitting in Da Vinci's pose), "Are you all together, or is it separate checks?" He takes up a common sacrilege for Christians when movies use the name of Jesus, and plays it for irony. Out of frustration at the gathering, he mutters "Jesus!" Actor John Hurt as Jesus responds, "Yes?" When Christ confides that one of them will betray him that night and the disciples ask, "Who?" Comicus shouts "Judas," which startles the betrayer, but Comicus continues, "Do you want a beverage?" Trying to paint their portrait, DaVinci persuades them all to sit on one side of the table. Comicus lingers behind Jesus with a silver serving platter shining like an aureola, the radiant Divine halo in many medieval paintings. Tellingly, the film culminated with a series of coming attractions, including *Jews in Space*, with a spaceship shaped like a Star of David engaged in a *Star Wars* parody. In the

46 יסודות / Foundations

follow-up *Spaceballs*, Brooks plays a cartoonish Yoghurt, proclaiming the blessing, "May the Schwartz be with you!" His sly joke about the princess of Druidia being a Druish Princess resulted Barf's (John Candy) old line, "Funny, she doesn't look Druish." Finally, as the face of Rabbi Tuckman (as opposed to Friar Tuck), a purveyor of sacramental wine, Brooks gleefully performs the wedding ceremony of Robin Hood and Maid Marian, celebrating getting "married in a hurry." He makes jokes about Lox and Bagels and introduces the merry men of Robin to *milah*, the latest rage that ladies love. When asked how circumcision is done, he answers, "I's a snap. I take my little machine [a tiny guillotine] and I take your little thing and I put it into this little hole here, and ... nip the tip."

Brooks says that he went into show business to make a noise, "to *pronounce myself*. I want to go on making the loudest noise to the most people. If I can't do that, I'm not going to make a quiet, exquisite noise for a cabal of cognoscenti" (Parish 222). According to Gene Wilder, Brooks aimed at setting off "bombs of laughter" (Tynan). Contrasting Brooks with his fellow New Yorker Woody Allen, Wilder says,

> Woody will take a bow and arrow or a hunting rifle and aim it at small, precise targets. Mel grabs a shotgun, loads it with fifty pellets, and points it in the general direction of one enormous target. Out of fifty, he'll score at least six or seven huge bull's-eyes, and those are what people always remember about his films. He can synthesize what audiences all over the world are feeling, and suddenly, at the right moment, blurt it out. He'll take a universal and crystallize it. Sometimes he's vulgar and unbalanced, but when those seven shots hit that target I know that that little maniac is genius.

In short, Brooks takes the baseball player approach with jokes: as long as you hit three out of ten, you were winning.

Kenneth Tynan has also contrasted the filmmaking of Allen and the sophomoric Brooks. He says, "Woody has become a professional, whereas Mel is still a brilliant amateur. *Amateurs* are people putting on parties with multimillion-dollar budgets." Brooks, however, envisions himself as more than a slapstick artist—he is an intellectual. He aims to please cinematic *cognicentia* with thoughtful laughter as well as robust explosions. The greater one's familiarity with the text, the more one enjoys his subtle allusions. In *Blazing Saddles*, in Mongo's existential comment about being a mere pawn, one recognizes a shadow of Ivan in Fyodor Dostoyevsky's *The Brothers Karamazov*. In a *New Yorker* interview, Brooks reveals how he combines intellectual allusions with basic slapstick.

> When I was going to do *The Twelve Chairs*, I needed a priest who takes the mother's dying confession about putting her jewels in a chair and then gives up everything to get those jewels. I had a scene with him and Ron Moody, and

Ron says, "Father Fyodor, shame on you! You took a woman's dying confession for personal gain. You're not worth spitting on!" And then Dom, in an ad-lib, said, "Well, you are." And he spit right back in Ron Moody's face [Shulman].

Deftly interweaving literary and cultural allusions with fart jokes and belching, he hides his sly references in plain sights. When Dr. Thorndyke speaks at a therapists' convention in *High Anxiety*, he drops the names of two actual psychoanalysts, Otto Rank and Richard von Kraft-Ebing, creating what scholar Stanley Corngold sees as complex cognitive pleasures aroused by the sudden realization of incongruity. The intellectually satisfying task of identifying an allusion to another text enhances this pleasure. When Brooks spoofs the quick merchandizing of films to videos in *Spaceballs*, he educes a delight of discovery when Dark Helmet (Rick Moranis) sees himself in the present on a video screen. His exaggerated double-takes multiply the mirth in the "We're in the Now-Now" scene. Brooks also exploits anachronisms with panache. In one meta-cinematic moment, seemingly non-diegetic music wafts in the background of cowboys crossing the desert. Suddenly, Count Basie and his orchestra appear out of nowhere playing "April in Paris." The unexpected breaking of the movie's illusions draws a knowing laugh.

After burlesquing the familiar and making it funny, parody requires an affection for the film genre. While shooting *Young Frankenstein*, Brooks exuded love for the movies spoofed: "I was five years old in 1931 when James Whale's *Frankenstein* came out ... that movie scared the hell out of me. I was really terrified," he recalled. "It was the scariest thing I saw in my life." Reveling in that experience, he said, "I'm a movie buff. I've watched all the great James Whale horror films over and over again. I love them because of his incredible portraiture, all the backlighting. They'd always have this sort of little halo of white light around the head" (Daly). Imitating Whale's black and white cinematography, paying homage to the "beautiful, gleaming, sweating gray stone castles" (Daly). The old horror scores combined with electricity noises and gadgets whirring brought him an Academy Award nomination for Best Sound.

Brooks has also expressed deep affection for his amanuensis, Alfred Hitchcock: "I told him that where other people take saunas to relax, I run *The Lady Vanishes*, for the sheer pleasure of it. He had tears in his eyes. I think he understood that I wasn't going to make fun of him. If the picture is a sendup, it's also an act of homage to a great artist. I'm glad I met him, because I love him" (Tynan). Brooks demonstrates his fondness for the director in *High Anxiety* by adding reality to the Hitchcockian thrills. His parody of *The Birds* focuses upon an "aspect of avian behavior primly ignored by Hitchcock." Hiring the same bird wrangler employed by Hitchcock, Brooks directs the flock of pigeons to chase him across a park, bombarding him with bird droppings. According to critic Kenneth Tynan the chaos of blitzing the actor with bird excreta (mayonnaise and chopped spinach) is best described by Barry Levinson, one of four collaborators on screenplay, who told him, "We have enough equipment here to put a man on the moon, and it's all being used to put bird droppings on Brooks." As Brooks' hero is pelted, one can see the beauty of the world and its incessant bird droppings are "very Jewish indeed. After all, birds have tormented Jewish heads since the days of Tobit. Mel Brooks has simply found a new wrinkle for a very old, very Jewish story from the *Apocrypha*" (Pinsker 254).

Much of Brooks' comedy erupts out of the excesses of the body with lust and gluttony. Not only did he abet America in coming to terms with the ubiquity of the fart, but he introduced the salaciously silly Lili von Shtüpp (as in *She Shtupps to Conquer*) (in Darrach). The brassy burlesque chanteuse of the Rock Ridge saloon boasts that Sheriff Bart will be like wet sauerkraut in her hands. "Tell me, Schatzie, is it twue what they say about the way you people are … gifted?" She says (sound of a zipper opening). "Oh, it's twue. It's twue." She offers him a long sausage/*schnitzengruben* and makes a German spectacle of herself. A cleavage-obsessed Governor in *Blazing Saddles* and a bosom-staring King Louis XVI in *History of the World, Part I* attest to his playful exploitation of the body. "Lots of other people said the campfire scene [in *Blazing Saddles*] was too vulgar," he said. "But the film allowed me to be the lovely Rabelaisian vulgarian that I am. I mean those cowboys farting allowed me for the first time to really exercise my scatological muscles. So, we had a bunch of guys eating a lot of beans and delivering a mighty symphony orchestra—music in the wind!" (David).

In her article "Spoofing and Schtik," *New Yorker* film critic Pauline Kael lambastes "schtik." According to Kael, the fraudulent nature of *schtick* is "the special bit, the magic gimmick that makes the old look new, the stale seem fresh; it is what will 'grab' the public." "Spoofing has become the safety net for those who are unsure of their footing," Kael says, and unlike satire, "spoofing has no serious objectives; it doesn't attack anything that anyone could take seriously; it has no cleansing power." Asked what he thinks of critics who complain about vulgarity, Brooks quips, "They're very noisy at night. You can't sleep in the country because of them" (Gross). When corrected by the interviewer that he had been asked about critics, not crickets, Brooks replied, "They're no good. And they can't make music with their legs" (Allen 67).

Parody, of course, differs from satire in its tone as well as its goal. Where parody pokes one in the ribs, satire sticks its finger in the eye, calling the viewer to recognize vice, folly, or ignorance. In his parodies,

Brooks sticks his fingers everywhere. He shoots a satiric arrow at racism in *Blazing Saddles*, casting Cleavon Little as the hip Sheriff Bart, the only African American in a bigoted Old West. Its brilliant, but often misunderstood, attack on bigotry provoked Turner Classic Movies to warn viewers of the film's use of the N-word and stereotyped characterizations. Host Jacqueline Stewart points out that anything superficially racist about the movie underlies its subversive intention. Offensive material is "explicitly stated by characters portrayed as narrow-minded, ignorant bigots." As Richard Pryor was one of the credited screenwriters, Stewart argues that the *modus operandi* of their collaboration shows that "absolutely nothing is off limits, and jokes can tackle every sensitive subject" (Welk). Michael Green highlights the satirical elements of the film. Brooks includes a parade of ethnic stereotypes, from "Mexican *bandidos*, Chinese laborers in straw cone hats, Arabs of ambiguous origin riding on camels, and, yes, a Jewish Native American" who speaks Yiddish (Mel Brooks himself). These diverse comic characters are not the butt of the joke, says Green. One is not ridiculing differences. What makes the movie so groundbreaking is how Brooks "satirizes racism; he shows how stupid it is" (Faulx).

Vulgar Pleasures

As scholar Maurice Yacowar argues, reassessing Brooks' "vulgarity" is overdue (vii). The British journalist G.K. Chesterton championed the "value of all vulgar notions, especially of vulgar jokes. When once you have got hold of a vulgar joke, you may be certain that you have got hold of a subtle and spiritual idea. The men who made the joke saw something deep, which they could not express except by something silly and emphatic. They saw something delicate which they could only express by something indelicate." Chesterton observes that vulgar comedies are "so subtle and true that they are even prophetic." With this in mind, if you really want to know what is going to happen in our society, do not read academic papers on sociology. If you want to know what will happen, watch the parodies of Mel Brooks as "if they were the dark tablets graven with the oracles of the gods. For, mean and gross as they are, in all seriousness, they contain what is entirely absent from all sociological conjectures of our time: they contain some hint of the actual habits and manifest desires" of real people (*All Things* 16). If we are really to find out what society will become, we will find it, not in the academic studies that analyze people but in the films that people study. Like Chesterton, Brooks sought to understand the jokes at which the mob laughs. For Chesterton and Max Beerbohm, the mob laughed at three overlapping sections, "jokes about bodily humiliation, jokes about things alien, such as foreigners, and jokes about bad cheese" (*All Things* 14).

According to Chesterton, Beerbohm thought he understood the first two forms,

> but I am not sure that he did. In order to understand vulgar humour it is not enough to be humourous. One must also be vulgar, as I am…. We do not laugh at the mere fact of something falling down; there is nothing humourous about leaves falling or the sun going down…. All the birds of the air might drop around us in a perpetual shower like a hailstorm without arousing a smile. If you really ask yourself why we laugh at a man sitting down suddenly in the street, you will discover that the reason is not only recondite, but ultimately religious. All the jokes about men sitting down on their hats are really theological jokes; they are concerned with the Dual Nature of Man. They refer to the primary paradox that man is superior to all the things around him and yet is at their mercy [*All Things* 13].

All of Brooks' jests about big bosoms, large penises, and bean-induced farts are actually theological jokes. While Steven Allen did not approve of these vulgarities, their incongruities point to the Dual Nature of human beings, the amazing oxymoron of the spiritual animal. They show that spiritual creatures also can have bodies which they cannot control.

For Chesterton, the laughter at foreigners, at difference *qua* difference, is an equally subtle and spiritual idea. One discovers the surprising truth of "a thing being like oneself and yet not like oneself." Nobody laughs at what is entirely foreign; nobody laughs at a Great Wall or a pyramid. It is funny to see the face of God disguised. When a writer colleague threatened him with "terminal violence," Brooks quickly jumped on a table, shouting, "So, I'm working with God now, a being who holds sway over life and death!" His nemesis demurred. Mel descended from his mountaintop with the last word: "God is a Jew too, you know" (Took 61).

In his collaboration with artist Ernest Pintoff, Brooks won the 1964 Oscar for their animated short *The Critic*. Brooks revives the old Jewish man, like an Old Testament patriarch, wandering into a foreign film house and encountering a modernist animated film. He talks back to the abstract images on the screen, muttering, "What is it, a squiggle? Nope. It's moving. It's a cockaroach. I'm looking at a cockaroach. I came to see a hot French picture with a little nakedness.What am I looking at here?" Scholar Henry Jenkins identifies Brooks as a vulgar modernist, as one of the untimely born popular artists locked outside the classical canon, due to their outsider status and clownish sensibility (151). Drawing upon the former senior critic of the *Village Voice*, J. Hoberman, the concept of "vulgar modernism" emerges as a popular, self-reflexive, intertextual pastiche of low brow culture. The Award-winning cartoon ridiculed experimental modern art through the lens of a crotchety critic. With his mock Russian Yiddish accent, Brooks yells back at a woman who tells him to be quiet, "I'm 71 lady and I'm gonna die soon," and continues his incessant grumbling.

The greatness of this cranky spectator comes through his kvetching at modernity, a stand-in for the vulgar audience against the elite. Brooks is a comedian who showcases his comedy, dismantling it for the pleasure of his spectators. Brooks breaks, even shatters, the codes and conventions of classical cinema, like a clown in a china shop, with his physical rowdiness and antic pranks. Like those in his film parodies Brooks incarnates the vulgar. He is the son of Aristophanes, "Rabelais, Chaucer, and Balzac." Brooks refuses to disown what is called "healthy vulgarity" when it occurs in Chaucer, but "childish smut" when it infiltrates the cinema. Chesterton once mused about a critic who remonstrated with him, saying with an air of indignant reasonableness, "If you must make jokes, at least you need not make them on such serious subjects." Chesterton replied he had it all wrong. All jesting rises out of the "sudden realization that something which thinks itself solemn is not so very solemn after all.… All the most grave and dreadful things in the world produce the oldest jokes in the world—being married; being hanged" (*All Things* 12). Chesterton avers that

> funny is not the opposite of serious. Funny is the opposite of not funny, and of nothing else. The question of whether a man expresses himself in a grotesque or laughable phraseology, or in a stately and restrained phraseology, is not a question of motive or of moral state, it is a question of … self-expression. Whether a man chooses to tell the truth in long sentences or short jokes is a problem analogous to whether he chooses to tell the truth in French or German. Whether a man preaches his gospel grotesquely or gravely is merely like the question of whether he preaches it in prose or verse [159].

Chesterton no doubt would agree that Mel Brooks should have been named Isaac. In Hebrew, *Yitzhak* means "Laughter." His parodic sermons preach truths of being human on screen, incarnating the spirit of laughter from our wonderfully vulgar flesh.

Filmography

The Birds. Dir. Alfred Hitchcock. Universal-International Pictures, 1963. DVD. Universal Studios Home Entertainment, 2012.
Blazing Saddles: 30th Anniversary Special. Dir Mel Brooks. Warner Bros., 1974. DVD. Warner, 2004.
Blue Angel. Dir. Josef von Sternberg. Universum Film A.G., 1930. DVD. Kino Lorder Films, 2007.
The Critic. Dir. Ernest Pintoff. Columbia Pictures, 1963. *YouTube*, April 10, 2015.
Destry Rides Again. Dir. George Marshall. Universal Pictures, 1939. DVD. Universal Studios Home Entertainment, 2003.

42nd Street. Dir. Lloyd Bacon. Warner Bros, 1933. DVD. Warner Archives, 2015.
Frankenstein. Dir. James Whale. Universal, 1931. DVD. In *Classic Monsters Collection*, Universal Studios Home Entertainment, 2015.
"From Here to Obscurity." *Your Show of Shows*, March 5, 1954, https://www.youtube.com/watch?v=tultp0xOml8.
Get Smart. Created by Mel Brooks and Buck Henry. Season 1 (1965). HBO DVD, August 52008.
High Anxiety. Dir Mel Brooks. Twentieth Century Fox, 1977. DVD. Twentieth Century Fox Home Entertainment, 2006.
History of the World: Part I. Dir. Mel Brooks. Twentieth Century Fox, 1981. DVD. Twentieth Century Fox, 2006.
The Lady Vanishes: Criterion Collection Special Edition. Dir. Alfred Hitchcock. Gaumont-British Picture Corporation, 1938. DVD. Video Service Corp., 2011.
The Producers. Dir. Mel Brooks. Embassy Pictures, 1967. DVD. Shout Factory, July 2, 2013.
Spaceballs. Dir. Mel Brooks. MGM/UA Communications Co., 1987. DVD. MGM, 2015.
"A Trolleycar Named Desire." *Your Show of Shows*, April 5, 1952. https://www.youtube.com/watch?v=zbV83yJ_fxk.
The Twelve Chairs. Dir. Mel Brooks. Universal Marion Corporation Pictures, 1970. DVD. Twentieth Century Fox Home Entertainment, 2006.
"Vacant Holsters." *Your Show of Shows*, directed by Nat Hiken and Max Liebman. n.d. https://www.youtube.com/watch?v=4eaHi7BRMfQ.
Young Frankenstein. Dir. Mel Brooks. Twentieth Century Fox, 1974. DVD. Twentieth Century Fox Home Entertainment, 2006.

WORKS CITED

Adler, Bill, and Jeffrey Feinman. *Mel Brooks: The Irreverent Funnyman*. Playboy P, 1976.
Allen, Steve. *Funny People*. Stein and Day, 1981.
Atlas, Jacoba. "Mel Brooks Interview." *Film Comment*, vol. 11, no. 2, March/April 1975, pp. 54–57.
Bergson, Henri. "La Rire." *Comedy*, edited by Wylie Sypher, Doubleday, 1956, pp. 61–192.
Bonnstetter, Beth. "Mel Brooks Meets Kenneth Burke (and Mikhail Bakhtin)." *Journal of Filmand Video*, vol. 63, no. 1, Spring 2011, pp. 18–31.
Chesterton, G.K. *All Things Considered*. John Lane, 1913. Cited parenthetically as *All Things*.
Chesterton, G.K. "On Mr. McCabe and Divine Frivolity." *The Collected Works of G.K.Chesterton*. Vol. 1, Ignatius Press, 1986.
Corngold, Stanley. *Complex Pleasure*. Stanford Press, 1998.
Daly, Steve. "You've Got Me: Mel Brooks." *Entertainment Weekly*, no. 529, March 2000.
Dandlin, Michael. "*Funny Man: Mel Brooks*." *Cineaste*, vol. 45, no. 1, Winter 2019, p. 68.
Darrach, Brad. "Mel Brooks." *Playboy*, February 1975. *The Stacks Reader*.http://www.thestacksreader.com/mel-brooks-the-playboy-interview/. Accessed January 15, 2023.
Davis, Ivor. "A Conversation with Mel Brooks." *Tablet*, June 28, 2016. https://www.tabletmag.com/sections/arts-letters/articles/a-conversation-with-mel-brooks Accessed January 15, 2023.
Desser, David. "Mel Brooks." *My Jewish Learning*. https://www.myjewishlearning.com/article/mel-brooks/. Accessed June 3, 2022.
Faulx, Nadya. "*Blazing Saddles*: The Best Interracial Buddy Comedy." *NPR*, February 7, 2014. https://www.npr.org/sections/codeswitch/2014/02/07/272452677/blazing-saddles-the-best-interracial-buddy-comedy-turns-40. Accessed June 4, 2022.
Fleishman, Philip. "Interview: Mel Brooks." *Macleans*, April 17, 1978, p. 8.
Freeman, Hadley. "Interview: Mel Brooks." *The Guardian*, December 4, 2021. https://www.theguardian.com/film/2021/dec/04/mel-brooks-on-losing-the-loves-of-his-life-people-know-how-good-carl-reiner-was-but-not-how-great. Accessed June 9, 2022.

Fussman, Cal. "The Comedians." *Esquire*, vol. 149, no. 1, January 2008, pp. 78–79.
Gehring, Wes. *Parody as Film Genre*. Greenwood, 1999.
Gross, Terry. "Mel Brooks." *Fresh Air*, NPR, November 23, 2022. https://www.klcc.org/npr-arts-culture/npr-arts-culture/2022-11-23/mel-brooks-says-his-only-regret-as-a-comedian-is-the-jokes-he-didnt-tell. Accessed November 23, 2022.
Hoberman, James. *Vulgar Modernism*. Temple University Press, 1991.
Jacobs, Samuel P. "Mel Brooks Still Laughing." *Newsweek*, vol. 158, no. 10, September 5, 2011.
Jenkins, Henry. "Mel Brooks, Vulgar Modernism, and Comic Remediation." *Companion to Film Comedy*, edited by Andrew Horton and Joanna Rapf, Wiley-Blackwell, 2013, pp. 151–71.
Kael, Pauline. "Spoofing and Schtik." *The Atlantic*, December 1965. https://www.theatlantic.com/magazine/archive/1965/12/spoofing-and-schtik/660738/. Accessed January 15, 2023.
Kennedy Center. "2009 Kennedy Center Honors: Mel Brooks." https://www.kennedy-center.org/artists/b/bo-bz/mel-brooks/. Accessed January 15, 2023.
Kosner, Edward. "*Funny Man*: Anything for a Laugh." *Wall Street Journal*, March 15, 2019. https://www.wsj.com/articles/funny-man-review-anything-for-a-laugh-11552658384. Accessed January 15, 2023.
Lindvall, Terry, Dennis Bounds, and Chris Lindvall. *Divine Film Comedies*. Routledge, 2016.
Pallies, Daniel. "Hybrid Theories of Pleasure." *Philosophical Studies*, vol. 178, no. 3, 2021, pp. 887–907.
Parish, James. *It's Good to Be the King*. John Wiley, 2007.
Pascal, Blaise. *Pensees*, edited by William Benton, University of Chicago P, 1952.
Pinsker, Sanford. "Mel Brooks and the Cinema of Exhaustion." *From Hester Street to Hollywood: The Jewish-American Stage and Screen*, edited by Sarah Blacher Cohen, Indiana UP, 1983, pp. 243–256.
Rabinowtiz, Dorothy. "Mel Brooks: Portrait." *Wall Street Journal*, May 16, 2013, D7.
Schulman, Michael. "Mel Brooks Writes It All Down." *The New Yorker*, November 28, 2021. https://www.newyorker.com/culture/the-new-yorker-interview/mel-brooks-writes-it-all-down. Accessed January 15, 2023.
Sennett, Ted. *Your Show of Shows*. Macmillan, 1977.
Took, Barry. *Comedy Greats*. Thorsons Publishing, 1989.
Tynan, Kenneth. "Frolics and Detours of a Short Hebrew Man." *The New Yorker*, October 22,1978. https://www.newyorker.com/magazine/1978/10/30/mel-brooks-frolics-and-detours-of-a-short-hebrew-man. Accessed June 4, 2022.
Wansink, Craig, and Terry Lindvall. *Old Men of the Bible*. Smyth/Helwys, 2019.
Welk, Brian. "*Blazing Saddles* Disclaimer." *Wrap*, August 14, 2020. https://www.thewrap.com/blazing-saddles-gets-intro-disclaimer-for-racist-context-on-hbo-max/. Accessed June 4, 2022.
Yacowar, Maurice. *Method in Madness*. St. Martin's Press, 1981.

קרעוו ןבילקעגסיוא
Selected Works
(1965–1991)

Old Man from Russia: This is cute.... This is cute.... This is nice.... What the hell is it? I know what it is! It's Garbage! That's what it is! Two dollars I've paid for a French movie, for a foreign movie and I've got to see this junk....
—*The Critic* (1963)

Got Smart

Mel Brooks, Ambivalent Parody, and the Cultural Politics of Foolishness

Kerry Soper

Mel Brooks was the first comedic film director I knew by name when I was a preteen growing up in the 1970s—probably because of the mental shock of seeing two of his raucous movies, *Blazing Saddles* and *Young Frankenstein*, within the same year (1974). At the time, I was simply amazed that films like this could be made (simultaneously silly, entertaining and smart). Now, looking back, I can understand better why Brooks' work had a special appeal to me and my friends: his brash parodies of genre films resonated with a generation of young people who had been raised on a glut of earnest and overwrought Hollywood entertainment. These silly-serious lampoons somehow seemed mainstream and alternative at the same time, offering comforting familiarity (cheerful rehashings of core types and conventions) and energizing irreverence (satiric deflations of each genre's blind spots, inflated character types and ideological agendas).

Later, when I was in college, I discovered that one of my favorite television shows while growing up—*Get Smart*—was also the product, in large part, of the Mel Brooks mind and method. And while this televisual spoof of the spy thriller genre/James Bond franchise is not seen as one of Brooks' major works, it deserves a careful reassessment, and can serve as a revealing case study of the mechanisms and cultural uses of ambivalent parody. To be specific, an analysis of *Get Smart* gives us the opportunity to explore how a Jewish comedic auteur helped to create a spy show that was both wholly crowd-pleasing and cheekily counterdiscursive—that created subtle (but ideologically and satirically significant) distance and difference between itself and the big screen spy thrillers it lampooned. Those subversive shifts can be seen in the construction of the show's earnest and foolish protagonist

(Maxwell Smart, Agent 86), in the expanded role played by its female lead (Agent 99), and in its jokey deconstructions of the spy thriller genre's core myths and ideals.

To begin, a bit of theoretical framing is in order on the cultural work performed by traditional film genres and the comedic parodies that mock them. For starters, genre films (like espionage thrillers or Westerns) functioned during the mid-20th century in Britain and the United States like modern-age fairy tales or myths, continually recycling a set of classical story templates and using emotionally powerful filmic tools to distill and amplify over time a set of archetypal characters, resonant narrative conventions, and powerful (and sometimes contradictory) cultural "truths." To elaborate, the

Dressed in trench coats, Maxwell Smart (Don Adams) and Agent 99 (Barbara Feldon) display Mel Brooks' brand of crowd-pleasing, but ultimately counterdiscursive parody in *Get Smart* (NBC [1965–69]; CBS [1969–70]). Michael Ochs Archives / Getty Images.

dominant film aesthetics of the era—cinematic spectacle and escapist realism—were especially good at harnessing the myth-making power of those stories to naturalize dominant cultural discourses and ideologies, making their values and ideals seem timeless, universal and natural (Hayward 80–83). While an older, Jungian theoretical frame might have ascribed those meanings to deep, universal roots, more recent genre studies/cultural studies approaches to cinema (which are shaped by neo–Marxist ideas) emphasize the cultural constructedness of those ideals, pointing to shallower semiotic roots: the profit-making and dominant culture-pleasing objectives of the entertainment industries that created them.

As an example, a studio like Eon Productions in Great Britain might purchase the rights to an already popular novel like *Goldfinger*, by Ian Fleming, with established genre archetypes and conventions; then, in the filmic adaptation, they would try to maximize the popularity, resonance and profitability of the text among core fans by harnessing an array of cinematic devices (camera angles and point of view, close ups, soundtrack, editing) to distill and amplify key archetypes and narrative tropes. While the novel might have been an ambivalent and sometimes ironic dissection of dominant cultural values (such as notions of masculinity, femininity and Western cultural exceptionalism), the drive to create a profitable, blockbuster spectacle at the filmic level had the effect of erasing most of those nuances; instead, it enshrined a set of distilled and idealized notions of violent/independent masculinity, sexist treatments of female identity, and jingoistic notions of Anglo-American cultural/political righteousness and superiority.

Psychoanalytic film theory gives us additional ways to think about the cultural appeal and power of a distilled, cinematic spy thriller as it syncs so powerfully with cultural anxieties, and taps into the psychological interests of core fans. Using a basic Freudian paradigm as a starting point, we could conjecture that a James Bond film in the early '60s served as a virtual site for individual wish-fulfillment and collective exploration of free-floating cultural anxieties. The cinema-going experience reinforced the dream-like sensations and power of the viewing experience, immersing audience members in darkness and exposing them to a powerful sound system and giant screen that created an almost out-of-body experience. The viewer, in effect, was transported into an escapist realm of affecting music, aestheticized violence, heroically exaggerated male protagonists and idealized (even literally gilded, in the case of Goldfinger) female objects of desire (Storey 75). In addition, giving qualified credence to Freud's core configuration of the mind, we could say that each part of the viewer's psyche is given something to fulfill its needs/desires: for the ego, an inflated hero with a set of extreme freedoms/privileges/abilities with which to identify; for the id (and its subdivisions of libido and Thanatos), spectacles of violence and sensuality; and for the superego, overarching justifications for all of this extra-legal, quasi-vigilante mayhem (licenses to do whatever was required to preserve Western cultural hegemony).

The film scholar Laura Mulvey fleshes out this view of the spy thriller's psychological appeal from a feministic perspective. In her essay "Visual Pleasure and Narrative Cinema," she asserts that midcentury, action-oriented genre spectacles catered especially to the psychological desires/fantasies of a patriarchal culture and male psyche. In particular, the amplified hero (who possessed exceptional fighting abilities, asserted his masculinity through society-cleansing violence, and had a license to womanize indiscriminately) invited narcissistic identification and the ever-renewing flow of objectified Bond-girls functioned as a voyeuristic spectacle for the male viewer (scopophilia). The implied rules about separate gender roles and privileges, moreover, were reinforced by narrative tropes and the behavior of the camera's objectifying lens: male protagonists were agents, capable of violence and meaningful action that could forward/resolve the narrative, while female characters were limited to serving as visual props/spectacles that passively tolerated the male gaze. These deeply ingrained, sexist "rules" were even enforced with predictable narrative tropes, such as female characters being punished through improbably extreme and symbolically-loaded means—like skin suffocation from being covered by gold—if they stepped beyond their stereotypical roles and tried to impact the narrative (Mulvey 719, 720).

One final, poignant layer to this psychoanalytic framing comes from Jacques Lacan, a psychoanalyst who took Freudian theory into poststructuralist territory. He saw the default nature of the human psyche as one of lack and discord, and suggested that as individuals emerge from childhood, they embark on a fruitless pursuit of solid identity/ego, an idealized romantic/sexual partner and sense of plenitude or purpose. As adults, these searches are conducted in the symbolic realm—through literature, art, film, and so on; and cinema, because of its capacity to create the sensations of dream-like wish fulfilment, is especially powerful in setting up and amplifying those expectations of fulfillment. Applying this to a film like *Goldfinger*, we could conjecture that instead of satisfying psychological needs—which can't be met in the first place—it took the average male viewer on a psychological roller coaster ride: first, a thrilling, temporary identification with an inflated hero, voyeuristic and overwrought fantasies of attaining an idealized romantic partner, and a righteous sense of society-saving purpose; then a sense of deflation upon return to normal life and its default sense of lack; and then, again, an anxious, addictive pursuit of the next cinematic high (Storey 84, 85). For the average female viewer, we can imagine an even more complicated psychological experience as one would be forced to see one's self through (or adopt the perspective of) a male gaze and learn in harsh ways some deep "truths" about gender roles and hierarchies.

At first glance, any comedic parody that lampoons one of these inflated genre spectacles would seem to be inherently subversive. A closer examination of the nature of parody reveals a more complicated picture, however—a symbiotic relationship between a parody and its target, and a spectrum of satiric treatments that exhibit different degrees of counter-discursiveness. Linda Hutcheon explores these complexities, arguing that because a parody relies on a viewer's awareness of the targeted cultural text, and inevitably repeats many of the core elements of the original work, it "always implicitly reinforces even as it ironically debunks" (Hutcheon xii). In other words, repetition—and a focus on triggering recognition—results in a celebration or reification of the popular text as much as its denigration. Hutcheon elaborates, nevertheless, that parodic texts are not all alike; some are more counterdiscursive than others, exhibiting perhaps a deeper animus in some cases towards its targets, or engaging in a more thorough deconstruction of a particular genre's core tropes and worldview. You can chart, in fact, a spectrum of ideological tones in parody—from "respectful to playful to scathingly critical"—and the most satiric/subversive modes are marked by a "repetition with critical distance, which marks difference rather than similarity" (Theory 6). As we'll see, Hutcheon's spectrum provides a way for measuring Brooks' treatment of key facets of the spy thriller in *Get Smart* against both its primary target (the mythic films in the James Bond franchise), and the early, milder conceptions of this show imagined by television executives (before Brooks' involvement). The data will support the claim that Brooks succeeded at using an auteur-like sensibility (contrarian, Jewish, irreverent, and sometimes furious) to create parodic films and television that were simultaneously crowd-pleasing and genuinely counterdiscursive.

Turning the focus to comedy—the realm of Mel Brooks and *Get Smart*—we can begin by describing briefly how he achieved the auteur-like clout to help create a parodic television show that achieved so effectively that balance between mainstream familiarity and irreverent subversion. Without digging too deeply into his biography, we can highlight two aspects of his background that resulted in the dual (ambivalent/satiric, mainstream/alternative) quality in his comedies: a prolonged childhood exposure to (and ambivalent affection for/fascination with) classical Hollywood genre films, and a contrarian and sometimes angry attitude toward dominant cultural ideals and power structures as a result of growing up with the double consciousness of a second generation Jewish immigrant.

Like many kids in an urban setting (NYC) in the late 1930s and early 1940s, Brooks spent most Saturdays watching double and triple features at a local, dumpy theater. He remembers subsisting on a "big diet of Western movies," and had omnivorous tastes across old Chaplin comedies, musicals, big spectacles and genre b movies. While he asserts that "even as a kid, [he] loved all movies, black and white, color, what have you" (Brooks 32), it might be more accurate to say that he had a love/hate addiction to mainstream cinema, some excessive and addled viewing habits, and an undercurrent of Lacanian dissatisfaction—as suggested by these descriptions of his cinema-going habits:

> I fell in love with the movies right there [at an old theater in Coney Island]. This was much better than real life. Who needs real life? ... My mother was always sending an older brother to drag me out. Sometimes I went there when it opened at 11:30 in the morning and stayed until nightfall starved to death, a splitting headache, but I couldn't take my eyes off the screen [McGilligan 10, 11, 17].

As Brooks grew into adulthood, that interest in film remained, with ongoing clues that he was attracted and repulsed in equal parts by those mainstream texts—and unable to look away. At the start of his professional career, for example, Brooks developed a reputation for being flakey and unavailable—in large part because he continued to see "all types of films incessantly, often going alone to kill an afternoon or evening" (McGilligan 91). And then later, when he had found a satisfying way to engage with that storehouse of beloved/hated texts—through ambivalent parody, he confirmed that there were antagonistic facets to his treatment of classical templates; for example, in describing his comedy in *Blazing Saddles*, he said that "we're trying to use every Western cliché in the book—in the hope that we'll kill them off in the process" (Dauber, *Jewish Comedy*, 130).

Key explanations for that underlying frustration can be found in his Jewish identity and experience. Like other minorities who fell in love with mainstream popular cultural texts that were often racist (in both subtle and overt ways), he perhaps suffered from a form of double consciousness—seeing himself through the condescending and mocking eyes of dominant cultural ideals and types (so vividly celebrated in genre film), while looking for ways to push back, rebut and carve out his own heroic identity. For example, after an eye-opening, traumatic stint serving in the military—where he saw the deeper realities of racism of both foreign and homegrown types—he became consumed by a low boiling fury and began to see "life now as a battle … with himself as the underdog leader of a personal mission seeking victory and vindication" (McGilligan 46). Later in life, friends noticed that same anger pulsing beneath his bright and irreverent comedy; they observed that "behind Brooks's bravado … was profound insecurity. Behind his façade as a perpetual amusant were depths of self-loathing and a fury at the world" (McGilligan 75).

Some of that self-loathing could have been an outgrowth of a lifetime of being exposed to idealized, filmic depictions of suave, hypercompetent and gentile/Caucasian heroes on the one hand and, on the other, having to witness a parade of less impressive Jewish character types and stereotypes. Close friends, in fact, confirm that "Brooks was obsessed with his height, his looks, and his religion, in that order" (McGilligan 90). It's as if the Lacanian diagnosis of the average person's sense of inadequacy—in the face of dream-like fantasies in cinema of heightened identity, romance and heroic purpose—was made even more acute for a doubly-conscious, minority, film buff like Brooks.

Assuming that Brooks' ethnic identity did play a significant a role in his love-hate relationship with classical Hollywood cinema, it seems appropriate that the strategies he developed in his humor for expressing that ambivalence—and occasionally pushing back in counterdiscursive ways—emerged according to Jewish comedic methods and worldviews. Some history can help to describe the tools Brooks inherited: to begin, in the late 19th century, most Jewish-themed humor was created and performed by non–Jews with the purpose of mocking and denigrating newly arrived, Eastern European immigrants. Stereotypes of greedy merchants, orthodox greenhorns with thick Yiddish accents dominated stage performances in a genre dubbed "Jewface" (because of its similarities to blackface and blatantly racist cartoons in magazines like *Puck* and *Harper's Weekly*). By the first and second decades of the 20th century, however, Jewish-themed humor developed a greater level of nuance and sympathy as second-generation immigrants filled theaters, protested those earlier brands of two-dimensional racism, and even became professional comedians, entering the relatively open doors of the entertainment world (Zax). Those early Jewish Vaudeville comedians, like Eddie Cantor and the Marx Brothers, were still limited to a degree by the Jewface stereotypes that they had inherited, as well as their own marginalized cultural status; nevertheless, they found clever ways to push back against a dominant culture and expand their palette of comedic devices and modes.

For starters, because second generation Jewish immigrants could be found in both the audience and the on the stage, Jewish-inflected jokes became nuanced, varied and occasionally subversive toward the dominant culture. Jewish performers, for example, began exercising an insider privilege and so the jokes about Jewish identity and culture could still be self-mocking, but now with a higher degree of particularity and sympathy. They could also wear the outward stereotype of Jewishness lightly—as a shallow mask, or an obviously exaggerated application of greasepaint eyebrows and mustache, as in Groucho Marx's case; then beneath that inherited shell of racist meanings, they could perform an array of subversive or sympathetic roles. Those new voices included wise fools, trickster figures, carnivalesque clowns, cheeky satirists and everyman underdogs. Common to many of those roles were a clever use of language: Yiddish terms and types, earthy vulgarity, witty and subversive wordplay, and deliberate misuses of English—in a mode of pseudo foolishness, often as a way to poke fun at dominant cultural figures, ideals and hypocrisies (Davies 147). Jewish comedy also tended to feature a carnivalesque earthiness, using celebrations of idiocy, foolishness and the grotesque to deflate idealized heroic types and inflated ideals. In other words, in most cases these devices were used to "punch up" instead of "punch down." As Theodore Reik, the famed Jewish psychoanalyst observed, Jewish humor almost never made fun "of physical handicaps or frailties ... [or] body deformities and ugliness"; instead, it punctured notions of perfection, power and heroism (Dauber, *Jewish Comedy*, 131).

In the 1930s and 1940s, as popular Jewish performers migrated into radio, film and television, parody served as an ideal mode for this array of Jewish-inflected comedy tools and attitudes. Indeed, it worked nicely as an ambivalent or vacillating mode of tribute/mockery for performers like the Marx Brothers, Sid Caesar and Mel Brooks who wanted to be both popular (pleasing a broad, mainstream audience, censors and cultural guardians), and also true to their own subversive impulses. Jeremy Dauber, a scholar who has written about both Jewish comedy and Brooks' career, elaborates on the logic of this productive marriage of Jewish sensibility and comedy genre:

> You can't be a master parodist without ... a deep familiarity and love for the material. And yet you have to be outside it as well: to feel estranged enough from it to point out its flaws, its ridiculous features, its aesthetic omissions and even its moral failures. In short, you have to be the loyal opposition: which is as good a way of describing a certain American Jewish attitude as any [*Mel Brooks: Disobedient Jew*, 2].

Turning our attention to Brooks and how he wielded these comedic tools, we can make a few caveats about applying the concept of auteur to his career in general, and to the making of *Get Smart* in particular. In film studies there is a large body of work that pushes back on the concept of the auteur—a single individual, usually a director/writer shaping the meanings of a filmic or televisual text. Critics have pointed out that the concept underappreciates the collaborative nature of these creative works, fixating instead on the "cult of the director." The concept can have a sexist bias, focusing primarily on the "genius" of male innovators or visionaries, and it often ignores the messiness and instability of meaning-making in a text (the various ways that those codings are resisted/lost for viewers or shaped by inherited genre tropes, intertextual overlap, and the cultural discourses that delimit or determine textual codings).

In the making of *Get Smart*, the qualifications about collaborative issues are especially valid since the record shows that Brooks, his agents, and the production studio (Talent Associates), oversold his contributions to the show. Buck Henry, the cocreator, for example, had an equal impact on the shaping of the text and ultimately devoted more time to the day-to-day running of the show during its first, most critical year. But because Brooks was the more recognizable, auteur-like figure in the mix, there was pressure to feature his name first in the creation credits—and so it was initially promoted as "created, written and produced by Mel Brooks" (McGilligan 222). By the time the show reached the public, this pitch had been amended to "created by Mel Brooks with Buck Henry," but it was only decades later that Brooks was able to apologize to Henry and set the record straight (McGilligan 538).

Brooks was also a tricky collaborator, often sowing as much chaos as he did productive innovation. He was averse to writing, for example, and thus developed the habits of a "talking" or "performing writer," leaving an assistant or cowriter to do the actual labor of getting things down on paper (McGilligan 77). In addition, he was spread too thin through mid-career (working on a surplus of projects at the same time), given to fits of rage at his collaborators, and being unreliable ("arriving late and lounging around, making phone calls to stockbrokers, griping to his agent, hobnobbing around the studio") (McGilligan 118, 172, 272).

Given those caveats, there a still some useful reasons to describe Brooks as a qualified auteur for this study. First, the concept a popular creator who achieves mainstream success while remaining true to a challenging comedic or aesthetic vision is accurate and helpful in exploring Brooks' subversive approach to creating *Get Smart*. After an apprenticeship as a writer in Sid Caesar's *Show of Shows*—which featured that array of Jewish comedic methods of parody and mockery from the margins described above—and the achievement of mainstream fame through his "2000-Year-Old-Man" comedy albums with Carl Reiner—he found himself in demand as a writer/director with a solid industry reputation and recognizable public identity. As Dauber describes, he still nurtured in his heart an unbridled fury towards an array of cultural injustices, racism, and inflated hierarchies, and was willing to test the limits of mainstream comedy, but he was savvy enough to do it in a sustainable and profitable way:

> He wants to lay waste to the place, to reduce it to ashes in the smoldering fire of his comic genius. But Brooks is no anarchist, no Groucho Marxist: his ultimate decision—following a path so resonant of so many other American Jewish success stories—is that the secret lies in constraining himself within the system, rather than working outside it [*Mel Brooks: Disobedient Jew*, 2].

McGilligan, his biographer, elaborates that Brooks could rein in the obnoxious and subversive sides of his personality when necessary, thus protecting his ongoing participation in the power structures of the entertainment industry: "In television and film scripts, talk-show appearances and advertising jobs, he'd try accenting the Nice Mal, the warm and fuzzy side of his personality" (McGilligan 195).

Secondly, the chaotic aspects of Brooks' creative style—the impromptu brainstorming, irreverent performing and disruptive methods—were aspects of his capacity to counterbalance the staid wittiness of a more cerebral collaborator like Buck Henry, as well as the conservative impulses of network producers and studio executives. To elaborate, Brooks apparently had no fear or lack of ego in the writer's room; he described his unapologetic style: "I was aggressive. I was a terrier, a pit bull terrier. I was unstoppable. I would keep going until my joke or my sketch was in the show. I didn't care if anybody else's was in or out" (Nesteroff 110). In sum, Brooks' carnivalesque energy and free-associating improvisations—and belligerent approach to negotiations with executives and producers—were key factors in his ability to create and protect the stealthily counterdiscursive energies and elements of an otherwise mainstream television show. Dauber elaborates on the disruptive qualities of Brooks' comedic worldview and methods: as an irreverent, fury-filled parodist he was willing to be "vulgar, obscene, or blasphemous" as a way of expressing a "broad, brave truth" about traditions or ideals that had become "too stuffed-shirt, a little too accreted, too iconic" (*Jewish Comedy*, 130). At the same time, as a savvy auteur seeking mainstream approval—and a Jewish entertainer coping with lingering double consciousness, perhaps—he had to maintain a familiarity, a "deep love for the material," and a thorough knowledge of the genres he was lampooning, in order "to hit the jugular while you're taking it down" (Dauber, *Jewish Comedy*, 130; Dauber, *Mel Brooks: Disobedient Jew*, 2).

So where can we identify the impact of Brooks' worldview and methods on *Get Smart*? First, we can compare original conceptions of the show, by the producers at Talent Associates, against the end product itself, after being shaped by the sensibilities of Brooks and Henry. Like executives at most mainstream production companies, the minds behind the original idea were trying to cash in on a national "spy craze"—an early '60s period that featured blockbuster James Bond films, such as *Goldfinger* (1964), and an array of other espionage-themed films and television shows: *The Man from U.N.C.L.E.*, *I Spy*, *The Avengers*, *Burke's Law* and *Honey West* (McCrohan 40). Dan Melnick, a key conceiver of the concept, for example, recalls that "I had the idea to satirize the James Bond genre because I was already a fan of the James Bond novels.... I enjoyed the real James Bond, so when I thought of satirizing, it was a way to extend James Bond" (McCrohan 11). In addition, he gave the show the working title of "Super Spy" and suggested it "ought to feature a beautiful girl agent, a la the James Bond girls" (McGilligan 223). Notice the lack of counterdiscursive distance or difference in this description; despite the use of the term "satirize," the goal was not to rebut, deconstruct or challenge—but instead, to capitalize on and extend an existing craze. "Super Spy," the original name for the show (though meant to be mildly ironic), for example, signals simply an extension/amplification of one of the core tropes of the Bond movies—an outsized hero with special abilities. Moreover, little thought seems to have been put into recasting the female lead in an alternative way; she was simply described/imagined as another Bond girl that would cater to the male gaze.

When Brooks first, and then later Henry, were brought on board as a way of attracting potential studio investors, creative power passed into the hands of cheeky auteurs. Key counterdiscursive shifts that they introduced, after a three-month creative gestation period, included a new name (that suggested cheekier, more subversive purposes), a more radical conception of the show's protagonist as a genuine fool, a stealthily nuanced construction of the female lead, and a genuinely silly-smart, satiric tone. For starters, Brooks' idea for the new title—"*Get Smart*"—had a surface meaning ("assign Maxwell Smart to the job"), but it also carried street-wise connotations drawn from urban, Jewish culture: be savvy, get streetwise, "wise up" (Brooks 150). On a subliminal level it might have even advertised the intellectual benefits of consuming smart parodies of mainstream genre entertainment: learning to see through the emotional and ideological manipulations of inflated archetypes and ideals.

The construction of the show's protagonist, and the casting of Don Adams in that role, also reflected Brooks' impulse to create critical, parodic distance from the James Bond archetype. Maxwell Smart, for starters, was designed by Brooks and Henry to be a sympathetic underdog with whom the average viewer could identify and sympathize. As a result, he was essentially a straight arrow: idiotic, for sure—but uncorruptible, naïve, and noble in his impulses (McCrohan 58). Brooks elaborated that "Buck Henry and I saw Max as earnest and innocent. He was noble and believed in justice. He was never on the take, and so his naivete or his dumbness worked for him" (Green 29). To recognize genuine parodic distance here, consider the contrast those innocent foundational qualities created from the world-wise cynicism and wink-wink opportunism of James Bond.

The casting of Don Adams, moreover, created a powerful satiric contrast to archetypal figures like Sean Connery: instead of a suave, physically imposing gentile, he was a diminutive, everyman figure from Jewish/Irish immigrant stock. Looking back on his years long performance of this character, Adams himself recognized—in common sensical ways that Lacan might affirm—how a comedic everyman alternative had the power to puncture inflated notions of Hollywood heroism:

> The average guy would fall over himself trying to be a spy. But they all look at James Bond and fantasize themselves as Sean Connery. Well, with me they could look at me and say, "I can understand that because that would probably be me" [Green 28].

While it is easy to see Maxwell Smart's beta male physique as a clear, visual counter to the inflated masculine ideal of a James Bond hero, the parodic and satiric functions of his mindset are a bit more complicated to unpack. To begin, Smart is not a nebbish—a male who is pitifully ineffectual, timid or submissive; instead, he is closer to a *schlemiel*—an inept or incompetent person who is delusional or unaware of his foolishness. He genuinely sees himself as suave and heroic, in other words—a brilliant spy and expert fighter (McCrohan 52). At times he slips into trickster figure or wise fool mode—as he scrambles to cover his mistakes, get himself out of a jam, or bluff an opponent—but that cleverness is always an expression of shallow guile rather than deep self-awareness.

The unchanging quality of Smart's genuine foolishness or delusional self-belief served several comedic functions. First, it allowed Adams to play the character straight, never trying to be funny in hammy ways. Brooks was very intentional about that strategy; in fact, he explained that Max "was always wrong, but always came out on top. He never played the joke and never shared with the audience that he was aware that what he was doing was funny. It was very real, character-driven comedy" (Brooks 150). Second, Smart's delusional mindset gave him a set of fixed, ridiculously conflicting character qualities (inflated self-belief butting up against deep incompetence) that served as a high concept character type to win over viewers, as well as a reliable joke-making mechanism (to sustain the show's multi-season run). On a satiric level, that gap between inflated belief and pathetic reality helped to reinforce one of Brooks' core satiric goals: to deconstruct the inflated qualities of the Hollywood template. And because Maxwell Smart was never capable of developing self-awareness, it was left to the viewer to "get smart," to use the Brooks' parodic treatment as a critical lens for watching, mocking and mentally deconstructing inflated Hollywood texts.

Turning our attention to Agent 99, played by Barbara Feldon, we can look for additional evidence that Brooks and Henry made critical counterdiscursive choices. For starters, as with any fundamentally ambivalent parody, or mainstream sit-com designed to attract the core audience of the overarching genre, there were the alignments with the classical template: she was a secondary character (without even a name), she was beautiful and feminine in ideal ways, and her inexplicable infatuation with/devotion to Maxwell Smart played into a male fantasy of "an attractive, all-accepting, all-supportive, loving, mommy/girlfriend/beautiful pal" (Green 41). A closer examination of her roles within the show, and relationship with Smart, however, reveals some critical distances/differences. To begin, Agent 99, as conceived by Brooks and Henry, was not the secondary, two-dimensional Bond Girl suggested by the executives at Talent Associates; instead, she was a central character who had the beauty of a stereotypical Bond Girl, but the smarts and complexity of Miss Moneypenny, Bond's long-term, motherly confidant back at headquarters. As a result, the producers of *Get Smart* cast an actress, Feldon, who could embody that hybrid identity—a "gorgeous showgirl with brains" who was famed for knowing her Shakespeare (Green 10).

As the show developed, Agent 99 exhibited other qualities, and adopted additional roles, that increased the distance between herself and the typical Bond Girl and sexist codings/Mulvey ascribed to that type. For example, she was genuinely smart and competent as a spy, and repeatedly had to bail Maxwell out of tricky situations (while often flattering Max that he was the hero). Max was usually oblivious to her contributions, of course, and these jokey dynamics served to both preserve and poke fun at a diehard fan's egotistical needs. The fact that she was never punished in a cosmic way for impacting/resolving the narrative was also significant; in episode after episode, she was smart, competent and quietly heroic. On a cultural level, that sustained articulation of a hybrid female action/spy hero had real significance, expanding the palette for future films and television shows and inspiring female viewers, who wrote reams of thank you notes to Feldon for being a feminist icon (Green 40).

Agent 99's romantic relationship with Max deserves some measuring as well. From a distance, it seems a bit backward for that era to have 99 be so content to hide her real name, fawn over Max perpetually (despite his ineptitude), and pine for marriage and a family. Within the show's peculiar balance between mainstream and alternative signaling, however, these qualities can be seen as clever ways to capitalize on hybrid ideals and compromises. She eventually weds Max in the series, for example, but she remained, as one chronicler of the show described, "a career spy even after she married, and even after she had children. For a married woman with children and a well-paid husband to keep her job is a rarity on television today. For 99 to have done it when she did it constituted a miracle" (McCrohan 65). There was also a pragmatic side to her self-effacing role in relation to Max. Like a screwball heroine, she was content to play the role of trickster figure and wise fool in order to navigate a sexist system, flatter/attract/bail out repeatedly a male companion and fly under the radar when it came to getting dangerous attention or credit. It was as if she saw the harsh, Mulveyian dynamics at work in this patriarchal genre ecosystem and figured out the best ways to survive and thrive. The fact that she "got cheekier" and less fawning towards Max over the years as an actress and a character, moreover, shows that her hybrid roles and screwball qualities were genuinely counterdiscursive in subtle but significant ways (Green 40).

Finally, Brooks' and Henry's core comedic tone (a mix of wittiness and low brow silliness) and key tools (irreverence, irony and absurdity) contributed to the text's critical distance from its target. While most heavily produced and mediated sit coms from the 1960s felt like they were created and written by committees (cliched characters and safe, predictable jokes), there was an intelligence, originality and auteur-like weirdness to *Get Smart*; it was clearly the product of creators who were testing limits, challenging convention. Brooks described that courage to swim against the current:

> I guess I'm most proud of the bold wit that Buck Henry and I laced through *Get Smart* without condescending to the lowest common denominator in intelligence so we could get big ratings. You know, the network concept: the lower the brain level of the show, the more people you're going to get to watch it. And we never caved into that. I mean, Buck and I were steadfast about it. I really had to amuse us first [Green 237].

While Brooks seems most eager to emphasize sophisticated wittiness of the show, it is also true that a spirit of juvenile irreverence and absurd silliness (which are most likely attributed to his influence) were key to both the show's success in attracting a broad audience, and in achieving a deceptively silly/joke-driven brand of deconstructive satire. To elaborate, television networks in the 1960s were notoriously resistant to edgy, innovative shows or the inclusion of topical, politically-engaged satire; executives lived in fear of alienating mainstream audiences, touchy advertisers and sensitive cultural guardians. As Buck Henry reported, "The cardinal rule in television is, don't offend the audience morally, politically, or esthetically—just don't offend them" (McCrohan 56). Leonard Stern, another producer of the show, elaborated that they had to pitch *Get Smart* as a "spoof" rather than a satire in order to make it past squeamish gatekeepers: "You could sell a spoof to the networks, but the idea of a satire made them uncomfortable" (McCrohan 57). Evidence of the tricky reality of those barriers can be seen in the fact that the first network they courted, ABC, passed on the show because the executives felt that its core concept—a series about a bumbling secret agent, would "appear too un–American" (McGilligan 229).

Brooks and Henry effectively hurdled those blockages by creating satire that was absurd and silly in cosmic and deconstructive, rather than topical, ways. Instead of poking fun at a particular politician or historical event/movement, in other words, they skewered timeless targets: mindless bureaucracy, clueless uses of authority, political factionalism, Cold War paranoia, and so on. And the tools used to make that commentary were absurd *schtick* (ineffectual cones of silence, shoe phones), elaborate wordplay (parodies of governmental doublespeak and excessive acronyms), and silly physical comedy and sight-gags (Smart accidentally winning elaborate fights against much better opponents). As one chronicler of the show explained, "As satire, *Get Smart* operated like a holograph, interweaving pointed commentary with shtick so goofy that you could stare right at it yet overlook the aggression by choosing to hold it at a different angle … it managed volumes by wielding its bayonets under whoopee cushions" (McCrohan 106).

The show was also successful at harnessing seemingly silly, running jokes to its core, satiric purposes of lampooning the inflated aspects of the spy thriller genre. The regular "would you believe?" gag used in almost every episode, for example, playfully deflated or deconstructed the overwrought tropes of a movie like *Goldfinger*:

> As soon as you're gone, by the use of sheer brute strength I shall be able to rip these chains from the wall in one minute. Would you believe it? One minute. Would you believe two minutes? How about a week from Tuesday?
>
> You better give up. This building is surrounded by forty Control agents. Would you believe thirty? One angry boy scout? Girl Scout?

In effect, the narcissistic admiration/anxiety elicited by watching a James Bond thriller is replaced by the democratic, relaxed laughter of Jewish-inflected parody. In addition, the dual silly/seriousness of this kind of comedic deconstruction suggests that this show is a kindred spirit to jokey satires about warfare and political conflict like *Duck Soup* or *Catch 22*.

In closing, perhaps it is the mainstream success of *Get Smart* as television show (running for five years and spawning many offshoots) that prevents cultural critics from recognizing its genuinely subversive qualities or celebrating it at the same level as later cinematic works by Brooks like *Blazing Saddles* or *Young Frankenstein*. Perhaps this study can help to remedy that underestimation, showing how difficult it was to camouflage alternative intentions within mainstream packaging while effectively leveraging auteur-like power, integrity, and even a bit of fury. In sum, *Get Smart* was a unique cultural text: a genuinely popular parody that offered fans both a taste of the tropes that attracted them to a popular Hollywood genre, as well as psychological relief from—and ideological alternatives to—its inflated and sometimes oppressive ideals.

Filmography

The Avengers. Created by Sydney Newman, ABC Television (series 1–3), Associated British Productions for ABC and ABC American (series 4), ABC Television Films for ABC and ABC American (series 5), ABC Television Films for American ABC and Thames (series 6), 1961–69.

Blazing Saddles: 30th Anniversary Special Edition. Dir. Mel Brooks. Warner Bros., 1974. DVD. Warner, 2004.

Burke's Law. Created by Frank D. Gilroy, Ivan Goff, and Ernest Kinoy, Four Star Television and Barbety, 1963–66.

Catch-22. Dir. Mike Nichols. Paramount Pictures, 1970. DVD. Paramount Pictures Home Entertainment, 2017.
Duck Soup. Dir. Leo McCarey. Paramount Pictures, 1933. DVD. Universal Studios Home Entertainment, 2012.
Get Smart. Created by Mel Brooks and Buck Henry, Talent Associates and CBS Productions (Season 5), 1965–69 and 1969–70.
Goldfinger. Dir. Guy Hamilton. United Artists, 1964. DVD. Twentieth Century Fox, 2009.
Honey West. Developed by Gwen Bagni and Paul Dubov. Four Star Television, 1965–66.
I Spy. Developed by David Friedkin and Morton Fine. Three F Productions, 1965–68.
The Man from U.N.C.L.E. Created by Sam Rolfe and Norman Felton. Arena Productions and MGM Television, 1964–68.
Young Frankenstein. Dir. Mel Brooks. Twentieth Century Fox, 1974. DVD. Twentieth Century Fox, 2014.
Your Show of Shows. Created by Sylvester L. Weaver, Jr. Max Liebman Productions, 1950–54.

Works Cited

Brooks, Mel. *All About Me! My Remarkable Life in Show Business.* Random House, 2021.
Dauber, Jeremy. *Jewish Comedy: A Serious History.* W.W. Norton & Company, 2017. Cited parenthetically as *Jewish Comedy.*
_____. *Mel Brooks: Disobedient Jew.* Yale University Press, 2023. Cited parenthetically as *Mel Brooks: Disobedient Jew.*
Green, Joey. *The* Get Smart *Handbook.* Collier Books, 1993.
Hayward, Susan. *Cinema Studies: The Key Concepts.* Routledge, 2013.
Hutcheon, Linda. *A Theory of Parody: The Teachings of Twentieth Century Art Forms.* University of Illinois Press, 2000.
McCrohan, Donna. *The Life and Times of Maxwell Smart.* St Martin's Press, 1988.
McGilligan, Patrick. *Funny Man: Mel Brooks.* HarperCollins, 2019.
Mulvey, Laura. "Visual Pleasure and Narrative Cinema." *Critical Visions in Film Theory,* edited by Timothy Corrigan, Patricia White and Meta Mazaj, Bedford/St. Martins, 2011, pp. 713–24.
Nesteroff, Kliph. *The Comedians: Drunks, Thieves, Scoundrels and the History of American Comedy.* Grove Press, 2015.
Storey, John. *Cultural Theory and Popular Culture.* University of Georgia Press, 2006.
Zax, Tayla. "Remembering the Days of Vaudeville and Jewface." *Forward,* December 8, 2015. https://forward.com/culture/325800/remembering-the-days-of-vaudeville-and-jewface/.

Springtime for Strangelove!
The Holocaust, Nazism, and Jewishness in the Films of Mel Brooks and Stanley Kubrick

NATHAN ABRAMS *and* MICHAEL LIPINER

Introduction

Filmmakers Mel Brooks and Stanley Kubrick share many similarities. They were born around the same time (1926 and 1928 respectively); they both grew up Jewish in New York during World War II; they were both self-taught filmmakers: Kubrick began his career as a professional photographer for *Look* Magazine before making documentaries while Brooks became a writer for several successful television shows before directing commercials where he "learned a little about how to deal with a camera, a set, and a crew" (165). And they both experienced antisemitism and had a deep fascination with the Holocaust and Nazism. Whereas Kubrick generally masked these references, Brooks was more explicit. Nonetheless, they both subverted audience expectations using parody, entropic or black humor, and violence. As we aim to demonstrate in this essay, both filmmakers similarly attempted to raise awareness about the Holocaust and Nazism while exploring Jewishness in their films, which were personal subjects for them both. However, because the Holocaust was too daunting a subject for them to tackle head-on, both filmmakers used black humor, which "informed much of the cultural transgression at the turn of the 1960s" (Fermaglich 10) to satirize Nazism and parody Hitler. Christiane Kubrick said of her husband: "And when he came to the Holocaust story, there was a moment when he realized he could not imagine it at all. He was too frightened, too horrified. And then you have to show it on the screen. And this is why he said he could not make it. He was too scared" (Piskorz 115). Brooks once admitted: "I can't make fun of the

Holocaust. It's too large, too heartbreaking. You can't really deal with it; it's too earth-shattering" (*All About Me!* 48). He added, "But I do use Hitler and Nazis and the guys who perpetrated the outrage. I make fun of them, showing what brutes and pigs they were" (Stratton 247).

These similarities lead the viewer to recognize the influence that Kubrick had on Brooks. By comparing Kubrick's *Lolita* (1962) and *Dr. Strangelove or: How I Learned to Stop Worrying and Love the Bomb* (1964) with Brooks' *The Producers* (1967) and *To Be or Not to Be* (1983), we will argue that, in the words of Lisa Ellert, Micayla Lander, and James B. McCauley, Kubrick and Brooks both used "veiled language and coded images to create cultural representations of the plight of the Jewish people" (Ellert, Lander and McCauley 75).

War and the Holocaust

Kubrick never served in the military, but he held a continuing fascination with it and war nonetheless (LoBrutto 32). He had a keen interest in reading about history and documenting it through photography during his adolescence and teens (Grinberg 209). When he lived in New York City's Greenwich Village between 1948 and 1955, he was exposed to bohemian ideas, existentialism, and the Beats, all of which may have contributed to what has been described as his anti-war stance. The filmmaker once reflected: "For all its horror, war is pure drama, probably because it is one of the few remaining situations where men stand up for and speak up for what they believe to be their principles." Kubrick read voraciously about the topic both for the films he made about war—*Fear and Desire* (1953), *Paths of Glory* (1957), *Spartacus* (1960), *Dr. Strangelove*, *Barry Lyndon* (1975), and *Full Metal Jacket* (1987)—but also those he did not, including Julius Caesar's conquest of Britain, Napoleon, and the U.S. Civil War.

World War II and the Holocaust were especially emotionally gripping and Kubrick read a lot about them both throughout his life (Grinberg 209). "I share the fairly widespread fascination with the horror of the Nazi period," Kubrick once said (Ciment 156). His family had immigrated to New York from Eastern and Central Europe, precisely those places devastated by the Nazis. His third wife, Christiane, has said that "Stanley knew of extended family members murdered by the Nazis" (Cocks, "Death by Typewriter," 190). In fact, The Holocaust Martyrs and Heroes Remembrance Authority in Israel records 59 "Kubriks" murdered in the Holocaust (Cocks, *The Wolf*, 20). Nathan Abrams has argued that, as a result, "He struggled with its impact and with his own understanding of himself as a potential Jewish victim, an innocent and accidental survivor of the Nazi genocide" (Abrahms 13). Louis Blau, lawyer and friend to Kubrick from 1958 until his death, stated, "Kubrick believed the Holocaust was the greatest disaster in history" (Archerd).

World War II also deeply affected Brooks. In 1944, he enlisted in the U.S. Army and was sent to Europe for combat engineering training and to deactivate enemy land mines. There, he experienced hostile antisemitism from some of his fellow soldiers. He also recalled witnessing a large number of Holocaust refugees: "They were starving. It was horrible" (Historical Vignette). Brooks' combat experiences greatly affected his antiwar ideology:

> War isn't hell. War is loud. Much too noisy. All those shells and bombs going off all around you. Never mind death. A man could lose his hearing.... You thought about how you were going to stay warm that night, how you were going to get from one hedgerow to another without some German sniper taking you out. You didn't worry about tomorrow.... I was a Combat Engineer. Isn't that ridiculous? The two things I hate most in the world are combat and engineering [Evans 197–98].

His three older brothers had also enlisted during World War II. One of them, Lenny, was captured by the Nazis and, not realizing he was Jewish, was fortunately sent to a prisoner of war camp where he survived (*All About Me!* 48). On returning home from military service, Brooks recalls weeping upon seeing the Statue of Liberty (*All About Me!* 70).

Survival of the Funniest—Heil-arious Hitler

Throughout his career, Brooks has had a penchant for lowbrow humor for which, as Maurice Yacowar argues, reassessing his "vulgarity" is needed (*Method*, vii). This type of humor was previously depicted in Kubrick's two black comedies—*Lolita* and *Dr. Strangelove*—which satirized German *émigrés*, Nazis, and Hitler, providing the template for Brooks' later parodies. Both filmmakers also similarly depicted satire in these films on the diegetic stage with actors playing multiple roles to manipulate their audiences and subvert formulaic expectations. In turn, this is ironically what the Nazis did with their use of rhetoric and propaganda.

Kubrick cast British-Jewish actor, Peter Sellers, in both of his early comedies. Given his talent for mimicry and knack for improvisation, Sellers ended up portraying a multitude of zany characters, some of whom were invented solely for the films and not found in the source material. In *Lolita*, Sellers' Clare Quilty is a perverse theatrical director who pines for the nymphet Lolita. To steal her away from Humbert, he adopts a series of theatrical disguises including a police officer, psychologist Dr. Zempf, and an unnamed voice on the telephone. Similarly, Humbert hides behind the persona of a cultivated Central European intellectual and married husband.

Dr. Zempf, a heavily accented German émigré fond of quoting Freud, is a precursor to Sellers' Dr. Strangelove, an (ex)-Nazi scientist who greatly admires Hitler but is now employed by the U.S. government in *Dr. Strangelove*. But in the over-the-top way that Sellers played them, it was if they had "stepped right out of the Jewish vaudeville tradition or a Marx Brothers movie" (Abrams, *Stanley Kubrick*, 101). Zempf, for example, wears thick-lensed glasses, so oversized that he must lift them to light a cigarette. Strangelove has an arm with a mind of its own that is unrepentantly Nazi and prone to off-the-cuff Sieg Heil salutes or strangling its owner. As Kubrick said of them, "Strangelove and Zempf are just parodies of movie clichés about Nazis" (Ciment 156). *Dr. Strangelove* was even to include a mass custard pie fight, which, although cut from the final reel, provided a model for the delivery and content of Brooks' movies (Broderick 181–82).

Although Dr. Strangelove has very little screen time, he controls the War Room from behind the scenes in a dark corner much like a theater director working the stage to instill his creative vision of the entire production. The cavernous room itself suggests an arena or maybe even a coliseum. After the deranged General Ripper (Sterling Hayden) launches a nuclear attack on Russia, Strangelove stage-manages his idea to hide in underground shelters and select only those "superior" to procreate, thus recreating Hitler's Master Aryan Race plan.

As Strangelove wrestles with his Nazi and American identities, other characters perform in dual roles. Sellers is literally playing both the U.S. president and Dr. Strangelove in the War Room while General "Buck" Turgidson (George C. Scott) appears to be a patriotic American but exhibits totalitarian traits. He uses Nazi-style rhetoric to justify to the American president (Sellers) Strangelove's Master Aryan Race Plan and discriminates against Russians, downplaying the Soviet Union's strength and tactics. In the presence of the Russian ambassador De Sadesky (Peter Bull), Turgidson tactlessly says: "Mr. President, if I may speak freely, the Ruskie talks big, but frankly we think he's short of know how. I mean, you just can't expect a bunch of ignorant peons to understand a machine like some of our boys. And that's not meant as an insult, Mr. Ambassador." Meanwhile, De Sadesky is a spy-in-hiding who snaps pictures of the War Room using a hidden camera while denying he is a spy.

Kubrick's early comedies also explore sexuality and perversion. *Lolita* is, after all, about rival pedophiles vying for the attention of an underage girl and her subsequent abuse, but it is infused with innuendo. The titular character is sent by her mother to Camp Climax (a moniker invented by Kubrick rather than the novel's author, Vladimir Nabokov) for what she proposes will be "isolation from boys." In *Dr. Strangelove*, General Jack Ripper (Sterling Hayden) confesses to Captain Lionel Mandrake (Sellers) that Russia's "plan" to infiltrate America's water systems with fluoride had come to him during sexual intercourse when he could not perform. Indeed, all the names in *Dr. Strangelove* contain some sort of sexual reference. As mentioned, Sellers' sexually perverted Quilty portrays Dr. Zempf, a feigned German-accented school psychologist (and a precursor to the actor's Dr. Strangelove) who manipulates Humbert by telling him that Lolita is sexually repressed. His name can be interpreted as *Senf* (German: mustard), as in "to cut the mustard" sexually but which also suggests heat and spiciness, another of the myriad sexual jokes that punctuated *Lolita*.

These films made a great impression on Brooks and his films, *The Producers* and his remake of the classic *To Be or Not to Be*, which were both musical parodies of Hitler and the Nazis.[1] Reviewing a recent biography of Mel Brooks, the critic Jesse Tisch observes, "with Brooks, excess was always the point"; "he was," Tisch continues, "built for overflow" (34). The same could be said of Sellers' comic persona and especially in his two films for Kubrick. The critic for the *New York Mirror*, for example, described Zempf as a "menacing Sid Caesar–type Viennese official" a decade after Brooks had been writing for Sid Caesar's "Your Show of Shows" in the early 1950s. This comedy show included the sketch, "The German General," in which Caesar was referred to as "mein general." Caesar would later play a comedic role as Chief Caveman in Brooks' *History of the World: Part I* (1981).

It was originally titled *Springtime for Hitler*,[2] but Brooks was forced to change it due to its controversial nature (McKenna). Indeed, upon its original release, *The Producers* was panned for bad taste and was a commercial failure. In response to heavy backlash regarding its comedic approach to Nazism and Hitler (Stratten 251), Brooks explained, "The way you bring down Hitler and his ideology is not by getting on a soapbox with him, but if you can reduce him to something laughable, you win" (*All About Me!* 183).

Brooks' protagonist Leo Bloom (Jewish actor Gene Wilder) shares some similarities with Humbert Humbert (James Mason) in *Lolita*. Both are classic nebbishes, stereotypically Jewish neurotics, who commit crimes to assuage their obsessive-compulsive disorders and schlemiel victimization: feelings of aloofness, inferiority, genuine unhappiness, and massive anxieties. Neither, though, address their Jewishness. They follow James Moshin's description of Jewish-Americans at the time who were "balancing their religious identity with their identity as part of a 'white ethnicity,' which often leads to cultural assimilation into a 'generic American identity'" (Moshin 24–25).

Both are also manipulated by others—namely Quilty (Sellers) and Max Bialystock (Jewish actor Zero Mostel). The former is a television producer with a sideline in pornography who specializes in seducing women and their young daughters. Humbert becomes so obsessed with him that *Lolita* is really about Quilty being bookended by his shouted name. Humbert and Quilty are doppelgängers, who skillfully conceal their dark pedophiliac crimes behind an "amiable mask," but are in fact obsessed with competitively pursuing and winning over their underaged female victims. Like Humbert and Quilty, Brooks' antiheroic Jewish-encoded protagonists-cum-criminals are Bialystock and Bloom, who engage in illicit sexual relations and pilfer their investors' money. Bialystock is a zealous and failing Broadway stage producer who immorally takes advantage of wealthy old ladies' deep pockets by enticing them with sexual advances.

Bialystock convinces Bloom to hire an ex–Nazi playwright Franz Liebkind (Kenneth Mars). His name, which "translates as 'love child,' a polite term for bastard" (Stratton 251), recalls that of Dr. Strangelove, implying either dubious parentage or pedophilia. Their characters are also similar. Dr. Strangelove, the titular ex–Nazi scientist who idolizes Hitler, in a momentary lapse, even addresses the U.S. president, Merkin Muffley (also played by Sellers), as "mein Führer." His comical "hand" protests Dr. Strangelove's compromise with the Americans, humorously wrestling over a lit cigarette or a circular slide rule or becoming involuntarily erect. Despite having crossed over, Strangelove continues to spout a Nazi-like eugenicist ideology.

Similarly, Brooks described Liebkind as "not only one of the worst writers that ever wielded a pen, but also a regenerate dyed-in-the-wool Nazi. He was madly in love with his Führer, Adolf Hitler, and always wore a World War II German helmet splattered with pigeon droppings" (*All About Me!*, 158). When Liebkind's play is accepted, he says to his birds (an important Holocaust referent [Boissoneault]), "Do you hear? We are going to clear the Führer's name!" The Nazi sympathizer, Liebkind, hysterically explains to Bialystock and Bloom, "I'm not responsible, I only followed orders!" Liebkind then sardonically bellows the patriotic song, "America the Beautiful." In doing so, Brooks follows Kubrick by satirically raising notions of dominant American hegemony via Nazis who immortalize Hitler's memory and conveniently ignore the terrible deeds he committed against humanity. He is like Dr. Zempf, who says to Humbert, "We Americans.... We believe that it is equally important to prepare the pupils for the mutually satisfactory mating and the successful child rearing," in a thick and affected Germanic accent. This idea also precursors America's "Strangelovian Master Race offspring" ("Indirected" 24) plan once they win World War Three.

But where Kubrick only dabbled in parody, Brooks takes it one step further. Their Nazi musical, titled *Springtime for Hitler—A Gay Romp with Adolf and Eva at Berchtesgaden*, features "[a] line of beautiful girls dressed as storm troopers [with] black patent leather boots: S[&]M." Thus, Brooks lampooned Riefenstahl's choreographed, glamorized images of the Third Reich's swastika military formations with dancers jubilantly line dancing and prancing on the diegetic stage. The "Springtime for Hitler" production begins with a musical celebration of Nazism. The chorus line sings: "And now it's Springtime for Hitler and Germany. Deutschland is happy and gay. We're marching to a faster pace. Look out—here comes the master race." This allusion to Hitler's Master Aryan Race plan mirrors Dr. Strangelove's similar "Master Race offspring" plan (mentioned previously) to select those deemed "fittest" to hide with the president's cabinet and military generals in underground mineshafts while awaiting nuclear war and the destruction of most of the world's population.

The musical is also infused by a "camp, homosexual sensibility in the mind of a sadistic, fascist leader" (Tatar 192). Hitler is played by Jewish actor Dick Shawn who flaunts his homosexuality with earrings and flamboyant, exaggerated gestures. This is achieved in part with Nazi Sieg Heils. Like Kubrick, Brooks comically depicts this salute to call attention to minority persecution. In *To Be or Not to Be*, they are repeated senselessly for comic relief, especially by Captain Schultz (Christopher Lloyd). In *The Producers*, while auditioning for the "Springtime for Hitler" musical, many actors dress the part of Hitler and disdainfully practice their "Heils." The salute is also sardonically impersonated by Lolita to her mother (an invented scene for the film) in protest of authority. Dr. Strangelove (an invented character for the film, which satirically broaches Cold War politics and the superpower arms race [Broderick 82]) attempts to suppress his gloved hand, which mockingly forms a *Heil* and rolls his wheelchair backwards in protest. In Kubrick's *Spartacus*, the Romans contemptuously extend their arms and exclaim, "Hail!" as an allegorical attack on "twentieth-century fascism" (Burton 8), specifically McCarthyism and its Hollywood blacklisting.

A Star Is Reborn

Decades later, Brooks would return to satirizing Hitler and the Nazis within the illusions of the theater in his remake of what he considered to be a "wonderful movie": *To Be or Not to Be* (1942) directed by Ernst Lubitsch, his "cinematic hero" (*All About Me!* 331). In this classic film, Lubitsch never identified "Jews" as victims, which partially accounts for Brooks wanting to remake the film. Brooks also stated that it was a "perfect picture for Anne [Bancroft, his non–Jewish wife] and me to co-star in," mirroring Kubrick casting his future wife, Christiane (a non–Jewish German in his dramatic war film, *Paths of Glory* [1957]).

Brooks opted to produce Lubitsch's remake and hired Alan Johnson to direct, who had previously choreographed his "Springtime for Hitler" number. Set in 1939 Warsaw, *To Be or Not to Be* featured Brooks and Bancroft as Frederick and Anna Bronski, actors whose theater company attempts to thwart the Nazis from destroying the Polish underground movement at the brink of World War II. The film's opening montage includes theater posters with titles that connect to *Lolita*'s main themes: "Gypsy Lovers," "Ladies," "Indiscretion," and "Naughty Nazis." As in *The Producers*, the opening scene in *To Be or Not to Be* features Frederick dressed in full garb as Hitler on the diegetic stage performing in a musical number about the Nazi invasion of Europe.

Like Kubrick, Brooks depicts complex characters representative of minorities who had to camouflage their true nature and feign roles to make them appear safe and acceptable to the ruling classes. Whereas Kubrick alluded to homosexuality in his early comedies (Quilty in *Lolita* and General Jack D. Ripper in *Dr. Strangelove*, respectively), Brooks overtly depicts this targeted and persecuted group. Sasha Kinski (James Haake, "the world's oldest working drag queen," according to his Twitter bio), is Anna's courageous gay costumer and hairdresser. His homosexuality is not discovered until he is forced by the Nazis to wear a pink triangle (a Holocaust marker), which he does without protest. With Sasha's characterization, Brooks brazenly and "explicitly refer[red] to the inclusion of gay men in the groups condemned to the Nazi death camps, a significant moment and one that would not have been possible in Lubitsch's 1940s version" (Richman).

When the Gestapo pursues Sasha, he frantically runs into the Bronski theater, screaming: "You've got to hide me. They're rounding up homosexuals and putting them in concentration camps!" The troupe quickly hides Sasha by applying makeup and dressing him as a woman for their musical number, "Ladies," an homage to the beautification of women. The film also reveals several Jewish families and members of the Polish resistance hiding in the theater basement to avoid being rounded up by the Nazis.

As befitting the times in which their films were made, Kubrick (and Lubitsch) refrained from overtly Jewish references in their films. Brooks, however, explicitly raises issues with Jewish sensibilities. An actor named Lupinsky (Lewis J. Stadlen) proudly wears his Jewishness on his sleeve. He makes the sign of a six-pointed star and wears the Nazi-enforced Yellow Star of David armband. When he is captured by the Nazis, he recites Shylock's famous soliloquy from *The Merchant of Venice* ("Hath not a Jew ..." doubling on the "medieval stock-type of the Jew as usurer" [Sicher 57], a stereotype also used by the Nazis in their propaganda). Although Brooks plays his recurring, familiar nebbish character in *To Be or Not to Be*, it can be surmised that his characterization of Frederick is not as Jewish as he is not targeted by the Nazis.

In the latter film's finale, the theater troupe hatches a plan to rescue its Jewish victims by performing a show with Frederick in disguise as Hitler and the actors as Nazi officers (mirroring Quilty's incarnations and Dr. Strangelove). The Jewish families and members of the Polish resistance dress as clowns and await a secret trap door. However, they are soon discovered by the diegetic audience and the troupe acts quickly to make them laugh and therefore be distracted by the "clowning around as foolish and silly Jews to the delight and scornful laughter of the Gestapo and Nazi officers" (Boerboom 106). Sasha (disguised as an SS officer) grabs an elderly Jewish woman disguised as a clown, places an extra yellow Jewish star on her, and yells, "*Juden!*" The audience bellows with laughter as members of the Polish resistance and Jews-disguised-as-clowns exit the theater and make it safely to England.

Furthermore, *To Be or Not to Be* breaks entirely free of comedy with a mini-documentary film-within-the-film shot in grainy black-and-white with real footage depicting the ramifications of war-torn Europe. This includes soldiers marching along ruined cities and other similar scenes with the actors in the film before the sequence resorts back to color and to comedy. It resembles those moments in *Dr. Strangelove* when Kubrick breaks entirely free from comedy to provide a realistic and historical picture of war. The sequences where a squadron of troops have been ordered by the president to attack Burpelson Airforce Base to prevent a preemptive strike on Russia are masterfully shot and provide much realism. Kubrick cleverly uses grainy black-and-white cinematography—bolstered by the lack of music and dialogue—with many quick edits, closeups, various angles, and shaky cams, resembling an historical documentary and recalling Holocaust footage and World War II battle scenes.

Moreover, more dramatic moments in *Dr. Strangelove* include, as mentioned, a Russian ambassador spy-in-hiding clandestinely taking pictures of the War Room. He mirrors Professor Siletski (José Ferrer), a Nazi spy who collects names from the Polish underground to give to the Gestapo. However, Frederick intercepts his plan by disguising himself as Siletski (who closely resembles Dr. Zempf in *Lolita*) and traveling to Germany to provide them with false names.

Frankensteinian Golems

An oblique theme running through Kubrick's and Brooks' films is that of the golem as a critique of war and Nazism. In *Lolita*, Kubrick inserted a scene in which Humbert, Charlotte and Lolita watch *The Curse of Frankenstein* (1957). It is a small moment but portends a theme that will inform much of his later work. Certainly, Kubrick's invented Dr. Strangelove can be read, in Brian E. Crim's words, as a "darkly comic, Germanic golem" (391), intent on creating a new "Monster" or superior Master Aryan Race to save political and military leaders from extinction amid global thermonuclear war with the Soviet Union. As a Germanic (and ex–Nazi) scientist, Strangelove mirrors Dr. Frankenstein and both concoct a plan to "procreate" which brings about death and destruction. While Frankenstein flees to hide from being murdered by his revengeful-driven Creature, Strangelove monstrously plans to hide in an underground bunker to escape total annihilation by world powers in retaliation for starting World War Three. The Soviets' Doomsday Device is also arguably a form of golem, technology run amok.

In the famous Jewish folklore legend, an artificial clay anthropoid—the golem—was created in the 16th century to counter antisemitism by Prague sorcerer and Jewish spiritual leader Rabbi Loew. It greatly influenced Mary Shelley's Frankenstein and the countless Golem remakes and reincarnations. In fact, Frankenstein's Monster has also been linked by scholars to the Jewish legend of the Golem (Toumey 423). Dr. Victor Frankenstein mirroring Loew also creates an artificial human. Paul Wegener then made *The Golem: How He Came Into the World* in 1920 (Friedman 50–51), influencing the string of Hollywood *Frankenstein* films which emerged beginning in the 1930s with (former theater director) James Whale's *Frankenstein* (1931) and *The Bride of Frankenstein* (1935). Since they were made just before and during the Nazi rise to power they have been interpreted as a critique of Nazi Germany and its fear of the cultural outsider (Winters 121–22).

Likewise, Brooks explored these themes in his black-and-white parodic film *Young Frankenstein* (1974), which used the same laboratory set and props from Whale's original film (Yacowar, *Comic Art*, 174). Baron Beaufort von Frankenstein (played by Jewish actor Gene Wilder) is Frankenstein's grandson who, like Strangelove and Quilty's German incarnations, tries to conceal his German identity by insisting that his surname is the Americanized "Fronksteen." He travels to his ancestral castle in Transylvania where he recreates his family's monstrous legacy with the help of oddball German-accented characters. This includes his assistant, Igor (played by Jewish actor Marty Feldman), and the sinister Nazi-like housekeeper, Frau Blucher (Cloris Leachman). The latter is an obvious play on Hannah Arendt's alias, Frau Blücher (Scott 170), whose surname was taken from her second husband, Heinrich Blücher.

In one scene, Brooks calls attention to historical Jewish persecution and draws Nazi allusions modeled on *Dr. Strangelove*. After it is discovered that Frankenstein has revived his grandfather's original Monster experiment, a committee hearing is formed to determine whether to subjugate and persecute the (Jewish) scientist. The committee chair states, "This man is different," before he is interrupted by an angry villager who allegorically echoes persecution of the Jews when he shrieks: "He's a Frankenstein! And they're alike! It's in their blood! ... What they really want is to rule the world!" The townspeople cheer in agreement before the chair introduces "the one man most qualified to judge the situation fairly."

This man is Police Inspector Hans Wilhelm Friedrich Kemp (Kenneth Mars, who played the Nazi Liebkind in *The Producers*) who is clearly modelled on Dr. Strangelove. Like his predecessor, Kemp wears a black suit and has a dark monocle (in place of Strangelove's dark sunglasses). He also has a black-gloved mechanical hand, which jerks uncontrollably with a crank and chain that needs readjustment, and which he constantly subdues. Although the committee hearing is set in Transylvania and the actors speak with English accents, Mars (like Sellers) speaks with a heavy German accent, often harshly, to parody Nazism using the same mechanical mannerisms analogous with Hitler, who "evinces stiff and rigid postures" (Tomasulo 114).

When Kemp meets Frankenstein, it is to interrogate him and he recalls Nazi Aryan race ideology: "It is not superstition that worries me, Herr doctor, but genes and chromosomes." As they play a game of darts, he bellows, "You are a Frankenstein!" and the (Jewish) scientist misthrows his arrow multiple times into a pane of glass with echoes of Kristallnacht. At the conclusion of their meeting, Kemp's gloved arm forms a Nazi Heil salute and, much like Strangelove, he wrestles to control it. Kemp soon leads an angry mob of villagers to lynch Frankenstein and his Monster. They break into his castle and pull Frankenstein's inert body from his machines before the Monster, now transformed after receiving part of his creator's brain, sings a moving soliloquy. Kemp and the mob themselves are quickly transformed and embrace their threatening Other "enemies." In doing so, Eric Michael Mazur asserts that Brooks' sappy ending taps into a post–Holocaust era Jewish fantasy of being accepted by the general society after unyielding oppression (94).

Like its precursors in *Dr. Strangelove* and *The Producers*, *Young Frankenstein* also uses the theater for comedic effect. When Frankenstein concocts a creative idea to impress the Bucharest Academy of Science with his Creation, he bellows, "My name is Franken-shtein!" in its correct German pronunciation. To demonstrate to the European committee that the Outsider undesirable is now "civilized," he and the Creature perform on the diegetic stage Jewish composer Irving Berlin's song, "Puttin' on the Ritz." Like classic Broadway artists, they dance and sing in choreographed unison wearing top hats and tuxedos with coattails. However, when a stage light bursts, the Monster becomes frightened and the audience soon "boos" and throws trash at them before chaining and imprisoning the poor Creature.

Like Kubrick's early comedies, *Young Frankenstein* also explores sexuality and perversion in a satirical fashion. Frankenstein's sexy lab assistant, Inga (Teri Garr), suggests that since the creature's body will have to be larger than normal to make it easier to operate on, it should have an enormous "*Schwanzstucker*," derived from the German, "Schwanz," meaning "tail," and "stuck," meaning "piece" (Alliata 186). This mirrors the multiple references to penises in *Dr. Strangelove*, such as Ripper's huge cigar and the given and family names of General Buck Turgidson who was originally to be called "Schmuck." There is also Strangelove's phallic arm that becomes involuntarily erect. When the creature consummates his relationship with Elizabeth (Madeline Kahn), she unexpectedly belts out the aria, "Ah, Sweet Mystery of Life" (composed by Victor Herbert who grew up in Stuttgart), comically confirming his well-endowed manhood. In the film's final scene, Inga asks Frankenstein what he received in a new operation he undergoes with the Creature. He simply smiles and hums as the camera zooms-in on a closeup with the sounds of their coitus followed by Igor blowing another phallic symbol, the ram's horn known in Hebrew as the Shofar.

Conclusion

Kubrick and Brooks shared similar views about war and the Holocaust, which were deep and personal subjects for both. They used black comedy to create cultural representations of the plight of the Jewish people by satirizing their stereotypes, as well as those of German *émigrés*, Nazis, and Hitler. Both filmmakers also similarly depicted satire on the diegetic stage with actors playing roles to manipulate both audiences and subvert formulaic expectations. In a series of ruses based on theatrical disguises, they turned fascist horror into hope. At times, Kubrick and Brooks also broke free entirely from comedy to raise serious issues about persecution and genocide by providing a realistic look at war. By drawing on the Golem folklore, they raised Frankenstein-related themes analogous to their outsider, Other, and allegorical Jewish victimization. The cast—both real-life actors and their respective diegetic roles—disguise themselves in multifaceted roles, including *nebbish* and *schlemiels*. However, in the end, it is their use of black, satirical comedy that universalized historical oppression and called attention to the Holocaust and the historical plight of Jewish people. There is much more to be said. For example, drawing upon both *Spartacus* and *2001: A Space Odyssey* (1968), Brooks satirizes historical events laden with Nazi and Holocaust references in *History of the World: Part I*. The comparisons demonstrate the extent of Kubrick's influence, and in this instance, on Brooks whose films, in turn, reveal an ongoing on-screen conversation and relationships with his cinematic master which helps us to deepen our understanding of Brooks' films and critique which pushes past Kubrick's. But this deserves a fuller investigation of the comparisons between two remarkable Jewish filmmakers of the 20th century.

Notes

1. We know from the Stanley Kubrick Archive, for example, that Brooks attended the premier of *Dr. Strangelove*. Another connection is Brooks' use of Slim Pickens, the B52 bomber pilot, in his *Blazing Saddles* (1974) whom he described as "one of the best Western comedy actors that ever lived ... the guy who rides Stanley Kubrick's atom bomb down to earth" (Brooks, *All About Me!*, 214).

2. "The Making of 'The Producers'" documentary (2002) is featured on the Special Edition DVD of *The Producers* (1967); dir. Laurent Bouzereau.

Filmography

Barry Lyndon. Dir. Stanley Kubrick. Hawk Film and Peregrine Films, 1975. DVD. Video Service Corp., 2017.
The Bride of Frankenstein. Dir. James Whale. Universal Pictures, 1935. Universal Pictures, 1931. DVD. Universal Studios Home Entertainment, 2014.
The Curse of Frankenstein. Dir. Terence Fisher. Warner Bros., 1957. DVD. Warner Bros. Home Video, 2005.
Dr. Strangelove or: How I Learned to Stop Worrying and Love the Bomb. Dir. Stanley Kubrick. Columbia, 1964. DVD. Columbia/Tristar Video, 2001.
Fear and Desire. Dir. Stanley Kubrick. Joseph Burstyn, 1953. DVD. Kino Lorber Films, 2012.
Frankenstein. Dir. James Whale. Universal Pictures, 1931. DVD. Universal Studios Home Entertainment, 2000.
Full Metal Jacket. Dir. Stanley Kubrick. Natant and Harrier Films, 1987. DVD. Warner Bros. Home Video, 2010.
The Golem: How He Came Into the World. Dir. Paul Wegener. Deutsche Bioscop, 1915. DVD. Reel Vault, 2015.
History of the World: Part I. Dir. Mel Brooks. Brooksfilms, 1981. DVD. Twentieth Century Fox, 2006.
Lolita. Dir. Stanley Kubrick. Metro-Goldwyn-Meyer, 1962. DVD. Castaway Pictures, 2007.

Paths of Glory. Dir. Stanley Kubrick. United Artists, 1957. DVD. Video Service Corp., 2010.
The Producers. Dir. Mel Brooks. Embassy Pictures, 1967. DVD. MGM (Video & DVD),2 003.
Spartacus. Dir. Stanley Kubrick. Bryna Productions, 1960. DVD. Universal Pictures Home Entertainment, 2018.
To Be or Not to Be. Dir. Alan Johnson. Brooksfilms, 1983. DVD. Twentieth Century Fox, 2006.
2001: A Space Odyssey. Dir. Stanley Kubrick. Metro-Goldwyn-Meyer, 1968. DVD. Warner Home Video, 2015.
Young Frankenstein. Dir. Mel Brooks. Gruskoff/Venture Films, Crossbow Productions, and Jouer Limited, 1974. DVD. Twentieth Century Fox, 2014.

Works Cited

Abrams, Nathan. *Stanley Kubrick: New York Jewish Intellectual*. Rutgers University Press, 2018.
Alliata, Michela Vanon. "The Uses of Parody and the Practice of Laughter in Mel Brooks's *Young Frankenstein*," in *Mary Shelley's Frankenstein, 1818–2018*, edited by Maria Parrino, Alessandro Scarsella, and Michela Vanon Alliata, Cambridge Scholars, 2020, pp. 178–192.
Archerd, Army. "Kubrick 'Memoir' Shocks Spielberg." *Variety*, June 18, 1999. https://variety.com/1999/voices/columns/kubrick-memoir-shocks-spielberg-1117503222/. Accessed July 11, 2022.
Boerboom, Samuel. "Not Just a Dresser—*To Be or Not to Be* and the Case of Sasha Kinski." *The Political Mel Brooks*, edited by Samuel Boerboom and Beth E. Bonnstetter, Rowman & Littlefield, 2019, pp. 67–86.
Boissoneault, Lorraine. "When the Nazis Tried to Bring Animals Back from Extinction." *Smithsonian Magazine*, March 13, 2017. https://www.smithsonianmag.com/history/when-nazis-tried-bring-animals-back-extinction-180962739/.
Broderick, Mick. *Reconstructing Strangelove*. Columbia University Press, 2017.
Brook, Vincent. "A Wave of Their Own: How Jewish Filmmakers Invented the New Hollywood." *Jewish Film & New Media: An International Journal*, vol. 7, no. 1, Spring 2019, pp. 48–80.
Brooks, Mel. *All About Me!* Random House, 2021.
Burton, Margaret. "Performances of Jewish Identity: *Spartacus*." *Shofar: An Interdisciplinary Journal of Jewish Studies*, vol. 27, no. 1, Fall 2008, pp. 1–15.
Ciment, Michel. *Kubrick*. Collins, 1983.
Cocks, Geoffrey. "Death by Typewriter Stanley Kubrick, the Holocaust, and *The Shining*." *Depth of Field: Stanley Kubrick, Film, and the Uses of History*, edited by Geoffrey Cocks, James Diedrick, and Glenn Perusek, University of Wisconsin Press, 2006, pp. 185–217. Cited parenthetically as "Death by Typewriter."
_____. "Indirected by Stanley Kubrick." *POST SCRIPT: Essays in Film and the Humanities*, vol. 32, no. 2, Winter/Spring, 2013, pp. 20–33. Cited parenthetically as "Indirected."
_____. *The Wolf at the Door: Stanley Kubrick, History, and the Holocaust*. Peter Lang, 2004. Cited parenthetically as *The Wolf*.
Crim, Brian E. *Planet Auschwitz: Holocaust Representation in Science Fiction and Horror Filmand Television*. Rutgers University Press, 2020.
Ellert, Lisa, Micayla Lander, and James B. McCauley. "The Very Rotten 1970s—Mel Brooks's Satire of Politics in the Age of Ford." *The Political Mel Brooks*, edited by Samuel Boerboom and Beth E. Bonnstetter, Rowman & Littlefield, 2019, pp. 53–66.
Evans, Art. *World War II Veterans in Hollywood*. McFarland, 2020.
Fermaglich, Kristen. *American Dreams and Nazi Nightmares: Early Holocaust Consciousness and Liberal America, 1957–1965*. UPNE, 2007.

Friedman, Lester D. "The Edge of Knowledge: Jews as Monsters/Jews as Victims." *MELUS/ Ethnic Images in Popular Genres and Media*, vol. 11, no. 3, Autumn 1984, pp. 49–62.
Grinberg, Marat. "Kubrick and Jewishness." *The Bloomsbury Companion to Stanley Kubrick*, edited by Nathan Abrams and I.Q. Hunter, Bloomsbury Academic, 2021, pp. 203–13.
Haake, James. "Bio." *Twitter*. https://twitter.com/gypsyhaake?lang=en.
"Historical Vignette 109—Mel Brooks Was a Combat Engineer in World War II." *U.S. Army Corps of Engineers*, August 2007. http://www.usace.army.mil/About/History/ HistoricalVignettes/SportsEntertainment/109MelBrooks.aspx. Accessed July 11, 2022.
LoBrutto, Vincent. *Stanley Kubrick: A Biography*. D.I. Fine Books, 1997.
Mazur, Eric Michael. *Encyclopedia of Religion and Film*. ABC-CLIO, 2011.
McKenna, Anthony Thomas. *Showman of the Screen: Joseph E. Levine and His Revolutions in Film Promotion*. University Press of Kentucky, 2016.
Moshin, James. "On the Big Screen, but Stuck in the Closet: What Mel Brooks's *The Producers* Says About Modern American Jewish Identity and Communicating the Holocaust." *Journal of the Northwest Communication Association*, vol. 35, Spring 2006, pp. 22–45.
Piskorz, Artur. "Kubrick: A True Artist. An Interview with Christiane Kubrick and Jan Harlan."*Revista Latente*, vol. 12, 2014, p. 115.
Richman, Darren. "Movies You Might Have Missed: *To Be or Not to Be*, Mel Brooks Second World War Comedy." *The Independent*, July 19, 2018. https://www.independent.co.uk/ arts-entertainment/films/features/movies-you-might-have-missed-to-be-or-not-to-be-mel-brooks-world-war-two-comedy-a8454796.html. Accessed July 11, 2022.
Scott, Joanna Vecchiarelli. "Alien Nation: Hannah Arendt, the German Emigrés and America." *European Journal of Political Theory*, vol. 3, no. 2, 2004, pp. 167–76.
Sicher, Efraim. "The Jewing of Shylock: Wesker's 'The Merchant.'" *Modern Language Studies*, vol. 21, no. 2, Spring 1991, pp. 57–69.
Stratton, Jon. "Haunted by the Holocaust: *Hogan's Heroes*, *The Producers*, *Fiddler on the Roof*." *Journal for Cultural Research*, vol. 22, no. 3, 2018, p. 247.
Tatar, Maria. "'We meet again, Fräulein': Hollywood's Fascination with Fascism." *German Politics & Society*, vol. 13, no. 3, Fall 1995, pp. 190–98.
Tisch, Jesse. "History of Mel Brooks: Both Parts." *Jewish Review of Books*, Winter 2020. https://jewishreviewofbooks.com/articles/5764/history-of-mel-brooks-both-parts/#.
Tomasulo, Frank P. "The Mass Psychology of Fascist Cinema—Leni Riefenstahl's *Triumph of the Will*." *Documenting the Documentary: Close Readings of Documentary Film and Video*, edited by Jim Leach and Barry K. Grant, Wayne State University Press, 1998, pp. 81–102.
Toumey, Christopher P. "The Moral Character of Mad Scientists: A Cultural Critique of Science." *Science, Technology, & Human Values*, vol. 17, no. 4, Autumn 1992, pp. 411–437.
Walker, Alexander. et al. *Stanley Kubrick, Director: A Visual Analysis*. W.W. Norton, 2000. Digital Edition.
Winters, Ben. "'There have been developments': Frankenstein's Monster Finds a (Mahlerian) Voice." *Interdisciplinary Humanities*, vol. 26, no. 2, 2009, pp. 116–27.
Yacowar, Maurice. *The Comic Art of Mel Brooks*. Crescent Moon Publishing, 2015. Cited parenthetically as *Comic Art*.
―――. *Method in Madness: The Comic Art of Mel Brooks*. St. Martin's Press, 1981. Cited parenthetically as *Method*.

Around a Proscenium
Representation and Distance in The Producers

MURRAY POMERANCE

Let us pass over the incontestably true: that as far as anybody is funny in this life, Mel Brooks is funny—is funny, thinks funny, knows funny, makes funny; also that Zero Mostel has the verve of a brass combo and the delicacy of Disney's dancing hippopotami; also that never until Gene Wilder have we seen a full-blown case of male hysteria; also that Mostel chasing Wilder around his office while Wilder screams for his blue blanket is gut-splittingly hilarious and shriekingly perilous; and also that the idea of producing a Broadway musical called *Springtime for Hitler,* even in order to lose money, is unspeakably preposterous, strange in the way that an alien presence could seem strange, completely over the top. More:

The Producers (1967).

for such a show, Hitler would have to be somewhat fey, if not utterly narcotized, and could be played, of course, only by Dick Shawn; as the playwright, Kenneth Mars with his Wehrmacht helmet and trained pigeons would walk a tightrope between unbelievably silly and terrifyingly true to life. All this has been finely masticated, accepted as canonical in the annals of American comedy, and gaped at by audiences that, watching with at least as much eagerness as the "Broadway theatre audience" we see depicted inside *The Producers* (1967), revere the thought of Bialystock and Bloom's intended fiasco having become a mega-hit. Take the film and its story as read.

To acknowledge the film's status in the history of American cinematic comedy we set aside any or all of the following (obviously cogent) lines of analysis:

- *The Producers* is entirely recursive, based in an idea as ridiculous for a film as *Springtime* is ridiculous as an idea for a Broadway show: *Come, let's watch a movie about a pair of zany guys mounting, of all insane things, a Broadway musical called "Springtime for Hitler"*....
- The energy running the motor mechanism of the plot is entirely characterological, based as much in casting as in composition, and further, every character has the sort of hyper-animated quality and style we are accustomed to find in cartoons—Mostel's Bialystock most of all;
- In their relentless mouthiness—of two contrasting kinds (tuba, let us say, and piccolo)—Mostel and Wilder typify the gabby Jewish borscht-belt comedian who remains embodied so faultlessly by Brooks himself. Bialystock and Bloom are not only Brooksian, then, but stand-ins for the Brooks we have already met and decided to love;
- The idea of making a bouncy and happily nostalgic stage musical about an abject monster is both outlandish and outrageous, not to say psychotic. Only thoroughgoing rapaciousness, as we see in Bialystock and Bloom's hungry eyes, can even come close to explaining. Seen from the point of view of any serious consideration of the horror of the Holocaust, the best one can say about the Bialystock-Bloom project is that it is ignorant. Bialystock and Bloom know this, however. They are rational to the hilt in predicting that such a musical will fail, predictably, but we can say they are also sympathetic enough at heart to understand it should fail, too. In the musical's success there is a dramatic irony and a moral challenge (which I intend to discuss);

- Since even a motion picture *about* the preparation and staging of so outré a musical property as *Springtime* is self-avowedly outré itself, we can have no very good reason for declining to believe that some accountant set his teeth off-camera into the already mega-successful Mel Brooks; that Brooks had a need for a flop (the Internal Revenue Service does wonders with film producers) and that therefore *The Producers* is itself an attempted failure that shockingly failed to fail.

However, what is really fascinating about *The Producers* is not its exaggeration, not its "insanity," not its *bravura* Rossinian musical quality, not the Brooks ensemble company in all its glory but something else that has strangely gained less attention than all these, while at the same time burrowing into the depths of our public and private conscience "that delighted Broadway theatre audience"—that audience and its unbridled guffaws.

What about those folks? And what about us, enjoying them enjoying? Because we *of course, axiomatically* enjoy *The Producers*. Is it true for this "Broadway audience" we stare at and for the cinemagoing audience staring that, as Walter Benjamin wrote, the "image of happiness is indissolubly bound up with the image of redemption," that "the past can be seized only as an image which flashes up at the instant when it can be recognized and is never seen again" ("Concept" 389; 390)? A flash—not a way of life. Watching *Springtime for Hitler* is the onscreen audience fashioning through the imagination some modish, thrilling, indeed unceasingly titillating bourgeois interior? The private citizen's drawing room, writes Benjamin, "was a box in the world-theatre" ("Paris" 168). Do we freely catch a ribald glimpse of something passing by, something even grotesque, delighted *because it is passing?*

Because the punch line of the story in *The Producers* is not fiduciary: an expensive production calculated to be a flop is in fact a hit, so that poor Bialystock and Bloom now have ballooning tax troubles. That would be, perhaps, a kind of accountant comedy. That is a source of humor, part of the set-up, but not the punch line. The punch line is that onscreen audience: the one that not only surprises our heroes and us by loving what they are supposed to hate but also, more originally, produces and manages so loving a response; the one that finds Hitler funny because—we can presume—its members rented seats and came to the theater *ready* to find Hitler funny. They knew where they were going. Thus, the "joy of Hitler" was for these private individuals an important illusion.

And associated with this punch is a second one that reflects upon those of us who profess to love the film, since we, too, come to watch *ready already* to find Hitler funny, because we are ready already to find that onscreen audience ready already. I do not mean to ask, "Is Hitler funny?" I mean to ask, "What is involved in finding Hitler funny?" Even better: "What is involved in being ready already to find Hitler (and the Nazi atrocity) funny?"

There are conflicting possibilities to be considered:

(1) Brooks may be suggesting to us seriously, straightforwardly, and intentfully what Bialystock and Bloom are suggesting, namely, that Hitler really is funny, really can be taken that way, and his film and the invented stage play it contains are mere affirmations of this "fact." Hitler is funny, in short, and there is nothing odd about anybody laughing at him. In such a proposition there is something Bergsonian, in the sense that a comedian (Brooks the filmmaker) has what could be called a philosophical more than a political interest; a comedian would "stand back" from the conventionally politicized perspectives that mark human affairs and lend gravity of one kind or another to concerns and propositions—say that a figure might affirm the truth of a statement (such as the Nazi affirmation about Jews) that almost everybody else can see is nonsensical. Comedy, this theoretical possibility would imply, involves backing off from historical horror into a kind of neutral zone, where one can see the kind of movement Bergson saw when he pointed to the source of laughter as a person's behaving like a thing—that is, to an abject loss of personhood. This "funny" Hitler is a puppet, as it were, clearly not a person in control of himself and not the engineer of six million deaths in concentration camps. Instead, a flamboyant and ill-tempered orator perched on a piece of wood and shrieking at millions. The one who offered what are obviously idiotic explanations for a national economic catastrophe, this *obvious idiocy be*ing the butt of the joke. The one with the preposterous mustache. "Look," Brooks could be saying, "this guy is patently and uncontestably ridiculous, so making a movie in which when finally he appears he will be a stage puppet who looks patently and uncontestably ridiculous is in no way eccentric." I will return to this theme shortly, but for the present it is enough to suggest that it is possible to conceive what lies under *The Producers* as a simple recognition of a humorous possibility that has not been generally accepted as politically correct. (To stress: I cite a conception that is possible. It would not be my claim that this conception underpins or reflects Brooks' choices as a filmmaker at all.)

Alternatively, and fraught, I think, with far more serious implication, is this logic:

(2) Bialystock and Bloom, and their brother under the skin Mel Brooks, know, definitively, that Hitler is not funny (funny, as in inspiring; merely odd; light-hearted). Not funny, not imaginable as funny, not

related to "the funny" at all. Hitler was a monster and (diegetically) now (1967), just more than twenty years after the war, he is a monster still. The proposition that from a healthily neutral stance one should give him full consideration as both human and funny requires a disavowal of the monstrosity, which means a disavowal of the Holocaust, but the camps have been seen; the gas chambers and ovens have been seen; the piles of gold jewelry and dental fillings have been seen; the corpses have been seen— George Stevens, who made *Woman of the Year* (1949), *A Place in the Sun* (1950), and *Shane* (1953) was one of the soldiers who liberated Dachau, and he saw with his own eyes. Hitler was and is the very opposite of funny. (Unless, of course, time makes everything funny, and we should be laughing at the eruption of Vesuvius, the beheading of Lavoisier, the Spanish Inquisition.)

Further, by this historical point in the late 1960s, humankind has agreed in general upon this negative reading, this negative reading need receive no special publicity as almost no one (no one a liberal thinker such as Brooks would have coffee with) would negate it. So there is no strangeness in Bialystock and Bloom's presuming that their Broadway audience—largely tourists; visitors from New Jersey—will think the same way, enthusiastically abhor the show or refuse to buy tickets for it, thus driving the project bankrupt. When at the curtain call the audience raves with delight, there is something sad and genuine about their shocked surprise. This is not only *not the outcome they predicted* as businessmen, it is an outcome *they were, and remain, unable to imagine* as moral people. Bialystock and Bloom want to make money, yes, and they will go to lengths. But they will not go *to any lengths*. Going to *any* lengths is what Hitler and the Nazis did.

Whatever "springtime" may seem to mean in *Springtime for Hitler*, the two savvy producers (savvy but not savvy enough) must surely recognize the puncturing ambiguity: Hitler did *spring* upon Czechoslovakia; he did *spring* upon Poland; he did *spring* upon France; and he worked hard to *spring* upon Britain. World War II *was* "spring time" for Hitler. Shockingly to them, the audience for *Springtime* is either happy and complacent about this, or painfully ignorant.

Let us presume that Brooks considered *The Producers* finally a frame for a satire, and that what is being satirized is the thoughtlessly conventional, rote disingenuous profession of "horror" at the Nazi atrocity. What can we think is being offered by Brooks, then, as he invokes the presence of a giddy audience such as this—what-me-worry? or too uninformed for words—watching and enjoying this particular show in a film that by its nature invokes the presence of people like us with our own historical knowledge and principled attitudes? The framing system of the film is that

Springtime is the obsession of two men who prance around a proscenium; that it is "staged" before a "Broadway audience" in a play-within-the-film inside that proscenium; that therefore this Broadway audience, as shown onscreen, reflects the film itself, and this audience for the film itself (our audience like that audience), is the outermost "rim" of the frame (see Goffman). Thus ... we are invoked; we are absolutely invoked; because just as the stage show provides pleasure for its paying customers (and not insignificantly because in forking out money for the tickets—in 1967 one would have paid about $12.00 for an orchestra seat, but inflation has driven that price up beyond $200 today) in direct response to them expecting that it would and to their generalized demand for pleasure, so *The Producers* provides pleasure for us, who expect all through it, with building enthusiasm, that something marvelous is on its way. We are ready, just as that diegetic audience came to the theater ready, to find *Springtime for Hitler* a gas, and in fact we go much further, taking delight in all the backstage machinations that bring it to life.

To centralize: nowhere in the film is a case made that the attraction of *Springtime* is (a) its silly plot, (b) its jejune score, (c) the caricatured performances, or (d) any critical comment that has been made or could be made about it. The attraction of the show is really one thing and one thing only: its title. Brooks carefully arranges that the stage work we and the audience see is faithful, wholly faithful, and unremittingly faithful to that title. There is no way to doubt that what drove this diegetic audience to buy tickets was the palpably ironic linkage of the word "springtime" with the word "Hitler." (Notably, verbal *schticks* are a trademark of Mel Brooks' whole comedic career.) Further, "springtime" is to be taken not as a moment for attacking, as I suggest above, but as index of the lovely season of green rebirth. ("Hitler will be reborn!")

Brooks' mise-en-scène sets this audience up for a fall—that is, *we will drop them.*

· We must remember how in the 1950s and 1960s the Broadway experience had a Jewish "flavor," so to speak, since a great deal of the caustic humor of the stage had a Jewish inflection (and a convincing number of creative and performative personnel identified with Judaism in some way). Further, it was taken as known in the 1960s that many in the Broadway audience were resident or local Jews from the City or New Jersey. As for Brooks' piece (he was born Melvin Kaminsky), the principal casting alone must be seen as telltale: Zero (Samuel Joel) Mostel, blacklisted in the 1950s and from September 1964 to 1972—immediately following his glowing success in *A Funny Thing Happened on the Way to the Forum* (where he played a "Jewish" Roman slave)—the internationally acclaimed (and immeasurably Jewish) Tevye in *Fiddler on the Roof,* did radio, movies, and theater (including Yiddish theater). Gene Wilder (Jerome Silberman) had performed since the age of eleven, and was here making his film debut. This film was very obviously two Jewish boys playing two Jewish boys mounting a show about Hitler for what they had to presume was a palpably Jewish audience.

Let us focus on this fictive audience as Mel Brooks constructed it and examine what its members must now be assumed to have been thinking and assuming.

(1) First, that whatever anybody wants to say about Hitler the Madman Monster, all that madness and monstrosity is—now in redeeming 1967—done and gone; history has let it pass by. Yes, yes, there were atrocities, surely, certainly; and perhaps we even know families directly touched by those atrocities, families wounded and scarred and haunted. But it's 1967–1968, we're thinking about the Vietnam War if we think about anything in the world outside ourselves. World War II and everything it involved is wrapped and done. Note how in 1976 when in his *Marathon Man* John Schlesinger has a single older woman screaming across 47th Street, "Der weisse Engel!," as she points to the evil Dr. Szell (Laurence Olivier), she is basically the only figure on the street who seems to have a memory. In sum, everyone knows we are at a safe distance form Hitler. Thus,

(2) Hitler he can be objectified and made the object of humor, just as is done with any and all subjects comedians joke about from a safe distance. Distance, in fact, is an essential ingredient in the joking, and there is no difficulty, now, on opening night, in the diegetic Broadway theater, in stepping back from Hitler. Nor is a moral issue raised in anyone's doing so. Again—not me speaking; I am trying to imagine what that audience must be imagined to have thought.

(3) More. When from a distance you think about it you must see that this Broadway audience is being given to enjoy, just as we are, a gala display of colorful choreographed movement, set to a stylish beat, with clear well-toned singing voices on a magnificently lit stage and with a rainbow of scenery—all this just simply wonderful no matter what anybody is actually saying through the words, no matter what blitheness or import one could assign to it. *Springtime* is finally, after all, BROADWAY, and in its own right Broadway is a legitimate attraction, here, now, and always. (This is the subtle import of Bialystock and Bloom's mounting their show *on Broadway*, not off-Broadway.) Brooks poses this hypothesis in full view of his film audience, because for them, explicitly, the idea of this particular musical ON BROADWAY *is* the attraction. Here is an ostensibly outré subject routinized, glamorized, and hermeticized by virtue of a Broadway presentation in a Broadway house and bouncing to a Broadway score. It has the imprimatur! But:

(4) We must recognize, too, that surely there are plenty of politically, socially, ethnically, and personally touchy subjects—I fear it is already an outrage for me to call the Nazis "touchy"—that would not under any circumstances make their way to Broadway, not today, not in the late 1960s. *The Abortionist's Tango. Lynching Birthday Party. Rape Melodies of 1968.* And so on. This, Brooks understands. And he knows in himself, has known since in his teens he saw it happen, how the Hitler episode—if it can be called that—is nothing but an atrocity. He has made vulnerable Bialystock and hypertouchy Bloom capable of understanding, too. Is there something being said in excess of conventional opprobria by using Jews as the key markers in this Broadway success? Because whatever else one might claim about Hitler, what is indisputable is that he hated, tortured, murdered, and profited upon the deaths of Jews especially. The show *Springtime for Hitler* is a coded reference to Jewry. It's a let's-make-fun-of-"Let's-Get-Jews." And thus:

(5) In order to love the show, the diegetic show and the show containing this show, one must be ready to make fun of "Let's Get Jews." In short, one must be ready to assume a Nazi stance, even in playful retreat from the everyday, for an hour or two, or at least take that stance as anodyne. Is Brooks not speaking to his movie audience in bold terms, then, saying in effect, "Watch yourselves! Watch the complacency with which you are prepared to, ready to, even eager to abandon the historical catastrophe of the past and pretend nothing was going on but play and games, some pleasure party in Germany!" And is he, we must wonder, putatively asking all this of his viewers for a reason? Does he not surmise that in our culture we have already, by 1967, gone too far amiss in our memory and consideration of the Holocaust? We have gone amiss, we have allowed ourselves to forget, we have pretended—and continue to pretend as we laugh at *The Producers*—that none of what happened under Hitler applies directly to us. We are not the victims, we are not them, we are not related to them, we are not of the same species as them.

We are the *Übermenchen* now.

To speak the speech of *The Producers* as an oratory, as a condemnation, as a prophecy, as an indictment, but to speak it not as a prosecutor but as a mere entertainer (a *mere* entertainer), is, more than arrogance, equivocation, perhaps an insurance of being heeded but not taken to task for saying what should be heeded. When with comedy we see ourselves configured as objects worthy of our own laughter, we divide ourselves as we watch, being in part akin to, identical with, the figures in that theater audience who are ridiculous and blameworthy in their laughter; and in part the sober witnesses watching them with our own critical laughter, a special laughter, to be sure. When there is criticism in a laugh the laughter has risen above guilt. It is hardly that through a comedic approach Brooks the orator will not be blamed for wounding, although he will not; it is that in hearing him we will be proud enough to laugh at ourselves from a purely hypothetical superior perch, a figment of our smart imagination, as though the plain truth of what is on display is really and, we hope, understandably, too far away to see.

Filmography

Fiddler on the Roof. Dir. Richard Lester. United Artists, 1966. DVD. MGM Canada, 2011.
A Funny Thing Happened on the Way to the Forum. Dir. Richard Lester. United Artists, 1966. DVD. MGM (DVD & Video), 2003.
Marathon Man. Dir. John Schlesinger. Paramount Pictures, 1976. DVD. Paramount, 2017.
A Place in the Sun. Dir. George Stevens. Paramount Pictures, 1951. DVD. Paramount, 2001.
The Producers. Dir. Mel Brooks. Embassy Pictures, 1967. DVD. MGM (DVD & Video), 2003.
Shane. Dir. George Stevens. Paramount Pictures, 1953. DVD. Paramount Pictures Home Entertainment, 2017.
Woman of the Year. Dir. George Stevens. Metro-Goldwyn-Meyer, 1942. DVD. Video Service Corp., 2017.

Works Cited

Benjamin, Walter. "On the Concept of History." *Walter Benjamin: Selected Writings*, Vol. 4 1938–1940, edited by Howard Eiland and Michael W. Jennings, translated by Edmund Jephcott et al., Harvard University Press, 2003, pp. 389–400.
_____. "Paris—The Capital of the Nineteenth Century." *Charles Baudelaire: A Lyric Poet in the Era of High Capitalism*, translated by Quintin Hoare, Verso, 1997, pp. 155–76.
Goffman, Erving. *Frame Analysis: An Essay on the Organization of Experience.* Harvard University Press, 1974.

Between the *Mensch* and the *Pícaro*
Greed, Deceit, and Friendship in Mel Brooks' The Twelve Chairs *(1970)*

Ralph Beliveau

Photographer Edward Fielding, in a brief bit of writing, explores "The Symbolism of the Empty Chair in Art." He says that he often uses a chair to imply human occupation of space, through its emptiness and absence. "The chair can symbolize loss or the hope of a return," he writes. "The chair can imply loneliness or a restful place to sit down after a long day or hike into the wilderness" (Fielding). Empty chairs abound in Mel Brooks' 1970 film *The Twelve Chairs*, arguably one of his least watched and discussed films. For many viewers the films that followed like *Blazing Saddles* and *Young Frankenstein* are a first stop, and the subsequent success of the stage version of *The Producers* brought attention back to Brooks' first film. *The Twelve Chairs* is something of an empty chair in audience experience with Brooks. Its absence in the discussion can perhaps be redirected fulfilling the hope of a return. The film is well worth re-consideration as a step in his wide-ranging body of work, revealing how Brooks translates humor across different cultural contexts. He also eventually reveals his affection for rogues, offering a powerful way to understand how he works as a maker of comedy.

Throughout his career, Mel Brooks made comedy by moving easily among different genres in two different senses of the word. From his early work, Brooks has been quite successful in television as well as comedy albums. His work on *Your Show of Shows* (1950–1954) and *Get Smart* (1965–1970) exist alongside several successful comedy albums that he made with Carl Reiner: *2000 Years with Carl Reiner and Mel Brooks* (1960), *2000 and One Years with Carl Reiner and Mel Brooks* (1961), *Carl Reiner and Mel Brooks at the Cannes Film Festival* (1962), *2000 and Thirteen with Carl Reiner and Mel Brooks* (1973), along with a later revival of the characters in 1997. Henry Jenkins, in considering Mel Brooks as an agent of "vulgar modernism," mentions that Brooks was a "media comedian" "in two senses of the word—in that he worked across many different media in the course of his career and in the sense that he constantly called attention to the nature of remediation across his works" (Jenkins 169).

One important notion of "genre" is the way Brooks reflexively used different media for comedic purposes. But the other notion of genre has a more reflexive side to it, where Brooks uses the conventions and gestures of a particular story type: for example, classic black and white horror films, westerns, sci-fi, and Hitchcock films. Occasionally his use of these genre elements is more formal and reflexive, like the silent movie tropes of *Silent Movie*, or the historical and biblical epics that shape *History of the World: Part 1*. These approaches to comedy fall more clearly under the idea of *parody*, where the use of imitation of the source work is the more direct object of criticism and transgression. Audiences are well suited to parody when their knowledge of the source material suffices as the object of humor.

The context for the kind of comedy in *The Twelve Chairs*, on the other hand, is less tied to a commonly recognized notion of film genre. At the same time, the film is more satire than parody, focusing more on commentary about the world in the film rather than the film itself. This becomes clearer through the way the structure of the film assembles its satirical criticism of historical events juxtaposed against some easily recognized cultural values.

Social Satire and Changed Identities in Twelve Chairs

The world depicted in *The Twelve Chairs* is what remains after the massive social upheaval of the Russian Revolution. Brooks' satire re-considers the immense social displacement caused by these turbulent politics. Its main thrust lies in its depiction of greed and critiques what greed will drive people to do in difficult circumstances. Its main plot begins with a dying woman who makes a startling confession. She calls for the local priest and for someone to bring her son-in-law to her and tells them this story: back when her aristocratic family was quite well off—before the revolution—she had a collection of extremely valuable jewels sewn into the seat of one of twelve dining room chairs to hide them from the Bolsheviks. This was at the onset of the revolution, so she was not able to rescue the jewels before the family had to leave and the chairs were subsequently taken up into the "property of the people." On her deathbed, she explains this to two people. First, she tells the story to her local priest,

Father Fyodor (Dom DeLuise), though the audience does not know what he was told, as he is seen to rush away from the house in a panic. However, when her son-in-law, Ippolit Matveyevich Vorobyaninov (Ron Moody) arrives, the audience hears the whole story. Vorobyaninov, no longer an aristocrat, is instead a bureaucrat. Also, the dying mother-in-law criticizes him for having been an indulgent spender of her deceased daughter's fortune.

The film's two central characters, Fyodor and Vorobyaninov work separately to plot how to get the chairs and recover the jewels. But then a third character is brought into the mix, Ostap Bender (Frank Langella), a homeless wanderer and con man who stumbles across Vorobyaninov at the site of his former mansion. Bender learns about the jewels, so he strikes an uncomfortable partnership with Vorobyaninov to help recover them. Meanwhile, Father Fyodor has shaved off his long beard and changed his appearance away from being a priest. He sets off to find the chairs on his own, while Vorobyaninov and Bender also set off on their own to locate the chairs.

Part of the satire is grounded in the way that the desire for the jewels brings to light several changes in social status among the characters who are now on the hunt. Each of them changes because of the political situation underpinning his actions. Father Fyodor transforms from being a local priest into just a citizen who desperately and deceitfully seeks the chairs, to the point of claiming at one point to be Vorobyaninov's first born son. He makes this claim in an office labeled "The Bureau of Furniture

From left: Tikon (Mel Brooks), Vorobyaninov (Ron Moody), and Ostap Bender (Frank Langella) plot before setting out on the hunt for treasure in *The Twelve Chairs* (1970).

Not Listed in Other Bureaus." That list, in true Mel Brooks–style, includes "The Bureau of Bureaus and Dressers." But when Fyodor arrives at the "Not Listed" Bureau, Ostap Bender has preceded him, and pretends to be the bureaucrat in charge. Bender gives Fyodor a forged shipping order that sends him off to Siberia to find the chairs.

Bender does not so much transform as much as he assumes various poses and identities that serve his con-man ways. When we first see him in the film, he is at a town square pretending to be a soldier who lost both an eye and a leg in the war. He reveals himself as a sham quickly when an attractive woman catches his eye ... and he lifts the eye patch to get a better look at her and reveals his intact leg from behind a curtain. Through most of the film Bender remains suited in what appears to be a military uniform, which was part of his routine begging for support as an injured veteran.

Vorobyaninov begins as the transformed ex-aristocrat turned bureaucrat. Early in the film, when he starts to look for the chairs, Vorobyaninov goes to the mansion he used to live in, where the chairs were last known to be. This is where he first meets Bender, who is talking to the caretaker of the place, Tikon (played by Mel Brooks himself). Tikon complains about being called "comrade" all the time, especially by people who don't know him. He says that he misses Russia, but he also misses his "Master," Vorobyaninov. He has flashbacks where Vorobyaninov repeatedly hits him, and when they finally meet, Tikon is overjoyed to be hit by him again. This is one of many elements in the film that leans toward slapstick comedy to display the social satire, the desirability of the old order of a highly classed society. The film makes fun of the notion of such a hierarchy letting everyone know their place:

> BENDER: Tell me, who lived here in the old days?
> TIKON: Oh, in the old days was my master, Ippolit Matveyevich Vorobyaninov. He was a marshal of the nobility! I loved him: he hardly ever beat us.

Via Tikon, we get a satirical picture of the old social structure versus the new. This helps to support an image of Vorobyaninov as being not very sympathetic. As he pursues the chairs, in league with Bender, he begins acting like a con-man. When Vorobyaninov and Bender need money to buy one of the chairs, they find themselves searching for ideas sitting in front of a statue of Dostoyevsky. Bender looks at it and tells Vorobyaninov that he should pretend to have an epileptic fit to draw sympathy—and money—from those passing by. Vorobyaninov initially says he will not lower himself to begging, but Bender yells at him that begging is something he has had to do his whole life and threatens to end their partnership if he does not comply. Vorobyaninov complies, and starts writhing on the ground, as Bender solicits the growing crowd to give, so Vorobyaninov can get medical attention. Part of Bender's chatter to solicit donations adopts the language of describing Vorobyaninov as a comrade, as a fellow citizen needing assistance. Again, the film's social satire is reinforced. Greed is clearly under the microscope in this film. The destructive force of the chase after the jewels sits differently in the three central characters. For Vorobyaninov, the chase is a desire for the glories of the past in which he had lived. He had been in a position of privilege that we can see in his own diffuse flashbacks and through the comic desires for that past expressed by Tikon.

Bender experiences the chase as an extension of his life as a rogue and a flim-flam artist. He is obviously quite skilled at what he does. Brooks is enough of a trickster to set this up with the scene where he pretends to be an injured vet, which is not really all that clever (or subtle) given what we later see in Bender's ability to be deceitful on many levels. Despite this, he is depicted in a way that remains charming. His intelligence and smooth style are designed to be attractive to audiences. Additionally, there is always the popular appeal of the rogue character as a type in adventure stories, more recently encountered in Han Solo in the *Star Wars* universe and Tyrion Lannister in the *Game of Thrones* universe. Such characters are appealing because of their abilities to break the social rules and fly in the face of social conventions. At the same time, they are appealing for their wit, for their ability to think and act in a way that critiques social norms, if not moving to out-and-out satire of conventions, usually accomplished through their subversion. This is fundamental to the appeal of Bender in all the versions of the character, from the initial novels he appears in during the late 1920s to the large number of adaptations that have been mounted of *The Twelve Chairs* over many decades.

In a story in *The Odessa Journal* from 2021, the roots of Bender's character are traced to a confidence man named Osip Shor who forged identities to get out of military service, posed as a chess master, and at one point, pretended to be a scientist who had developed a breed of chicken with no feathers, thus skipping the need to be plucked. Shor shared an apartment with the brother of Yevgeny Petrov, who with Ilya Il'f wrote the novel *The Twelve Chairs*. Bender, it should be noted, is something of a folk hero in Russia, becoming "part of Soviet/post–Soviet literary folklore and he remains popular today. Numerous monuments to Il'f and Petrov (as well as to Bender) have been erected in various cities across the former Soviet Union" (Mulcahy 190). Perhaps Ostap Bender could be thought of as a parallel to the fictionalized versions of Bonnie and Clyde, or other criminal figures who develop into folk tale figures. In her discussion of the novel,

Amy Sargeant observes that "[i]ndeed it is easy to read Ippolit (Vorobyaninov), provisionally, structurally as Sancho Panza to Ostap's Don Quixote, and yet easier still to regard Ippolit as Huck Finn to Ostap's Tom Sawyer (and to read Ostap as one of the numerous conmen populating Twain's adventure stories)" (Sargeant 53). In the case of Ostap Bender in Brooks' film, greed motivates his actions, while an attractive sense of style and cunning obscures the more prurient part of his motivations.

For Fyodor, the chase is portrayed by Brooks as a more comic endeavor, being partially dependent on the broad kind of physical comedy that is offered in the performance of Dom DeLouise. The chase sequences in the film between Fyodor and Vorobyaninov are sped up, suggesting a kind of physical comedy connected to the silent film era, right from the start when we see Father Fyodor do a pratfall to the groin on the fence as he tries to flee the scene where he has learned about the jewels in the chair. Without a partner, Fyodor specializes in other aspects of broad physical comedy.

All these characters are subsumed in a film narrative that involves a chase and a heist. Much of the humor is derived from the frustrations that happen along the way. By the time we reach the end, it is hard to be surprised by the failure of the search. The jewels in the last chair had been found by a civic organization head, who used the money to build a substantial social club for workers, spending much of it on chess sets and beautiful furniture. When Vorobyaninov and Bender learn the fate of the fortune, it's not surprising to feel sympathy for them while viewing the transformation of the pre–Revolutionary class system into a massive bureaucratic state. The result that the bureaucracy won out in the end is disappointing.

The conclusion, however, brings attention to an underlying structure that runs throughout the film. The relationship between Vorobyaninov and Bender comes to the fore. Though their failure in the search threatens to put an end to their partnership, at the last moment it is resurrected. They part with nothing to show, broke from the chase. But as Bender begins to walk away, Vorobyaninov spontaneously slips into his *schtick*, dropping to the ground and pretending to have an epileptic seizure. Bender turns back and takes up his role as the huckster, calling the gathering audience to give money to care for this sad and stricken individual.

Brooks and Culture-Crossing Satire

Many people familiar with Brooks and his work are aware of the reach back into Jewish ethnic origins in his humor. But by and large, he is probably more thought of as a satirist and especially a parodist of media culture. His most familiar film work directly reflects on familiar Hollywood genres: westerns with a shot of blacksploitation in *Blazing Saddles*, gothic horror in *Young Frankenstein* and *Dracula: Dead and Loving It*, space opera science fiction in *Spaceballs*, classic history and adventure films in *Robin Hood: Men in Tights* and *History of the World Part One*, espionage in his TV work on *Get Smart* and the film *High Anxiety* (specifically riffing off of Hitchcock films), silent movies in … well, *Silent Movie*, and even Broadway depictions in *The Producers*. Even the earlier work with Carl Reiner is playing with audio/radio interview formats with a nod toward *The Candid Microphone* (ABC, 1947–1948; CBS 1950), the precursor to *Candid Camera* (ABC, 1960–1975).

The Twelve Chairs is notable because it does not appear to be a parody of an existing genre in and of itself. There are certainly moments that reflect on other film conventions, such as the over-cranking sped-up shots during chase scenes, which strongly recall older film comedy conventions. It is also an unusual item in the canon of Brooks' films, because it was an adaptation of a novel, particularly known in Russia and the Soviet Union, along with other eastern European cultures, but is not as widely known in the United States. The way that Brooks came to read the novel is a story in itself. Brooks mentions that he was part of a club, a gourmet society in the 1950s and 1960s that met in Chinatown in New York every Tuesday (Buss). Brooks mentions that the group included several writers, some of whom were famous, such as Joe(seph) Heller, the author of *Catch-22*, and Mario Puzo, the author of *The Godfather*. Brooks was introduced to another member, Julie Green, whom Brooks knew previously. Green was a diamond merchant who also read extensively. According to Brooks, Green had "read everything ever printed that was good. And it was Julie Green who had finished reading *The Twelve Chairs*.… And he said, 'Hey Mel, it might even make a movie!' I said, 'Eh.' And I read it, and I was really thrilled with it. I loved it. I loved the adventure. And I said, 'It's got a great plot! You've got to follow these 12 chairs!'" (Buss). For Brooks the appeal of the plot appeared to marginalize the challenges that would be faced in "Americanizing" the novel to make a film comedy.

The notion that there were several ways in which cultures would need to be bridged seems less of an issue in the final film than might have been the case since we are quite used to different kinds of conventional "cheating" (for example, think Romans and evil characters talking with British accents). The signs that appear in the film, such as the labels on Vorobyaninov's mansion that has been transformed into a retirement home, and the endless doors that line the hallway of the "Bureaus of Furniture" are in English. There are also different uses of accents from different actors, with Ron Moody and Mel Brooks usually using modified Russian accents (though speaking English, of course) and Langella and DeLuise not affecting much of an accent at all. But these are film conventions to which audiences have long grown accustomed.

There also is the challenge that faced Brooks of translating the humor and satire from the novel into humor appropriate for an American film comedy audience. And here, there is a secondary challenge as well: what happens to the literary conventions fundamental to Il'f and Petrov's novel, *The Twelve Chairs*? How did Brooks adapt this novel into his film? One of these important literary frames is the idea of the *picaresque*. The etymology of *pícaro*, the Spanish term that goes back to the 16th century, picks up its modern sense in the early 19th century. Typically, the *picaresque* displays the following seven characteristics: it is often written in first person by a character of low social standing who gets by living with his wits and rarely has a job; the plot is organized by connected episodes and might even seem plotless; there is very little character development; the story is executed in plain language and seen as being realistic; there is usually a satirical edge to the story; and the *picaro* operates on the edge of criminality, but as a character is seen as a sympathetic outsider, not contained by social conventions (Thrall and Hibbard). *Pícaros* are actually quite practical constructions. "A pícaro does not ask great philosophical questions about why things happen but accepts his circumstances as they are: 'I have two hands,' a pícaro says; then he thinks what he can do with them, and does it" (Yovanovich 26).

Brooks adopts these characteristics to serve the purposes of the social satire that he uses to drive the comedy in his film. Clearly, Bender is the central *pícaro*, but these characteristics are also distributed through other characters and the overall structure of the film. The plot of the search for the jewels gives the film momentum and structure, while the film narrative remains episodic in its execution. Brooks' use of elements of the *picaresque* to inform his choices is still quite unusual when set against the rest of his canon.

Another set of influences on *The Twelve Chairs* is one closely connected to Brooks' own autobiography. He was raised by parents who had arrived as Jewish immigrants from Russia. As Robert Mulcahy writes, "As an outsider Jewish-American comic with ethnic roots in Eastern Europe, Brooks has crafted an identity of considerable appeal to a large, diverse audience over his long career. As the son of first-generation immigrants from the former Russian empire, Brooks had an appreciation and image (however idyllic) of the pre–World War II era of his parents' generation" (Mulcahy 188). It may be why on the 50th anniversary of the release of *The Twelve Chairs*, Brooks said, "I got letters over the years from people who had seen it on television. And they're always these wonderful, emotional letters of how much they loved it and 'Where has this picture been?' It's all very nice. Of all the movies I've made, it's one of my top favorites" (Buss). Perhaps the reason *The Twelve Chairs* remains a top favorite is because of the deep connection with his own family history and the notions of borders that comes with immigration and ethnic differences.

In "Chasing the Wealth: The Americanization of *Il'f* and Petrov's *The Twelve Chairs*," Robert Mulcahy focuses on these border issues. Brooks, he argues, "wisely opted for the generalization of human foibles. The result is a film that focuses on the universal themes of obsessive greed and transnational brotherhood, while also engaging in social satire" (189). I would also suggest its uniqueness among his other work helps to keep it different for him. Perhaps the struggles it faced to find an audience makes it feel to him more like an underdog or an underachiever.

The Twelve Chairs *as Art Film*

One question that is asked about this Mel Brooks film is why it was not well received by audiences and some critics on its release. Even critics who were positively inclined toward the film and toward Brooks mixed positive and negative aspects in their reviews (McGilligan). Perhaps, as Robert Mulcahy suggests, "the film lacks a strong audience draw. Such as a leading romantic couple to maintain the interest of an American audience that flocks to romantic comedies" (Mulcahy 199). In the *Los Angeles Times*, Donald Liebenson wrote, "Lacking the cult popularity of *The Producers* and the satirical feel of Brooks' later comedies, it was quickly relegated to back-bin obscurity upon its initial video release." In an article focused on Mel Brooks and Woody Allen, Dave Kehr in 1982 suggested that modern comedies, more broadly, "were never made for critics, but what's changed, I think, is that the new comic style is actively hostile to most of the established critical values. Comedies now flaunt their arbitrary organization, their thinness of character, and their lack of content—almost as if they were trying to keep intellectuals out" (9). This is interesting to consider since it seems tailored to especially those picaresque characteristics in *The Twelve Chairs*.

It is possible that one of the hurdles the film faced had to do with how it was perceived. Set in Russia/the Soviet Union, shot in what was Yugoslavia, with characters who dressed and acted foreign, audiences thought that this was going to be a foreign art film, possibly with subtitles. That was perhaps no problem for urban centers, but made the film less successful in other parts of the United States. As Brooks offered, "It never crossed the George Washington Bridge. It became like a little art film. It played New York. It played big cities like Boston, New York, L.A., San Francisco. But it never really played any cities that didn't have an art theater. So it didn't get any real distribution" (Buss).

So is *The Twelve Chairs* an art film? By most conventional definitions of art films, it is not. Typically, art films are made with a priority placed on aesthetics, often exhibiting experimental techniques, and are not designed for mass audiences. They are usually marked and understood as different from mainstream Hollywood films (Willinsky 4). Often foreign films are seen as "art house cinema" because of the differences in aesthetic sensibilities and languages that are part of the experience. By those standards *The Twelve Chairs* would not be an art film in the strict historical sense.

More importantly, though, there is an example of a take on "art cinema" that was part of Mel Brooks work in the 1960s and brings to the forefront how he might have perceived the notion. In 1962, Brooks had attended a screening of Animation shorts by Norman MacLaren, the Canadian animator. As Brooks told it to *The New Yorker*, "Three rows behind me ... there was an old immigrant man mumbling to himself. He was very unhappy, because he was waiting for a story line and he wasn't getting one" (Tynan 106). The mumbled complaining became the source for Brooks voiceover for the animated film, *The Critic*, in 1963. In it, animator Ernie Pintoff presents a series of abstract geometric shapes moving around the frame. Brooks, improvising and adopting a heavy Yiddish accent, expresses his frustration at the abstract art film. The result is a hilarious notion of what happens when a not-art-film person is confronted with an experimental or art film.

The Critic was enormously successful, and Brooks and Pintoff received the Academy Award for an Animated Short in 1964. The short brings together the ethnic humor that Brooks had been honing. And, of course, it is an art film, so it succeeds in what Henry Jenkins (164–65) called Brooks' ability to effect "comic remediation," in a juxtaposition of vulgarity and modernism: "a cranky Jewish old man trying to make sense of Ernest Pintoff's abstract, experimental animation: 'What the hell is this? Must be a cartoon.'" He expresses curiosity and outrage, trying to interpret the action through a series of metaphors and analogies (from birth and sex to cockroaches), dismissing the abstract art as "dirt," "Trash," "Junk," and "Filth." Jenkins points out how the film plays to both the sophisticated filmgoer and the viewer who would share the Critic's opinion (Jenkins). It's this doubling that achieves comic remediation.

The Mensch *and the* Pícaro

Brooks is, in many instances, just like Ostap Bender, better off certainly but still maintaining his ability to make films, and to make art, at

אויסגעקליבן ווערק / Selected Works (1965–1991)

sometimes high risk. It clearly shows how Bender in *The Twelve Chairs* resonated with Mel Brooks, as a rogue artist who succeeds on the basis of his wits. Perhaps we could also see a bit of autobiography in Brooks' *The Twelve Chairs*. "While picaresque works are not straight-forward autobiographies, they have autobiographical dimensions that captivate readers, turning readers into extensions of the pícaro and his or her play with life" (Yovanovich 24). This may be why, among all his work across television, records, movies, and musicals that *The Twelve Chairs* gives us an insight into how Brooks sees himself as a creator, constructed somewhere between the vulgarity of his ethnic, physical sense of humor, and the modernist trappings of mainstream media making. He is part thoughtful, honorable, and honest *mensch*, and part sly, deceitful, and manipulative *pícaro*.

Audio Recordings

Reiner, Carl, and Mel Brooks. *Carl Reiner and Mel Brooks at the Cannes Film Festival*. Capitol, 1962.
Reiner, Carl, and Mel Brooks. *2000 and One Years with Carl Reiner and Mel Brooks*. Capitol, 1961.
Reiner, Carl, and Mel Brooks. *2000 and Thirteen with Carl Reiner and Mel Brooks*, Warner Bros, 1973.
Reiner, Carl, and Mel Brooks. *2000 Years with Carl Reiner & Mel Brooks*. Capitol, 1960.

Filmography

Blazing Saddles: 30th Anniversary Special Edition. Dir. Mel Brooks. Crossbow Productions, 1974. DVD. Warner, 2004.
The Critic. Dir. Ernest Pintoff. Columbia, 1963. YouTube, April 10, 2015, https://www.youtube.com/watch?v=PramR5oxn50Check.
Dracula: Dead and Loving It. Dir. Mel Brooks. Columbia, 1995. DVD. Warners Home Video, 2008.
Get Smart. Created by Mel Brooks and Buck Henry. Talent Associates, CBS Productions (Season 5). NBC, 1965–1969; CBS, 1969–1970.
High Anxiety. Dir. Mel Brooks. 20th Century Fox, 1977. DVD. 20th Century Fox Home Entertainment, 2006.
History of the World: Part 1. Dir. Mel Brooks, 20th Century Fox, 1981. DVD. 20th Century Fox Home Entertainment, 2006.
The Producers. Dir. Mel Brooks. Embassy Pictures, 1968. DVD. MGM, 2021.
Robin Hood: Men in Tights. Dir. Mel Brooks. 20th Century Fox, 1993. DVD. 20th Century Fox Home Entertainment, 2006.
Silent Movie. Dir. Mel Brooks. 20th Century Fox, 1976. 20th Century Fox Home Entertainment, 2006.
Spaceballs. Dir. Mel Brooks. MGM, 1987. DVD. MGM, 2015.
The Twelve Chairs. Dir. Mel Brooks. Universal Marion Corporation Pictures, 1970. DVD. 20th Century Fox Home Entertainment, 2006.
Young Frankenstein. Dir. Mel Brooks. 20th Century Fox, 1974. DVD. Sony Pictures Home Entertainment, 2014.
Your Show of Shows. Created by Sylvester L. Weaver, Jr. Max Liebman Productions. NBC, 1950–1954.

Works Cited

Buss, Andrew. "Mel Brooks Revisits *The Twelve Chairs* for Its 50th Anniversary: 'It's One of My Top Favorites.'" *Consequences*, October 28, 2020. https://consequence.net/2020/10/mel-brooks-interview-the-twelve-chairs/.

Fielding, Edward. "The Symbolism of the Empty Chair in Art." *LinkedIn*, December 4, 2019. www.linkedin.com/pulse/symbolism-empty-chair-art-edward-fielding/.

I'lf, Ilya and Yevgeny Petrov. *The Twelve Chairs*. Federal Publishing House, 1928

Jenkins, Henry. "Mel Brooks, Vulgar Modernism, and Comic Remediation." *A Companion to Film Comedy*, edited by Andrew Horton and Joanna Rapf, John Wiley & Sons, 2012, pp. 151–171.

Kehr, David. "Funny Peculiar." *Film Comment*, vol. 18, no. 4, July–August 1982, pp. 9–11, 13–16.

Liebenson, Donald. "Finding Long-Lost Treasure Among 'The Twelve Chairs.'" *Los Angeles Times*, July 6, 1997. https://www.latimes.com/archives/la-xpm-1997-jul-06-ca-10019-story.html.

McGilligan, Patrick. *Funny Man: Mel Brooks*. Harper Perennial, 2020.

Mulcahy, Robert. "Chasing the Wealth: The Americanization of Il'f and Petrov's *The Twelve Chairs*." *Border Crossing: Russian Literature Into Film*, edited by Alexander Burry and Frederick H. White, Edinburgh University Press, 2016, pp. 188–201.

"Osip Shor: The Story of the Real Prototype of the Great Schemer." *The Odessa Journal*, June 20, 2021, n.p. https://odessa-journal.com/osip-shor-the-story-of-the-real-prototype-of-the-great-schemer.

Rodriguez González, Félix. *Spanish Loanwords in the English Language: A Tendency Towards Hegemony Reversal*. De Gruyter Mouton, 2017.

Sargeant, Amy. "4 x 12 Chairs." *Interfaces: Image-Texte-Language*, vol. 34, no. 1, 2013, pp. 49–59.

Thrall, William, and Addison Hibbard. *A Handbook to Literature*. The Odyssey Press, 1960.

Tynan, Kenneth. "Profiles: Frolics and Detours of a Short Hebrew Man." *The New Yorker*, October 30, 1978, pp. 46–130.

Willinsky, Barbara. *Sure Seaters: The Emergence of Art House Cinema*. University of Minnesota Press, 2001.

Yovanovich, Gordana. *Play and the Picaresque: Lazarillo de Tormes, Libro de Manuel and Match Ball*. University of Toronto Press, 1999.

Brooks, Gogol, and Dali

Surrealism, Simulacra, and Simulation in Blazing Saddles *(1974)*

Sue Matheson

When the ground-breaking and Emmy Award–winning *Get Smart* ended unexpectedly in 1970,[1] its co-creator Mel Brooks could not find work. Comedy had become unfashionable on television, and Brooks found he was suddenly "a starving artist"—an art-house film director waiting for his first "real commercial hit" (201). "I was back in New York, walking down Fifty-seventh Street, right after a rainstorm, watching the rainwater travel down the gutter to the sewer," he said, "[and] I heard a voice behind me say, 'Hiya, Mel. What are you doing, looking for change?'" (203). It was his agent David Begelman, co-head of the newly formed Creative Management Associates, who took him out for lunch, asked him to read a screenplay (called *Tex X* by Andrew Bergman), and reminded him that he "ow[ed] a fortune in alimony" (*Disobedient* 101). Brooks reluctantly agreed he had to take the job, Begelman agreed Brooks could hire Bergman and work with a gang of comedy writers, and suddenly the struggling filmmaker was again on his way to the top. The project came to be known as *Blazing Saddles*. Brooks had the chutzpah and artistic currency to retain the rights to the movie's final cut, but making *Blazing Saddles* with Warner Bros. was not easy. The film failed during its first screening with the Studio's executives. It was a "disaster!" Brooks told Brad Darrach during his 1975 *Playboy* interview, "We showed it first to the studio brass. Ten of them in a small screening room. Now the first really big joke in the picture comes when the white cowboy says, 'How 'bout a good ole n[-----] work song?' And the black labor gang, as one man, begins to sing 'I get no kick from champaaagne.' That's a tremendous joke. But in the screening room, nothing. *Gornisht*! Not a titter. I said, we 'have just entered 4C on the Titanic.' The next 90 minutes was a non-laugh riot. When the lights went up, I had sweat circles the size of Rhode Island under my arms."[2]

Brooks was saved by his producer Mike Hertzberg, who immediately booked a public screening for that evening. When Brooks insisted the screening be canceled, Hertzberg said, "No! Invite more people. Let normal people see it. Then we'll know" (in Darrach). Grabbing a phone, Hertzberg instructed his staff that he was going to run the picture again in a larger viewing theater, and that he wanted it packed with at least two hundred people: secretaries, janitors, cleaning women, waiters—anyone but studio brass. According to Brooks, at 8 p.m., two hundred and forty people were "jammed into this room…. Frankie Laine sings the title song, with the whip cracks. Laughs begin—good laughs. We go to the railroad section. The cruel overseer says to the black workers, 'Let's have a good old n[-----] work song.' Everybody gets a little chilled. Then the black guys start to sing 'I get no kick from champagne' … [T]hat audience was like a Chagall painting. People left their chairs and floated upside down, and the laughter never stopped" (Tynan).

Budgeted at $2.6 million, *Blazing Saddles* became Warner Bros.' money maker that summer, ranked sixth on the 1974 Box Office list and grossing $16.5 million ("History"). The following summer, *Blazing Saddles* earned another $10.5 million domestically and then another $8 million in 1979.[3] Its lifetime gross totals $119,616,663 (Box Office Mojo). *Blazing Saddles*' reviewers, however, were not enthusiastic on its February 7, 1974, release. *Esquire*'s John Simon found the film's vulgarity offensive. According to Simon, "[n]o mention of *Blazing Saddles* can be brief enough. Mel Brooks's film … is a model of how not to make a comedy. It is like playing tennis not only without a net but also without a court and twenty balls simultaneously. All kinds of gags—chiefly anachronisms, irrelevancies, reverse ethnic jokes and out-and-out vulgarities—are thrown together pell-mell, batted about insanely in all directions, and usually beaten into the ground" (145). He complained, "[I]n one of our better theatres, a civilised-looking [sic] audience laughed loudest and longest at a scene in which a bunch of cowboys sit around a campfire eating beans. One after another, they raise their backsides a bit and break wind, each a bit louder than his predecessor. If this is what makes audiences happiest, all future for the cinema is gone with the wind" (145). Roger Ebert of the *Chicago Sun-Times* also objected, grumbling, "[t]here are some people who can literally get away with anything—say anything, do anything—and people will let them. Other people attempt a mildly dirty joke and bring total silence down on a party. Mel Brooks is not only a member of the first group, he is its lifetime president. At its best, his comedy operates in areas so far removed from taste that (to coin his own expression) it rises below vulgarity."

Ebert also found the movie undisciplined. "Its structure is a total mess," he said. "It's a crazed grabbag of a movie that does everything to keep us laughing except hit us over the head with a rubber chicken." Gary Arnold of *The Washington Post* thought *Blazing Saddles* "a messy and antiquated gag machine." Vincent Canby of *The New York Times* said, "The trouble is that [it] has no real center of gravity ... it looks as if it includes every gag thought up in every story conference. Whether good, bad or mild, nothing was thrown out." Canby concluded Brooks' "brashness is rare, but his use of anachronism and anarchy recalls not the great film comedies of the past, but the middling ones like the HopeCrosby 'Road' pictures. With his talent he should do much better than that." Time, however, has vindicated Brooks. In 1975, the film was nominated for one Photoplay Award, two BAFTA Awards, and three Oscars at the 47th Academy Awards.[4] It won the 1975 Winner of the Writers Guild of American Award for the Best Comedy Written Directly for the Screen.[5] In 2006, *Blazing Saddles* was deemed "culturally, historically, or aesthetically significant" by the Library of Congress and selected for preservation in the National Film Registry.

Generally, critical conversations about *Blazing Saddles* have focused on Brooks' social commentary. For example, in "*Blazing Saddles* as Postmodern Ethnic Carnival," Bill Hug argues that "carnival in *Blazing Saddles* dismantles the Western's conventions and themes, destroying ethnic, narrative, and even 'factual' boundaries," questioning concepts of social, political, moral, and religious order. Rock Ridge, he says, becomes "a kinder, gentler community, which Bart and Jim have saved not only from

Olson (David Huddlestone) and Harriet Johnson (Carol Arthur) find themselves at a loss for words when Bart (Cleavon Little, right) announces he is their sheriff in *Blazing Saddles* (1974).

governmental and corporate corruption but the ethnic and racial corruption implicit in western narrative itself" (65; 78). In *Mel Brooks: The Disobedient Jew*, Jeremy Dauber finds in *Blazing Saddles* an essential statement of American Jewish tension caused by "affection for the mainstream and alienation from it" (3): playing "chaos for comedy," *Blazing Saddles* provides insight into "a certain kind of racism endemic to the American imagination" (100).

The film's aesthetic issues, however, continue to call for critical attention. In 1974, Jan Dawson of *Film Monthly Bulletin* found *Blazing Saddles*' loosely structured narrative highly problematic, pointing out Brooks' "satirical talent still seems more appropriate to the undisguised fragmentation of the revue format than to the cumulative structures of even a skeleton narrative development," noting "one suspects that the film's gradual disintegration derives not—as has been suggested—from its makers inability to end it so much as their inability to stop laughing at their own jokes" (120). Asserting Brooks had shown "better visual craftsmanship in his two earlier features, THE PRODUCERS and THE TWELVE CHAIRS," Daniel Golden of *Jump Cut* also thought "*Blazing Saddles* falls apart as a movie." "[A] deliberate travesty of a genre that has done a pretty fair job of self-parody in recent years," a "movie within a movie," *Blazing Saddles* "chases its own tale over the horizon," he said. "[It] is just too sloppy and self-indulgent, despite its burlesque of its own fictive world.... There are lots of laughs, even for non–New Yorkers, but there's too much *shtick*."

Brooks disagreed with his critics' assessments—publicly and vehemently. In *Film Comment*, Brooks told Jacoba Atlas, "I made a conscious effort to be brilliant" and insisted *Blazing Saddles* was "the result of meticulous construction, especially in the scriptwriting stage" (54). About his critics, Brooks said, "If they really knew my work, you could not say zany Mel Brooks and seriously discuss *The Twelve Chairs*, *The Critic*, or certain aspects of the early *Show of Shows*, when tragedy and comedy met so beautifully. I object ... because I think you could call Picasso zany because he's not a naturalistic painter, or dull. Or you could call Dalí zany. But they're great artists and we've got to learn that abstract comedy or surrealistic comedy is not necessarily cheap" (in Parish 197).

In *commedia dell'arte*, the zani, who amuses his audiences with farting, burping, and snoring, is a simpleton or the village fool who keeps company with lunatics, buffoons, and jugglers. *Blazing Saddles* contains zanis, but as Brooks points out, their behavior should not be considered cheap slapstick. Like Picasso's and Dalí's art, *Blazing Saddles* is serious play. As Kenneth L. Eggener remarks, in America, Surrealists were described as the Marx Brothers of the art world, while comedians like the Marx Brothers were hailed as "native" Surrealists, owing to their own "amusing lack of logic" (39). Brooks' reference to Dali in particular calls for careful consideration, as he would have been familiar with the artist's work and his hijinks.

As Brooks grew up in Brooklyn, Dali "spent his winters at The St. Regis New York, delighting, bewildering and outraging a captivated city" (Dannatt). Shuttling between New York and Los Angeles, he created jewelry, designed clothes and furniture (including a sofa in the form of actress Mae West's lips), painted sets for ballets and plays, wrote fiction, produced a dream sequence for the Alfred Hitchcock thriller *Spellbound* and designed displays for store windows (Dannatt). A one man-theater, the artist was notorious for his outrageous eccentricity, his self-promotion, and most of all his zany stunts. In Europe before the Second World War, he was remembered for "seducing many ladies, particularly American ladies, but these seductions usually consisted of stripping them naked in his apartment, frying a couple of eggs, putting them on the woman's shoulders and, without a word, showing them the door" (Bunuel). In New York, "crowds jostled six-deep on 5th Avenue" to admire Dali's rendering of a woman with a "head of roses complete with red lobster telephone" in the Bonwit Teller department store's windows. "It was in these windows, in 1939, that Dalí staged possibly his most famous New York stunt, climbing into a bathtub in a window and then crashing through the plate glass—with the bath—to thunderous applause" (Dannatt).

Post-war, Dali's zany social satire remained part and parcel of the Big Apple's gestalt. In 1962, he wore a golden robe and lay on a bed in a Manhattan bookstore helping to sell *The World of Salvador Dalí*, a book he produced with Robert Descharnes; in 1965, he dressed Andy Warhol up in an Incan headdress, tied him to a spinning wheel, and poured paint all over him. Recognizing Mel Brooks as a kindred spirit with the phrase shouted by Max Bialystock (Zero Mostel) in *The Producers*—"If you got it, flaunt it"—Dali acted in a Braniff Airlines commercial in 1967. In 1969, he then took to walking a giant anteater through New York's streets and subways.

As a New Yorker, Brooks "hated, hated, *hated* Hollywood" (McGilligan 104) but he knew "[i]f you were a Jewish intellectual, whose parents had immigrated from Russia, you could like my pictures, but there were hardly any of those in Amarillo, Texas, where you gotta play in one of their three or four theatres or else you're outa luck. You gotta break into one of the John Wayne houses or you ain't ever gonna break out" (McGilligan 300). In the commentary of the 30th Anniversary Special Edition of *Blazing Saddles*, he compares his experience of agreeing to write and direct *Blazing Saddles* to that of Charles Dickens who took a job writing *A Christmas Carol* for a magazine. "[T]his better be the best movie I ever wrote," he said, "I wanted to make sure that people don't think I'm selling out.... I wrote *The Twelve Chairs*, and I wrote *The Producers* and at that time everything was, I thought, at a very lofty level of writing" ("Scene-Specific Commentary"). "I decided [*Blazing Saddles*] would be a surrealist epic," Brooks told Kenneth Tynan of *The New Yorker*. "It was time to take two eyes, the way Picasso had done it, and put them on one side of the nose, because the official movie portrait of the West was simply a lie. For nine months we worked together like maniacs. We went all the way" (Tynan).[6] He encouraged Norman Steinberg, Andrew Bergman, Richard Pryor, and Alan Uger to write "the craziest shit" as the character-centered screenplay for *Blazing Saddles* developed (McGilligan 310). He told them, "We should write dangerously, that's what this is all about" (Liebenson).

Brooks' earlier collaborations with Caesar's writers who shared "the same background, the second-generation Russian-Ukrainian-Jewish intellectual heritage" stood him in good stead (Tynan). Mel Tolkin, in particular, had encouraged Brooks to read the Russian Greats—Leo Tolstoy, Fyodor Dostoyevsky, Aleksandr Pushkin, and Nicolai Gogol. For Brooks, *Dead Souls* was "a revelation." Gogol's proto-surrealism and -absurdism deepened his knowledge of the comic grotesque and the creative possibilities of chaos, encouraging him to work towards greater violations of causal reasoning, bizarre juxtapositions, incongruities, non-sequiturs, irrational situations, and expressions of nonsense. In 1975, Brooks asked Darrach, "Where would I be today if it wasn't for Nikolai Gogol? ...he showed me how crazy you could get, how brave you could be. Son of a bitch bastard! I love him!" "I love Gogol's great eye for idiot behavior," Brooks said. "Gogol said that life is so tragic, so stupendously sad that we'd better laugh a lot and enjoy ourselves. You either get a sense of humor [*sic*] going or you go under."

As Brooks points out in *All About Me!*, Gogol "had a tremendous understanding of the human condition. And the other side was absolute madness. Just madness! Insanity. He would write about a nose that could speak. Gogol was not bound by the rules of reality, yet he understood how the heart beats, why it beats" (190). Reading Gogol and talking with Tolkin also made Brooks want "to achieve more"—he wanted to be an "American Molière," the new Aristophanes, and "in the Fifties, the great foreign movies began to arrive. Rossellini's *Open City*, De Sica's *The Bicycle Thief*, films by Fellini, Bergman, Kurosawa, the French New Wave." Impaling foreign pictures was a comic staple of *Your Show of Shows*: "La Bicycletta,"[7] a parody of Vittorio De Sica's *The Bicycle Thief* (1948), showcases Sid Caesar (a Pedrolino), Imogene Coca (a Franceschina), and Carl Reiner (a Pierrot), clowning as three poverty-stricken, working-class Italians in post–War Rome. After fifteen minutes of zany double-talk about poverty and joblessness and much coveting of Reiner's shiny new bicycle and its irresistible horn, the three are unmasked—they are all bicycle thieves.

The Hollywood Western was also a familiar target for Caesar's writers. Parodying the Western came naturally to Caesar who insisted his character types be "rendered simply and boldly," their traits "coarsely exaggerated without the complexity that accompanies human beings" (Caputi 176–77). "Technicolor Westerns"[8] is a monologue, its story patterned after Western melodrama. Caesar first asserts "there's a certain type of picture that Hollywood makes which is sure fire, cannot miss … the story is always the same." A popular type, he is a cowboy, his arch enemy, a gunman—the comic reversal occurs when his faithful horse outdraws the outlaw. "Vacant Holsters," aired on *Caesar's Hour*,[9] spoofs the revenge Western. In it, Caesar is a near-sighted vigilante, a comic type who loses his Coke bottle–thick glasses and has to peer through the bottoms of beer mugs to find the villain and have a shoot-out.

Creating a comic V-effeckt[10] out of "special kinds" of vulgarity, Brooks and his writers pushed *Your Show of Shows*' stock characters beyond their limits, making the Western types in *Blazing Saddles* so tasteless viewers could not identify with them. Purposely insensitive, paradoxical, absurd, and cruel, its satire is grounded in unpredictability, emphasizing the ridiculousness (or unlikeliness) of its characters and their situations. The Hollywood saloon girl, for example, is a decorative, politely presented, and sympathetic type—an angel of the ale-house who ensures men mind their manners while drinking and gambling. Grotesquely exaggerated, Lili von Shtupp (Madeline Kahn) is a jaded *nymph du prairie*. Her name carrying blatant sexual connotations,[11] she is a sex clown, her discarded lovers, disappointed Augustes whom she stooped to shtupp. Straddling a chair on stage, dressed in a black Merry Widow, garters, fishnet stockings and high heels, Brooks' bawdy grotesque belongs in the sordid fleshpots of Joseph von Sternberg's *Der blaue Engel* (1930) and Bob Fosse's *Cabaret* (1972). Burlesquing Frenchy (Marlene Dietrich) in George Marshall's *Destry Rides Again* (1939), von Shtupp agrees to prostitute herself by seducing the town's sheriff. Working on stage in her underwear and a see-through boudoir robe, trimmed with sequins and ostrich feathers, she is dressed to be in a back room with the boys, but she is "[t]ired" of men, worn out by an absurd number of suitors, "thousands" of them, "again and again." Hers is the dirtiest song Brooks says he ever wrote.[12] A nymphomaniac who confides that she is "not a wabbit," Von Shtupp complains stage door Johnnies have exhausted her with "their comings and goings and goings and comings." Everything below her waist is "kaput."

Roasting Dietrich as a German national—and recalling *The Producers*' musical parody, *Spring Time for Hitler* on Broadway—Brooks juxtaposes the cowboys in the saloon and the singer with a Preussischer Garde-Pionier chorus line. Four German officers, dressed in double-breasted, Dunkelblau Waffenrocks (decorative Brandenburg cuffs) and pointy Prussian Pickelhaube helmets from the 1880s, join von Shtupp on stage and surreal social satire (focused on gender issues) follows. Synchronized with matching costumes, haircuts and lampshade moustaches, the "goddess of desire's" bodyguard are not romantic figures. Supporting characters, they repeat her lines with military precision and tell her needy, cheering fans to stop bothering their idol. The chorus leader shouts, "Give it break! Can't you see she's sick? She's better alone!" He scolds, "Can't you see she's pooped?" In sync, the ensemble dances with the same military precision in their jackboots, using their Karabiner 88s to protect the star from her lovers. At the end of the number, they scoop up von Shtupp, and carry her off stage ... and then back on again for a quick bow ... and then back off again.

Unlike her chorus line whose American English is perfectly pronounced, Kahn lampoons Dietrich's sultry, German accent. Every "r" is a "w," even in the invitation von Shtupp pens to Bart. When Lamarr asks the chanteuse if she can seduce and abandon the new sheriff, she replies, "Is *Bismawk* a *hewing*?"[13] She later reports to Lamarr, "It's like wet *sauewkwaut* in my hands. *Tomowwow mowning* he'll be my slave." Drawing on the banquet and the sausage, favored carnival images in Rabelais' *Gargantua*, von Shtupp's insatiable sexual appetite is also incongruously juxtaposed with her offer of an outrageously large and drooping banger for breakfast. Bart, however, rejects her Pantagruelian offer of a sixteenth sausage. When he makes his escape, he has to ask her to stop clinging to him and making a "German spectacle" of herself. Dietrich's habit of donning menswear, declaring herself "much more alluring in these clothes," too is a comic target ("Marlene Dietrich"). When she is not working at the saloon, von Shtupp appears in a three-piece sack suit. Its jacket, vest, and trousers should all be made of the same material, but her vulgar, bright yellow vest and a large bowtie with purple polka dots overturn the respectable, conservative values of her jacket's navy pinstripe. Offstage, backstage, and onstage, she is a clown.

Taggart's Lords of Misrule are also highly exaggerated, one-dimensional types. Associated with the body's orifices, "the gaping mouth, loins and anus" (Harpold), their clowning inverts the noble values associated with the Western's cowboy. A Feast of Fools, their infamous farting scene demonstrates all the key elements of *Gargantua*'s banquets— exaggeration, excess, and hyperbole. *Blazing Saddles*' February 17, 1973, shooting script specifically draws our attention to the riders' vulgarity, emphasizing "[t]he only SOUND WE HEAR is a *vulgar symphony* of eating, grunting, belching and *farting*" (*Script*, italics mine).[14] The cowboys swill coffee, gobble down heaps of baked beans, and fill the range with

"PFFTs," modulated "PBBBBTs," assertive "THPPTPHTPHPHHPHs" and blaring "BRRRTs." Their explosive action stops only when Taggart (Slim Pickens) emerges from his tent and ends their festivities. Waving his hat about to dismiss the stench, he declares, "I'd say you've had enough."

Brooks' politician is another vulgar hieroglyph associated with the anus. Governor Petomane (Mel Brooks) is named after William J. Le Petomane, a French flatulist (professional farter) famous for his ability to seemingly fart at will (Classical gas). Petomane, combined the French verb *péter*, "to fart" with the *-mane*, "-maniac" suffix, translates to "fartomaniac." Full of hot air, his colleagues too are flatulent. Stopping these grotesques from harrumphing in Petomane's office, Lamarr inverts the high and the low, the oral and the anal: "Gentlemen," he says, "please rest your sphincters." Kidding *Playboy* that encouraging farting promotes *heteroglossia*, Brooks, channels Petomane, declaring, "[f]arts are a repressed minority. The mouth gets to say all kinds of things, but the other place is supposed to keep quiet. But maybe our lower colons have something interesting to say. Maybe we should listen to them. Farts are human, more human than a lot of people I know. I think we should bring them out of the water closet and into the parlor, and that's what I did in *Blazing Saddles*" (in Darrach). Brooks reminds Darrach, "before *Blazing Saddles*, America had not come to terms with the fart. Wind was never broken across the prairie in a Ken Maynard picture. In every cowboy picture, the cowboys sit around the campfire and eat 140,000 beans and you never hear a burp, let alone a bloozer. For 75 years these big, hairy brutes have been smashing their fists into each other's faces and blasting each other full of holes with six-guns, but in all that time, not one has had the courage to produce a fart."

Promoting associative spectatorship, *Blazing Saddles* deliberately upsets its viewers' expectations of narrative unity. A master of juxtaposition, Brooks prevents viewers' cause-and-effect analysis by placing his subjects either side by side or near one another to create unexpected and incongruous effects, encouraging associative spectatorship. He also uses exaggerated elements of surprise and *non sequiturs* to ridicule the Western's *status quo*. For decades, Gene Autry's Cowboy Code of Honor, Hopalong Cassidy's Creed for American Boys and Girls, and Roy Rogers Riders Club Rules had created heroes who promoted polite civility on and off the celluloid range. Cowboys, according to Autry's Code, were well-mannered, well-adjusted, highly principled individuals. A cowboy would "never shoot first, hit a smaller man, or take unfair advantage … never go back on his word or a trust confided in him … always tell the truth … be gentle with children, the elderly, and animals … not advocate or possess racially or religiously intolerant ideas … help people in distress

... be a good worker ... keep himself clean in thought, speech, action, and personal habits ... respect women, parents, and his nation's laws ... [and] be a patriot" (Reynolds).

Shocking audiences into laughter, no Riders Rules are observed when Taggart and his farting hoodlums ride into town, "a-whompin' and a-whompin' every livin' thing that moves within an inch of its life." In Rock Ridge, Van Johnson (George Furth) sums up "what's been happening": the sheriff has been "murdered, crops burned, stores looted, people stampeded, and cattle raped." Upending polite society, Taggart and his gang are an anti-community. They do not hesitate to shoot first, hit a small man, or take unfair advantage of the unarmed townsfolk who flee from them. They look forward to raping "the shit out of the women" later at the Number Six Dance.

Juxtaposed with Taggart's men, Brooks' clean-living, anal-retentive townsfolk are also designed to alienate their viewers. As the Waco Kid points out, the citizens of Rock Ridge are also Western icons: "simple farmers ... people of the land ... common clay of the New West." American Yeomen, they should embody the ideals of the American Character, but, lacking the sharpness of its intellect, they cannot. Curiously clannish and unspeakably vulgar, they are small-town types, all bearing the surname Johnson. Terribly inbred, they are "morons." Or, as Bart says, "sooooooo stupid." Not self-reliant or inventive, refusing to help others, they inexplicably expect others to help them. Before Bart agrees to stop Mongo breaking up the town, Van Johnson shouts, "The fool's going to.... I mean the sheriff's going to do it!"

Appointed the carnival king, Bart tames Mongo with a candygram, but he is not a clown character borrowed from *commedia dell'arte*, a simple scapegoat to be sacrificed with his faithful sidekick in the end by his retinue of idiots. Cleaning up a town tainted with incest, Rock Ridge's sheriff is himself dirt-free. As Martin Pumphrey observes in the Western, "[h]eroes may be dusty but not dirty. Their clothes may be worn but not greasy. They seldom sweat. Above all, they have always just shaved" (53). Freshly shaven, tubbed and scrubbed, Bart glistens like a matinée idol as he rides his palomino to Rock Ridge. Signaling virtue, his appearance is not only presentable; it is overly clean and comically glib.

Made entirely of leather, Bart's wardrobe (as one-dimensional as the type it represents) is high camp, introducing "a new standard: the idea of style, theatricality" (Sontag 527). The artifice of the sophisticated, spotless, golden suede worn by the newly minted lawman on his way to Rock Ridge offers camp's "comic vision of the world" (Sontag 527), lampooning the look made famous by Roy Rogers and Gene Autry. His yoked shirt, adapted from the traditional cotton garment worn by the vaquero, and his pants are color coordinated with his horse. Even his Stetson appears to be made of suede. In Rock Ridge, Bart's leatherwear is amplified again. Following comedy's rule of threes, his gun belt and matching suede pants and shirt are topped off by a 1950s Roy Rogers fringed leather jacket when he visits Lily von Shtupp.

Highly exaggerated, Bart's look is alienating, but Bart himself is not. Pitted against robbers, outlaws, bandits, self-serving politicians, a corrupt attorney, racist and incestuous morons, and a nymphomaniac, he is modelled after another multi-dimensional lawman played against the town sheriff's type. Like Jimmy Stewart's Destry, Bart is a well-rounded character who upholds the Cowboy Code. Viewers are invited to identify with him—and who wouldn't? Embodying the American Character, he is intelligent, self-reliant, ethical, upwardly mobile, hardworking, enthusiastic, tolerant, and inventive. Bart's character arc is also modelled on Destry's attractive trajectory. Like Destry, Bart is an optimistic self-starter who has to prove himself worthy of being a sheriff. Like Destry, Bart perseveres despite the difficulties believing the citizens he protects will accept him. The Waco Kid warns Bart that Rock Ridge, populated with racists, will not change, but Bart proves him wrong. As Hug observes, Bart's urbane sophistication overturns social stereotypes (72), and the townsfolk join him and stop Lamarr's evil scheme. Like Destry, he confounds his opponents with his civility. But when all the Johnsons announce they "need" him to stay and be their sheriff, Bart rides West, demonstrating the restlessness that has always been an important element of the American Character.[15]

As Brooks points out, satiric comedy serves the two parts of his audience equally and simultaneously: the part that gets every film reference and all of the subtext, and the other part that has never seen or heard of any related films (211). In *Blazing Saddles*, he and his writers carefully recycled musical styles, objects, technologies, iconic scenes, dialogue, camera angles, art direction—essentially everything—associated with the Western. Building blocks, these references make the overall movie greater than the sum of its parts. There is an incongruous church scene filled with concerned citizens set in the same church used for a similar gathering in *High Noon* (1952). *The Treasure of the Sierra Madre* (1948) is also referenced in a paraphrased quote, "We don't need no stinking badges." When Mongo is chained to the bars of a detention cell, Bart hangs up wanted posters, one of which was seen in *Rio Bravo* (1959). His office and jailhouse were also used in *El Dorado* (1966) shot at Old Tuscon Studios. By accident (or not), Lyle (Burton Gilliam) wears the same costume as James Drury in *The Virginian* (Revue Studios 1962–63; Universal Television 1963–71): black pants, hat, and a vest with a red shirt. In 1981, Jean Baudrillard could have been thinking of *Blazing Saddles*, when he observed that "[c]inema plagiarizes and copies itself ... remakes its classics, retroactivates its original myths" ("Simulacra" 47). Belonging to a larger body of work in which films are exchanged not for the real world but for one another, *Blazing Saddles* is part of "an uninterrupted circuit without reference or circumference" ("Simulacra" 6).

Brooks also recycled films outside the Western's scope in *Blazing Saddles*. References to *Der blaue Engel* (1930) and Mark Sandrich's *Top Hat* (1935), Bob Fosse's *Cabaret* (1972), *The Wide World of Sports*, *Looney Tunes* cartoons, Esther Williams' water ballets, and the Busby Berkeley dance routine also remind viewers of the limitations of characters' knowledge and the absoluteness of their own. Brooks remembers, "We threw crazy comedy bits into the mix. In one scene Bart becomes Bugs Bunny. We just stole it, but it was a Warner Bros. cartoon so we knew we could get away with it" (208). He and his writers even recycled the names of film stars to broaden *Blazing Saddles'* cinematic moment. Olson Johnson is an allusion to comedians Ole Olsen and Chic Johnson, who starred in H.C. Potter's *Hellzapoppin'* (1941) and influenced Brooks' comedic style; Van Johnson was named after the popular song-and-dance actor typecast as "the fresh-faced, well-mannered nice guy" that *IMDb* says "you always wanted your daughter to marry!" (Van Johnson).

A film constructed from the debris of other texts, *Blazing Saddles* is unified by the surreality determined by the juxtapositions of its parts. As Roderick Heath observes, when Bart on horseback encounters Count Basie and his Orchestra playing sophisticated "foreground" music in a bandstand in the desert, "[l]ayers of history and art collapse together in one perfect surrealist gesture." Here and throughout *Blazing Saddles*, the purpose of Brooks' bricolage is parody, not pastiche. Contrasted with the suave sophistication of Cole Porter's "April in Paris" and Count Basie's Orchestra, *Blazing Saddles'* title song is a parody of the blue-collar country and western ballads, sung by Frankie Laine, a popular baritone who belted out theme songs for film Westerns[16] and the theme song for the television series, *Rawhide* (CBS, 1959–1966). The tune's simple-minded lyrics introduce the action about to take place: the good guy's "job" is "to offer battle / To bad men near and far." Wearing "a shining star," he will conquer fear and hate, turning "our night into day." Resembling the opening of *Rawhide*, this opening number exaggerates the sound of a whip cracking, before the film's titles catch fire like those at the beginning of *Bonanza* (NBC, 1959–1973). On fire, *Blazing Saddle's* parody opens almost exactly where the frontier fairy world of *Once Upon a Time in the West* (1968) ends, with Brooks' camera on the locomotive, showing the railroad and its workers.

Rock Ridge is arguably the most essential item of *Blazing Saddle*'s bricolage. Shot on the same outdoor sets as Michael Crichton's *Westworld* (1973), *El Dorado* (1966), *High Noon* (1952), *Rawhide* (CBS, 1959–1965), *Bonanza* (NBC, 1959–1973) and *Gunsmoke* (CBS, 1952–1961; 1962–1975), parts of *Blazing Saddles* were filmed on Laramie Street at Warner Brothers Burbank Studios and at Old Tuscon, another popular location for shooting Westerns located six miles west of Tuscon, Arizona. Typically consisting of one street, one bank, one hardware store, and one saloon, towns in Westerns shot on these lots were constructed to provide adequate accessibility for film cameras and their crews. As a visual lane for shot setups, Rock Ridge is not an exception to this rule. Aptly, it has only one of every type of building. Comically, its ice cream parlor boasts only one flavor of ice cream.

Remarkably, Rock Ridge appears to be real until it is compared to one of the booming frontier communities it is supposed to resemble. In 1881, the town of Tombstone had a bowling alley, four churches, an icehouse, a school, two banks, three newspapers, and an ice-cream parlor, alongside 110 saloons, 14 gambling halls, and numerous dance halls and brothels ("Old Tombstone"). Its robust civic grid featured Freemont Street, Allen Street and Toughnut Street running from West to East, intersected by 2nd Street, 3rd Street, 4th Street, 5th Street, and 6th Street running from North to South. In 1882, Dodge City consisted of eight streets (Cedar, Vine, Spruce, Walnut, Chestnut, Front, Locust, Maple) intersected by four numbered avenues (2nd, 3rd, 4th, and 5th), Falladora Avenue, and Military Avenue ("Old Tombstone"). Clearly, audiences are meant to learn little about the historic American West in *Blazing Saddles*. Rendered surreal, Rock Ridge is a-historical, its surreality, hyperreal—its "[s]imulation [being] no longer [one] of a territory, a referential being or a substance ... [but] the generation by models of a real without origin or reality" ("Simulacra" 1).

As Baudrillard points out, the hyperreal consists of four types of simulacra. Simulacra of the first order clearly counterfeit the real and are recognizable as illusions, copies, or place markers. In simulacra of the second order, distinctions between the real and its copy begin to break down because of the proliferation of simulacra which misrepresent and mask the reality they imitate, but in spite of this, the real continues to be recognizable and may be accessed. In the third order, simulacra or representations of the real masks *the absence* of the real. In the fourth order, simulacra has no relation to any reality whatsoever—"it is its own pure simulacrum" ("Simulacra" 6).

Bart, the Waco Kid, the townsfolk, and the railroad workers make what they believe are first order simulacra, building "an exact replica of the town of Rock Ridge, every building, every store front, every rock and every tree right down to the orange roof on Howard Johnson's outhouse" in the desert to trick Taggart and his gang. The next morning, they have constructed a simulation of Rock Ridge in the desert, consisting of two-dimensional Hollywood flats painted to look like three-dimensional storefronts. Misrepresenting the reality of Rock Ridge, its false fronts, boasting windows and doors, are clearly second order simulacra, lacking support jacks and sandbags, being propped up behind with pieces of lumber that act as crude stage braces. Standing in front of the flats, Bart declares the simulacrum "a perfect copy" before he realizes the counterfeit lacks citizens. More replicas are added. The townsfolk "make perfect copies" of themselves and place their life-size stand ups outside the storefronts and in the street. A stand up of a horse at a hitching post is also added.

Ironically, Taggart and his gang gallop "a-whompin'" and "a-whumpin'" into the simulation, "wrecking havoc on the town, engaging in joyful carnage and senselessly mutilating innocent cardboard cutouts" (*Script*). Even though the stand ups they trample face the camera (and not the horsemen), the cowboys do not recognize they are destroying replicas until Taggart tries to kick a door open—and its false front collapses. Then he yells, "It's a fake! We've been suckered in!" Absurdly, the irony does not dissolve. Instead, Taggart's discovery that Rock Ridge is "a fake" is compounded while the film continues.

As Baudrillard notes, simulation starts with the radical negation that the sign has value ("Simulacra" 6). Like a carefully constructed set of dominoes falling, every reference to the real in *Blazing Saddles* is negated, becoming "calculated chaos" on screen. Brook's comic controls, built into the action's design, intensify its tension in a series of catastrophes. As Anthony Caputi points out, in *commedia* "the piling up of catastrophes has the effect of suggesting the world is rich in surprises. As these surprises rush in on the beholder they generate a state of excitement, not unfairly if a bit hyperbolically described as a frenzy" (143). Brooks produces this comic frenzy in controlled stages, in which each catastrophe expressed as a carefully choreographed fight. The first catastrophe begins with "the fake town of Rock Ridge EXPLODING in a symphony of cataclysmic destruction. Pieces of the town soar through the air, walls collapse and dummies fly in all directions" (*Script*).

Accordingly, the "Black Bart Brawl" follows. Bart, the Waco Kid, and the townsfolk rush into the replica and pummel the cowboys. Fights in Westerns are meant to purge communities of their weaknesses, but instead of defeating Taggart and his gang, the townsfolk, "a-whompin' and a-whumpin," only become part of the fray. As Brooks says, "With *Blazing Saddles*, we moved the truth out onto the street" (207). Upending the

Western's morality play, the settlers prove they are as uncivilized as the cowboys. On Rock Ridge's street, men punch one another, and women hit cowboys with sticks. Von Shtupp is seen singing with a group of German soldiers who are inexplicably not involved in the action. Then Mongo tips over a life-size, plastic replica of a horse, unseating its rider, and instead of diminishing, the violence snowballs. Brooks cuts to a crane shot which pulls back, rupturing the realism that has been the Western's trademark for over a century.

In *Blazing Saddles*' "Scene-Specific Commentary," Brooks remarks when "the camera pulls back and shows you this is a movie, it's like a Pirandello." *Blazing Saddles* becomes a film-within-a-film, its buildings with walls and roofs are seen among Hollywood flats with working doors and windows. Announcing "the death sentence of every reference" ("Simulacra" 6), Laramie Street takes the place of the makeshift replica of Rock Ridge built at Old Tuscon Studio. Warner Bros. backlot appears as the shot continues to widen: first, the sound stages neighboring Laramie Street are shown, then the streets in the backend of the lot, and finally Burbank's water tower and Burbank itself become visible. As the camera pans and then zooms in towards a soundstage, Rock Ridge is radically redefined, becoming part of Baudrillard's fourth order.

More walls (physical and metaphorical) are broken, destroying Hollywood's fantasy of real space on screen. Brooks says, "What I did when the gunfight spilled over onto the Busby Berkeley set with the fifty dancers was what Picasso did when he painted two eyes on the same side of the head" (in *Disobedient* 105). Like Picasso, Brooks fractures the screen's two-dimensional picture plane to convey other dimensions of filmmaking at work in a movie. Cutting from the crane shot of Laramie Street to the interior of an adjacent soundstage, another crane shot records a gay director, his crew, and his gay actors, dressed in top hats and tails, resetting the action of a Busby Berkley musical. When the camera begins to roll, Brooks' second catastrophe occurs. The wall of the soundstage collapses, and "The Black Bart Brawl" pours into what should be "a closed set."

At this moment in the February 17, 1973, shooting script, the director, Buddy Bizarre (Dom DeLuise), screams, "Is this some kind of grotesque joke?" And grotesque it is: juxtaposed, both casts and the crew are exaggerated types. Taggart aptly replies, "Piss on you, I'm workin' for Mel Brooks!" punching Bizarre, who screams "not in the face," and the chorus leader calls, "Come on girls." Following Brooks' stage direction, "[t]he Western types and the chorus boys start mixing it up" (*Script*) the action becomes simply irrational. Two saddled horses are pulled across the stage, a cowboy and dancer fight, make up, and go on a date, two fully-clothed dancers perform a synchronized water ballet in one of the fountains, the

Johnsons' wives continue swatting Taggart's men with sticks, and Mongo, hoisting a struggling victim over his head, carries him about in the crowd.

Having collapsed and combined genres, casts, and crews, *Blazing Saddles* snowballs even more—to "new self-reflexive heights" (McGilligan 332). As Baudrillard points out, "it is dangerous to unmask images, since they dissimulate the fact that there is nothing behind them" ("Simulacra" 5). Brooks escalates the comic frenzy, making it more precarious by moving it from the sound stage to the Studio's commissary where the action is no longer safely contained on a set. Here, actors (in and out of costume), commissary staff, and fans from a studio tour fight again. An actor, cast as Hitler and eating his lunch in his costume and make up, establishes the scene's surreality, telling a friend, "They lose me right after the bunker scene." Immediately, the Black Bart Brawl pours in the lunchroom's door, and Brooks' third catastrophe begins. "It is a riproaring beauty of a fight": juxtaposed, "the [Western's] Good Guys and the Bad Guys [are] engaged in fisticuffs ... many of the dancers from the thirties set have been swept along in the fracas," and other actors and extras join in "wearing a variety of costumes: [among them,] Bathing Beauties in bikinis, Tarzan and Cheetah, confederate soldiers, Southern belles, thirties gangsters, six Munchkins out of the 'Wizard of Oz'" (*Script*).

Brooks uses *commedia's* food pranks to escalate the simulated frenzy. Cream pies have been a slapstick staple since Ben Turpin was slapped with one in *Mr. Flip* (1909). After the commissary's baker is pied, the fight acquires Rabelaisian proportions. Heaps of custard, mounds of whipped cream, and plates of food fly through the air. The camera cuts to the members of the tour leaving the Commissary: they all have been participating. Actors, characters, and the public smash and overturn tables of food. Every character slammed with a pie becomes a grotesque, wearing an exaggerated mask made of whipped cream, and Taggart "who slides down the food counter ... is covered with an assortment of foods.... Yankee Bean Soup, coleslaw, Tuna Surprise" (*Script*).

Further disrupting the notion that characters, actors and viewers belong to discrete states, it is said that *Blazing Saddles* became a happening. As the actors and characters involved in the pie fight escape the Studio's lot and race into Burbank, a man in a sweater who was not an actor is said to have wandered into the scene at the Warner Bros. Gate #2 Entrance. He stood on the sidewalk, observing the actors. After being asked to leave, he complied but returned and re-entered into the shot. Brooks finally sent out a waiver for him to sign and left him in the movie ("Trivia"). He can be seen by the light pole as the characters stream past him—another wall is broken as he becomes an audience-within-an-audience observing the action on Olive Avenue in a film-within-a-film. Lamarr, whose custard mask has mysteriously become even more pronounced, is the last person to run past him. In character, Harvey Korman crosses Olive Avenue and hails a cab, saying to the driver, "Take me off this picture." After the taxi exits the shot, Bart, who has not been pied, follows, a shining cinematic anachronism galloping his absurdly spotless palomino in pursuit.

It is dark when Lamarr's cab arrives at Grauman's Chinese Theatre, located on Hollywood's Walk of Fame at 6925 Hollywood Boulevard. Here, Brooks demolishes the fourth wall, as the Western's signs and symbols that spilled out of Warner Bros. in the theater. Fourth order simulacra, cattle, a surreal sight gag that appeared earlier in the church and again in the saloon in Rock Ridge, stand lowing incongruously in a roped-off part of the lobby. Having removed his custard mask, Lamarr attempts to blend in with the people waiting to see *Blazing Saddles* at Grauman's. Seated in the theater, he becomes an audience member, but as a villain, he cannot escape his destiny. Seeing Bart on screen gallop up outside the theater, he "bolts out of his seat and up the aisle" and attempts "to leave ... flying out just as Bart begins to enter" (*Script*). His showdown with Bart should have taken place on screen. Instead, Brooks' final catastrophe, *Blazing Saddles'* shootout occurs outside the theater. Poking fun at the Western's offer of regeneration through violence, Lamarr is shot in the crotch. Emasculated on the Walk of Fame, he dies on Douglas Fairbanks, Jr.'s, cement marker. Deflating that star's manhood, Lamarr's last words are: "How did he do such fantastic stunts with such little feet?!"

As Peter Brook points out in "The Deadly Space," "[t]heatres, actors, critics and public are interlocked in a machine that creaks, but never stops" (40). After Bart and the Waco Kid enter the theater to see the movie's ending (both hoping it will be happy), they, like Lamarr, cannot escape their destinies. One minute, Bart and his sidekick are seated and enjoying the film; in the next, Bart is part of the action on screen bidding the Johnsons a fond farewell. The Kid, who was eating popcorn with Bart in Grauman's Theatre, appears in the next scene reclining on a hay bale. At the Livery Stable, he waits with his theater popcorn for Bart to invite him to go "nowhere special." In the movie's final scene, they ride into an uninhabited desert and dismount at a fork on a dirt road where a uniformed chauffeur opens the back door of a stretch limousine, and they climb in. Bryan Bradander thinks this juxtaposition of the Cadillac "[a]n odd and fantastic ending for a cowboy movie set in 1874,"; Brooks says is it "one of the private peaks of the movie," adding, it "still makes me cry. I'm all puddled up as they drive off in the red sunset" (Bradander).

"Happy endings do not impress us as true, but as desirable," Northrup Frye says. "[T]hey are brought about by manipulation" (170, 178). As Frye points out, Hollywood's synonym for *anagnorisis* is its "gimmick" which provides the type of ending that Hollywood studios insist every comedy must have. With Bart and the Kid no longer on screen, movement, harmony and rhythm coalesce into a surreal image much more powerful than words, asserting the realities of the objective external world and the American Dream. Illogically and startlingly juxtaposed with the dusty desert wasteland, the shiny black Cadillac is a *deus ex machina* and a Surrealist Object, a ready-made more powerful than words—being at once an incongruous and quintessential symbol of American mobility and success. Every American knows that Bart and the Kid riding off into the sunset in it are not leaving. They have instead arrived.

In *America*, Baudrillard observes that "[i]t is not the least of America's charms that ... the whole country is cinematic. The desert you pass through is like the set of a Western.... To grasp its secret, you ... should begin with the screen and move outwards" (56). While the Cadillac westers through the sagebrush, the crane shot tilts up, reminding us of the Western's poetic place in America's imaginary. Its lens-flare, self-declaring, creates a halo for the butte (recalling Monument Valley), already backlit by the setting sun. What are we laughing at? Gogol's Governor in *The Inspector General* would say ... ourselves. Half a year after *Blazing Saddles* was released, the Dalí Theatre-Museum in Figueres, Spain, opened its doors—not surprisingly, one of its most popular exhibits was a long black Cadillac that rained inside itself whenever a visitor dropped a coin into a slot (Meisler).

As Jeremy Dauber wisely points out, "Brooks would not be the genius he is if his work didn't raise artistic questions at the highest level" (*Disobedient* 3). Self-regulating and self-designing, Westerns have always embodied the American Dream, their frontier worlds promising settlers a better life, opportunities to reinvent one's self, and upward social mobility. Self-deprecating, *Blazing Saddles*' sureality not only critiques the greed and racism of Manifest Destiny's nation-building activities, it also speaks to Americans' anxieties about the discrepancy that lies between their country's epic intent and its actual condition. Not bound by the rules of reality, *Blazing Saddles* confirms James Shevill's observation in "Notes on the Grotesque: Anderson, Brecht, and Williams," that the American grotesque continues to "[flow] from a basic American optimism about the possibilities of democracy, religion, money, goods, power" (237).

Offering renewal through laughter, *Blazing Saddles* continues to turn its audiences into Chagall paintings. In final analysis, its social satire not only "smashed racism in the face" ("Trivia")[17]; it continues to kid us about our participation in and complicity with the American Dream. Ironically, *Blazing Saddles* is also a testament to the resiliency of the Western. Brooks' audiences are still "crack[ing] up at some of the [film's] dangerous gags," because they, like Brooks, have watched and enjoyed Westerns.[18] In

126   אויסגעקליבן ווערק / Selected Works (1965–1991)

"The Frames of Comic Freedom," Umberto Eco points out, "what remains compulsory, in order to produce a comic effect, is the prohibition of spelling out the norm. It must be presupposed both by the utterer and by the audience. If the speaker spells it out, he is a fool or a jerk; if the audience does not know it, there is no comic effect" (6). Brooks, of course, can never tell us that the Western that was his breakthrough is really a ready-made, designed to challenge (and maybe change) our long-held and cherished beliefs (about ourselves). That is part of the shared culture we know too.

A gateway movie, a comedy classic, a trailblazing cult film, and the ultimate Western spoof. *Blazing Saddles* is not cheap humor. It is, as Brooks says, "a juxtaposition of hypocrisy, greed, flat-out fun and clichés that [he had] been watching since [he] was 3 years old." Somewhere, I hear Howard Johnson in Rock Ridge saying Brooks knows that he knows that we know that he knows that we know what *Blazing Saddles* is really all about. Then Brooks himself says, "It's still paying for my beans … in video."

Can you hear the comic rimshot? *Vershteh?*

Notes

1. *Get Smart* (NBC, 1965–1969; CBS, 1969–1970).
2. Instead of "Swing Low Sweet Chariot" or "Camptown Races," Bart and the black railroad workers sing Cole Porter's "I Get a Kick Out of You." This leads to the white cowboys demonstrating what they wanted to hear by singing "Camptown Races," and dancing around like idiots, oblivious to the black, Chinese and Irish workers laughing at them, until Taggert arrives and yells at them to stop. Then, to drive the point home that they are being treated like slaves, Bart and Charlie sing "Camptown Races" on the hand cart after being sent to find the quicksand after being told that unlike the horses, they are expendable.
3. See "'Blazing Saddles' in $10,288 on New Trail," *Variety*, March 28, 1979, p. 7; "Big Rental Films of 1979," *Variety*, January 9, 1980, p. 21; Jennifer Martin, "The No. 1 Movie from the Year You Were Born," CBS News, November 22, 2022, https://www.cbsnews.com/pictures/the-number-one-movie-from-every-year/26/; https://www.the-numbers.com/market/1974/top-grossing-movies.
4. *Blazing Saddles* was nominated for Photoplay's 1975 Gold Medal (Favorite Movie) and BAFTA's 1975 Film Award for Best Screenplay (Mel Brooks, Norman Steinberg, Andrew Bergman, Richard Pryor, and Alan Unger). Cleavon Little was nominated for BAFTA's 197 Film Award for Most Promising Newcomer to Leading Film Roles. Madeline Kahn was nominated for Best Actress in a Supporting Role; John C. Howard and Danford B. Greene for Best Film Editing; John Morris (music) and Mel Brooks (lyrics) for Best Music, Original Song.
5. The script for *Blazing Saddles* was co-written by Brooks, Andrew Bergman, Richard Pryor, Norman Steinberg, and Alan Uger.
6. Brooks' interest in and affinity for the absurd had been encouraged when he was working for Sid Caesar. *Your Show of Shows*' writer's room was at times a surreal experience. Lucille Kallen remembers, "To command attention, I'd have to stand on a desk and wave my red sweater, Sid boomed, Tolkin intoned, [Carl] Reiner [the show's recently installed second banana comic who had become a frequent attendee at the writer's conferences] trumpeted, and Brooks, well Mel imitated everything from a rabbinical student to the white whale of *Moby Dick* thrashing about on the floor with six harpoons sticking in

his back" (Parish 72). Larry Gelbart recalled, "We were able to be urbane. Between us we read every book. Between us we saw every movie. Between us we saw every play on Broadway. You could make jokes about Kafka or Tennessee Williams" (Maslon 77).
    7. "La Bicycletta" (15:04) aired on *Your Show of Shows* on December 23, 1950.
    8. "Technicolor Westerns" aired on the *Admiral Broadway Revue*, March 4, 1949. It is available on *YouTube* at https://www.youtube.com/watch?v=WHmCrjftnio. [AU: Same notes for 8 and 9 OK?]
    9. "Vacant Holsters" (NBC, n.d.). It is available on *YouTube* at https://www.google.com/search?q=sid+caesar+western+youtube&rlz=1C1CHBF_enCA976CA976&oq=sid+caesar+western+youtube&gs_lcrp=EgZjaHJvbWUyBggAEEUYOTIHCAEQABiiBD IHCAIQABiiBNIBDzE0ODQ4OTI0NzJqMGoxNagCALACAA&sourceid=chrome &ie=UTF-8#fpstate=ive&vld=cid:ff29c276,vid:4eaHi7BRMfQ.
    10. V-effeckt or *Verfremdungseffekt*, credited to Bertolt Brecht, defamiliarizes audiences with the performances they are watching. In "Alienation Effects in Chinese Acting," Brecht described the v-effeckt being produced by performing "in such a way that the audience was hindered from simply identifying itself with the characters in the play. Acceptance or rejection of their actions and utterances was meant to take place on a conscious plane, instead of, as hitherto, in the audience's subconscious" (Willett 91).
    11. In Yiddish, shtupp, which means to push, carries sexual connotations.
    12. Kahn's hilarious torch song, "I'm Tired," is a parody of "I'm the Laziest Gal in Town" by Cole Porter, which Dietrich sang in Alfred Hitchcock's *Stage Fright* (1950), and Dietrich's signature song, "Falling in Love Again" from *The Blue Angel* (1930).
    13. As Jeremy Dauber reminds us, the joke in Sid Caesar's popular send-up of *Shane* is that Shane succeeded because he ate herring (*Disobedient* 100).
    14. This section of *Blazing Saddles*' script is also available in Patrick McGilligan's *Funny Man* on page 330.
    15. John Murray, the 4th Earl of Dunmore, the colonial governor of Virginia, noted to Lord Dartmouth in 1774, Americans "for ever imagine the Lands further off are still better than those upon which they are already settled." He added that "if they attained Paradise, they would move on if they heard of a better place farther west" (Miller 77).
    16. Laine sang the title songs of several Western films, among them, *High Noon* (1952), *3:10 to Yuma* (1957), *Man Without a Star* (1955), and *Gunfight at the O.K. Corral* (1957).
    17. Gene Wilder says of *Blazing Saddles*, "They've smashed racism in the face, but they're doing it while you laugh."
    18. Of *Blazing Saddles*, Brooks, who grew up during the Golden Age of the Western and found them "flat-out fun," says, "basically, it's me taking a look at the West based on all the cowboy movies I've seen in my life. Maybe 6,000" ("*Blazing Saddles* Deflated").

FILMOGRAPHY

The Bicycle Thief. Dir. Vittorio De Sica. Produzione De Sica, 1948. DVD. Sony Pictures Home Entertainment, 2003.
Der blaue Engel (1930). Dir. Joseph von Sternberg. Universum Film A.G., 1930. DVD. Kino Lorber Films, 2007.
Blazing Saddles: 30th Anniversary Special Edition. Dir. Mel Brooks. Crossbow Productions, 1974. DVD. Warner, 2004.
Cabaret (1972). Dir. Bob Fosse. ABC Pictures and Allied Artists, 1972. DVD. Warner Home Video, 1998.
Caesar's Hour. Created by Sylvester L. Warner. Max Liebman Productions. NBC, 1954–57.
The Critic. Dir. Ernest Pintoff. *Mel Brooks—The Critic* (1963). *YouTube*, April 10, 2015, https://www.youtube.com/watch?v=PramR5oxn50Check.
Destry Rides Again. Dir. George Marshall. Universal Pictures, 1939. DVD. Universal Studios Home Entertainment, 2003.

אויסגעקליבן ווערק / Selected Works (1965–1991)

El Dorado. Dir. Howard Hawks. Laurel Productions, 1966. DVD. Paramount Pictures Home Entertainment, 2017.
Get Smart. Created by Mel Brooks and Buck Henry. Talent Associates and CBS Productions (Season 5). NBC, 1965–1969; CBS, 1969–1970.
Gunfight at the O.K. Corral. Dir. John Sturges. Paramount Pictures, 1957. DVD. Paramount, 2003.
Gunsmoke. Created by Norman Mcdonnell and John Meston. CBS Productions, Filmmaster Productions, Arness and Company (1959–61), The Arness Company (1961–64). CBS, 1952–1961; 1962–1975.
Hellzapoppin'. Dir. H.C. Potter. Universal Pictures, 1941. DVD. Reel Vault, 2015.
High Noon. Dir. Fred. Zinnemann. Stanley Kramer Productions, 1952. DVD. Team Marketing, 2015.
Looney Tunes. Created by Leon Sclesinger, Hugh Harmon and Rudolf Ising. Warner Bros., 1930–present.
Man Without a Star. Dir. king Vidor. Universal Pictures, 1955. DVD. Universal, 2016.
Mr. Flip. Dir. Gilbert M. "Bronco Billy" Anderson. Essanay Films, May 8, 1909. *YouTube.* https://www.youtube.com/watch?v=2fo2fG3t0eE. Accessed February 17, 2011.
Once Upon a Time in the West. Dir. Sergio Leone. Euro International Films (Italy) and Paramount Pictures (United States), 1968. DVD. Paramount, 2017.
Open City. Dir. Roberto Rossellini. Minerva Film and Joseph Burstyn & Arthur Mayer. DVD. eOne Films, 2002.
The Producers. Dir. Mel Brooks. Universal Marion Corporation Pictures, 1970. DVD. Image Entertainment, 2000.
Rawhide. Created by Charles Marquis Warren. CBS Television Network Productions. CBS, 1959–1966.
Rio Bravo. Dir. Howard Hawks. Warner Bros., 1959. DVD. Warner Home Video, 2010.
Spellbound. Dir. Alfred Hitchcock. Selznick International Pictures and Vanguard Films. DVD. MGM (Video & DVD), 2008.
Stage Fright. Dir. Alfred Hitchcock. Warner Bros., 1950. DVD. In *The Ultimate Collection.* Universal Pictures Home Entertainment, 2017.
"Technicolor Westerns." Admiral Broadway Review. Season 1 (March 4, 1949). *YouTube,* https://www.youtube.com/watch?v=WHmCrjftnio.
3:10 to Yuma. Dir. Delmar Daves. Columbia Pictures, 1957. DVD. Columbia Pictures, 2002.
Top Hat. Dir. Mark Sandrich. RKO Radio Pictures, 1935. DVD. Warner Bros. Home Video, 2009.
The Treasure of the Sierra Madre. Dir. John Huston. Warner Bros., First National, 1948. DVD. Warner Bros. Home Video, 2010.
The Twelve Chairs. Dir. Mel Brooks. Universal Marion Corporation Pictures, 1970. DVD. Image Entertainment, 2000.
"Vacant Holsters." *Sid Caesar: Your Show of Shows / Caesar's Hour / Admiral Broadway Revue. YouTube,* https://www.youtube.com/@sidcaesaryourshowofshowsca2250. Accessed July 8, 2017.
The Virginian. Created by *Charles Marquis Warren.* Revue Studios 1962–1963; Universal Television 1963–1971. NBC, 1962–1971.
Westworld. Dir. Michael Crichton. Metro-Goldwyn-Meyer, 1973. DVD. Paramount, 2017.
The Wide World of Sports. Created by Edgar Sherick. ABC Sports. ABC, 1961–1998.
Your Show of Shows. Created by Sylvester L. Weaver, Jr. Max Liebman Productions. NBC, 1950–54.

Works Cited

Arnold, Gary. "'Blazing Saddles' on a Dead Horse." *The Washington Post,* March 7, 1974, B15.
Atlas, Jacoba. "Mel Brooks Interview." *Film Comment,* vol. 11, no. 2, March/April 1975, pp. 54–57.

Baudrillard, Jean. *America.* Translated by Chris Turner, Verso, 1988.

_____. "The Precession of Simulacra." *Simulacra and Simulation,* translated by Sheila Faria Glaser, University of Michigan Press, 1994. https://0ducks.files.wordpress.com/2014/12/simulacra-and-simulation-by-jean-baudrillard.pdf. Cited parenthetically as "Simulacra."

Belth, Alex. "BGS: Playboy Interview: Mel Brooks." *Alex Belth's Bronx Banter.* http://www.bronxbanterblog.com/2013/12/20/bgs-the-playboy-interview-mel-brooks/.

"Big Rental Films of 1979." *Variety,* January 9, 1980, p. 21.

"Blazing Saddles." *Box Office Mojo.* https://www.boxofficemojo.com/title/tt0071230/?ref_=bo_se_r_1. Cited parenthetically as *Box Office Mojo.*

"Blazing Saddles." *THE NUMBERS.* https://www.the-numbers.com/movie/Blazing-Saddles#tab=summary.

"'Blazing Saddles' in $10,288 on New Trail." *Variety,* March 28, 1979, p. 7.

"BlazingSaddles.pdf." *thescriptlab.com,* 2023. https://thescriptlab.com/wp-content/uploads/scripts/BlazingSaddles.pdf. Cited parenthetically as *Script.*

Bradander, Bryan. "Cadillac played key role in 'Blazing Saddles.'" *USA Today,* May 11, 2014. https://www.usatoday.com/story/driveon/2014/05/11/blazing-saddles-cadillac-40th-anniverary/8820003/.

Brook, Peter. *The Deadly Space.* Touchstone, 1968.

Bunuel, Luis. "Quotes." https://www.bfi.org.uk/features/luis-bunuel-quotes.

Canby, Vincent. "Screen: 'Blazing Saddles,' a Western in Burlesque.' *The New York Times,* February 8, 1974. https://www.nytimes.com/1974/02/08/archives/screen-blazing-saddles-a-western-in-burlesque.html.

Caputi, Anthony. *Buffo: The Genius of Vulgar Comedy.* Wayne State Press, 1978.

Carson, Johnny. Interview with Mel Brooks. [Video]. February 13, 1975. YouTube. https://www.youtube.com/watch?v=WYuv-8SjjPg.

"Classical Gas: Galton & Simpson's Le Pétomane—Comedy Chronicles." *British Comedy Guide.* https://www.comedy.co.uk/features/comedy_chronicles/classical-gas-galton-simpson-le-petomane/.

Dannatt, Adrian. "Dali in Manhattan." *BEYOND: The St. Regis Magazine,* no. 4, 2014. https://magazine.stregis.com/the-surreal-life-of-dali-in-new-york/.

Darrach, Brad. "Mel Brooks: The Playboy Interview." *Playboy,* February 1975. *The Stacks-Reader.* http://www.thestacksreader.com/mel-brooks-the-playboy-interview/.

Dauber, Jeremy. "How *Blazing Saddles* Deflated Western and Gentile Notions of Masculinity: On the Political Context and Playfulness of Mel Brooks's 1974 Parody." *Literary Hub,* March 20, 2023. https://lithub.com/how-blazing-saddles-deflated-western-and-gentile-notions-of-masculinity/. Cited parenthetically as "*Blazing Saddles* Deflated."

_____. *Mel Brooks: Disobedient Jew.* Yale University Press, 2023. Cited parenthetically as *Disobedient.*

Dawson, Jan. "Blazing Saddles." *Film Monthly Bulletin,* vol. 41, January 1974, pp. 120–21.

Eco, Umberto. "The Frames of Comic Freedom." *Carnival!,* edited by Umberto Eco, V.V. Ivanov and Monica Rector, Mouton de Gruyter, 1984, pp. 1–9.

Eggener, Keith L. "'An Amusing Lack of Logic': *Surrealism* and Popular Entertainment." *American Art,* vol. 7, no. 4, Autumn 1993, pp. 30–45.

Frye, Northrup. *The Anatomy of Criticism: Four Essays.* Princeton University Press, 1957.

Harpold, Terry. "The Grotesque Corpus." *Perforations,* vol. 2, no. 3, 1992. http://www.pd.org/Perforations/perf3/grotesque_corpus.html.

Heath, Roderick. "The Producers (1968) / Blazing Saddles (1974)." *Film Freedonia,* April 21, 2022. https://filmfreedonia.com/page/5/.

"History." In *"Blazing Saddles." AFI Catalogue.* https://catalog.afi.com/Catalog/moviedetails/54998.

Hug, Bill. "*Blazing Saddles* as Postmodern Ethnic Carnival." *Studies in Popular Culture,* vol. 36, no. 1, Fall 2013, pp. 63–81.

Liebenson, Donald. "Mel Brooks Went Too Far—But Only Once." *Vanity Fair,* November 30, 2021. https://www.vanityfair.com/hollywood/2021/11/mel-brooks-memoir-interview.

Mambrol, Nasrullah. "Jean Baudrillard and Film Theory." *Literary Theory and Criticism*, August 2, 2018. https://literariness.org/2018/08/02/jean-baudrillard-and-film-theory/.
"Marlene Dietrich as Amy Jolly Wearing a Men's Tuxedo with Top Hat in ' Morocco' (1930)." *Vintage Everyday*, December 27, 2020. https://www.vintag.es/2020/12/marlene-dietrich-morocco.html. Cited parenthetically as "Marlene Dietrich."
Martin, Jennifer. "The No. 1 movie from the year you were born." CBS News, November 22, 2022. https://www.cbsnews.com/pictures/the-number-one-movie-from-every-year/26/.
Maslon, Laurence. *Make 'Em Laugh*. Hachette Book Group, 2008.
McGilligan, Patrick. *Funny Man: Mel Brooks*. HarperCollins, 2019.
Meisler, Stanley. "The Surreal World of Salvador Dalí." *Smithsonian Magazine*, April 2005. https://www.smithsonianmag.com/arts-culture/the-surreal-world-of-salvador-dali-78993324/.
Miller, John. *Origins of the American Revolution*. Little, Brown, 1944.
Nachman, Gerald. *Seriously Funny: The Rebel Comedians of the 1950s and 1960s*. Pantheon Books, 2003.
"Old Tombstone." *Tombstone Web: Tombstone Arizona Information. tombstoneweb.com*. https://tombstoneweb.com/tombstone-map/. Cited parenthetically as "Old Tombstone."
Parish, Robert. *It's Good to Be the King: The Seriously Funny Life of Mel Brooks*. John Wiley & Sons, 2007.
Pumphrey, Martin. "Why Do Cowboys Wear Hats in the Bath? Style Politics for the Older Man." *The Book of the Western*, edited by Ian Cameron and Douglas Pye, Studio Vista, 1996, pp. 50–62.
Reynolds, Bill. "Cowboy Codes from Western Heroes." *Western Horseman*, October 4, 2017. https://westernhorseman.com/culture/out-west/cowboy-codes-from-western-heroes/.
"Scene-Specific Commentary By Mel Brooks." *Blazing Saddles: 30*th *Anniversary Special Edition*. Dir. Mel Brooks. Crossbow Productions, 1974. DVD. Warner Bros. Home Video, 2002. Cited as "Scene-Specific Commentary."
Schevill, James. "Notes on the Grotesque: Anderson, Brecht, and Williams." *Twentieth Century Literature*, vol. 23, no. 2, May 1977, pp. 229–38.
Simon, John. "The Lower Shallows." *Reverse Angle: A Decade of American Films*. Clarkson Potter, 1982, pp. 140–45.
"Smart Money." *Time*, October 15, 1965. https://web.archive.org/web/20180503014149/http://content.time.com/time/magazine/article/0,9171,834525,00.html.
Sontag, Susan. "Notes on 'Camp.'" *Partisan Review*, vol. 31, no. 4, Fall 1964, pp. 515–530.
"Trivia." *Blazing Saddles* at *IMDb*. https://www.imdb.com/title/tt0071230/trivia/?ref_=tt_trv_trv.
"The Twelve Chairs." *AFI*. https://catalog.afi.com/Catalog/moviedetails/23558#:~:text=A%20box%2Doffice%20chart%20in,markets%20as%20%241%2C848%2C172%2C%20to%20date.
Tynan, Kenneth. "Frolics and Detours of a Short Hebrew Man." *The New Yorker*, October 22, 1978. https://archive.ph/LL0Si#selection-4483.479-4491.693.
"Van Johnson." *IMDb*. https://www.imdb.com/name/nm0004496/bio/?ref_=nm_ov_bio_sm.
Weiler, A.H. "Mel Brooks Goes West." *The New York Times*, November 26, 1972. https://www.nytimes.com/1972/11/26/archives/mel-brooks-goes-west-mel-brooks-goes-west.html.
Willett, John, ed. and trans. *Brecht on Theatre*. Hill and Wang, 1964.

Parody, Pastiche, and Intertextuality in Mel Brooks' *Young Frankenstein* (1974)

FRANCES PHEASANT-KELLY

Introduction

Young Frankenstein (1974) is an Academy-nominated comedy horror that was critically acclaimed on its release and was selected for preservation in the Library of Congress National Film Registry in 2003. Through a combination of approaches, the film primarily imitates the James Whale productions of *Frankenstein* (1931) and *Bride of Frankenstein* (1935), both in its narrative content and visual effects but also in its cinematography and German Expressionist features. In addition, it replicates the iconic characterization of the Whale films and utilizes the same laboratory setting that featured in the 1931 production. At the same time, it exploits a broad range of horror codes and conventions in its *mise-en-scène* as well as depicting places traditionally associated with horror, namely Transylvania. The soundtrack also depends on the generic signifiers of horror whilst cinematography invites associations with early cinema, notably through the use of monochrome filmstock, vertical and horizontal wipes and iris shots.

As well as referring to the horror film, *Young Frankenstein* draws upon other genres, specifically, the Hollywood musical and film noir while its sexual innuendoes constitute humorous moments that reflect the relaxation of the Hays Code prior to the time of its release, and are consistent with certain British traditions of 1960s comedy, namely the *Carry On* film series. Further, its emulation of several iconic sequences from Whale's *Frankenstein*, notably the "It's alive!" scene, exaggerates their melodramatic aspects. However, there are other significant aspects of Brooks' version that suggest it is not merely comedic parody but pays homage to Whale's interpretation of Mary Shelley's novel, notably invoking it directly in the film's title. Indeed, as Mel Brooks himself states, "Of all my films, I am the proudest of this one. We set out to make a beautiful period picture, with all the craftmanship of James Whale's 1930s films" (Brooks 3). He also comments that "we [Gene Wilder and himself] talked about being very faithful to the tempo and the look of James Whale's marvelous films, *Frankenstein* from 1931 and *Bride of Frankenstein* from 1935" (Brooks 25). Engaging theoretically with scholarship on parody, homage and intertextuality (Allen; Dyer; Hutcheon) and referencing Michaela Alliata's (2020) related study of the film, this essay analyzes *Young Frankenstein* both in relation to Whale's earlier versions, and to other forms. Focusing on characterization, *mise-en-scène* and cinematography, it argues that as well as parody and intertextuality, aspects of homage are fundamental to the film's aesthetics.

Between Parody, Homage and Intertextuality

Despite its various elements of intertextuality and homage, and coming under the broader category of remakes (see Eberwein), *Young Frankenstein* is consistently ranked as a parody with Lester Friedman and Allison Kavey noting that "film buffs and scholars alike usually accord Mel Brooks's *Young Frankenstein* [...] the top spot in any listing of horror film parodies" (156). This is due to clear instances of imitation that are consciously rendered comedic. Relatedly, Kamilla Elliott states that "[n]umerous critics have argued that Gothic literature is already parodic and that Gothic film adaptations of it are more so" (24). Elliott explains that *Young Frankenstein* draws upon an earlier parody of the Frankenstein narrative, *Abbott and Costello Meet Frankenstein* (1948). As she notes, this earlier film had "already parodied Gothic architecture and film sets, ludicrously oversizing the door handles of Frankenstein's castle and redoubling their size as knockers. *Young Frankenstein* parodies this parody, redoubling their size and sound yet again, and then redoubling the visual parody with word play: 'What a great pair of knockers!' The visual-verbal parody further parodies psychoanalytical symbolism and Freudian readings of Gothic Architecture" (27).

Parody is one of multiple forms of appropriation in the arts, which are often consciously generated, with Richard Dyer listing some of these as including plagiarism, emulation, pastiche, fakes, forgeries, hoaxes, and homage (24). However, he divides these into two categories: those that are concealed, not textually signaled, and evaluatively open (including plagiarism, fakes, forgeries, hoaxes), and those that are unconcealed, textually signaled and evaluatively predetermined (including parody, emulation, homage, travesty, burlesque and mock epic) (24). While he notes some interchangeability between parody and pastiche, Dyer makes a distinction between "works that imitate to make fun, mock, ridicule or satirize (parody) and those that do not (pastiche)" (40). As he further explains, pastiche is a copy that "imitates other art in such a way as to make consciousness of this fact central to its meaning and affect" (4). For the purpose of emphasizing the distinction between the two, he draws on a definition of parody by Simon Dentith which describes it as "any cultural practice which provides a relatively polemical allusive imitation of another cultural production or practice" (in Dyer 40).

Linda Hutcheon expands on this to note "what is remarkable in modern parody is its range of intent—from the ironic and playful to the scornful and ridiculing. Parody, therefore, is a form of imitation, but imitation characterized by ironic inversion, not always at the expense of the parodied text" (6). However, Margaret Rose takes issue with certain aspects of Hutcheon's definition, suggesting that Hutcheon does not fully address the comic character of parody (238). Meanwhile, Friedman and Kavey contend that "an exaggerated imitation of a previous film for comic effect, as exemplified in *Young Frankenstein*, fulfils any basic definition of parody" (156).

These various perspectives are extended in relation to Brooks' film by Michela Vanon Alliata who argues that they "do not correspond entirely to the way in which parody operates in *Young Frankenstein*, primarily because the tone is always outlandishly comic—parody is never aligned with satire—but especially because of the freedom with which Brooks treats the original text, ranging from mockery to respectful admiration. Relying as it does on irony and low comedy, parody here seems closely related to the modern notion of the burlesque, an umbrella term employed [...] to describe different kinds of humorous imitation" (180). She notes that the film resorts to stand-up comedy and *double-entendres* as well as identifying instances of intertextuality, these including the way that the character of Frau Blücher "is modelled on Judith Anderson's portrayal of the manipulative Mrs Danvers in Hitchcock's *Rebecca*" (Alliata 185). Despite a focus on humor and laughter, Alliata indirectly references several examples of homage: first noting that Brooks' film "was shot in black and white to stylistically mirror the 1930s classic Universal horror films, especially James Whale's *Frankenstein* and *The Bride of Frankenstein*" (181). Second, she notes Brooks' use of the original equipment from Whale's films (181) and remarks that the film is a "loving tribute to his cinematic forebears" (182). Like Alliata, Bruce Hallenbeck observes that "[w]hat makes this film such an affectionate homage to its source material is the fact that Brooks went to the trouble of recreating the monochrome look of the old Universal horrors, right down to the usage of Kenneth Strickfaden's actual lab equipment from the original *Frankenstein*. Brooks also employed old-styled opening credits and scene transitions that would have been at home in early thirties films, such as wipes, irises and numerous fades to black. The photography by Gerald Hirschfeld also evokes the period, as does the musical score by Brooks's favorite composer, John Morris" (108).

While Brooks seems committed to recreating Whale's style, there are minor inconsistencies. For example, it is noted that the cover of the *Lancet* that Dr Frederick Frankenstein (Gene Wilder), Victor Frankenstein's grandson, is reading while on the train to Transylvania does not correspond to those of the 1930s but is instead contemporaneous to the film (Perciaccante et al 736). Nonetheless, there are a significant range of elements that constitute homage. As Dyer explains, homage involves "the deliberate recognition and appreciation of a specific predecessor, where such practice is no longer the cultural norm" (37). Thomas Leitch elaborates further, explaining that the homage "accept[s] the original text's authority on its own terms […] [its] primary purpose is to pay tribute to an earlier film rather than usurp its place of honor. Like readaptations, homages situate themselves as secondary texts whose value depends on their relation to the primary texts they gloss; the difference is that the hallmark of readaptations is fidelity in transcription, whereas a faithful homage could be a contradiction in terms" (47). Leitch continues that homages "present themselves as valorizations of earlier films which are in danger of being ignored or forgotten" (47), and that "homages […] only acknowledge one earlier text" (54). Although Brooks' adaptation draws on other texts, the director constantly reiterates the importance of Whale's aesthetic approaches to *Frankenstein*, both in his adaptation of the film and in his account of making it such that the earlier film takes precedence. As Leitch goes on to state, "Homages deal with the contradictory claims of remakes—that they are just like their original, only better—by renouncing any claim to be better" (49).

Both parody and homage are closely connected to intertextuality, which, as Graham Allen outlines, refers to the way that all texts relate to others (although he subsequently acknowledges the complexity of the term). As he notes, "[t]exts, whether they be literary or non-literary, are viewed by modern theorists as lacking any kind of independent meaning […] Meaning becomes something which exists between a text and all the other texts to which it refers and relates, moving out from the independent text into a network of textual relations. The text becomes the intertext"

(1). Given its references to other genres, Brooks' film therefore involves a range of imitative forms, but its attention to homage is generally understated in scholarly discourse. It is argued here that while *Young Frankenstein* displays instances of all three forms of imitation, apparent in its cinematography, narrative content, visual effects and *mise-en-scène*, and is unquestionably parodic, it is also essentially an homage to Whale's films, and thus extends previous academic scholarship on the film which usually positions the film solely as parody.

Young Frankenstein

Principally, the narrative of *Young Frankenstein* offers a version of Mary Shelley's novel that draws visually and narratively on both of Whale's films as well as referring intertextually to a range of other genres. In synopsis, the film follows the work of Victor Frankenstein's grandson, Frederick, who, like his grandfather, attempts to reanimate dead tissue. There are several similar or identical scenes in Brooks' remake but also parodic and slapstick moments that are distinctive. The opening credits feature an image of a mountain top castle, accompanied by classic horror-style music composed by John Morris and Gothic-like typography, and is filmed in monochrome. As the camera pans across the castle's archways, the melodramatic score persists together with the inclusion of further horror iconography, including thunder and lightning and a medium close-up of a clock striking midnight. Following this, the camera pans in close-up alongside a coffin labelled "Baron Von Frankenstein" before the coffin lid suddenly opens in a jump-scare. This latter scene intertextually recalls the opening scenes of both Tod Browning's *Dracula* (1931) as well as those of Terence Fisher's Hammer Horror version of *Dracula* (1958). Inside the coffin, a skeleton clings to a box (containing, it transpires, a will) which it comically refuses to let go. Thereafter, an iris shot opens a scene absent in both the novel and Whale's film versions and establishes a new context for the monster's lineage by presenting Wilder as a scientist, Dr Von "Fronkensteen," his exaggerated alternative enunciation of the name being the first conscious attempt at parody. Narratively, his rejection of the usual Frankenstein pronunciation represents a dismissal of his grandfather's experiments as the work of a "madman." Like Dr Waldman (Edward Van Sloan) in Whale's version, the scientist is delivering a lecture, deliberating on the structure and function of the brain and paralleling the "abnormal" brain discussion in the earlier film. The introduction therefore provides a connection between Whale's original film version and Brooks' adaptation in line with Thomas Leitch's comment that "[m]ost remakes try to be readily intelligible to an audience that has never heard of their originals, but ideally they provide additional enjoyment to audiences who recognize their borrowings from their sources" (41).

Homage

Instances of homage, parody and intertextuality therefore occur frequently throughout the film, with direct tributes to Whale's versions of Shelley's novel. Brooks insisted that the film was shot in black and white "to salute those great Universal Pictures movies of the 1930s" (39). He also aimed for lighting effects equivalent to those of Whale, noting of Gerald Hirschfield's cinematography "every one of them was backlit like James Whale with the angelic glow behind the actors' heads. He just really knew how to do it" (Brooks 107). Overall, the *mise-en-scène* intertextually recalls earlier horror iconography although there are specific aspects that mirror Whale's films. For example, the cobbled streets and archways of Transylvania appear similar to the setting of Whale's film although Brooks notes that "the scale of the set actually outdid James Whale's *Frankenstein* in size and Transylvanian detail" (111). While there are marked differences between the respective films' resolutions, there are crossovers in their narratives; for example, the way that the townspeople congregate angrily to chase the Creature. *Young Frankenstein* involves another meeting of the townspeople, where one villager states "we still have nightmares from five times before," one assumes intertextually referring to those killings in Whale's as well as previous film versions of the Frankenstein narrative. In addition, the visual style echoes that of *Frankenstein*. One of the most significant examples is the cinematography and framing inside the mountain top laboratory. Here, extreme long shots of cavernous interiors and precipitous vast staircases draw upon the aesthetics of Whale's *Frankenstein* whereby characters appear small and vulnerable. Relatedly, the expressionist features of Whale's originals are replicated through shadows—a typical example occurs in a nighttime scene when Frederick and his assistants, Inga (Teri Garr) and Igor (Marty Feldman) recapture the escaped Monster (Peter Boyle)—after leaving the blindman's hut, the Monster returns to the village, lured by the sound of violin music (referencing *Bride of Frankenstein*) and casting a gigantic shadow against the houses.

Such features also manifest in the graverobbing scene, itself drawn directly from Whale's 1931 film (and absent in Shelley's novel). While this opens Whale's film, Brooks introduces it partway through in a shortened sequence, visualizing first a hanging corpse and then its subsequent burial. Just as Henry Frankenstein and his deformed assistant, Fritz

(Dwight Frye), illicitly watch the burial from a distance in Whale's film, so too do Frederick and Igor. In Brooks' film, Feldman's unusually prominent and misaligned eyes substitute for Fritz's wide-eyed manic stare while the character likewise sports a hunched back. Entering the cemetery, they then disinter the body, where, also like Whale's version, the crosses marking the graves are positioned at odd angles though they lack the low angle perspective of the earlier film that exaggerated their expressionist tropes. The scene then reverts to parody as Igor comments that "it could be worse—it could be raining," just as a torrential downpour occurs. Further scenes of homage ensue: first, when Igor sketches what the Monster might look like, the drawing being similar to Whale's Creature in its size and long arms (suggested by his short jacket sleeves); and second, as Frederick sends Igor to procure the brain of "Hans Delbruck." In a scene replicating Whale's original, Igor breaks into a "brain depositary" where three (rather than two) brains in glass jars are lined up. As instructed, Igor retrieves the jar containing Delbruck's brain but then, like Whale's version, is startled (here by the lightning which illuminates his own reflection in a mirror) and drops the jar. Igor then takes the jar labelled "abnormal brain," which is viewed in close-up, exactly like Whale's version.

The most significant element of homage, however, occurs when Frederick and Inga locate a concealed passageway. In the passageway they come across a line of skulls, corresponding to a similar series of skulls in Dr Waldman's office in Whale's *Frankenstein* (visible when Elizabeth [Mae

Discovering Frankenstein's laboratory, which featured in James Whale's 1931 original film version of *Frankenstein* (courtesy of its designer, Kenneth Strickfaden).

Clarke] and Victor [John Boles] visit Waldman). Opening another door, they enter Frankenstein's cobweb-laden laboratory where Mary Fairclough notes the correlation between the spectacle of reanimation in Whale's version and that in Brooks' adaptation, enhanced in that both have an audience, which differs from Mary Shelley's novel (401).

As noted by Alliata and Hallenbeck, Brooks attained access to the original equipment while the way it is filmed adds to a sense of respect for Whale's original. Reverence is suggested by the characters themselves—as the camera pans across the setting, an awestruck Frederick comments quietly, "So this is where it all happened," while alongside sounds of electricity sparking and crackling, the voice of Colin Clive, who played the doctor in Whale's original *Frankenstein*, is audible: "Just think! A dead brain ready to live again in a new body"; "Look! No blood, no decomposition." This sequence of *Young Frankenstein* therefore particularly valorizes Whale's *Frankenstein* and situates itself as a secondary text (Leitch 47). The laboratory becomes central in the film as the site where the Monster is recreated, the Monster having many of the same pronounced physiognomic features as Whale's original. These include a prominent forehead and neck scars, though a zip is used in lieu of the neck bolt. When Frederick is raised to the roof with the assembled corpse, he assumes a cruciform shape, arms outstretched, a cross-shaped shadow falling across the laboratory, and exclaims, "Tonight, we shall ascend into the heavens, we shall mock the earthquake, we shall command the thunders" (in Brooks 46). This subtly alludes to Henry Frankenstein's (Colin Clive) words in Whale's film, "Now I know what it feels like to be God" (although this scene was cut from the 1931 print). Likewise, when the Creature does become reanimated, a slow zoom into closeup of its moving hand replicates the corresponding scene in Whale's original. So too does Frederick's exclamation of "It's alive! It's alive!" follow the 1931 film. When Frederick instructs the Creature to sit up, it does so with its arms outstretched, echoing the mannerisms of Boris Karloff's Creature. Likewise, Peter Boyle's Creature adopts the same mechanical gait as Whale's original, brought to the spectators' attention in the "Puttin' on the Ritz" scene.

Here, to display the Creature's skills to a theater audience at the Bucharest Academy of Science, Frederick instructs it to "walk heel to toe," thus highlighting the similarity of gait with Karloff's Monster. The scene is a further significant example of homage in the way that Frederick is introduced to the audience by the Master of Ceremonies (Norbert Schiller), who imitates Edward Van Sloan's introduction to Whale's *Frankenstein*. In Whale's original, a prologue was added to the start of the film which did not change the story but indicated to audiences that the story was a fantasy and not possible in reality. This intended to address claims of blasphemy from various state censors and the Hays office regarding the creation of life. The use of the prologue was an ideal solution to keep the film narrative intact but mitigate the allegedly persuasive capacity of the film. Edward Van Sloan, who plays the part of Dr Waldman, emerges from behind a curtain version, stating, "How do you do? Mr. Carl Laemmle feels that it would be a little unkind to present this picture without just a word of friendly warning." A second strategy was used to further remove Whale's film from realism and circumvent the censors. As Friedman and Kavey note, the opening prologue was deliberately artificial: "starting with a blatantly theatrical setting and a direct address to an invisible audience disrupts the illusion of the fourth wall and clearly identifies what follows as an artificial construct" (108). In Brooks' version, both the Master of Ceremonies and Frederick likewise emerge from behind a curtain to address the theater, the spectator placed in the position of the diegetic audience, thus emulating *Frankenstein*'s prologue. Despite its different ending, Brooks' film also draws on *Bride of Frankenstein*, notably in its stylization of Elizabeth (Madeline Kahn) whose white-streaked hair in the closing scenes is identical to that of Elsa Lanchester, who played the Bride in *Bride of Frankenstein*. Overall, the film thus fulfils a definition of homage as "the deliberate recognition and appreciation of a specific predecessor, where such practice is no longer the cultural norm" (Dyer 37).

Intertextuality

If *Young Frankenstein* draws primarily on specific scenes from Whale's two films, it also exploits conventions of the horror film in general, as well as referencing other genres. Key examples of horror iconography include the use of thunder and lightning, the sound of howling wolves, swirling mist, a cobweb-laden *mise-en-scène*, a close-up of a full moon, and a clock striking midnight. In particular, the castle's archways and flaming torches echo the horror genre's tropes. Certain aspects are consistent with the horror film. For example, when Frederick leaves the train at "Transylvania" station, mist swirls around and old-style gas lamps flicker, creating an unsettling ambience. At the same time, a dragging sound is audible, the mist and darkness contributing to a sense of fear. This is further suggested when Frederick turns up his collar—as if chilled—and looks alarmed at the sound. A rapid zoom in to a close-up of his face, his eyes widening in fear is a typical horror technique, before the camera cuts to a close-up of a cloak-clad Igor, emphasizing his unusual, bulbous eyes.

As well as the horror genre, there are references to the musical, the Western and to film noir. The most notable of these intertextual references occurs when Frederick introduces the Creature in the aforementioned scene at the Bucharest Academy of Science. Both Frederick and the Creature wear top hat and tails, and perform a tap routine to "Puttin' on the Ritz," a dance in a musical originally performed by Fred Astaire. The scene caused conflict between Wilder and Brooks, with Brooks considering that "it was too far outside of our salute to the back-and-white classics" (28) but ultimately proved successful, with James Heffernan describing it as "the most outrageous and certainly one of the most original departures from Mary Shelley's novel" (156). Heffernan goes on to state that "on the one hand, Astaire's combination of sexual charm and urbane sophistication is about as far from Mary Shelley's repulsive giant as anything can be. On the other hand, the episode exemplifies what the creature has become in popular culture: 'a source of immensely popular entertainment [...] We are captivated not by transgression as such but by the starring performance of it. In the tap dance of *Young Frankenstein*, the creature acts out transgression for an audience, theatrically breaching the wall between savagery and sophistication'" (156). There are further musical interludes in the film that recall other genres. For example, towards the end of the film Elizabeth sings "Glory Glory Hallelujah" ("Battle Hymn of the Republic"), which is more usually associated with American Civil War narratives and Westerns.

There are also allusions to film noir, evident in the scene at the train station when Frederick bids farewell to Elizabeth as he departs for Transylvania. Even though the sequence is overtly parodic, the rain-soaked platform, steam-filled surroundings, low-lit monochrome *mise-en-scène*, and the costumes and exaggerated melodramatic figure behavior of Frederick and Elizabeth are suggestive of *film noir*: Frederick wears a raincoat and fedora while Elizabeth's costume of feathers, fur and jewel-bedecked headdress recalls the classic femme fatale. Meanwhile, in a subsequent line in the film Frederick asks Igor, "Would you give me a hand with the bags," to which Igor responds, "Sure, you take the blonde, and I'll take the one in the turban," in imitation of Groucho Marx. Moreover, as noted, *Young Frankenstein* emulates cinema of the 1930s in its adoption of various cinematographic techniques. As Brooks states, "I ended up going back to James Whale, as I so often did on this movie. I went back to the old-fashioned, 1920s editing techniques—the iris outs, the spins, and the wipes. Not only did they lend the film a feeling of authenticity to Whale's era, they also helped me move seamlessly between comedy and art" (151). In terms of characterization, as also commented on by Alliata, Frau Blücher is consciously modelled on Mrs. Danvers in Hitchcock's *Rebecca* (1940) with Brooks noting that "we asked her to play Frau Blücher like Judith Anderson's domineering and cold Mrs. Danvers" (83). According to Allen, "intertextuality provides a new vision of meaning, and thus of authorship and reading: a vision resistant to ingrained notions of originality, uniqueness, singularity and autonomy" (6). Nonetheless, one might argue that, on the one hand, many of these intertextual moments are inflected with Brooks' recognizable style while, on the other hand, they also contribute to sustained support for Whale's vision.

Parody and Innuendo

As noted, the film is overtly parodic. This trope is established in the opening scenes where a skeleton in a coffin clasps tightly a box, not only suggesting that the skeleton has agency but also that it is reluctant to hand over its inheritance. The following scene too has comedic implications with Wilder conforming to the mad scientist stereotype when he performs unethical abusive procedures on a volunteer—the "patient," an elderly man, is rendered unable to respond to physical or verbal abuse (because of a nerve-impulse blocking device attached to his neck) but his anguish still registers in his facial expression. Meanwhile, in frustration at a medical student's persistent questions about his grandfather's work, Frederick accidentally slams a scalpel into his thigh in a fit of anger and then tries to cover up his pain, quickly dismissing the class. When handed the will from his great grandfather (in the same box that the skeleton was reluctant to relinquish), Frederick departs for Transylvania, invoking the above-mentioned farewell to Elizabeth, his fiancée, at the train station. Every potential emotional interaction between the two is rendered parodic: Elizabeth refuses to be kissed because of smudging her lipstick, she halts his embrace because of her hair and dress, and ultimately, they touch elbows as a restrained form of affection before she chokes on steam emitted from the train. Frederick's ensuing train journey stops first at New York and then Transylvania, playfully ignoring temporal and geographic incongruities. On arrival at Transylvania, Frederick asks a local boy if he has the right station, inquiring, "Pardon me boy. Is this the Transylvania station?" The young boy initially responds in a broken German accent then reverts to a U.S. accent, thus accentuating the reflexive nature of the film. At the same time, the boy's response of "Ja, ja, Track 29, do you want a shine?" refers to the Glen Miller song "Chattanooga Choo Choo" which contains the lines "Pardon me boy. Is that the Chattanooga Choo Choo? Track 29! Boy, you can give me shine" (in Brooks 34). As Alliata explains, "parody is a self-conscious and self-reflexive practice that involves the intention of the artist in the encoding, as well as the interpretative activity of the reader in the decoding" (179). Pronunciation and language continue to be a significant aspect of characterization—not only in Frederick's insistence on the pronunciation of "Fronkensteen" but also in the encounter between Frederick and his assistant Igor who demands that his name is pronounced "eyegor" rather than "eegor." When meeting Igor, Frederick slaps him on the back before realizing that Igor has a pronounced hump and informs him that he is a "rather a brilliant surgeon" to which Igor appears puzzled: "Your hump," points out Frederick; "what hump?" Igor responds, his hunched back actually changing sides in a later sequence. Igor then tells Frederick to "walk this way" before handing the latter his shortened walking stick and awkwardly descending some steps with a pronounced limp (exactly like Fritz in *Frankenstein*).

The play on words and innuendo continues, first in Inga's comment of "werewolf" on hearing wolves howling en-route to the castle. "Werewolf?" asks Frederick to which Igor replies, "There wolf!" and points off screen. Second, when the two, together with Inga, reach the mountain top laboratory, Igor bangs one of the huge door knockers, and Frederick comments, "What knockers!!" to which Inga replies, "Thank you, doctor." Thereafter, the door creaks open and the housekeeper, Frau Blücher (Cloris Leachman), introduces herself. At the sound of her name, the horses rear up as if fearful—indeed, whenever her name is mentioned, the horses rear, recalling the scene in Todd Browning's *Dracula* when the villagers respond equally fearfully to the mention of the name "Dracula" by crossing themselves.

Perhaps reflecting the focus on the Creature's hand to show the first signs of life (and Henry in *Bride of Frankenstein*), as well as the emphasis in Henry Frankenstein's comments when he discusses the Creature in *Frankenstein*: "with a body I made with my own hands, my own hands!," hands seem to be prominent in the film. For instance, when Frederick and Igor disinter the body, they wheel the coffin through the streets of Transylvania when the coffin suddenly topples, and the corpse's arm sticks out. Just at that moment, the two are apprehended by a police officer who insists on shaking Frederick's hand though, in this case, it is the hand sticking out of the coffin. The word "hand" crops up several times in their conversation, with the police officer, satisfied that all is in order, commenting, "If you have everything in hand." So too does the town inspector (Kenneth Mars) have a mechanical arm that he must manipulate into position, and as Brooks states, was "a takeoff on Lionel Atwill's intense, one-armed inspector in the 1939 *Son of Frankenstein* [1930]" (87). Relatedly, Hallenbeck notes that "the scene in which he plays darts with Frankenstein is a pitch-perfect parody of a nearly identical scene in *Son* [*of Frankenstein*] in which Atwill plays darts with Basil Rathbone" (108). Innuendo also occurs during the reanimation scene when Frederick instructs Inga to "elevate me," where, despite the sexual connotations, he obviously means to raise the platform to the roof. It surfaces too in discussion about the seven-foot Monster having an enormous "Schwanzstucher," a term for the Monster's genitals invented by Brooks (Alliata 186).

The Creature itself is subject to further parodic scenes, the most prominent being related to the drowning sequence of Whale's original. State censor boards in Massachusetts, Pennsylvania, and New York partially cut the scene in Whale's version where the young girl Maria (Marilyn Harris) is accidentally murdered whereby the drowning scene remained intact but the shot of the monster throwing Maria into the water was cut (Vieira 70). However, as noted by David Lewis (in Curtis 154), the scene of the Creature sitting with Maria subsequently followed by her father carrying her body implied that he had raped her, with Whale successfully arguing for its retention, at least until 1938. As James Curtis recounts, when the film was reissued in 1938 under the auspices of the PCA, the drowning scene was removed completely and was only recovered in 1985 in the British Film Institute archives (157). Having watched the film in its original format as a child in 1932 (Brooks 10), Brooks, however, would have been aware of the intact drowning scene which engendered sympathy for the Creature—his version subverts this poignant moment: an extreme low angle shot from inside a well (offering a different perspective to the lakeside setting of Whale's film) looks up to frame the child, Helga (Anne Beesley), and the Creature looking down into the well, throwing petals. Having thrown in all the petals, Helga asks the Creature, "What shall we throw in now?" Here, a closeup shows the Creature's eyes move laterally and look offscreen, as if it has had an epiphany, and is parodic because of his apparent knowingness (which is analogous to audience expectations that he will throw the child into the well). Effectively, the Creature's seeming awareness of what has gone before "acknowledges the authority of [its] model[s] by refusing to imitate it directly and instead [calls] attention to [its] own artifice" (Leitch 49). The scene, therefore, through humor, also venerates the original and illustrates a combination of parody and homage. This sequence intercuts with scenes of the anguished parents frantically searching for their daughter. Meanwhile, Helga insists that the Creature sit on a seesaw and, as it duly slumps down, the child on the other end of the seesaw is comically catapulted through an open window to land in bed.

Similar humor arises when the Creature enters the cottage of a blind man (Gene Hackman) who offers him wine, soup and a cigar, a parody of the scene featuring a blind hermit (Oliver Peters Heggie) in *Bride of Frankenstein* (Brooks 91). In quick succession, the blind man accidentally pours hot soup in the Creature's lap, spills its wine, and ignites its hand, mistaking it for a cigar, causing the Creature extreme distress. The sequence intertextually refers to the Creature's fear of flames that led to the murder of *Frankenstein*'s Fritz (who taunted the Creature with a burning torch) and is iterated several times in Brooks' version, again when the Creature is later captured and a warden holds a match to him, causing the Creature to kill him. Finally, as Elliott notes regarding the Gothic parody, Elizabeth's response to the Monster towards the end of the film "parodies Freudian conflations of phobia and desire when she bursts from terror and revulsion into rhapsodic song after being mounted by the film's well-endowed monster" (30). The ending, which deviates significantly from Whale's films, sees Frederick transfer part of his brain to the Creature, rendering the latter as articulate and cultured. While the Creature is paired with Elizabeth—whose hair is now identical to that of Elsa Lanchester—Frederick marries Inga who, like Elizabeth during her seduction by the Creature, bursts into song with "Sweet Mystery of Life" on her wedding night, implying that Frederick has attained the Creature's "Schwanzstucher" in the transference process.

Conclusion

Young Frankenstein has clear elements of parody and intertextuality as well as frequent examples of slapstick humor and innuendo. While there are narrative and visual parallels with *Frankenstein* and *Bride of Frankenstein*, there are also significant differences, particularly in the film's resolution and the insertion of musical interludes. However, in line with Leitch's claims regarding homage, one might equally argue that *Young Frankenstein*'s "primary purpose is to pay tribute to an earlier film rather than usurp its place of honor" (47). This becomes apparent through Brooks' account of making the film and through close following of aesthetic details in Whale's films, notably the inclusion of the original Strickfaden laboratory, early cinematographic techniques, and lighting effects, expressionist tropes, characterization and *mise-en-scène* that replicate Whale's films. Overall, while constituting comedy, *Young Frankenstein* situates itself as a "secondary text[s] whose value depends on [its] relation to the primary texts [it] gloss[es]" (Leitch 47). It thus valorizes Whale's films and takes "seriously the classic status of [its] originals and the idea of film classics generally" (Leitch 50).

Filmography

Abbott and Costello Meet Frankenstein. Dir. Rowland V. Lee. Universal Pictures Company, 1939. DVD. In *Complete Legacy Collection*, Universal Studios Home Entertainment, 2014.

Bride of Frankenstein. Dir. James Whale. Universal Pictures, 1935. DVD. In *Universal Classic Monsters: The Complete 30-Film Collection.* Universal Studios, Home Entertainment, 2014.
Dracula. Dir. Tod Browning. Universal Pictures, 1931. DVD. Universal Studios Home Entertainment, 2014.
Dracula. Dir. Terence Fisher. Hammer Film Productions, 1958. DVD. Warner Home Video, 2005.
Frankenstein. Dir. James Whale. Universal Pictures, 1931. DVD. Universal Studios Home Entertainment, 2000.
Rebecca. Dir. Alfred Hitchcock. Selznick International Pictures, 1940. DVD. Video Service Corp., 2017.
Son of Frankenstein. Dir. Rowland V. Lee. Universal Pictures, 1939. DVD. Universal Studios Home Entertainment, 2014.
Young Frankenstein. Dir. Mel Brooks. Twentieth Century Fox, 1974. DVD. Twentieth Century Fox, 2014.

Works Cited

Allen, Graham. *Intertextuality.* Routledge, 2011.
Alliata, Michela Vanon. "The Uses of Parody and The Practice of Laughter in Mel Brooks's *Young Frankenstein.*" *Mary Shelley's Frankenstein 1818-2018,* edited by Maria Parrino, Alessandro Scarsella and Michela Vanon Alliata, Cambridge Scholars Press, 2020, pp. 178-192.
Brooks, Mel. *Young Frankenstein: The Story of the Making of the Film.* Black Dog & Leventhal, 2016.
Curtis, James. *James Whale: A New World of Gods and Creatures.* University of Minnesota Press, 2003.
Dyer, Richard. *Pastiche.* Routledge, 2007.
Eberwein, Robert. "Remakes and Cultural Studies." *Play It Again Sam: Retakes on Remakes,* edited by Andrew Horton and Stuart McDougal, University of California Press, 2022, pp. 15-33.
Elliott, Kamilla. "Gothic-Film-Parody." *Adaptation,* vol. 1, no. 1, 2008, pp. 24-43.
Fairclough, Mary. "Frankenstein and the 'Spark of Being': Electricity, Animation, and Adaptation." *European Romantic Review,* vol. 29, no. 3, 2018, pp. 339-407.
Friedman, Lester, and Allison Kavey. *Monstrous Progeny: A History of the Frankenstein Narratives.* Rutgers University Press, 2016.
Hallenbeck, Bruce. *Comedy Horror Films: A Chronological History, 1914-2008.* McFarland, 2009.
Heffernan, James. "Looking at the Monster: 'Frankenstein' and Film." *Critical Inquiry,* vol. 24, no. 1, 1997, pp. 133-158.
Horton, Robert. *Frankenstein.* Wallflower Press, 2014.
Hutcheon, Linda. *A Theory of Parody: The Teachings of Twentieth-Century Art Forms.* University of Illinois Press, 2000.
Hutcheon, Linda, and Siobhan O'Flynn. *A Theory of Adaptation.* Routledge, 2013.
Leitch, Thomas. "Twice Told Tales: Disavowal and the Rhetoric of the Remake." *Dead Ringers: The Remake in Theory and Practice,* edited by Jennifer Forrest and Leonard Koos, State University of New York Press, 2002, pp. 37-62.
Rose, Margaret. *Parody: Ancient, Modern, and Post-Modern.* Cambridge University Press, 1995.
Perciaccante, Antonio, Alessia Coralli, Philippe Charlier, Otto Appenzeller, and Raffaella Bianucci. "Young Frankenstein and The Lancet." *Lancet,* no. 392, 2018, p. 736.
Vieira, Mark. *Forbidden Hollywood: The Pre-Code Era (1930-34): When Sin Ruled the Movies.* Running Press, 2019.
Weaver, Tom, Michael Brunas, and John Brunas. *Universal Horrors: The Studio's Classic Films, 1931-1946.* McFarland, 2007.

Comedic Film Criticism, Filmed
Mel Brooks' Love of Cinema in Silent Movie *(1976) and* The Critic *(1963)*

MATTHEW CIPA

"THE SOUNDTRACK INVENTED SILENCE."
—Robert Bresson (*Notes on the Cinematograph*, 28)

"If the eye is entirely won, give nothing or almost nothing to the ear. * One cannot be at the same time all eye and all ear.

*And *vice versa*, if the ear is entirely won, give nothing to the eye."
—Robert Bresson

In *Silent Movie* (dir. Mel Brooks, 1976), director and recovering alcoholic Mel Funn (Mel Brooks) and friends Marty Eggs (Marty Feldman) and Dom Bell (Dom DeLuise) convince the head of failing production studio Big Pictures Studios (played by Sid Caesar) to make the first silent picture in decades. If the film is a success, it will help the studio avoid a takeover, thereby ensuring its continued existence and revitalizing Funn's career and artistic stature. Throughout, the intrepid trio recruit stars like Burt Reynolds, James Caan, Liza Minnelli, Anne Bancroft, and Paul Newman for their film. After a series of hijinks which threaten to destroy the picture being made, *Silent Movie* concludes with a triumphant premiere. Big Pictures Studios is saved, and Mel Funn's artistic genius, called into question by his propensity for drinking and the apparent "unfilmability" of his idea, is restored to the pantheon of great filmmakers. But we, the spectators, never see the film being made—we see the rapturous applause, the slapstick laden pursuit in gathering stars, and the skewering of producers. The film itself is never something to which we are treated, even in part.

Mel Brooks is often touted as a satirist and parody-generator *par excellence*. His treatment of targets—B-Grade horror films in *Young Frankenstein* (1974), the Western in *Blazing Saddles* (1974), Alfred Hitchcock in *High Anxiety* (1977), and swords-and-sandals epics in *The History of the World, Part 1* (1981)—is motivated less by caustic evisceration and more by love and appreciation. *Silent Movie*, too, operates in this domain. Spectators need not see the film that Funn and Co. are making, because *Silent Movie* is not about that film. A paean to the artform of silent filmmaking, Brooks' film being made and set in '70s Los Angeles at the highpoint of New Hollywood and "gritty realism," dour and weighty themes, experimental filmmaking techniques, and disregard for budgets that grew out of the socio-political-cultural upheaval of the time affords a renewed appreciation of the glories of silent movies. As Henry Jenkins observes, in *Silent Movie* the jokes in the film often "depend on our anticipation of sounds" (167) and so "the gags in *Silent Movie* often play upon audience consciousness of the absence of sound" (168). The film sets out this form of cinema not as archaic—a historical curiosity—but as a uniquely expansive mode of cinematic storytelling, being expansive not only in the formal and creative possibilities that await (especially in making a silent film in the sound era), but expansive, too, in its possibilities for comedy.

An ode to silent filmmaking, *Silent Movie* engages with films and techniques from the bygone cinematic era that it references in elegantly and intelligently designed comedic set-pieces. It demonstrates Brooks' awareness (and self-awareness) of star personae, of the ways in which sound can be used through presence and absence, and the *joi de vivre* that defines his comedy. When Funn, Eggs, and Bell try to attain the services of Marcel Marceau, the only moment in which dialogue breaks through the canvas of sound effects, music, and silence occurs. Marceau responds with a defiant, even insulted "Non!"

In order to better understand the critical-appreciative tendencies of Brooks' movies, this essay examines in detail the ways in which *Silent Movie* is a silent cinematic laboratory; it also interrogates an animated short, *The Critic* (director, Ernest Pintoff), in which Brooks voices a disgruntled spectator watching and trying to make sense of an abstract film. Bearing in mind how *Silent Movie* and *The Critic* function as works of film criticism filmed, the absence of Brooks' material voice in *Silent Movie* and Brooks' uses of absorption and theatricality, two concepts drawn from the work of art historian Michael Fried, are also considered.

Filming Criticism

In order to understand the ways in which *Silent Movie* and *The Critic* function as film criticism filmed, one must ask: what is the task of film criticism—what does it aim to do, what are its achievements, and what is its relation not only to the film it criticizes, but also to the spectator interacting with work, critic, and criticism? Inheriting arguments by Noël Carroll and Peter Lamarque, Stephanie Ross highlights the functional multiplicity of criticism in its creation and consumption, noting that for practical reasons one might consult a review when deciding which film to see or which streaming series to spend time with, and that one might also consult criticism after-the-fact to "refine and deepen our understanding of works we've already encountered" (4). For Alex Clayton and Andrew Klevan, good criticism possesses a variety of characteristics:

> the best criticism deepens our interest in individual films, reveals new meanings and perspectives, expands our sense of the medium, confronts our assumptions about value, and sharpens our capacity to discriminate. Moreover, it strives to find expression for what is seen and heard, bringing a realm of sounds, images, actions and objects to meet a realm of words and concepts. Engaging with film through criticism therefore means involving ourselves not simply with a series of points and arguments but with language and style [1].

Clayton and Klevan conceive of criticism as something that is written, but here it should be noted that *Silent Movie*, written, directed, and starring Brooks, is also a work of cinematic criticism. The spectator's experience is shaped by the language and style of Brooks' critique of filmmaking, the narrative of the film, the examples and references peppered throughout, and the unique design of his comedy. In *The Critic*, Brooks' irritated cinemagoer narrates his reservations about what is appearing before him: as the abstract shapes and colors move across the screen, we are invited to see the things he sees and experience what he does.

As outlined, critical practice has a functional dexterity that goes far beyond snap evaluative judgments. It is as much about articulating an appreciation as it is fostering and cultivating that appreciation in others—an appreciation that does not just involve a particular film, but one that can be interwoven with the medium of film itself, a cluster of works, the work of a particular director, performer, cinematographer, and so on, so as to better refine the means by which critical judgements are made. Ross is also attuned to these observations, noting that criticism can address individual works as well as greater, broader topics—genres, movements, oeuvres—and that one way in which to think about the multifunctionality of criticism is as a continuum that links the simplest critical judgments (for example, good/bad) to "increasingly detailed accounts setting out how and why works are to be savored, where this involves contextualizing those works, parsing their properties, proposing interpretations, and estimating their significance" (4–5).

Silent Movie and *The Critic* operate at different points on this continuum. The complexity of *Silent Movie* demands the viewer appreciate it as a work in and of itself, understanding the references to other films and individuals central to silent film. It also invites making sense of Brooks' own relation to these topics as he functions as a filmmaker and critic who has chosen not to express his appreciation of the form in words, but instead to film it and show us. Demonstrating his understanding and love of silent film, his decision to remove his material voice in *Silent Movie* is the most elegant way to appreciate silent film—deploying his critical and authorial voice through the silence of a silent film.

The Critic is somewhat simpler in that it comedically appraises a popular critical tendency and a particular form of film. After a brief introduction of a varying-colored backdrop with geometric shapes and patterns changing position and design, the first words of our skeptical critic are uttered: "What the hell is this?" At once incredulous and less than complimentary—"This is cute, this is cute, this is nice; what the hell is it? Oh, I know what it is. It's garbage!" and "It must be some kind of symbolism. It must be symbolic of junk"—Brooks' eponymous critic provides spectators a play-by-play of his interpretation and appreciation of what we are watching. When the critic speculates that the agile, abstract shapes on-screen represent "birth, it's a bug, it's two things they, they like each other. Two things in love" we may well see things the same way. The other unseen spectators within the short film, however, do not have much gratitude for their fellow cinema-goer's insights. He is often encouraged into silence, with other diegetic spectators urging the critic to "shh!" while others still are somewhat more direct: "Hey, could you shut up?"

Arguably, there is little spectatorial "space" to consider how the critic's view of the film differs somewhat from our own—in part, because *The Critic* is not just what is on-screen, it encapsulates the abstract shapes dancing before us and Brooks' critic commenting on them. When he questions the intentions of the abstract film's author—"Why does he waste his time with this? He should do something constructive, like drive a truck, or make a shoe"—and draws his final conclusions ("I don't know much about psychoanalysis, but I'd say this is a dirty picture") we experience, given the practice of criticism is part of *The Critic* itself, a dialogue. The film the critic watches and for which he ultimately has disdain, has made a statement—the author making a statement through it (putting aside the question of whether the author is the director of *The Critic* or some other diegetic author)—and the critic has responded. This dialogic form throughout the short film breaks down the margins between diegetic and non-diegetic elements.

There is also a dialogic quality to *Silent Movie*. Part of the illumination, appreciation, and celebration of the distinctiveness of silent film in *Silent Movie* is apparent in the way in which Brooks' selection of material

150   אויסגעקליבן ווערק / Selected Works (1965–1991)

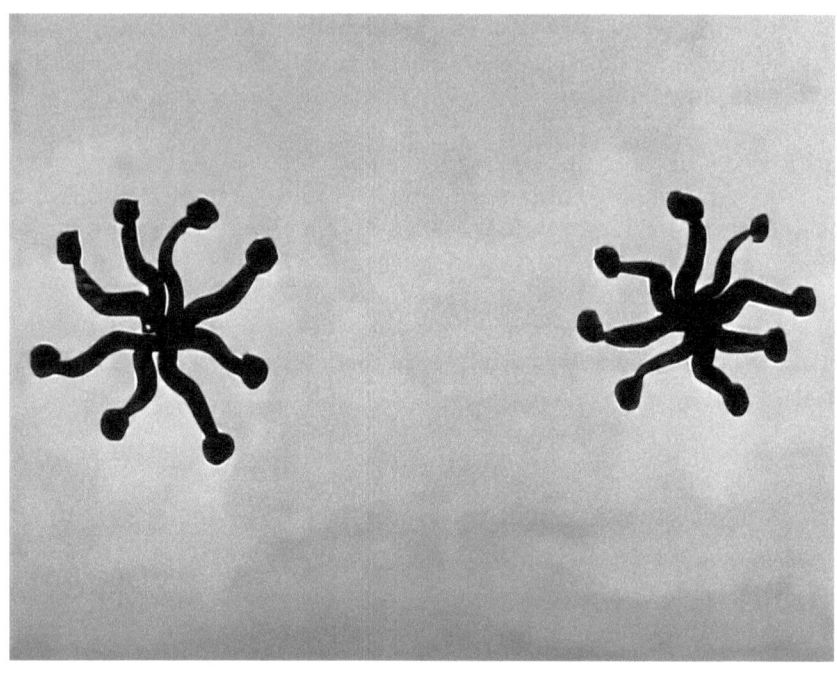

"Two things in love" in *The Critic* (1963).

to reference and incorporate into his own work identifies his own understanding of the topic. Experiencing *Silent Movie*, we witness Brooks' response to the material he has chosen, turning it as though it were on a lathe to satisfy his own comedic needs. Doing so, he embeds himself and his film firmly within a tradition for which he has a great deal of respect, from which he receives a great deal of joy, and in which he finds aesthetic value. *Silent Movie*'s adoption of the conventions and figures of silence and sound is evidence of Brooks' admiration and understanding of this mode of filmmaking and its comedic potential. Spectators are treated to long-winded conversations between the central three characters, only to have the briefest of intertitles capture what was apparently said. In the spirit of Bresson, the reduction or constraint of sound, of the demands on the ear, heightens the demands on the eyes. Here, the film's slapstick comedy flourishes in the visual, with set pieces involving a blind man who, having used a public bathroom, emerges, and confused, selects the wrong dog, or a sequence involving a Coca-Cola vending machine that launches cans at a supersonic velocity (at groin height, of course). Often, such action is supplemented by a light orchestral accompaniment that supplements the chaos on-screen, or even adds to it by setting the rhythm of the performers who knowingly respond (as Funn, Eggs, and

Bell do when they skip in time to the music, striding in unison down a hospital hallway).

Dialogue requires a voice and a listener. Where is the voice in *Silent Movie*? How is it Brooks is heard? Writing about Plato's dialogues, John T. Lysaker notes that a dialogue contains the original presented thought as well as its reinterpretation from one's interlocutor, and that the beautiful, rhythmic back-and-forth creates something new in and of itself (114). He further remarks that "[d]ialogues thus exemplify a certain kind of life, one mediated and ordered by all that speech can accomplish and haunted by all that it cannot, whether in practice or principle" (114). In the context of certain types of comedy—parody, homage, the kind of joyous-appreciative comedy which I would suggest is one of Brooks' hallmarks—we see this form of dialogic life cinematically recreated. The original material (slapstick comedy itself, the silent films being referenced) is reinterpreted by the filmmaker—the original thought's meaning, intention, and effect reconstituted by Brooks. This dialogic structure also underpins the act of criticism, whereby the effect of some topic or work of art is explored. In *Silent Movie*, both of these types of responses overlap and exist in one dialogue.

Addressing the selection of critics (the reasons why we choose to spend more time with certain critics over others), Stanley Kauffmann writes:

> Our reason for reading some critics instead of others is usually our respect for the perception and intellect to be found in some and not others. Obviously these criteria are not in question, but, pursuing them, we tend to ignore the way in which opinions mine the insights. Often we quite knowingly dig through dense writing in order to mine the insights. But when the writing itself is good, the criticism does more than illuminate its subject more succinctly: it blesses us with beauty—no other term will do—that is an endorsement of the whole being of art [42].

These comments resonate with Noël Carroll's observation that "the object of criticism is what the artist has done" and therefore "what the artist has done should be construed in terms of whether and how it is an achievement (or failure)" (51). Brooks' successful realization of a silent film comedy evidences his understanding of his topic. Displaying the best sensibilities of silent film comedy, *Silent Movie*, fixed diegetically and as a historical artefact in the context of sound film, demonstrates Brook's adeptness with the comedic possibilities of sound, music, and his own voice.

Simon Critchley aims to understand the humanity of humor, writing that "[i]f humour is human, then it also, curiously, marks the limit of the human. Or, better, humour explores what it means to be human by moving back and forth across the frontier that separates humanity from animality" (29). He continues, observing, "[h]umour is precisely the exploration of the break between nature and culture, which reveals the human to be not so much a category by itself as a negotiation between categories" (29). Following this line of thought, comedy, too, has a dialogic form—a negotiation, a reinterpretation, an interlocution. *Silent Movie*'s ever-deepening layers then bless us with a particular expression of beauty—a cinematic beauty informed by silence, and articulated critically, cinematically, comedically, and dialogically (all at once) by Brooks. What is it, though, about Brooks' multifaceted voice—as star, filmmaker, critic, and comedian—that is so important to considering *Silent Movie* as a work of film criticism filmed?

Voiceless Bodies, Bodyless Voices

Mel Brooks has a star persona that has been refined across the course of a many decades-long career in comedy, radio, television, and film. Among other things, his star persona is produced by the individuality of his comedy, his appearance, and critically, his voice. Richard Dyer writes that "audience foreknowledge, the star's name and her/his appearance (including the sound of her/his voice and dress styles associated with him/her) all already signify that condensation of attitudes and values which is the star's image" (126). Any number of characteristics are placed into the melting pot to produce the stardom of any given individual, and so the spectator's awareness (and, perhaps, the star's self-awareness) of such hallmarks shape the way in which, for example, a star performer's persona will melt into or assimilate with a character.

Dyer proposes there are three ways in which the star image is used in the construction of character: selective use, perfect fit, and problematic fit. The first involves the film's use of "character and the rhetoric of film" to emphasize certain features of the star and de-emphasize or ignore others. The second deciphers how "all the aspects of a star's image fit with all the traits of a character" (129). The third recognizes a disjuncture between star and character in which the star overwhelms the character as "powerfully" and "inescapably present" and the ways in which the "always-already-signifying nature of star images more often than not create[s] problems in the construction of character" (129).

Silent Movie demonstrates Brooks' understanding of star personae, especially his own. While elements of what I say here are no doubt informed by hindsight and Brooks' comedic output after *Silent Movie*, he nevertheless enjoyed in the earlier stages of what was to grow into a widespread and iconographic popularity by identifiability based on his voice. It grew gravellier, "growlier," and throatier as the years passed, but even in the '70s, it had a distinctiveness that was part of the stardom of Mel Brooks. In *The Critic*, Brooks' vocal performance, even with the accent applied, would have been familiar to audiences because of his comedy albums which included popular bits like "The 2000-Year-Old Man," created and performed with his comedy partner Carl Reiner. The awareness, then, to remove a recognizable feature from what was his first starring role on-screen, demonstrates a playful, comedic, cinematic, and critically intelligent awareness of certain characteristics that constitute his identifiability and stardom.

James Naremore notes how "in silent movies, actors needed to make their few words rise out of their gestures, never forgetting that meaning lay in their eyes and at their fingertips" (48). This practice was due, in part, to the inheritance of acting techniques from the theater, but was even more indebted to the constraints of the then "soundless" medium itself. In *Silent Movie*, Brooks' awareness of the conventions of silent filmmaking—the way in which gestural aspects of performance respond to the constraints of silence—is played for laughs. Attuned to this element of his stardom, we still hear his voice—it is difficult in moments in which Funn is wildly gesticulating on-screen, speaking with great verve and "volume," not to hear in our mind's ear Brooks' affect, or read any subsequent intertitle without the memory of how he sounds. This is clearer and more potent an effect the more familiar we are with him and as is the case of one's relation with and knowledge of any star. As in Dyer's account of stardom, there is a compelling dilemma mined for comedic purposes as much as it points out Brooks' removal of his voice demonstrates his selective use of his star qualities as they relate to the character of Funn through their absence. In short, Brooks' reflexive self-awareness illustrates what is a problematic fit between star and character for Dyer.

Of course, the relation between performer and character is a persistent and complex one in the study of screen art. Andrew Klevan follows Stanley Cavell's observations about performance, suggesting that "characters have no existence apart from the particular human beings on screen, and no life apart from particular performers who incarnate them. Character and performer are inextricably intertwined; they coalesce" (4). Cavell himself notes that "[t]he screen performer explores his role like an attic and takes stock of his physical and temperamental endowment; he lends his being to the role and accepts only what fits; the rest is nonexistent" (28). As Naremore observes, "[i]n the silent cinema... 'speech' require[s] a special technique. One of the actors' jobs [is] to speak occasionally, giving slightly exaggerated ostensiveness to tiny expressive movements of eyes, face, and hands" (48). Brooks' ability to respect and understand the conventions of silent filmmaking while exploiting them for laughs is evidenced in a delightful dancing sequence between Feldman's Eggs and Anne Bancroft. Eggs' pursuit of women in the film is only ever met with that perennially humorous experience, rejection. Here though, he enjoys some success. Bancroft first partners with Funn for a tango until he dips her head (accidentally) onto a table and spins her (shot sped-up) into the club's kitchen. She emerges after the collision partnered with Eggs. The first sequence with Funn is shot using full-body two shots, in which their bodies are tightly framed, and closer shots showing the two dancers primarily from the shoulders up to emphasize their faces. When Eggs takes over, the dance then attains a micro-level of movement. Instead of dancing with their bodies which now remain still, Eggs and Bancroft dance with their eyes, making full use of Feldman's bulging, misaligned pair. He moves his eyes around first, and then, in a call-and-response form of the dance, Bancroft responds, crossing her eyes, then darting them from side-to-side, before concluding with a bright grin.

Brooks' critique of silent film in *Silent Movie* also relies on his continued presence as the author/filmmaker/critic of the work. For Cavell, "stars of every magnitude ... have provided the movie camera with human subjects—individuals capable of filling its need for individualities, whose individualities in turn, whose inflection of demeanor and disposition were given full play in its projection" (35). Brooks' centrality in a character so closely connected to his star persona, without one of the most identifiable characteristics of his stardom, seems to resist the kind of performer-character assimilation that Klevan and Cavell remark upon. But this, as Cavell

Marty Eggs (Marty Feldman) and Anne Bancroft dance the tango with their eyes in *Silent Movie* (1976).

comments, is in fact appropriate. Brooks' retention of his individuality reminds his viewers of his authorship in performance and direction. Brooks' decision to remove his voice, evidence that he understands and is a worthwhile critic of the silent film, dispenses with what is iconographic to better serve the film—that is, at the same time, the piece of criticism—he has made.

For Roland Barthes, the individuality of one's voice—the "grain" as he terms it—goes beyond the materiality of the vocal chords and the sounds it produces: "[t]he 'grain' is the body in the singing voice, in the writing hand, in the performing limb" (276). Here it should be noted that there is an embodied, full-bodied, physiological quality to the grain—the individuality, the subjectivity, the essence—of one's voice. Enhancing Brooks' individuality, his stardom (central, if partial), his directorial voice, his authorial voice, and his critical voice sound in a chorus of silence as one, and so *Silent Movie* becomes a multi-faceted, multi-valent, multi-functional work of cinematic and critical art. As Kaufmann observes earlier, one reason to watch this piece of film criticism filmed, is because its author is an individual whose comedic sensibilities evidence his understanding of its cinematic heritage deemed aesthetically valuable from the opening credits. The removal of Brooks' material voice is highly appropriate because *Silent Movie* is less about its plot and more about the conventions of silent filmmaking—after all, individuals making a silent film themselves need not be silent. Charles Affron remarks that

> screen acting need not be limited by the flatness of the screen image. So much in the film medium conspires to free the actor, to relieve him of the burdens of naturalistic portrayal, to grant him the metaphorical power of great painting and sculpture, to offer him the high style of classical theatre and opera [3].

Paralleling the persona of the star with the character they are portraying, Affron suggests when watching stars like Lillian Gish, Greta Garbo, and Bette Davis, we "savor the delight of their rhythms and rhymes, the flow of their contours" (4). This diegesis and non-diegesis, a flowing, dialogic back-and-forth between the internal mechanics of plot and narrative and the external interests in silent film comedy, may also be attributed to the voice of Mel Brooks. Brooks may not possess the same sorts of rhythms, rhymes, and contours as Gish, Garbo, or Davis, but his individual comedic sensibility is evident in *Silent Movie*.

Absorption, Theatricality, and Film Criticism, Filmed

Responding to the (artistic and critical) work of Robert Morris, art historian Michael Fried develops his idea of theatricality, arguing that "the largeness of the piece, in conjunction with its nonrelational, unitary character, *distances* the beholder—not just physically but psychically. It is, one might say precisely this distancing that *makes* the beholder a subject and the piece in question ... an object" (154). Richard Rushton has brought Fried's observations about theatricality and its opposite—absorption—more firmly into the domain of film. Rushton notes how for Fried, cinema is apparently removed from the possibility of theatricality (227). According to Rushton, absorption is a term reserved for works of art "that try to present themselves as though they are not explicitly intended to be viewed by an audience" (227) whereas theatricality denotes "works of art that are conscious of, and which actively acknowledge, being looked at; they demonstrate to the audience that they are mere artefacts, made-up objects that are being paraded before an audience" (227).

Clarifying how these categories of art operate in relation to film, Rushton offers three definitions that inherit and extend Fried's observations. Non-theatrical cinema (generally speaking a correlate to classical fiction or narrative cinema) involves films which are experienced by audiences in "a state of absorption: the characters in a classical fiction film do not acknowledge the presence of the audience and therefore the audience members can believe that they are invisibly, secretly watching events unfold before them" (230). Theatrical cinema regards films that are "exhibitionist": "films that confront the audience in the form of trick effects, gripping chases, spectacular stunts, and demonstrations of events 'that could only ever happen on film'" (230). The third category is anti-theatrical cinema: "that form of cinema which takes neither absorption or theatricality for granted. It is that form of filmmaking which in many circles is referred to as 'modern' cinema.... It is the form of cinema that is aware both of the limitations and possibilities posed by the absorption/theatricality distinction" (230).

Silent Movie and *The Critic* are prime examples of cinema's interactions with theatricality and absorption. They display in differing ways the modernist tendencies of anti-theatrical cinema, joining the works of directors like Jean-Luc Godard, Sergei Eisenstein, Michelangelo Antonioni, John Cassavetes, Hou Hsiao-Hsien, Jacques Tati, Chantal Akerman, and many more. These hallmarks include "reflexivity, a capacity for irony, pastiche, self-reflection, of 'putting everything in quotation marks'" (Rushton 239). Here it should be noted that the relation between spectator and films displaying these modernist tendencies is extremely active. Rushton notes:

> what is essential to the modernness of the modern cinema...[is] the tendency of a work (a film, a painting) to go outside of itself in order to stretch the possibilities of what it can be, and furthermore, to stretch the capacities of the spectator's possibilities of what (or where, when, how) she/he can be [244].

Rushton describes this (borrowing Fried's terms) as a double bind, that is, an "approach that puts in question both the possibility of absorption and the possibility of theatricality" (244). At base, this double bind is a dialogue. Of course, such dialogues manifest themselves in many ways as films specifically reach outside themselves, shaping the interaction amongst spectator, work, and author.

In *The Critic*, we are witness not only to a film but also to an audible (though invisible) witness of that film. The film therefore is not simply what is visually represented—an animated, abstract work—because Brooks' unimpressed critic comments on it. The possibilities of spectatorial positioning in relation to *The Critic* shifts: viewers can eschew the critic's comments and focus on the specific work or consider the abstract figures and Brooks' spectator in tandem, engaging with the film's reflexive critique on spectatorship and the nature of criticism itself. *Silent Movie*'s relationship with criticism motivates a different kind of dialogue because of its unique engagement with theatricality and absorption. *Silent Movie* reaches out to a heritage of filmmaking that is afforded new possibilities because it is made in an era of sound. It reflexively examines stardom as a topic via cameos and in terms of authorship. Brooks' film is modern and anti-theatrical, because the spectator is constantly offered different possibilities in the richness of comedic details, the play between the presence and absence of sound, and the way in which there is no clearly demarcated line between diegesis and non-diegesis. One of the unique characteristics of comedy—and especially the form of comedy in which Brooks works—is that it is knowing, appreciative, and intelligent not just in terms of its "target" (in this case silent filmmaking) but also in the way in which it constantly plays to audiences. That is, *Silent Movie* draws spectators in and reaches out to them: it is theatrical at points, non-theatrical at others, and even aims in other moments for absorptive reception by the spectator. It is film criticism, filmed.

FILMOGRAPHY

Blazing Saddles: 30th Anniversary Special. Dir. Mel Brooks. Crossbow Productions, 1974. DVD. Warner, 2004.
The Critic. Dir. Ernest Pintoff. *Mel Brooks—The Critic (1963)*. YouTube, April 10, 2015, https://www.youtube.com/watch?v=PramR5oxn50Check.
High Anxiety. Dir. Mel Brooks. Twentieth Century Studios, 1977. DVD. Twentieth Century Fox Home Entertainment, 2006.
The History of the World, Part 1. Dir. Mel Brooks. Brooksfilms, 1981. DVD. Twentieth Century Fox, 2006.
Silent Movie. Dir. Mel Brooks. Crossbow Productions, 1976. DVD. Twentieth Century Fox Home Entertainment, 2006.
Young Frankenstein. Dir. Mel Brooks. Twentieth Century Fox, 1974. DVD. Twentieth Century Fox, 2014.

Works Cited

Affron, Charles. *Star Acting: Gish, Garbo, Davis*. E.P. Dutton, 1977.
Barthes, Roland. "The Grain of the Voice." *The Responsibility of Forms: Critical Essays on Music, Art, and Representation*, translated by Richard Howard, University of California Press, 1985, pp. 267-277.
Bresson, Robert. *Notes on the Cinematograph*. Translated by Jonathan Griffin, New York Review of Books, 1975.
Carroll, Noël. *On Criticism*. Routledge, 2009.
Cavell, Stanley. *The World Viewed: Enlarged Edition*. Harvard University Press, 1979.
Clayton, Alex, and Andrew Klevan. "Introduction: The Language and Style of Film Criticism." *The Language and Style of Film Criticism*, edited by Alex Clayton and Andrew Klevan, Routledge, 2011, pp. 1–26.
Critchley, Simon. *On Humor*. Routledge, 2002.
Fried, Michael. "Art and Objecthood." *Art and Objecthood*, University of Chicago Press, 1998, pp. 148–172.
Jenkins, Henry. "Mel Brooks, Vulgar Modernism, and Comic Remediation." *A Companion to Film Comedy*, edited by Andrew Horton and Joanna E. Rapf, Wiley-Blackwell, 2013, pp. 151–171.
Kauffmann, Stanley. "The Critic as Writer: Four Notes." *Salmagundi*, no. 137/138, 2003, pp. 41–47.
Klevan, Andrew. *Film Performance: From Achievement to Appreciation*. Wallflower Press, 2005.
Lysaker, John T. *Philosophy, Writing and the Character of Thought*. University of Chicago Press, 2018.
Naremore, James. *Acting in the Cinema*. University of California Press, 1988.
Ross, Stephanie. *Two Thumbs Up: How Critics Aid Appreciation*. University of Chicago Press, 2020.
Rushton, Richard. "Early, Classical and Modern Cinema: Absorption and Theatricality." *Screen*, vol. 45, no. 3, 2004, pp. 226–244.

"The Hitchcock picture to end all Hitchcock pictures"
Mel Brooks' High Anxiety *(1977)*

THOMAS GROCHOWSKI

Alfred Hitchcock's "Last" Film?

In 1976, Alfred Hitchcock released what would be his final film, *Family Plot*. His health had been failing him, and with the changes to Hollywood combined with his advancing years, it was only his third film since *Torn Curtain* a decade earlier. Hitchcock's final project, an adaptation of the Canadian Ronald Kirkbride's spy novel *The Short Night*, had originally been planned out in the late sixties, with shooting expected to take place in Finland, where part of the novel is set. However, Hitchcock opted to put off making the film, going to his home country to make *Frenzy*, and while various scriptwriters took on the *Short Night* project, Hitch returned to California to work on *Family Plot*. But in the summer of 1979, he told his assistant director and production manager Hilton Green that he was unable to continue to do the film, and he asked Green to tell Lew Wasserman (whose MCA corporation owned Universal and had represented Hitchcock for most of his Hollywood career) that he couldn't finish it.

However, there was another Hitchcock project being made in the late seventies, over at 20th Century–Fox studios, and it was made with Hitchcock's approval and modest support. One might even argue that Mel Brooks' *High Anxiety* (December 1977) is in fact *the* last Hitchcock film. Following their parodic takes on the western with *Blazing Saddles*, the classic thirties-era Universal horror films with *Young Frankenstein*, and the golden age of silent film comedy with *Silent Movie*, Brooks and his team of writers wanted to continue with genre parody. According to Brooks' recent memoir, he became excited when someone in the room suggested Hitchcock. Brooks enthusiastically agreed, saying: "He *is* a genre" (276). He took a lunch meeting with Hitchcock mainly to get his blessing, and the two subsequently met regularly in Hitchcock's offices to discuss ideas and gags for the film. Hitchcock's most noted gag suggestion, a delightful bit where the hero makes a jump onto a ferry to escape his pursuers, only to realize that his ferry is going *inbound* instead of *outbound*, was never filmed, being too expensive. While Hitchcock was still hoping to make *The Short Night* at the time of *High Anxiety*'s release, I wonder if he had felt that he should give Brooks the last word on the "Hitchcock film," much the way that *Blazing Saddles* is spoken of (albeit erroneously) as the last word on the Western.

High Anxiety received generally mixed reviews upon its release. It was funny, yes, but it did not have the outrageousness of *Blazing Saddles* nor the surprising humanism of *Young Frankenstein*. In addition to pointing out how the film paled in comparison to those earlier films, some critics argued that because Hitchcock's films are so loaded with droll, if dark, humor, there was no real reason to parody them. Roger Ebert, in his review, argued that it is not worthwhile to spoof "a director of such sophistication that half the audience won't even get the in-jokes the other half is laughing about" (rogerebert.com). "Being so self-aware," Vincent Canby wrote, "Hitchcock's films deny an easy purchase to the parodist" (30). Canby, however, admits that given how he observed "five-and-ten-year-olds" who didn't know anything about the Frankenstein films of yesteryear "collapsing with laughter" (30) at *Young Frankenstein*, he didn't think this would affect the way *High Anxiety* would be received. As one of those ten-year-olds who saw *High Anxiety* on its release—it is the first film I remember seeing at a theater on my own with friends, no adult supervision—I can safely say that Canby was correct in his assumption.

Only in this century has Brooks' work become more critically studied in academia. (Contrast the ounces of books on his films to the pounds of books on Woody Allen's work since the late seventies.) Earlier works have generally been slim trade-book volumes such as Nick Smurthwaite and Paul Gelder's *Mel Brooks and the Spoof Movie* and Neil Sinyard's *The Films of Mel Brooks*. David Desser and Lester Friedman's *American Jewish Filmmakers* examines the careers of four sons of Eastern European Jewish immigrants: Brooks, Allen, Sidney Lumet, and Paul Mazursky. Their chapter on Brooks delves deeply into the significance of Brooks' Jewish identity in the context of his film work, with discussion of his early career days in the Catskills and his experiences working as a writer for Sid Caesar. First published in 1993, *American Jewish Filmmakers* was published in a second edition just around the time Brooks was bringing *The Producers* to Broadway; over the chapter's fifty pages, the authors give about two to an extended discussion of *High Anxiety* (in contrast to the six on *Blazing Saddles*, which also figures in their discussion of Brooks' position as a cultural outsider and how it has informed all his work).

The recent wave of scholarship on Brooks is a very welcome addition to film studies. Arthur Symons, in his innovative study *Mel Brooks in the Cultural Industries*, argues that Brooks has been a masterful adapter, a "multimedia survivor" (3). Symons argues that we must consider Brooks' work across media: sketch comedy on television, TV genre parodies, sitcoms, audio media, and most recently, his Broadway success (*The Producers*) and failure (*Young Frankenstein*). Especially interesting is Symons' discussion of Brooks' lesser-known television work: his Robin Hood sitcom from the seventies, *When Things Were Rotten* and his late-eighties sitcom about a struggling hotel, *The Nutt House*. Symons offers a critique of adaptation studies, which its emphasis on textuality and not on the perspective of the adaptor. Much of *Mel Brooks in the Cultural Industries* focuses on the Brooksian perspective, situating Brooks in the broader context of the culture industries of the late 20th and early 21st centuries, the dynamic between artistic needs and commercial imperatives (especially for "presold" content to ensure success in film and television). Symons examines Brooks' capacity for "prolonged adaptation" (21), wherein Brooks repurposes his earlier work into different media contexts. The clearest example is the transformation of Brooks' 1967 cult classic *The Producers* into a multi–Tony-winning Broadway musical in 2001 (which in 2005 became a film adaptation, directed by the stage production's director Susan Stroman). Symons also details Brooks' gifts as an adapter/parodist from his days working for Sid Caesar (whose sketch series *Your Show of Shows* often featured parodies of popular films and TV shows) and his work with Caesar co-star and co-writer Carl Reiner in creating the 2000-Year-Old Man "routine," which initially began as an improvisational bit done at parties but became a series of record albums which were repurposed into an animated short film, and whose persona can be seen in several of Brooks' films and in his multiple–Emmy-winning role as Uncle Max in the nineties sitcom *Mad About You*.

Yet in his discussion of Brooks as a survivor and creator of prolonged adaptations, Symons barely addresses *High Anxiety*, and when he does it concerns Brooks as a performer rather the film's imitation of Hitchcock. Regarding a comic scene at San Francisco Airport, Symons addresses how Brooks adapts his 2000-Year-Old Man persona, transforming his successful academic protagonist into a loud stereotypically Jewish man. Concerning another scene where Brooks' protagonist sings the movie's theme song, Symons claims that the performance is adaptation of Brooks' Frank Sinatra imitation, then known to audiences from his appearances on talk shows such as Dick Cavett's. (It's not so much the voice Brooks imitates as the way Sinatra plays with phrasing: as his character sings, "hey ... ziety," one imagines Sinatra cutting off syllables as he sings.) Symons never discusses the film as a Hitchcock adaptation; in fact, he doesn't mention the film in the context of Hitchcock at all. This is curious, especially since he refers to Brooks' status as "survivor" in comparison to Hitchcock's own calculated, reputation-enhancing moves in Hollywood (10). It is unfortunate that in his chapter on "the rise of parody and the fall of Mel Brooks the Director," he devotes many pages to *Blazing Saddles* and *Young Frankenstein*, then skips to 1987 as a marker for Brooks' "fall," writing several pages on *Spaceballs* and finishing with Brooks' last two films, *Robin Hood: Men in Tights* and *Dracula: Dead and Loving It*—ignoring not only *High Anxiety* but also *History of the World Part I* which followed it and *Silent Movie* which preceded it. While Symons is largely correct to suggest that Brooks' eighties and nineties films were generally inferior to those of the Kentucky Fried Theater, the L.A.-based sketch comedy troupe responsible for the first *Airplane!* film and the *Police Squad!* series that eventually spawned three *Naked Gun* films, *High Anxiety* would be worth a more detailed discussion even in *that* context. Given that Symons is discussing Brooks' adaptive style across different media, a discussion of *High Anxiety* as a Hitchcock parody, and as a partial return to sketch-comedy format of his early years (with several set-pieces done in direct imitation of iconic Hitchcock scenes like *Psycho*'s shower-murder rather than directly advancing the plot) would further Symons' argument and would likely mark this transitional period of Brooks' critical "fall," given the mixed reviews it received.

Among other recent examples of Brooks scholarship, one can find similar omissions of *High Anxiety*. Noted Brooks scholar Beth Bonnstetter has published important essays on *Spaceballs*, *Blazing Saddles*, and *History of the World, Part I* (see Bonnstetter, "Of Structures, Stories, and *Spaceballs*"; Bonnstetter, "Mel Brooks Meets Kenneth Burke (and Mikhail Bakhtin)"; Ott and Bonnstetter, "'We're at Now, Now'") but not any extensive discussion of *High Anxiety*. In the recent anthology Bonnstetter co-edited with Samuel Boerboom, *The Political Mel Brooks*, there is hardly a mention of *High Anxiety* in its ten chapters. It's been over a decade since the publication of Robert Alan Crick's *The Big Screen Comedies of Mel Brooks*, a comprehensive critical (if fannish) assessment of all the films Brooks directed. Is it possible that the only extended *academic* analysis of *High Anxiety* remains Maurice Yacowar's chapter from his book-length study of Brooks from the early 1980s? The best I could find is an awkwardly translated essay from a Polish journal concerning Brooks' use of parody in the film, one that does not contain much more concrete insights than Yacowar, though this may be due to its translation (Piwińska).

Although the recent Brooks scholarship has ignored *High Anxiety*, it nonetheless provides some fruitful means through which we can interpret the film. I wish to draw on Ott and Bonnstetter's concept of "parodic tourism" (from their analysis of *Spaceballs*) to discuss the various Hitchcock references Brooks employs. Before doing so, I will address some of the theoretical issues of adaptation from Thomas Leitch and Kamilla Elliott, in particular Elliott's use of the concepts of "micro-adaptation" and "compendium." While generally dismissed as amusing though derivative of Hitchcock, *High Anxiety* is not simply an affectionate homage to "the Master" but an important examination of Hitchcock's significance. The film is also an examination of critical Hitchcock themes, though turned on their heads, in particular the role of the camera in creating in the audience a self-consciousness of the act of looking. In its mocking of psychoanalysis, *High Anxiety* also upends, albeit timidly, constructions of gender.

Before discussing some of the theoretical perspectives important to my discussion, a brief plot summary will be helpful. Brooks' protagonist, Richard H. (for Harpo) Thorndyke, is a prestigious psychiatrist and professor, who moves to Los Angeles to run the Psycho Neurotic Institute for the Very *Very* Nervous, taking over for the recently deceased Dr. Ashley. Thorndyke's "driver and sidekick" Brophy (Ron Carey) suggests that Ashley may have been the victim of foul play, and Thorndyke's encounters with the staff, notably Dr. Montague (Harvey Korman) and Nurse Diesel (Cloris Leachman), serve to make him question things further. He has reason to be suspicious: as it will be revealed later, the duo (who are involved in a sadomasochistic sexual relationship) have been bilking their wealthy clientele while keeping the rate of patient recovery to (according to Montague) "once in a blue moon." They are also willing to kill those who would expose them: they were responsible for Ashley's death, and they arrange for the killing of another colleague, Dr. Wentworth (Dick Van Patten), who seeks to leave the hospital because he has become too afraid of what is going on. Thorndyke also is reunited with his old professor "Professor Little Old Man" (Lillolman, played by *Your Show of Shows* co-star Howard Morris), who learns that Thorndyke still suffers from his fear of heights and high places, or "high anxiety." When Thorndyke goes to San Francisco to attend a medical conference, he is accosted by Victoria Brisbane (Madeline Kahn), who claims her wealthy industrialist father is a virtual prisoner there, and that she has not been allowed to visit. Thorndyke is being shadowed by a man called "Braces" (co-writer Rudy De Luca), a hired killer in Diesel and Montague's employ. When Thorndyke realizes that Victoria's father is not the same patient he met at the institute, Braces observes this discovery and reports to Diesel, who orders him to commit a murder at the hotel and frame Thorndyke for it. Thorndyke goes on the run when he is accused of murder, but because the front-page photograph of the killing, taken by Brophy (a shutterbug), can actually prove Thorndyke's *innocence*, Diesel tells Braces to kill the doctor. Thorndyke survives the attack and manages to return with Victoria to Los Angeles, where they confront Diesel and Montague's henchman Norton (Lee Delano), who is about to throw Victoria's father out of the belfry of the institute's tower. Lillolman helps Thorndyke realize that his true fears are not of heights, and he is able to rescue Brisbane; Norton is knocked unconscious, and Montague surrenders after Diesel rather dramatically charges out of the tower, riding a broom, to her death. Thorndyke and Victoria marry, with the film's final shot being of the pair in their honeymoon suite.

Adaptation Theory: From Continuum to Compendium

In *Film Adaptation and its Discontents*, Thomas Leitch outlines a "continuum" taxonomy of different types of adaptations, where an adaptation may be classified along the continuum between adaptation and allusion, with the acknowledgment that films can employ all the different parts of the continuum. He makes this latter argument with an extended discussion of Luhrmann's William Shakespeare's *Romeo + Juliet*, but his larger point is that many films can be analyzed in this manner. In between the two poles are celebrations, adjustments, neoclassical imitations, revisions, colonizations, deconstructions, analogies, parodies/pastiches, and "secondary, tertiary, and quaternary imitations" (120). (The 2005 Stroman film of the Broadway version of *The Producers* would be called a tertiary imitation.) Working off Kamilla Elliott's theoretical approaches/modes as presented in *Rethinking the Novel/Film Debate* and Gerard Genette's taxonomy of transtextuality, Leitch seeks to construct a "grammar that would either break down adaptation into nonevaluative modes like Elliott's or at least provide a stronger rationale for the difference between intertextual and hypertextual relations," a grammar that propounds to describe "hypertextual relations as they shade off into the intertextual" (95). However, Leitch himself recognizes that the slope between adaptation and allusion really is slippery, that the delineation between these two "points" is much less clear than adaptation studies has claimed (126).

Although Leitch discusses Brooks' work only in the context of "parody and pastiche," *High Anxiety* does incorporate many modalities along Leitch's continuum, beyond parody, pastiche, and allusion. It certainly is a celebration of Hitchcock's work (one that very much imitates Hitchcock's style), and an adjustment of the story of *North by Northwest*, by presenting that film's basic plot only in its second half. While two other films provide *High Anxiety*'s narrative, its overall conception is of a piece with the vision of *North by Northwest* screenwriter Ernest Lehman: "I wanted to write a definitive Hitchcock film—the Hitchcock film to end all Hitchcock films" (Brady 200). For Lehman, the idea was to pull out all the stops that had become associated with Hitchcock, which were Brooks and his writers' intention as well. *North by Northwest* is the culmination of one of the critical "plot formations" (to use Robin Wood's terms) of Hitchcock's *oeuvre*, that of the falsely accused man—in particular the falsely accused man who becomes mixed up with an espionage plot. It's a plot that Hitchcock first told in *The 39 Steps* and then in *Saboteur*. Brooks, like Lehman before him, is following in the Hitchcockian tradition, since Hitchcock very liberally reworked source material for his own purposes.

Leitch notes that "parody can be successfully deployed and recognized even in small doses within larger texts" (119). These "small doses" may be called "micro-adaptations," a term Kamilla Elliott uses in her discussion of Tim Burton's first *Alice in Wonderland* film. For Elliott, these micro-adaptations are central to the film's meaning, because "they determine the narrative structure" of it (197). Another term Elliott uses to describe the Burton film is "compendium," referring to its double meaning as a brief treatment of a subject and an inventory—a collection of micro-adaptations. In the case of Burton's *Alice*, Elliot perceives micro-adaptations of the then-recent Tolkien and Lewis adaptations, *The Wizard of Oz, Honey I Shrunk the Kids, Buffy the Vampire Slayer*, and even videogame narratives, as well as more generally the narrative structures of "the *bildungsroman*, the anti–Cinderella story, and the mythological hero plot" (195). Given the many micro-adaptations of Hitchcock in *High Anxiety*, we can address the criticism of those who see the film as more likely a pastiche than a parody, critics such as Pauline Kael, who in her review of the film argued that Brooks was simply demonstrating his knowledge of movies (73). Elliott's concept of compendium, alongside Ott and Bonnstetter's concept of parodic tourism, may offer a means of critical interpretation of Brooks' film in relation to Hitchcock's work.

High Anxiety is loaded with narrative, stylistic, and verbal micro-adaptations of Hitchcock and other cultural texts. The three films that form the major hypotexts for Brooks are *North by Northwest, Vertigo*, and *Spellbound*. Thorndyke's arrival at the Institute echoes the arrival of Gregory Peck's character as the new head of the psychiatric hospital of *Spellbound*, though it turns out the man is an amnesiac who has falsely remembered himself as the real director's killer. Thorndyke's fear of heights—itself related to a childhood trauma, like Peck's amnesiac—is a defining characteristic of *Vertigo*'s protagonist Scottie, played by James Stewart. The film's villains order their hired killer to commit a murder in public, while wearing a Thorndyke mask. Thorndyke's own arrival—after a confrontation with Braces, who takes off the Thorndyke mask and hands him the murder weapon, laughing as he enters a hotel elevator—fully connects Thorndyke to his Hitchcockian namesake, Roger O. Thornhill, Cary Grant's ad executive-mistaken-for-spy-mistaken-for-killer of *North by Northwest*. Brooks also adapts the three films in important stylistic ways. The last-minute therapy session between Thorndyke and his mentor visually represents the climbing of the stairs of Scottie and Madeline/Judy in *Vertigo* but also recalls the "ski-slope" therapy session between the amnesiac and doctor in *Spellbound*; the "high anxiety" imagery of Thorndyke's falling parodies Scottie's animated nightmare in *Vertigo*; and Thorndyke's arrival in the lobby moments after the murder Braces has committed wearing the mask is an imitation of how Thornhill is set up for the stabbing of Lester Townsend at the U.N.

In addition to the narrative and stylistic borrowings from these central three films, *High Anxiety* contains a compendium of micro-adaptations of other Hitchcock films. Nurse Diesel is an echo of Mrs. Danvers from *Rebecca* and to a lesser extent Alex Sebastian's mother in *Notorious*; the killer Braces evokes Barry Foster's Bob Rusk (the "necktie killer") in *Frenzy*, and his attempted murder of Thorndyke in a phone booth also recalls the attempted murder of Grace Kelly's Margot in *Dial M for Murder*, which also ends in the assassin being killed with a sharp object; in her first scene, Victoria Brisbane behaves like an exaggerated version of Annabella Smith in *The 39 Steps*, demanding Thorndyke get down on his knees and go toward the window to close the shades. Dr. Wentworth's death is preceded by a scene that shows him in Diesel's office, pleading to be allowed to leave the Institute; the shadow of the window seems to trap Wentworth as he says, "I feel like I've been caught in a web!" The framing of Wentworth in shadow is a direct allusion to a shot in *Suspicion*, as Joan Fontaine's Lina returns to her home, devastated by her presumption that her husband Johnnie is not merely a gambler and a thief but also a murderer. Prior to his death, Wentworth is shown driving in the rain, in horrid conditions reminiscent of those Marion Crane drives through on her way to her doom. Wentworth is killed because he is a "man who knew too much." When Thorndyke learns that his hotel room reservation has been changed to a higher floor at the hotel, he is told that a "Mr. MacGuffin" called and changed it, "MacGuffin" famously being the term Hitchcock used to describe any "thing" that the main characters are seeking, like a piece of microfilm in *North by Northwest*. After being set up for murder, Thorndyke calls Victoria and asks to meet him at the "north by northwest corner" of Golden Gate Park—a meeting that does not take place because he is attacked by birds.

The film also inventories an apparently random selection of other cultural texts. In addition to her connection to Mrs. Danvers, Nurse Diesel also recalls Louise Fletcher's Nurse Ratched from *One Flew Over the Cuckoo's Nest*, and her death scene recalls Margaret Hamilton's Wicked Witch of the West, flying on her broom in *The Wizard of Oz*. The plot point of Brooks' predecessor's plans to make changes at the Institute—sidetracked by Diesel's claim that Ashley wanted to change the drapes only—recalls Minelli's adaptation of William Gibson's novel *The Cobweb* (see Crick 112; also Kael 73). The hotel desk clerk (Jack Riley) calls out for the bellboy Dennis (co-writer and future director/producer Barry Levinson) by calling out "oh, Dennis" in a direct imitation of Jack Benny calling out to Dennis Day, one of the singers on Benny's long-running radio and television comedy show. Brophy's blowing up of the photograph to show that Thorndyke was in the hotel's glass elevator at the time when Braces committed the murder is an exaggeration of a similar scene from Michelangelo Antonioni's *Blow-Up*, and the picture's status as a front-page story also recalls Henry Hathaway's newspaper picture *Call Northside 777*, where James Stewart's reporter uses a newspaper photograph, blown up to show the date of a newspaper being held by a newsie in the picture (talk about self-awareness!) to help free a man wrongly convicted of murder. Even in these apparently arbitrary allusions, Brooks employs them to draw comparisons and to enforce our awareness of *High Anxiety* as a self-conscious film, one the calls for us to engage with it as a text, not just as a story. Or, we might suggest, a *tour* of Hitchcock's art.

Parodic Tourism

In their discussion of *Spaceballs*, Ott and Bonnstetter discuss the concept of parodic tourism, a textual practice "which invites viewers to actively *participate* in structured, intertextual allusions" (312). In their reading, *Spaceballs* works off the science fiction genre, itself "a form of leisure and pleasure [involving] visual journeys to extraordinary places" that contains at least the "potential ... to activate a tourist gaze" (315). While ostensibly a parody of the first-produced *Star Wars* trilogy, *Spaceballs* really functions as a "meta-science-fiction film, where the extraordinary object of the tourist gaze is not the fictional universe of the story, but science fiction films themselves," a "cultural museum that takes the audience on a tour of science-fiction texts, of their underlying codes" (315).

As is the case with what we might call conventional tours, *Spaceballs* "has several built-in-stops" where its central narrative "appears not to be progressing" (316), but Ott and Bonnstetter posit that the film incorporates the touring process by representing the tourist in the person of the film's villain Dark Helmet and the tour guide in the person of his "wing man" Colonel Sandurz (forgive me), most famously in the scene where, after having overshot their targets by jumping to Ludicrous Speed, Sandurz suggests that they find them by watching a videocassette of the film itself, via a "new breakthrough in home video marketing: instant cassettes ... out in stores before the movie is finished." This famous self-reflexive moment, where the two central villains watch the first half of the film (at fast-forward speed, if not Ludicrous Speed) and come to the point where "we're at now, now," watching themselves watching themselves, is a critical aspect of what makes *Spaceballs* different even from earlier Brooks parodies such as *Blazing Saddles*, which concludes with the western narrative suddenly spilling out onto the Warner Brothers' studio lot. For Ott and Bonnstetter, the entire film is aware of itself as a construction, built as a "tour" of the genre as part of its parody, with the discussion of merchandising becoming part of the film's satiric and prophetic edge.

Following Ott and Bonnstetter, we can make a similar claim about *High Anxiety* as a form of parodic tourism as well. Once again Brooks seems to be following tradition: when Universal opened its theme park in 1965, the studio included a revamped tour and featured Hitchcock's work, with the Bates Motel remaining a fixture at both theme park locations. *High Anxiety* may not be as allegorically a tour of Hitchcock in the way that *Spaceballs* is a tour whose subject is the sci-fi film genre (there is no stand-in for the audience-tourist, for example), but it too takes its

In the famous shower-murder sequence in *Psycho* (1960), Marion Crane (Janet Leigh) stands in the shower, oblivious to the figure behind the curtain (left) who has just entered the bathroom.

audience through a tour of Hitchcock's iconic work. As in *Spaceballs*, *High Anxiety* provides sequences that are structured mainly for the purpose of being looked at much as tourists must look at the views on a tour, including scene reenactments or set reproductions if they are on a movie studio tour. (A popular stop at Universal allows the tourist to "fall" off the Statue of Liberty like Norman Lloyd's spy in *Saboteur*.) For Ott and Bonnstetter, a crucial aspect of parodic tourism is the way that it provides a coping strategy for the postmodern world, a world saturated by images. In relation to *Spaceballs*, *High Anxiety* is an ur-text of parodic tourism, telling a mainly cogent story while peppering its text with multiple allusions to Hitchcock films and other popular cultural texts ranging from *The Wizard of Oz* to *One Flew Over the Cuckoo's Nest* to Jack Benny's radio/tv program, and also taking "breaks" in the central narrative to offer detailed homages to specific iconic Hitchcock scenes. While Canby is correct about the reactions of ten-year-olds to the film, who laughed without necessarily getting every Hitchcock reference, tourists of *High Anxiety* will in fact get a more "enriched" experience of specific exhibits (Ott and Bonnstetter 317) if they know to what these exhibits refer.

While Crick is correct to claim that *High Anxiety* contains a well-structured narrative, even he admits that the most popular scenes in the film do not advance the plot, and thus are akin to the "built-in stops" Ott and Bonnstetter discuss regarding *Spaceballs*. In two of the most famous such scenes, Brooks transforms Hitchcockian acts of violence into comic set pieces. Having arrived at the hotel for the medical conference, Thorndyke keeps asking Dennis the bellboy to bring him a newspaper, but Dennis keeps ignoring the request and gets increasingly angered by Thorndyke's persistent asking. Soon after settling into his room, Thorndyke undresses to take a shower; Brooks shoots the sequence in an identical fashion to Hitchcock in the famous murder from *Psycho*. Shots of Thorndyke disrobing, the shower, and various close-ups of his body are edited much as Hitchcock edited the shots of Marion Crane. Right on cue (at least for audiences taking this tour), a silhouette appears behind the curtain: it is Dennis, holding a rolled-up newspaper, shrieking, "Here's your paper!" repeatedly, as the blows fall on Thorndyke. Brooks also mimics the final shot of the victim, moving from a tight closeup of the eye, circling away, to reveal the full face; since Thorndyke is not dead, he gives the scene's punchline: "That boy gets no tip." Later, after the murder for which he has been set up, Thorndyke sits on a bench in Golden Gate Park. He is waiting for Victoria Brisbane to arrive, when pigeons begin to gather, slowly. Their arrival in the frame takes the audience/tourists "back" to the 1962 Hitchcock film, but when suddenly a dropping appears on Thorndyke's shoulder, the audience is also taken back to *Blazing Saddles* and the famous baked beans scene. Thorndyke begins to make a run for it, but the birds keep shitting on him. The plot point that began the scene—the intended meeting of Thorndyke with Victoria, as he tries to stay out of jail for murder—has been itself shit on, for the sake of one of the larger laughs the film presents. These "stops" on the "Hitchcock tour" might arguably blunt the terror and shock of the violence of the original films, but by 1977, Hitchcock had become an institution, his work commodified by Universal itself via tourism.

Another scene that also appears not to advance the plot nonetheless resonates with Brooks' interests in "playing" with Hitchcock: the scene at the hotel bar where Thorndyke sings "High Anxiety." Yacowar points out that several critics didn't see the scene as particularly Hitchcockian, but he argues that it is very much in keeping with ideas and forms found in Hitchcock. Indeed, he sees the song paralleling Doris Day's performance of "Que Sera Sera" in *The Man Who Knew Too Much* (1956). More in line with gendered expectations, Yacowar suggests that in this moment, Thorndyke, or rather, Brooks himself, "is a Hitchcock hero, suave like Robert Donat, Bob Cummings, Jimmy Stewart, Cary Grant, and capable of public grace" (163). This "romantic self-projection points to the hero-identification and vicarious wish-fulfillment that is crucial to Hitchcock's casting and romance" (163). Numerous biographers have discussed the contrasting personas of Hitchcock's two most famous leading men, Stewart and Grant, and of Hitch's desire to "be" like the latter but generally seemed fated to be more like the former, especially Stewart's Scottie of *Vertigo*. Desser and Friedman, writing about *High Anxiety*, discuss how Brooks "inject[s] his particular brand of Jewish humor" in an environment that is comparatively "ethnically stale" (146), when considering Hitchcock's casting of actors like Grant and Stewart, but also Donat, Rod Taylor, Grace Kelly, Tippi Hedren, and Janet Leigh—though they mistakenly refer to the Catholic, Jesuit-educated Hitchcock as an "archetypal Wasp director" (162). These "stops" along the "tour," which supposedly have nothing to do with the film's plot, are very much tied to the film's themes.

The varied micro-adaptations of Hitchcock in *High Anxiety* serve not merely as signposts. Brooks is not simply showing off his knowledge of film, as Kael suggests he is. Rather, Brooks mimics Hitchcock's visual style to reinforce the significance of Hitchcock's themes, notably that of the dynamic between audience and central characters. Brooks describes Hitchcock's camera as "another one of his characters" (289) itself. What made Hitchcock stand out so much among even the most critically acclaimed Classical-era Hollywood directors was the way he implicated his audience in the process of revealing his narrative. Where many dramatic films of that era effaced their making, using an editing style that

"The Hitchcock picture to end all Hitchcock pictures" (Grochowski) 171

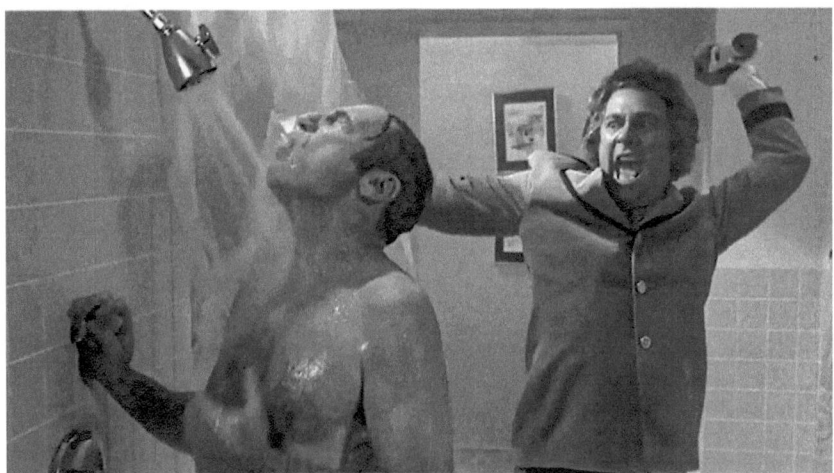

With the shower curtain pulled away in *High Anxiety* (1977), the bellboy Dennis (Barry Levinson) is about to attack Thorndyke (Mel Brooks) with the newspaper Thorndyke kept asking him to bring him. Holding both actors in the two-shot and identifying the attacker creates one of the biggest laughs in the movie.

was as unobtrusive as possible, Hitchcock's films put his audience in many uncomfortable circumstances through point-of-view editing. In some films, notably *Rear Window*, this was very much the intent; consider the iris shot of Raymond Burr's Lars Thorwald looking directly at the camera representing the telescopic camera lens of James Stewart's L.B. Jeffries, as Thorwald realizes he has been watched and (correctly) suspected of murder by his neighbor. There is often a sense of how the audience is snooping in on private scenes in a Hitchcock film. As Robert Stam and Roberta Pearson point out, we the audience "do not merely watch [Jeffries] performing actions; we perform the identical action—looking" (140).

The camera/audience-as-voyeur is prominent in Hitchcock's visual style going back at least as far as his first prominent silent film *The Lodger*, as he often presents secret actions and conversations that emphasize their privacy and often increase tension. The long shot of the Rutland publishing office that shows Marnie opening the safe and stealing money while a cleaning woman begins to mop the floor comes to mind; the audience is as helpless to warn Marnie (or the cleaning woman?) as Jeffries is helpless regarding Lisa's entry into Thorwald's apartment. In *The Lodger*, the Buntings have growing concerns about their new boarder as they hear him pace above their living room; Hitchcock represents this by using glass for the floor to show what they can hear but what the audience cannot. The Bates Motel features the infamous peephole allowing Norman to look at

Marion unobserved. In a very stylized moment from *North by Northwest*, Hitchcock uses a camera movement of an overhead shot just as the villain Vandamm and his assistant Leonard discuss what the former will do with his girlfriend Eve, now that they know she is a spy: as the camera moves upward, Vandamm explains, "This matter is best disposed of at a great height, over water." It is a scene overheard by Thornhill, who has been attempting to prevent Eve from getting on Vandamm's plane overseas.

In *High Anxiety*, Brooks uses the camera in much the same manner, comically pointing to its voyeuristic tendencies. Shortly after they learn from Braces that Thorndyke knows about the false Arthur Brisbane, Diesel and Montague discuss what to do while having coffee and dessert. The camera's point of view is from underneath the glass coffee table, which is filled with plates and cups; as Diesel and Montague put their "stuff" down, they block the camera's view, and the camera must move around to "find" them again. The dialogue is reminiscent of a scene in *Notorious* between Alex Sebastian and his mother when they discover that his wife Alicia is in fact a spy, and the use of the glass is an evocation of the scene from *The Lodger* described above. The scene ends abruptly and comically, with Diesel forcefully placing down a large tray, completely cutting off the camera's view.

An earlier dinner sequence begins with a long shot outside the dining room of the main building, where the staff have gathered for dinner. As the camera slowly moves in, it continues through the glass, crashing through the window, causing the members of the dinner party to "stare at us reproachfully" (Yacowar 157). Thus, "Brooks draws attention to our intrusion" (157) and makes us overtly aware of what Hitchcock often does in a more subtle fashion: how the camera, especially Hitchcock's camera, creates complicity for the audience in the central characters' moral choices, many of which are questionable. The film closes with a shot of Thorndyke and Victoria Brisbane (now Mrs. Thorndyke) about to make love in their honeymoon suite, and as the camera tracks back, the crewmembers are heard whispering, "Be careful!" and crashing through the room's window, again drawing reproachful looks.

In addition to comically pointing to the way Hitchcock's camera implicates his audiences, *High Anxiety* considers a topic of significance in many Hitchcock films, that of psychoanalysis. It was an important topic for Brooks, who himself often cited his experiences in psychotherapy as crucial for achieving some measure of emotional stability. (Brooks has also spoken of having suffered some form of PTSD as a World War II combat soldier.) Yacowar argues that in its exploration of a Hitchcockian theme of childhood trauma's impact on adults (like the Peck character in *Spellbound*), *High Anxiety* is "one of Brooks's most personal and revealing works" (161) in its reflection of Brooks' position as a social outsider, a son of European immigrant Jews, who seeks acceptance in mainstream American society amid various traumas from his past.

High Anxiety also playfully critiques psychoanalysis in its representation of how many of the educated characters, trained in a medical field, seem to have issues that take them toward a child-like state. In writing about *Rear Window*, Stam and Pearson note cinema's historical connection with psychoanalysis and dreamwork: working off the theories of Baudry, they write, "The cinema ... constitutes the approximate material realization of the unconscious goal of returning to an earlier state of psychic development" (139). The male characters especially have issues related to infantilism. (Indeed, Lillolman's dramatic therapy session reveals to Thorndyke that "it's not heights I'm afraid of—it's parents!") Thorndyke calls for "momma" in his dreams as he confronts his acrophobia; Montague cries out for "mommy" as Diesel spanks him in their bondage play; the killer "Braces" is named that because he wears braces on his teeth, a rarity for adults in 1977; Brophy behaves like a well-meaning, child-like sidekick, "not smart enough to have a mental breakdown," as Thorndyke points out; and Dennis the bellboy's attack on Thorndyke in the shower is a classic temper tantrum. Additionally, in an amusing moment during his keynote speech at the psychiatrists' convention, Thorndyke and his colleagues are reduced to baby-talk in a discussion surrounding topics such as penis envy when one attendee brings his young daughters to the speech.

After he sings the title song at the hotel lounge, Thorndyke demurs at Victoria Brisbane's suggestion that he should have become an entertainer, by saying, "the big bucks are in psychiatry." Indeed they are, as the film's central plot concerns the corruption at the Institute, which is partly related to the sexual "deviancy" of Diesel and Montague; they bilk their wealthy patients, who never get well. They are in a sense the "id" to Thorndyke's "ego," acting rapaciously in their efforts to collect as much of "the real money" as possible. When Thorndyke reviews a patient history with Montague, bringing the patient in for an interview, Montague re-ignites the patient's symptoms of neck pain and visions of werewolves by furtively shooting him with balled paper and putting plastic teeth in his mouth, playing the part behind Thorndyke's back as the patient recoils in horror.

In addition to emphasizing the psychological deviancy of many of its characters, *High Anxiety* also comically upends gender roles, in ways that offer an ambivalent statement regarding gender construction. Hitchcock criticism has long debated his work's representations of gender and sexuality as well, going back at least to Laura Mulvey's landmark "Visual Pleasure and Narrative Cinema," first published in 1975.[1] Montague wears

Diesel's underwear as part of their bondage play. Diesel challenges gender conventions in the way she wields power and in her mannish moustache (a touch put in by Leachman herself). In interviews (see Yacowar), Brooks has mentioned the way he lived out a fantasy in playing Thorndyke, since he got a chance to play up being a character such as Cary Grant's in *North by Northwest*. However, we can also connect Brooks to several "Hitchcock blondes," not just Grant, or Stewart, or Donat. I have mentioned Yacowar's observation about Thorndyke's singing recalling Doris Day as much as it evokes Sinatra. Early in the film, after his arrival at LAX, he meets Brophy, who repeatedly snaps photos of his new boss. Thorndyke is at first confused but then subsequent shots show him explicitly posing. Brophy's shutterbug hobby connects him to *Rear Window*'s photojournalist Jeffries, while the styled posing of Thorndyke comically suggests Grace Kelly's Lisa Carol Fremont, who models and works in the fashion business. Brooks also "plays" Kelly's character Margot in *Dial M for Murder*, in the scene where Thorndyke's phone call to Victoria is interrupted by Braces' attempt to strangle him. In the Hitchcock film, Margot's husband calls her solely to get her on the phone so that she may be strangled from behind. He listens to the struggle, waiting for the killer's signal that the job is done, a signal that never comes because Margot finds a pair of scissors, on which the killer is eventually impaled. Brooks has Thorndyke, on a payphone, suddenly attacked by Braces, and Victoria listens, thinking it's an obscene phone call, which both repulses and arouses her. (The call ends with Braces also impaled on a sharp object, a piece of broken glass from the phone booth.) The bird attack connects Thorndyke/Brooks to Tippi Hedren, and as discussed above, he also very directly plays Janet Leigh in the shower sequence of *Psycho*. In his play with psychoanalysis, Brooks destabilizes the notions of identity, sexual and even ethnic, as Yacowar notes.

    Hitchcock famously said that his movies were not slices of life, but slices of cake. *High Anxiety* offers a multi-tiered cake, reflecting back on Hitchcock's capacity for making his audience both entertained and uncomfortable. For writers like Crick, the film's success lies in its cogent story, one that can hold up well even for audiences that don't know Hitchcock's work. For tourists in the know, the film offers even richer pleasures, but that does not necessarily make it a "mere" pastiche. In its repurposing of Hitchcock, Brooks follows in the master's footsteps by molding his source material into his own, giving his Brooksian take on the significance of Hitchcock's camera and the many complex themes found in his work. It's not "the Hitchcock picture to end all Hitchcock pictures" (Brian De Palma refuses to let it be so), but rather, *High Anxiety* is a reminder of what Hitchcock accomplished in his half-century of filmmaking.

Note

1. Tania Modeleski's new chapter on *Marnie* in the third edition of her important *The Women Who Knew Too Much* demonstrates the continued significance of Hitchcock in feminist theory, as she further articulates the ambiguities in Hitchcock's gender/sexuality representations. There are many more critical examinations of the complex questions of gender and sexuality in Hitchcock's work, but space does not permit me to address them all here.

Filmography

Airplane! Dirs. Jim Abrahams, David Zucker and Jerry Zucker. Paramount Pictures and Howard W. Koch Productions. DVD. Paramount, 2017.
Alice in Wonderland. Dir. Tim Burton. Walt Disney Pictures, Roth Films and Zanuck Company, 2010. DVD. Walt Disney Studios Home Entertainment, 2010.
Blazing Saddles: 30th Anniversary Special Edition. Dir. Mel Brooks. Crossbow Productions, 1974. DVD. Warner, 2004.
Blow-Up. Dir. Michelangelo Antonioni. Metro-Goldwyn-Meyers, Premier Productions, Carlo Ponti Productions, Bridge Films, 1966. DVD. Video Service Corp., 2017.
Buffy the Vampire Slayer. Dir. Fran Rubel Kuzui. Sandollar Productions and Kuzui Enterprises, 1992. DVD. Twentieth Century Fox, 2017.
Call Northside 777. Dir. Henry Hathaway. Twentieth Century Fox, 1948.
The Cobweb. Dir. Vincente Minnelli. Metro-Goldwyn-Mayer, 1955. DVD. Warner Archives, 2011.
Dial M for Murder. Dir. Alfred Hitchcock. Warner Bros., 1954. DVD. Warner Bros. Home Video, 2009.
Dracula: Dead and Loving It. Dir. Mel Brooks. Gaumont, Brooksfilms and Castle Rock Entertainment, 1995. DVD. Warner Bros. Home Video, 2008.
Family Plot. Dir. Alfred Hitchcock. Universal Pictures, 1976. DVD. Universal Studios Home Entertainment, 2006.
Frenzy. Dir Alfred Hitchcock. Universal Pictures, 1972. DVD. Universal Studios Home Entertainment, 2006.
High Anxiety. Dir. Mel Brooks. Twentieth Century Studios, 1977. DVD. Twentieth Century Fox Home Entertainment, 2006.
History of the World Part I. Dir. Mel Brooks. Brooksfilms, 1981. DVD. Twentieth Century Fox, 2006.
Honey I Shrunk the Kids. Dir. Joe Johnston. Walt Disney Pictures and Silver Screen Partners III, 1989. DVD. Walt Disney Studios Home Entertainment, 2005.
The Lodger: A Story of the London Fog. Dir. Alfred Hitchcock. Gainsborough Pictures, 1927. DVD. Desert Island Films, 2012.
Mad About You. Created by Paul Reiser and Danny Jacobson. In Front Productions (1992–1999), Nuance Productions, TriStar Television (1992–1999), NBC, 1992–1999.
The Man Who Knew Too Much. Dir. Alfred Hitchcock. Filwite Productions Inc. and Spinel Entertainment, 1956. DVD. Universal Studios Home Entertainment, 2006.
North by Northwest. Dir. Alfred Hitchcock. Metro-Goldwyn-Mayer, 1959. DVD. Turner Classic Movies, 2010.
Notorious. Dir. Alfred Hitchcock. RKO Radio Pictures and Vanguard Films, 1946. DVD. Video Service Corp., 2019.
One Flew Over the Cuckoo's Nest. Dir. Miloš Forman. Fantasy Films, 1975. DVD. Warner Bros. Home Video, 2010.
Police Squad! Created by David Zucker, Jim Abrahams, and Jerry Zucker. Paramount Television. ABC, 1982.
The Producers. Dir. Mel Brooks. Embassy Pictures, 1967. DVD. MGM (Video & DVD), 2003.

176 אויסגעקליבן ווערק / Selected Works (1965–1991)

Psycho. Dir. Alfred Hitchcock. Shamley Productions, 1960. DVD. Universal Studios Home Entertainment, 2012.
Rear Window. Dir. Alfred Hitchcock. Patron, Inc., 1954. DVD. Universal Studios Home Entertainment, 2009.
Robin Hood: Men in Tights. Dir. Mel Brooks. Brooksfilms and Gaumont, 1993. DVD. Twentieth Century Fox Entertainment, 2009.
Romeo + Juliet. Dir. Bas Luhrmann. Bazmark Productions, 1996. DVD. Twentieth Century Fox, 2003.
Saboteur. Dir. Alfred Hitchcock. Frank Lloyd Productions and David O. Selznick Productions, 1942. DVD. Universal Studios Home Entertainment, 2007.
Silent Movie. Dir. Mel Brooks. Crossbow Productions, 1976. DVD. Twentieth Century Fox, 2006.
Spaceballs. Dir. Mel Brooks. Metro-Goldwyn Mayer, Brooksfilms and Industrial Light and Magic, 1978. DVD. MGM, 2015.
Spellbound. Dir. Alfred Hitchcock. Selznick International Pictures and Vanguard Films. DVD. MGM (Video & DVD), 2008.
Suspicion. Dir. Alfred Hitchcock. RKO Pictures, Inc., 1941. DVD. Warner Bros. Home Video, 2009.
The 39 Steps. Dir. Alfred Hitchcock. Gaumont-British Picture Corporation, 1935. DVD. Criterion, 2012.
Torn Curtain. Dir. Alfred Hitchcock. Universal Pictures, 1966. DVD. Universal Studios Home Entertainment, 2006.
Vertigo. Dir. Alfred Hitchcock. Alfred J. Hitchcock Productions, 1958. DVD. Universal Studios, 1999.
The Wizard of Oz: 70th Anniversary Edition. Dir. Victor Fleming. Metro-Goldwyn-Mayer, 1939. DVD. Warner Home Video, 2009.
Young Frankenstein. Dir Mel Brooks. Gruskoff/Venture Films, Crossbow Productions, Inc., and Jouer Limited, 1974. DVD. Twentieth Century Fox, 2014.
Your Show of Shows. Created by Sylvester L. Weaver, Jr. Max Liebman Productions. NBC, 1950–54.

Works Cited

Boerboom, Samuel, and Beth Bonnstetter, eds. *The Political Mel Brooks*. Rowman and Littlefield, 2019.
Bonnstetter, Beth. "Mel Brooks Meets Kenneth Burke (and Mikhail Bakhtin): Comedy and Burlesque in Satiric Film." *Journal of Film and Video*, vol. 63, no. 1, 2011, pp. 18–31.
⸺. "Of Structures, Stories, and *Spaceballs*: Parody as Criticism of Genre Film and Myth." *Sith, Slayers, Stargates, + Cyborgs: Modern Mythology in the New Millennium*, edited by David Whitt and John Perlich, Peter Lang, 2008, pp. 190–210.
Brady, John. *The Craft of the Screenwriter: Interviews with Six Celebrated Screenwriters*. Simon & Schuster, 1982.
Brooks, Mel. *All About Me! My Remarkable Life in Show Business*. Ballantine, 2021.
Canby, Vincent. "Mel Brooks in *High Anxiety*" (Review). *New York Times*, December 26, 1977, p. 30.
Crick, Robert Alan. *The Big Screen Comedies of Mel Brooks*. McFarland, 2002.
Desser, David, and Lester Friedman. *American Jewish Filmmakers*. 2nd edition, U of California P, 2002.
Ebert, Roger. "*High Anxiety*." rogerebert.com. https://www.rogerebert.com/reviews/high-anxiety-1978.
Kael, Pauline. "The Current Cinema: Fear of Heights." *The New Yorker*, January 9, 1978, pp. 70, 73–74.
Modleski, Tania. *The Women Who Knew Too Much: Hitchcock and Feminist Theory*. 3rd edition, Routledge, 2016.

Mulvey, Laura. "Visual Pleasure and Narrative Cinema." *Screen*, vol. 16, no. 3, 1975, pp. 6–18.
Ott, Brian, and Beth Bonnstetter. "'We're at Now, Now': *Spaceballs* as Parodic Tourism." *The Southern Communication Journal*, vol. 72, no. 4, 2007, pp. 309–327.
Piwińska, Maria. "Entertainment in the Media: Parody in 'High Anxiety' by Mel Brooks." *Zeszyty Prasoznawcze*, vol. 60, no. 4, 2017, pp. 866–879.
Sinyard, Neil. *The Films of Mel Brooks*. Exeter Books, 1987.
Smurthwaite, Nick, and Paul Gelder. *Mel Brooks and the Spoof Movie*. Proteus, 1982.
Stam, Robert, and Roberta Pearson. "Hitchcock's *Rear Window*: Reflexivity and the Critique of Voyeurism." *Enclitic*, vol. 7, no. 1 1983, pp. 136–145.
Symons, Arthur. *Mel Brooks in the Cultural Industries*. Edinburgh UP, 2012.
Wood, Robin. *Hitchcock's Films Revisited*. Revised edition, Columbia UP, 2002.
Yacowar, Maurice. *Method in Madness: The Comic Art of Mel Brooks*. St. Martin's Press, 1981.

Hitchcock, Brooks, and Pure Cinema

Douglas C. MacLeod, Jr.

> "The length of a film should be directly related to the endurance of the human bladder."
> —Alfred Hitchcock

Introduction

Not generally remembered for his cinematic wit, Alfred Hitchcock did periodically direct comedies (*The Trouble with Harry* [1955]), incorporate comedic moments in his suspense thrillers (Joseph and Herbie speaking about the ways they would murder each other in *Shadow of a Doubt* [1943]), and add silly, sometimes downright ridiculous, monologues at the beginning and ending of each *Alfred Hitchcock Presents* (1955–1962) episode. As Mel Brooks points out in *All about Me!: My Remarkable Life in Show Business*, when talking about *High Anxiety* (1977), his parody of Hitchcock as genre, Hitchcock was "very funny," and his films "used a lot of dark humor to heighten the tension" (278). The way Hitchcock was able to combine nail-biting thrills with scenes of dry hilarity was through his use of what he called "pure cinema," a type of storytelling, using filmic techniques Brooks would need to embrace to produce a proper parodic homage to "The Master of Suspense." Painstaking and thorough, Brooks watched "every Hitchcock film over and over again" (289) to be able to emulate the look and style of Hitchcock's pictures; and, ultimately, *High Anxiety* successfully houses takeoffs of all Hitchcock's unforgettable moments. Parodying such films as *Spellbound* (1945), *Strangers on a Train* (1951), *Rear Window* (1954), *Vertigo* (1958), *North by Northwest* (1959), *Psycho* (1960), and *The Birds* (1963), *High Anxiety* is "an act of homage to a great artist" who "could really manipulate an audience's emotions [by going] from light comedy to stark drama" (279), using "pure cinema" and techniques like subjective camerawork, montage, and the implementation of the MacGuffin to excite the masses and evoke nervous laughter.

Hitchcock's and Brook's Pure Cinema (Subjectivity)

In a 1963 interview with director and film aficionado Peter Bogdanovich, Hitchcock defines pure cinema as "complementary pieces of film put together, like notes of music make a melody" ("Peter Bogdonovich interviews Alfred Hitchcock [1963]"). As abstract as that may sound, Hitchcock believes to compose a filmic melody, editing needs to take place; however, Hitchcock suggests continuity editing is not the way to accomplish this specific goal. He says, "There are two primary uses of cutting or montage in film: montage to create ideas—and montage to create violence and emotions" ("Peter Bogdonovich interviews Alfred Hitchcock [1963]"). To clarify Hitchcock's definition, Bruce Isaacs in his 2020 book about dramatic homages to Hitchcock titled *The Art of Pure Cinema: Hitchcock and his Imitators*, points out, "[f]or Hitchcock, like Dulac, a cinema of movement was also a cinema of rhythm and sensation" (17). Hitchcock "explicitly aligns pure cinema with montage, or the creative possibilities of editing," which "seeks to interrupt the flow of a normative spectatorial perception" (Isaacs 19). In turn, Hitchcock's cinema converts viewers into the "flawed protagonist," watching his or her mark with a "perverse" and "fragmented, decentered, and inadequate gaze," rather than with a contrived "omniscience" (19).

To illustrate his suggestion, Isaacs speaks to Hitchcock's classic *Vertigo*, which is considered a visual manifestation of one man's fall into psychosis and obsession; and how Hitchcock uses montage, dolly movements, and shot/reverse shots to place viewers into that man's shoes (19). Prominent Hitchcock scholar Robin Wood similarly writes, in *Hitchcock's Films Revisited*, how Madeleine (Kim Novak), the object of Scottie's (James Stewart—the protagonist's) obsession, "is presented as a dream, in some sense; and she becomes our dream as well as Scottie's" (114), and claims the effect we are feeling is "intensified by Hitchcock's use of camera" (114) when Scottie follows/stalks Madeleine through San Francisco. The scene Wood and Isaacs discusses is twenty-five minutes of Scottie following Madeleine through the streets of San Francisco, without any dialogue: a totem of Hitchcock's canon and the purest of Hitchcock's cinematic endeavors. This sequence not only allows us to see Scottie's seedy stalking abilities but also makes us the seedy stalker, ominously lurking behind this ethereal and mysterious blonde woman who is now the object of our dangerous affection. Hitchcock uses subjective camera techniques, placing the audience in the perspective of the protagonist so we experience Scottie's emotions, which is only one element of the pure cinema that lay at the heart of Hitchcock's story making.

Another, more devious, example of Hitchcock's use of the subjective occurs when Bruno (Robert Walker) stalks and kills Miriam (Pat Hitchcock), Guy's (Farley Granger) libidinous wife, in *Strangers on a Train*. Bruno is calmly smoking an ever-phallic cigar, sitting at a bus stop in front of Miriam's house, contemplating how he will murder Miriam. Within seconds, we are placed into Bruno's shoes; we see Miriam's bedroom light go out and she leaves with two suitors. A bus enters the frame and we learn that they want to get on to go to their destination. We have to improvise, and we enter the bus. The bus stops at a carnival; we hang back while Miriam and her boy-toys get out of the bus and run into the park. Calmly prepared to take her life, we see an opportunity to pounce and leisurely stroll into the carnival.

We are not always given Bruno's perspective, however. If that were the case, montage and pure cinema would not exist, and Hitchcock's philosophical understanding of the cinematic process would be broken. So the camera's point of view goes back and forth between the viewers seeing through Bruno's eyes and then seeing Bruno following the three "friends." Hitchcock builds suspense in these moments; however, these shots contain glimmers of what Neil Badmington would call "Hitchcock's magic." Badmington points out the "films clearly have a hold, a pull, a power; the somehow call viewers back for another look, another account, even when all the angles appear to have been covered" (3).

As Bruno walks into the carnival and lights his cigarette, we see and hear Miriam getting an ice cream cone and asking the boys to purchase a hot dog to satisfy her "craving a little bit more." One of the boys stupidly says, "Craving for what?" Immediately after this comic moment, Miriam sees and admires Bruno and what is known as "the Kuleshov effect" takes place in that she looks at him and he looks at her, him being the hungry cat and she the emboldened (and sexually excited) mouse. Without conversation, they flirt, but he is stopped by a petulant cowboy-hatted child holding a balloon and a toy gun. The linear montage is momentarily sidetracked when the boy points the plastic weapon at him and says, "Stick 'em up! Bang! Bang!" Bruno, appalled and annoyed by the intrusion, takes his cigarette and while the boy walks away, he aptly pops the boy's balloon much to the dismay of the tot, and much to the elation of the viewers. It is a moment of visual comedy that heightens the suspense of the moment, which eventually leads to Miriam's gruesome strangulation by her eager stalker. It is also a moment of pure cinema in which actions speak louder than words: not only is pure cinema used to create suspense and horror;

it is also used to make moments of hilarity that increase or decrease the tension in a scene. Wes D. Gehring in *Hitchcock and Humor: Modes of Comedy in Twelve Defining Films* speaks of four comedic modes used by Hitchcock: dark comedy; personality-based comedy ("the clown character"); screwball comedies; and, reaffirmation parody. Reaffirmation parody/comedy, according to Gehring, is not as broad as the type Brooks uses in his films and does not undercut the genre itself. Reaffirmation comedies provide poignant insights into the genres they are parodying. Although Bruno is a *homme fatale*, not a *femme fatale*, *Strangers on a Train* has multiple motifs associated with *film noir*: there is a dark mood, the presence of crime, a victim is under suspicion, an ambiguous protagonist, the theme of violence, the murder is ceremonious, the film is associated with dreams in the way that it is filmed and disorients the spectator (Borde and Chaumeton). While Bruno's not-as-nefarious act against the child is laughable, it is also a violent moment directed towards a child.

In Brooks' *High Anxiety*, subjective camera use is not as prominently displayed; however, that is not to say it is not used at all, and, very much like Hitchcock, Brooks uses it to enhance story, suspense, and humor. Like with Scottie in *Vertigo*, Dr. Richard Thorndyke (Mel Brooks), the protagonist of the film, has a crippling fear of heights. Throughout *Vertigo*, Scottie's acrophobia is displayed with his subjective viewpoints being represented by a dolly zoom effect. Meg Shields remarks for *Film School Rejects*, a popular website for cinephiles and amateur filmmakers, that dolly zooms "are an in-camera illusion achieved by combining a wide-angle zoom lens, steady zoom, and a dolly. By dollying and zooming in opposite directions, the foreground elements appear to stay the same size while the background appears to squeeze or stretch." One of the more famous scenes in *Vertigo* happens at the end of the movie, when Scottie is trying to get up the spiral staircase with Judy (also played by Kim Novak). While walking up and dragging Judy, Scottie decides to look down to the floor below, and a dolly zoom effect happens, creating a vertiginous sight: the dolly zoom is used to give the effect that the stairs and the ground are not connected. Scottie immediately stops looking; if he continues, his acrophobia will act up again to the point of psychological paralysis. The same can be said for Thorndyke, who is forced by his mentor Dr. Lilloman (Howard Morris), to take a look at the view from his new office. He is told to look down to the ocean below, which scares Thorndyke to the point of falling into a psychologically-induced spiral abyss, similar to the one Scottie falls into while having a fever dream in *Vertigo*. Admittedly, the dolly zoom is not used for Thorndyke's form of vertigo, but there are multiple scenes where we become Thorndyke looking down and feeling the effects of his fear, including at the end of *High Anxiety* when he is trying to save

Arthur Brisbane (Albert J. Whitlock) from the grips of Norton (Lee Delano), the half-mustached orderly. Thorndyke, while tracing the back wall as to not look down and get an attack, notices a broken step, so he decides to jump to the next one, which is seemingly just fine. When he lands, however, the wooden step cracks and he falls through. He looks down and we become Thorndyke looking at our dangling feet. We can see we are really high up and we are not able to hold on, that is until Dr. Lilloman ("Little Old Man") tells us why we have our acrophobia. We are no longer Thorndyke, who finally loses his fear after his memory of falling from his high chair while his parents incessantly fought each other (the nebulous psychoanalysis being a common occurrence in many Hitchcock films as a way to explain the entire story away so the main characters could be married at the end, without interruption).

Subjectivity in *High Anxiety* is also used when characters look directly into the camera or when the camera wants to see something it cannot easily see. One of the funnier moments of the film comes when the camera is trying to see Nurse Diesel (Cloris Leachman) and Dr. Charles Montague (Harvey Korman) from underneath a glass table. As they are frenetically talking about what they are going to do to ensure their innocence, they are picking up and moving objects around on the table, which then continuously covers the lens of the mobile camera: coffee cups, a coffee pot, a cookie plate, a creamer, a sugar bowl, and then finally a strudel tray. The suspense comes in the form of them hatching a plan to frame Thorndyke for a murder, but it is hard to keep up with their plan because of the constant movement, which also adds to the humor. Another subjective

Dr. Thorndyke (Mel Brooks) experiences vertigo in *High Anxiety* (1977).

moment in the film happens earlier and is discussed by Mel Brooks in his memoir. Brooks decided "to emulate ... the way Hitchcock often moved his camera in slow, stealthy push-ins." So

> [o]ne good example is a slow camera move from outside into the institute's dining room through a glass door. Slowly but surely, the camera gets closer and closer to the dining room. Unfortunately, it doesn't stop, and crashes through the glass door. Everybody in the dining room—myself, Harvey, Cloris, Dick Van Patten, etc.—all look to where the camera crashed through the glass. The camera guiltily withdraws, absolutely mortified by its mistake. The cast goes back to eating as if nothing happened. It always gets a great laugh [289].

In essence, the camera is us, we become characters in Brooks' film, and we are then humorously added to the story to the point of becoming a part of the joke. Thus, Brooks also understands the subjective and how it is used in pure cinema.

In a 1969 interview at the National Film Theater with Bryan Forbes, Hitchcock was asked by an audience member, "Why have you never made a comedy?" His reply was simple: "But every film I make is a comedy!" ("Alfred Hitchcock and Bryan Forbes [1969]"). How is that possible? Jeffrey Michael Bays on his blog for *Medium* remarks that Hitchcock recognizes "even the most deadly of situations have an undercurrent of facetious wit, using comedy to actually heighten the suspense" in "Humor: Hitchcock's Secret Weapon." According to Bays, the types of humor Hitchcock uses are understatement, the dramatization of trivial details, a balance between laughs and tension, a beginning that is comedic, and a use of macabre characters. Although his assessment that Hitchcock's humor is "specifically aimed at the audience" is somewhat problematic, Bays' perceptions about how humor is used in his films makes it clearer how Hitchcock sees his own work and how Mel Brooks (along with several others) can write, direct, and produce a film like *High Anxiety*, his masterful "tribute," according to the trailer, of both Hitchcock and Hitchcock's perceptions about the importance of pure cinema.

Hitchcock's and Brooks' Pure Cinema (Montage)

The concept of montage was not developed by Alfred Hitchcock; the technique itself was used years prior, most especially by Russian filmmaker Sergei Eisenstein. In his seminal work *Film Form: Essays in Film Theory*, Eisenstein says montage

> the most powerful compositional means of telling a story ... is a syntax for the correct construction of each particle of film ... is simply an elemental rule of

filmorthograhy for those who mistakenly put together pieces of as film as one would mix ready-made recipes for medicine, or pickle cucumbers, or preserve plums, or ferment apples and cranberries together [111].

He also claims filmmakers need to move away from traditional linear ways of making films and think about how they can break away from formulaic techniques to ensure they are producing both poetic and political messages. After writing a comprehensive shot-by-shot analysis of his most famous "The Odessa Steps" sequence from *The Battleship Potemkin* (1925), he speaks about montage from the perspective of a Soviet filmmaker during a time of great ideological upheaval:

> The Soviet cinema is now passing through a new phase—a phase of yet more distinct Bolshevization, a phase of yet more pointed ideological and essential militant sharpness. A phase historically logical, natural and rich in fertilizing possibilities for the cinema, as most notable of arts [124].

Montage, thus, became an artistic way to create a language that is both rhythmic and propagandistic in its construction, having a dual purpose by building a cohesive story while at the same time ensuring a partisan agenda moving in one direction.

Hitchcock had a similar agenda; however, his work is not political in a partisan sense. He does see the pure nature of the filmic language and the importance of montage in achieving that goal, but he uses it more as a way to lure the audience into becoming a part of the story rather than just a politicized objective viewer. An example of this is demonstrated in *Strangers on a Train*'s beginning sequence.

A Diamond taxi cab pulls up in front of the train station to let out someone who obviously comes from money based on the fact he is helped out by a porter and he is wearing fancy spats. All the audience sees is his feet. Then another Diamond taxi cab pulls up: another man who comes from money; however, this time we see two tennis rackets come out. He is a sports figure with sensible shoes; like with the first character, viewers are not made a privy to this second character's face. The music starts to build up to and the cuts begin. The man with the spats is walking toward the left of the screen with a confident stride; the man with the sensible shoes is walking to the right of the screen with a sense of urgency. Hitchcock makes it known that these are serious men with an agenda to get to their respective destinations. Next, they are in the train station: Spats, then Sensible. Spats goes onto the platform; then Sensible follows. They do not know each other, but Hitchcock is setting it up that viewers are going to get to know these two men intimately. The train begins to move forward; it is on its way and so are the men (we are along for the ride). The orchestral music is bombastic and it cuts through the scene like a knife. On the train, Spats walks through one of the cars and he finds a seat. He stretches out and crosses his legs (the crisscross becomes a major motif throughout). Then, Sensible (Guy/Farley Granger) walks through the same car and sits across from Spats (Bruno/Robert Walker), stretches out, and accidentally taps Spats' spats. It is this small accidental nudge, this chance encounter, that causes the film to begin; the exposition, rhythmically, is fast-paced and deliberate, which sets the stage for the rest of the film. The montage itself is parallel in the way of timing between Bruno's shots and Guy's shots, which also foreshadows the amount of doubling that takes place in the film; although different people, they are the same or at least similar to each other in their motivations and their drive. Pure cinematic techniques, most especially montage, are representative of the characters, their personalities, the pacing of the film, and how the movie's plot is going to unfold to what is one of the most horrific and hilarious endings in cinematic history: Bruno and Guy's brutal fight for Guy's lighter on an out-of-control carousel.

The climax, a chaotic montage sequence, has a merry-go-round spinning at break-neck speed after a carousel carnie gets accidentally shot and killed. Bruno and Guy fight for Guy's lighter; Bruno plans to plant the lighter (adorned with a crisscross of tennis rackets) at the scene of Miriam's murder. We are on the merry-go-round with them; we are in danger. While the fight is taking place, an old man crawls under the carousel to get to the middle where the lever is to stop it from spinning (he stops briefly to wipe his nose); a boy laughs it up while whipping around and around; Guy and Bruno hold on to the carousel for dear life while they are in fisticuffs; and, ultimately, the merry-go-round becomes a steaming pile of rubble. And yet, all the police care about is the lighter. There is complete carnage, but the good news is the police are able to solve the case, and Guy can finally live happily-ever-after with his new love: the happy ending trumps a life of misery.

Brooks has a similar exposition in *High Anxiety* to that of *Strangers on a Train*. The film starts off with a TWA flight landing onto a runway. It is an immediate montage of the plane, of the landing gear, of the pilot's hands, the plane descending from the standpoint of the passengers. The smiling faces of the passengers are visible through their windows but as the plane continues its descent, the camera pans over to the horrified face of Dr. Richard H. Thorndyke (a direct homage to Roger O. Thornhill in *North by Northwest*), played by Brooks himself (which is a reference to Alfred Hitchcock who always placed himself in his own films). The words in the credits are made up of spirals, another common motif in Hitchcock's work (including *Strangers on a Train*), but these particular credits are telling viewers Brooks' parodic focus will be *Vertigo*. The bombastic music emulates Bernard Herrmann's familiar orchestral scores. Within minutes, and because of Brooks' abrupt use of pure cinema, the audience is already aware *High Anxiety* is having fun with Hitchcock and his films.

Brooks also establishes that Hitchcock, himself, is a genre (276). The term "Hitchcockian" has been used a countless number of times in a multitude of books, articles, interviews, and commentaries in recognition that not only is Hitchcock an auteur, but he is also his own style of filmmaking (Isaacs also alludes to this in *The Art of Pure Cinema*, where he writes about directors who are what he calls imitators of Hitchcockian cinema, like Brian DePalma and Dario Argento). The pilots land the plane. The camera is positioned behind them so we see the runway in front of them (yet another cinematic motif in Hitchcock's work in which viewers regularly see his protagonists behind the steering wheel of an out-of-control automobile). In this case, though, the pilots have complete control over the plane while viewers are experiencing Thorndyke's high anxiety through the imagery; viewers are feeling what Thorndyke feels even when all is going smoothly.

Thorndyke leaves the plane and enters the airport lobby, where a woman sees him and starts screaming, which startles him. The woman lifts up her umbrella as if it were a knife and runs toward Thorndyke. He is ready to defend himself from the attack but the woman is just excited to see another person coming off of the plane. Hitchcock has used the screaming woman in multiple films (most notably in *Psycho*) but makes this moment funny in that Brooks uses "the Kuleshov effect" for a comedic outcome. David Bordwell's comprehensive website on cinema speaks to Russian film director Lev Kuleshov's fascination with constructive editing (montage) "because that shows that cinema can call on the spectator's tacit understanding to assemble the separate shots. Kuleshov realized that we will build a sense of the scene's space and action out of separate shots without need for the comprehensive view supplied by an establishing shot" (Thompson and Bordwell). The spectator, in this case, understands this comedic and parodic moment is another homage to Hitchcock's use of pure cinema to evoke "violence and emotion," sans the violence. Brooks, like Hitchcock, also establishes himself as a genre, as an auteur. Audiences prior to watching *High Anxiety*, have seen or know about *Blazing Saddles* (1974), *Young Frankenstein* (1974), and *Silent Movie* (1976), and more than likely have a similar respect for the forms of cinema with which Brooks is having fun. The audience knows when they are watching an Alfred Hitchcock film, and the audience knows when they are watching a Mel Brooks film. And both understand visual storytelling (pure cinema) helps audience awareness to happen.

The beginning of the film does not end with the screaming woman. Thorndyke gets flashed in the airport bathroom by a man posing as a cop;

he gets tripped up at the end of an escalator (we see his feet and the feet of other patrons, which happens in the beginning sequence of *Strangers on a Train*); he walks from one end of the airport to another. As this is happening, we are only seeing parts of him: his hands, his back, his face, his legs, his torso. John Morris' loud score plays to a loud crescendo. Thorndyke finally walks out of the airport, the music ends with the closing of the doors (like with Guy's tapping of Bruno's foot), and he says with perfect comedic timing, "What a dramatic airport!" This is a moment of self-reflection in a self-reflective film, a regular occurrence in much of Hitchcock's movies. Hitchcock realizes his movies are movies. They are not real life; they are not representative of real life. They are visually constructed stories, pieces of film put together to create narrative.

Pastiche or Parody?

Richard Allen, in his essay "Hitchcock's Legacy" from the anthology *A Companion to Alfred Hitchcock*, is clear about why Hitchcock is so enduring:

> Like the German expressionist filmmakers, Hitchcock combined an authorial and stylistic self-consciousness expressed in the ideal of a cinematic narration eschewing dialogue, which he dubbed "pure cinema," with an understanding of the "disreputable" origins of cinema in the fairground and its unique appeal as a form of attraction or spectacle that is linked to gaming or play and to the shadow world of forbidden desire [572].

The rest of Allen's essay delves into Hitchcock's connections to not only German Expressionism but also European Art Cinema (French New Wave is an example of this), Postclassical Hollywood, Postmodern Surrealists. Hitchcock is a master of pastiche; he and his films pay homage to those that preceded him and them. In fact, so is his audience. And, so is Brooks, who is his audience. In turn, *High Anxiety* becomes a parody of a pastiche that utilizes pure cinematic techniques, like subjective camera work, montage and the MacGuffin, to introduce the story, the characters, the pacing, and the constructed language that is film. In the case of Hitchcock, he primarily creates suspenseful films that have elements of humor while Brooks, in the case of *High Anxiety*, creates humor that has elements of suspense.

One can argue Brooks, in *High Anxiety*, is also filming scenes of editorial meta-parody of the French New Wave movement, having knowledge of the connections French film critics and directors writing for the *Cashiers du Cinema* had with Hitchcock's work during the 1960s and 1970s. Right as Brophy (Ron Carey) is introduced, he takes photos of the newly arrived Thorndyke, who at first acts like a celebrity being hounded by the paparazzi but then embraces the moment by posing as if he were one of the three characters in François Truffaut's *Jules and Jim* (1962). Truffaut is a major director of the Nouvelle Vague while also having the distinction of performing an in-depth interview of Hitchcock in 1966 about Hitchcock's entire canon of work titled *Hitchcock/Truffaut*, which was filmed and became a more commercialized documentary in 2015. The picture-taking sequence mentioned above is also a direct but more subtle reference to Hitchcock's *Rear Window*, a film that places photographic images and pure cinema techniques to the forefront to ensure thrills, chills, and giggles.

Brooks is not always subtle, however. He very much recognizes the importance of music to Hitchcock's montages. While Thorndyke and Brophy are on the road, viewers learn more about the diegetic story. Thorndyke, who is now the new administrator for an asylum ("The Psycho-Neurotic Institute for the Very, Very Nervous") is taking over for a Dr. Ashley, who mysteriously passed away from a heart attack even though he was in "tiptop shape," at least according to Brophy. Brophy candidly says he believes Ashley was "a victim of foul play." Like in the shower scene in *Psycho*, which becomes a brilliantly funny parodic moment in *High Anxiety* when a bellboy wildly "stabs" Thorndyke with a newspaper while he is in the shower, ominous music fills the car. Thorndyke and Brophy seem to be able to hear the non-diegetic orchestra. They both look around confused until Thorndyke looks out the window to see a bus filled with Los Angeles Symphony Orchestra members aggressively playing the threatening arrangement. According to Isaacs, when speaking about Hitchcock's early silent films, he claims Hitchcock's use of sound and music is just an extension of his experimentation in using film form to produce pure cinema:

> Experimental sound design within the European avant-garde cinema explored nonnaturalistic soundscapes, asynchronic and contrapuntal relations between sound and image, and in some cases radically ambiguous or open sound images, whether such images were rooted in concrete sounds or increasingly complex, abstract musical accompaniment. It is natural to expect that in his early sound films Hitchcock would follow suit. In his desire for a pure cinema, sound was merely one further element of an artistic form with unlimited potential. This is to suggest that Hitchcock's experimentation with sound was a natural extension of his experimentation with the visual image in his silent films [166].

Isaacs focuses on the use of violins in *Psycho*, and how Hitchcock redefines Sergei Eisenstein's understanding of how music is used to enhance story:

A musical composition organized through counterpoint is often thought to contain greater depth, complexity, and subtlety. In his description of the image-sound relation "as music," Hitchcock seems to depart from Eisenstein et al.'s more instrumental notion of visual/sound counterpoint, or at least to expand on the model of counterpoint Eisenstein in particular seems to use interchangeably with cinematic montage. For Eisenstein, counterpoint in sound and image relation, serving the aegis of intellectual montage, should be dialectical; that is, the relationship should create a new concept of the whole. But in his own break from image-sound synchronization, Hitchcock seems to conceptualize the image-sound relation as musical counterpoint rather than dialectical montage [168].

The same happens in *High Anxiety*. Thorndyke and Brophy hearing what is generally a non-diegetic musical composition is representative of this. Brooks makes the vigorously-played music non-diegetic, then extra diegetic and then diegetic, which makes the film violently funny and overtly understanding of how Hitchcock used music in montage to his advantage.

Hitchcock's and Brook's Use of Pure Cinema (the MacGuffin)

Hitchcock's MacGuffin is a major component of all of his works not only because it drives the plot but also because of its comedic effect, in that it ultimately means absolutely nothing to the narrative; it has no real significance whatsoever. Examples of this include the following of Scottie's friend's wife in *Vertigo*; the stolen money in *Psycho*; the lighter in *Strangers on a Train*; the murder across from L.B. Jefferies' (James Stewart) apartment in *Rear Window*, and, strangely enough, the birds in *The Birds*. In the case of *High Anxiety*, the MacGuffin is the "changes" Dr. Ashley wanted to make at the asylum before his untimely and mysterious demise. These "changes" are brought up multiple times throughout the beginning of the film, but the viewers are not made aware of them early on to ensure the story and plot can move forward. The MacGuffin is another component of pure cinema Brooks picks up but, in this case, it is used for an actual purpose: comedy rather than suspense. The "changes" and Thorndyke's acrophobia are truly nothing but are used for something rather than nothing, which somewhat differs from Hitchcock's filmmaking methodology. In a way, this is why Brooks' film is more parody rather than a pastiche. These concrete, yet abstract, narrative devices are a way to move forward the humor rather than to drive the suspense.

One could also argue the psychoanalysis angle in *High Anxiety* could be the MacGuffin. Hitchcock regularly seems to use pseudo-science as

MacGuffins in his films, most notably at the end of *Psycho* when Norman's belief that he is his mother is dryly explained away by the psychiatrist, and in *Spellbound*, where the entire film is based on the practice of psychoanalysis. One scene in Brooks' work has Thorndyke under hypnosis in an attempt to cure his high anxiety. Dr. Lilloman tries to tell Thorndyke to fight through the fear and Thorndyke does so, literally. He gets into a physical fight with Lilloman, and they start formally boxing until the jaded Dr. Montague, the man who wanted to replace Dr. Ashley, comes in and stops the fight (he becomes a referee and eventually dings a boxing bell with Lilloman's pipe). This scene is a direct parody of the dream sequence created by Surrealist painter Salvador Dali for *Spellbound*. As Barbara Creed suggests in her essay "The Untamed Eye and the Dark Side of Surrealism: Hitchcock, Lynch, and Cronenberg," like the Surrealists, Hitchcock was "fascinated with the art of illusion" (125). The dream sequence is representative of this in that it may be a set piece but "the events surrounding this sequence are even more surreal that the nightmare" (125). These set pieces, which are staples of Hitchcock's work, could be deemed as MacGuffins as well, which gives more fodder for Brooks' comedic agenda and allows the film to build to its matrimonial conclusion. Brooks' set pieces include:

1. Thorndyke goes to San Francisco, a favorite place of Hitchcock's, to a conference, where he meets up with Victoria Brisbane (Madeliene Kahn), the daughter of Arthur Brisbane, who is a patient in the asylum because he thinks he is a cocker spaniel (the following of Madeliene in *Vertigo*);

2. the pigeons going on the "attack" by excessively shitting on Thorndyke, who finds temporary shelter in a park field house, that is until he is able to go into "Cable Car Cleaners" to get his suit dry cleaned (the menacing crows on the jungle gym behind Tippi Hedren and that attack the children as they run away from the school in *The Birds*);

3. the conference where Thorndyke is trying not to speak about penis envy and breasts while children are sitting in the audience, and the murder at that conference in the hope Thorndyke gets framed (the auction scene where Thornhill [Cary Grant] makes a ruckus to get out of a sticky situation and the stabbing murder at the United Nations to frame Thornhill in *North by Northwest*);

4. the phone booth sequence where Thorndyke is close to getting murdered by the man with the braces (Rudy DeLuca) (the phone booth sequence in *The Birds* along with two set pieces from films not spoken about in the introduction: the sloppy attempted killing in *Dial M for Murder* [1954] and the woman's more explicit strangulation in *Frenzy* [1972]);

5. the final tower sequence where the real Arthur Brisbane is going to be murdered (the end of *Vertigo*, which is Scottie's nightmare happening over and over again);

6. and, when Thorndyke sings "High Anxiety," a set-piece created by Brooks that adds his authorial touch to his own movies (musical numbers are used frequently by Brooks, most famously when Dr. Frankenstein and the Monster sing "Puttin' on the Ritz" in *Young Frankenstein*, which in and of themselves can be MacGuffins because they do not drive the story but just add to the comedic value of the film).

All of these scenes have direct correlations to Hitchcock and the only reason why they are funny is because of those correlations. The reasoning for each set piece is to make viewers laugh at the parodic nature of the moment and nothing more, which makes each a perfect representation of Hitchcock's MacGuffin.

Conclusion

High Anxiety ends with a marriage, like several of Hitchcock's movies, which reiterates that Brooks' film is a comedy and that Hitchcock's movies (other than a select few like *Vertigo*, *Psycho*, and *The Birds*) are indeed comedies: popcorn movies filled with intrigue, mayhem, and murder; as well as ridiculous moments like that of the camera going through the wall of the motel where Victoria and Thorndyke are honeymooning. At the end of *Strangers on a Train*, *North by Northwest*, *Spellbound*, and *Rear Window* marriages take place but in sarcastic ways, as if they have to be added for the sake of being added. Pure cinema and the techniques that represent it—subjectivity, montage, and the MacGuffin—are tossed aside to ensure all is right with the world and the order of things is back on track.

But maybe the marriages themselves are just MacGuffins in disguise. Do they really matter to the story or are they just endings to films that, ultimately, do not matter at all? Who knows? Who cares? All I know is that at the end of watching the pure cinema of Alfred Hitchcock and his magnificent parody directed by the "Master of Comedy," Mel Brooks, WE WIN!

Filmography

Alfred Hitchcock Presents. Created by Alfred Hitchcock. CBS (1955–60; 1962–64); NBC (1960–62; 1964–65).
The Battleship Potemkin. Dir. Sergei Eisenstein. Mosfilm, 1925. DVD. Reel Vault, 2015.

192 אויסגעקליבן ווערק / Selected Works (1965–1991)

The Birds. Dir. Alfred Hitchcock. Alfred J. Hitchcock Productions, 1963. DVD. Universal Studios Home Entertainment, 2012.
Blazing Saddles: 30th Anniversary Special Edition. Dir. Mel Brooks. Crossbow Productions,1974. DVD. Warner, 2004.
Dial M for Murder. Dir. Alfred Hitchcock. Warner Bros., 1954. DVD. Warner Bros. Home Video, 2009.
Frenzy. Dir. Alfred Hitchcock. Universal Pictures, 1972. DVD. Universal Studios Home Entertainment, 2006.
High Anxiety. Dir. Mel Brooks. Twentieth Century Studios, 1977. DVD. 20th Century Fox Home Entertainment, 2006.
Jules and Jim. Dir. François Truffault. Les Films du Carrosse and SEIF, 1962. DVD. Alliance, 2005.
North by Northwest. Dir. Alfred Hitchcock. Metro-Goldwyn-Mayer, 1959. DVD. Warner Home Video, 2000.
Psycho. Dir. Alfred Hitchcock. Shamley Productions, 1960. DVD. Universal Studios Home Entertainment, 2012.
Rear Window. Dir. Alfred Hitchcock. Patron Inc., 1954. DVD. Universal Studios Home Entertainment, 2009.
Silent Movie. Dir. Mel Brooks. Crossbow Productions, 1976. DVD. Twentieth Century Fox Home Entertainment, 2006.
Spellbound. Dir. Alfred Hitchcock. Selnick International Pictures and Vanguard Films, 1945. DVD. Criterion, 2002.
Strangers on a Train. Dir. Alfred Hitchcock. Transatlantic Pictures, 1951. DVD. Warner Home Video, 2011.
The Trouble with Harry. Dir. Alfred Hitchcock. Alfred J. Hitchcock Productions, 1955. DVD. Universal Studios Home Entertainment, 2006.
Vertigo. Dir. Alfred Hitchcock. Alfred J. Hitchcock Productions, 1958. DVD. Universal Studios Home Entertainment, 2012.
Young Frankenstein. Dir. Mel Brooks. Gruskoff/Venture Films, Crossbow Productions and Jouer Limited, 1974. DVD. Twentieth Century Fox, 2014.

Works Cited

"Alfred Hitchcock and Bryan Forbes (1969)." *The Hitchcock Zone*, October 3, 1969. https://the.hitchcock.zone/wiki/Alfred_Hitchcock_and_Bryan_Forbes_(1969)#:~:text=Alfred%20Hitchcock%20was%20interviewed%20at%20the%20National%20Film,lectures%20sponsored%20by%20John%20Player%20%26%20Sons.%20Video.
Allen, Richard. "Hitchcock's Legacy." *A Companion to Alfred Hitchcock*, edited by Thomas Leitch and Leland Poague, Wiley, 2011, pp. 572–591.
Badmington, Neil. *Hitchcock's Magic*. University of Wales Press, 2011.
Bays, Jeffrey Michael. "Humor: Hitchcock's Secret Weapon." *Medium*, April 23, 2021. https://medium.com/life-and-the-performing-arts/humor-hitchcocks-secret-weapon-94a0bde4e5e6.
Borde, Robert, and Etienne Chaumeton. "Towards a Definition of Film Noir." *Film Noir Reader*, edited by Alain Silver and James Ursini, Limelight, 1996, pp. 17–26.
Brooks, Mel. *All About Me! My Remarkable Life in Show Business*. Ballantine Books. 2021.
Creed, Barabra. "The Untamed Eye and the Dark Side of Surrealism: Hitchcock, Lynch, and Cronenberg." *The Unsilvered Screen: Surrealism on Film*, edited by Graeme Harper and Robert Stone, Wallflower Press, 2007, pp. 115–133.
Eisenstein, Sergei. *Film Form: Essays in Film Theory*. Translated by Jim Leyda, Harcourt, Brace, & World, 1949.
Gehring, Wes D. *Hitchcock and Humor: Modes of Comedy in Twelve Defining Films*. McFarland, 2019.
Isaacs, Bruce. *The Art of Pure Cinema: Hitchcock and His Imitators*. Oxford University Press, 2020.

"Peter Bogdanovich interviews Alfred Hitchcock (1963)." [Video]. *YouTube*, uploaded by FYchord, October 23, 2020. https://www.youtube.com/watch?v=Yjm_Nf0bfQk.

Shields, Meg. "How Does the Dolly Zoom Work?" Film School Rejects, January 3, 2021. https://filmschoolrejects.com/dolly-zoom/#:~:text=Dolly%20zooms%20are%20an%20in-camera%20illusion%20achieved%20by,while%20the%20background%20appears%20to%20squeeze%20or%20stretch.

Thompson, Kristin, and David Bordwell. "What Happens Between Shots Happens Between Your Ears." *David Bordwell's Website on Cinema*, February 4, 2008. http://www.davidbordwell.net/blog/2008/02/04/what-happens-between-shots-happens-between-your-ears/.

Wood, Robin. *Hitchcock's Films Revisited*. 1989. Columbia University Press, 2002.

The Court Jester's Tale
History of the World, Part I *(1981)*
as Epic, Parody, and Epic Parody

A. Bowdoin Van Riper

History of the World, Part I is rarely included in discussions of Brooks' parodies. A baggy, shambling, undisciplined film, it resembles nothing so much as a collection of blackout sketches linked by Brooks' manic presence in multiple roles. At first viewing, *History* barely even tries to be a coherent narrative, let alone one with the precision timing and pitch-perfect tone of *Young Frankenstein* or the magnificently orchestrated anarchy of *Blazing Saddles*. On closer examination, however, it is very much part of Brooks' ongoing experiment with cinematic parody: one that lampoons the historical-epic film while taking satirical swipes at narrative conventions that run through nearly *all* popular history.

Like *Blazing Saddles*, Brooks' *History* is a parody of a genre. It sends-up the mega-budgeted, cast-of-thousands historical epic invented by D.W. Griffith, made famous by Cecil B. DeMille, and given new life in the 1950s and early 1960s as new technologies and the challenge of television led Hollywood to (re)embrace spectacle. Also like *Blazing Saddles* (but unlike *Young Frankenstein* and most of Brooks' later parodic films), it suggests certain films in broad, abstract ways without specifically referencing them. The voiceover narration evokes a half-dozen different Biblical epics; the episodic structure is lifted from Irwin Allen's *The History of Mankind*; and the staging of the palace scenes in imperial Rome and pre–Revolutionary France acts as visual callbacks to films such as *Land of the Pharaohs*, *Quo Vadis*, and *The Three Musketeers*. Where classic Hollywood historical epics are relentlessly serious and scrupulously high-minded, Brooks' versions of the same story are relentlessly anarchic, bawdy, and scatological. *History of the World, Part I* is the "march of mankind" as it might unfold if written by the Lord of Misrule, stage-managed by the "rude mechanicals" of *A Midsummer Night's Dream*, and performed by a cast of horny teenage boys.

The film's pervasive, aggressive assault on "propriety" and "decency"—its jokes about urine-wielding art critics, dropped tablets, mounds of excrement, unwanted erections, and perpetually horny aristocrats—are not (just) a search for lowest-common-denominator laughs. They are at the core of Brooks' parodic message: impertinent reminders that the Great Men and Great Women of history were messy, fallible, idiosyncratic humans. *History of the World, Part I* is history as seen through the eyes (and recounted in the idiom) of a court jester, whose job is to remind the powerful that they, too, are mortal.

Genre, Prestige, and the Historical Epic

It has become fashionable, in discussing popular music and popular fiction, to dismiss genre as a set of arbitrary categories, imposed by publishers' marketing departments to make their jobs easier, and accepted by retail chains or the same reason. Genre exists, the glib assertion goes, to relieve the marketer, the retailer, and—by implied extension—the consumer of the need to think. Specifically, it relieves them of the need to consider the merits of the individual work *as* an individual work, by reducing it to an example of a broad category. The underlying proposition for the consumer (again, implied rather than directly stated) is "[t]he consumer of genre entertainment is undiscerning. *Any* work that falls within the genre will, likely, satisfy *any* fan of that genre."

The problems inherent in this view of genre are too numerous, and too obvious, to merit attention here. Decades of scholarship have established that genres are defined by stocks of characters, situations, plot tropes, and stylistic elements: a visual and narrative language shared by creators and consumers alike.[1] The relationships between genres and the subgenres that comprise them, the deliberate mixing of genres within a single work, and the knowing deconstruction of genre tropes for the amusement of fans familiar with them have all been parsed in detail.[2] On a purely practical level, in the realm of everyday life, the proposition that consumers of genre entertainment are (within their chosen genre) undiscerning omnivores is patently absurd to anyone who knows, or is, such a consumer. Fans of Agatha Christie's "Miss Marple" are unlikely to reach for, let alone enjoy, Ed McBain's "87th Precinct" *just* because crimes are committed, and solved, in both. Sam Raimi's *Evil Dead 2* (1987) and Taika Waititi's *What We Do in the Shadows* (2014) exist in the same hybrid subgenre (horror-comedy) but speak to different fanbases.[3]

All that said, the idea of "genre as arbitrary marketing category" *does* have analytical value. It achieves that value, ironically, when applied to works outside traditional "genre entertainment" categories such as science fiction, romance, horror, mystery, and crime.[4] "Literary fiction," for example, has emerged in recent decades as a genre label applied to work as an assertion that it is as distinct from "fiction" proper as (say) the fantasy of J.R.R. Tolkien, the crime novels of Donald E. Westlake, or the Westerns of Max Brand. The "literary fiction" label, however, is attached less to shared structures and tropes than to shared perceptions of "seriousness" and "quality."[5] The same argument could be made of "erotica," whose famously vague boundaries have more to do with the reader's (and society's) response to a given work than with the content of the work itself.[6] Both "literary fiction" and "erotica" are quasi-genre designations that do their marketing and promotional work by appealing to consumers' anxieties about taste and (by extension) class. The same, from mid-1910s to the mid-1970s, was true of the Hollywood's historical-epic films.

"Historical epic" is less a genre than an intersection of a genre (historical drama) and a style (epic). The two elements of the term "historical epic" are completely severable. *Madame Curie* (1943) and *Picnic at Hanging Rock* (1975) are historical dramas without being epics; they are grounded in specific historical times and places, but their physical settings are bounded, their characters human-scaled, and their dramatic stakes relatively small. *Grand Hotel* (1932) and *Advise and Consent* (1962) are epics without being historical; they are set in the present but feature larger-than-life characters competing on a grandly scaled stage for high stakes. Both historical dramas and epics come wrapped in a sense of *gravitas*: the former because of their narrative kinship to schoolbooks, Bible stories, and newspapers, the latter because of their association with opera and Shakespeare. They carry an (often unearned) expectation that audiences can learn both historical truths and moral lessons from them while they are entertained, which in turn gives them an indelible air of prestige.[7]

More than "literary fiction" or "erotica," however, historical epic films share a definable set of features that make them a distinct genre. These include an episodic narrative, richly detailed and opulently staged settings, an unwavering focus on Great Events, a strongly developed moral theme, and an uncompromising sense of seriousness.[8] These qualities are so central to the historical epic that they manifest not only in such paradigmatic examples such as D.W. Griffith's *Intolerance* (1916), William Wyler's *Ben-Hur* (1959), and Hugh Hudson's *Chariots of Fire* (1981), but also in what is arguably the genre's most bizarre outlier: Irwin Allen's fractally weird *The Story of Mankind* (1957).

Based on Hendrik Van Loon's best-selling popular history book, then a quarter-century old, Allen's film lifted its plot from Stephen Vincent Benet's "The Devil and Daniel Webster." Where Benet's story revolved around the soul of an impoverished New England farmer, however, Allen's film had the fate of the entire human race hanging in the balance. The Devil (Vincent Price), acting as prosecutor in a celestial courtroom, argued that the recent invention of the "super H-bomb" capped a long history of depravity that justified humankind's extinction. The "Spirit of Man" (Ronald Colman) argued the case for the defense by citing humankind's equally long history of art and science, its ceaseless curiosity and pursuit of justice. Vignettes involving key moments in human history—reused footage from previous Warner Brothers films, or new scenes shot by Allen using name stars as historical figures—serve as "evidence" and make up the bulk of the film.

The Story of Mankind is remembered today for its painful attempts at comic relief (Groucho Marx, as a fast-talking Peter Minuit, buys Manhattan from a nameless "Indian chief"), bizarre casting (Edward Everett Horton as Sir Walter Raleigh), and the exuberantly hammy performances (Agnes Moorhead, as Elizabeth I, confronts a Spanish envoy played by Cesar Romero). It was intended, however, as a serious attempt to compress the entire sweep of human history into a running time of only 100 minutes. It stretches from prehistory to the Second World War, and its lineup of historical characters is drawn from the canon of "Great Men" that populated textbooks of the era: Khufu (of Great Pyramid fame), Hippocrates, Caesar, Cleopatra, Nero, Joan of Arc, Columbus, Shakespeare, Newton, Marie Antoinette, Lincoln and Hitler.

The speeches of the celestial characters, which give the film its narrative continuity, also set its tone. The High Judge (Cedric Hardwicke) intones: "Take heed and listen well. Time runs swiftly. The fate of man is now laid at the doorstep of man, himself." The Spirit of Man sums up millions of years of prehistory this way: "Man had lived though many ages before the first dawning of reason led him toward the warmth of the fire. After an infinity of groping in the darkness, man was beginning to find some answers. To understand the values which lay in group living and mutual assistance." The Devil introduces Nero as a "flatterer, maniac, rapist, pervert, matricide, arsonist, bigamist, and sometimes accomplished musician and singer for all social occasions" and sets up the arrival of Europeans in the New World in equally sardonic terms: "[t]hen came the red man, fighting for his very survival, and the white man, determined to take away this so-called God-given heritage, used the foulest of methods. Rather confusing, don't you think?"

Notwithstanding its reception, and its casting of Harpo Marx as Isaac Newton, the *intent* of *The Story of Mankind* was clear. It aspired to seriousness because the historical epic was, by long tradition, a genre steeped in seriousness, that—as a result—conferred an air of prestige and (in the cultural, rather than the economic sense) class. So it largely remained until 1981, when Mel Brooks got his hands on it.

History of the World, Part I *as Genre Parody*

A genre film provides a set of familiar, recognizable elements that can be used as framework and backdrop for a wide range of stories. The audience's familiarity with the elements enables them to be introduced with little or no explanation: What they are, what they signify, and how they will function within the story can all be taken for granted, leaving more time to tell the story itself. Genre-parody films depend on the same familiarity, deploying the familiar tropes in order to subvert them. Jim's (Gene Wilder) famous speech in *Blazing Saddles*, consoling Bart (Cleavon Little) after his cordiality to the townspeople has been met with racist insults, works as comedy because it starts as a pitch-perfect imitation of a hundred speeches in a hundred earlier films—"You've got to remember that these are just simple farmers. These are people of the land. The common clay of the new West"—before pausing for the briefest of beats and taking a wickedly sharp left turn: "You know … morons." The same dynamic is at work in the Monty Python troupe's *Life of Brian* (1979) when a Roman soldier (John Cleese), after discovering the Judean hero (Graham Chapman) painting anti–Roman graffiti on a building, pedantically corrects his Latin grammar and orders: "Now write it a hundred times … if it's not done by sunrise, I'll cut your balls off."

Brooks, in *History of the World, Part I*, plays the genre-parody game of deployment and subversion on multiple levels, starting with the structure of the film itself. Like *The Story of Mankind*, *How the West Was Won* (1962), and *The Bible: In the Beginning* (1966), *History of the World* is composed of stand-alone episodes that are chronologically separated and narratively distinct from one another, with few (if any) characters appearing in more than one. Like those earlier films, it focuses on familiar episodes where the audience can be counted on to already have a broad sense of the setting, plot, characters, and tone. The five principal segments are introduced (in on-screen title cards, another staple of historical epics) as the Stone Age, the Old Testament, the Roman Empire, the Spanish Inquisition, and the French Revolution. Beneath these superficial signs of order, however, the film's actual organization is chaotic. The "Stone Age" segment runs for eight minutes, and "Spanish Inquisition" segment for ten. The "Old Testament" segment is a single, one-minute blackout gag. The

"French Revolution" segment, by contrast, runs for nearly thirty minutes, and the "Roman Empire" segment for close to forty.

The segments appear in chronological order, but within them time and space are flexible. The "Stone Age" segment spans more than a million years without changing the actors or the characters they play. The last three minutes of the "Roman Empire" segment shift from Rome to Jerusalem for the sake of a three-minute gag involving the Last Supper. Leonardo Da Vinci appears—1400 years early and identified only by his stage-Italian accent—as part of the gag, but Oedipus has already appeared (500 years late) on the streets of Rome. Continuity of both space and time are reduced to tatters at the end of the film, where Jacques (Brooks) is rescued from the guillotine by Josephus (Gregory Hines), an Ethiopian slave from the "Roman Empire" segment, still dressed in Roman costume and driving the same horse and cart he used in Rome. Brooks lampshades the gag by asking Josephus, who befriended the (different) character he played in Rome: "How did you get here from the Roman Empire?" Josephus' grinning reply completes the collapse of space and time and tramples whatever fragments of the fourth wall have managed to remain standing: "Don't be square, *mon cher*! Movies is magic!"

The tone of the individual segments is as uneven as their pacing and structure. "The Stone Age" is a string of pantomimed gags involving a group of cave-dwellers led by Sid Caesar that contrast absurdly with deeply serious voiceover narration delivered, with a completely straight face, by Orson Welles. "The Old Testament" is a single, brilliant sight gag: Brooks, as short, schlubby Moses, awkwardly holding up three carved tablets. "The Lord, the Lord Jehovah has given unto you these fifteen—" he declares, only to be interrupted by one tablet slipping from his grasp and smashing at his feet. "Oy! Ten! Ten commandments for all to obey!" There are similarly broad visual gags in "The Roman Empire," including one involving a giant marijuana joint, but its comedic backbone is a nonstop stream of verbal humor: jokes, puns, double entendres, and volleys of lines between "stand-up philosopher" Comicus (Brooks) and a half-dozen other characters. "The Spanish Inquisition" is staged like an excerpt of a musical, with the torturers (led by Brooks as Torquemada) singing in *Broadway Melody* style, nuns in white swimsuits and bathing caps doing an Esther-Williams-esque synchronized-swimming routine, and Jewish prisoners lamenting their plight in a patter song reminiscent—in form, not content—of "Ya Got Trouble" from *The Music Man* or "Moses Supposes" from *Singin' in the Rain*.

The Inquisition segment highlights a second level at which the construction of *History of the World* deploys and then, with great precision, subverts the conventions of the historical epic. Each individual segment of the film can be read as a free-standing, self-contained lampoon of the conventions of a particular subset of historical dramas. The targets of "The Old Testament" and "The Roman Empire" are obvious: Biblical epics like *The Ten Commandments* (1956) and *Ben-Hur* (1959) in the former case, sword-and-sandal extravaganzas like *Quo Vadis* (1951) and *Cleopatra* (1963) in the latter. "The Stone Age" spoofs first the "Dawn of Man" sequence from *2001: A Space Odyssey* (1968) and *One Million Years B.C.* (1966), along with generic "cave man" tropes like marriage-by-conquest (knocking the bride-to-be unconscious with a club).[9] "The French Revolution" sends up the conventions of swashbuckling royal-intrigue dramas like *The Three Musketeers*, *A Tale of Two Cities*, and *The Prisoner of Zenda*: decadent aristocrats, imperiled virginity, uncanny doppelgangers, and narrow escapes.

"The Spanish Inquisition" seems, at first viewing, to be the exception to this pattern: a simple exercise in the absurdity juxtaposing pitch-dark subject matter and cheery presentation. The fact that it delivers not just *a* musical spoof, but precise, recognizable (at least to fans) recreations of three different styles of cinematic musical suggests, however, that there is more going on. The answer lies in the set design and costuming, which mimic those of 1960s gothic-horror films such as *Black Sunday* (1960) *The Pit and the Pendulum* (1961), *The Tower of London* (1962), and *Witchfinder General* (1968). The threat of torture—sometimes averted, sometimes caried out—features prominently in the films and even more prominently in their advertising, with imagery hinting at bondage and grotesque violations of the protagonists' bodies. Brooks' dungeon scenes undercuts, and mocks, the promises of lurid sex and violence with which such films tease would-be viewers.

The Inquisition's prisoners in *History of the World* are middle-aged Jews—heavily bearded, unwashed, dressed in rags—rather than glamorous heroes and heroines with perfect teeth and flawless skin. The torture they are threatened with is actually inflicted, but in cartoonish ways that (right down to the use of enormous wooden mallets) evoke the memory of Warner Brothers cartoon shorts. The prisoners' patter song tells of worse indignities, already performed:

> I was sitting in a temple
> > I was minding my own business
> > > I was listening to a lovely Hebrew mass.
>
> Then these papist persons plunge in,
> And they throw me in the dungeon,
> And they shove a red-hot poker up my ass!
> Is that considerate?
> Is that polite?
> And not a tube of Preparation-H in sight!

The lyrical cleverness of the song, like the visual absurdity of three side-by-side breaking wheels spinning (with a prisoner bound to each) like reels in a slot machine, disperses the sense of dread that is the stock-in-trade of the Technicolor-Gothic horror films being parodied. Brooks substitutes laughter for the voyeuristic thrill of witnessing (or imagining) sexualized violence disguised as "historical atmosphere."

The third level of genre-parody in *History of the World* is its use of title cards and voiceover narration. Both are commonplace in historical epic films, as tools for framing the onscreen action. The latter is particularly commonplace in deliberately episodic films like *The Story of Mankind*, *How the West Was Won* (1962), and *The Bible: In the Beginning* (1966), where it provides continuity between episodes occurring in different eras and featuring different characters and plotlines.[10] John Huston, voicing *both* the offscreen narrative and the offscreen voice of God in *The Bible*, achieves the ultimate in narrative authority—textual or verbal.[11]

The voiceovers in *History of the World* are written in conscious imitation of those in serious historical epics and delivered—completely deadpan—by Orson Welles. The first words of the narrative, spoken over the opening of "The Stone Age" as day breaks over East Africa and the first bars of Strauss' *Also Sprach Zarathustra* swell on the soundtrack, recap the wordless message that Stanley Kubrick uses in the opening scenes of *2001: Space Odyssey*. "The ape rose," Welles intones as hairy bipeds stand and stretch, silhouetted by the rising sun, "and became man." The introduction to "The Roman Empire," backed by the sound of tympani and trumpet, would not feel out of place in any of Hollywood's mid-century depictions of the classical world: "Rome, vortex of modern civilization! Rome, the fountainhead of culture! Rome, blazing pronouncement of mankind's most glorious achievements!"

Brooks' subversion of the device comes not in his use of it, or the lines he gives Welles to deliver, but in the juxtaposition of the spoken words on the soundtrack and the actions depicted onscreen. The stone-age hominids labeled "Our Forefathers" by a title card stretch their arms, beat their chests, and then drop their hands to waist level and vigorously masturbate before dropping to the ground in a state of post-orgasmic bliss. Welles' rapturous pronouncements about the exalted glories of Rome fade out, along with the drums and horns, as the camera's gaze sweeps over a Roman street scene. The sign over an elaborate doorway advertises the business within: an "V and X Cent Store." A hawker (Barry Levinson) standing beside an assortment of carved marble pillars barks at passersby, exhorting them to "columns! Columns! Columns! Get your columns here! Ionic! Doric! Corinthian! Put a few talents down in front, turn any hovel into a showplace!" A few stalls later, a barber (Sid Gould) enumerates his services: "Haircuts, shaves, shampoos ... *bloodletting*?" A soothsayer's booth and a used-chariot lot share space with a banner on the Temple of Eros, advertising its annual orgy and buffet ("First Served—First Come"). The largest crowd, however, is gathered around an artisan (Pat McCormick) waving a section of bronze tube and extolling the virtues of a new product: "Yes, citizens, plumbing! It's the latest invention to hit Rome! It moves water from one place to another!" Get on the bandwagon, he urges them, and "pipe the shit right out of your house!" Vortex of culture, indeed.

Taking the Piss: Brooks' History as Historical Commentary

Mel Brooks released his first feature film, *The Producers*, in 1967, the year when the New Hollywood Era flared into existence, leaving the last vestiges of the Studio Era (including the Production Code) crumbled in its wake.[12] His timing was fortuitous. *The Producers*—with its cheerfully amoral heroes, "Springtime for Hitler" production number, and scenes of Max Bialystock (Zero Mostel) *schtupping* little old ladies—would have been unthinkable a decade earlier and a hard sell even a few years before. The newly unbuttoned Hollywood of the late '60s and '70s was fertile ground for Brooks' wickedly funny cinematic assaults on propriety and good taste. The countercultural optimism of the late sixties and early seventies also resonated—even after it curdled into cynicism in the aftermath of Kent State, the Pentagon Papers, and Watergate—with Brooks' relentless championing of the "little guy" and skewering of wealth, power, and pretension. Released in the last months of that era, *History of the World, Part I* exemplifies both elements of Brooks' work.

Historical-epic films—like history textbooks, historical pageants, historic-house museums, local historical societies, and countless other forms of popular history—present a streamlined, sanitized, sterilized view of the past. They depict history with all the tangles combed out, all the uncertainties banished, and all forms of "unpleasantness" skimmed over or discreetly hidden. The elites are noble and high-minded; the underclasses are hard-working and grateful; and villains—where they enter the story—are redeemably misguided or irredeemably evil, but never motivated by bigotry, greed, or naked self-interest. There are exquisite gowns (but no sweatshops), rosy-cheeked children (but no childhood diseases), and streets filled with horse-drawn carriages (but no gutters filled with manure). Everybody speaks in complete sentences. Nobody does things that involve bodily fluids.

Brooks, in *History of the World*, machine-guns this genteel, polished, version of the past with a steady stream of what its architects would—with a curled lip and a pained expression—describe as "vulgarity." His characters piss, shit, belch, fart, and scratch themselves in public. They get jerked around by their bosses, disrespected by government officials, and swindled by shady merchants. They get stoned on the job, have erections at embarrassing moments, and make passes at people they barely know. They are capable of cleverness, generosity, and self-sacrifice, but they also say and do boneheaded things for ill-considered reasons. They're too busy trying to keep money in their pockets, food in their bellies, and maybe (just maybe) a willing companion in their beds to worry over-much about "mankind's most glorious achievements," let alone "blazing pronouncements" of them. They are not the plaster saints that populate traditional historical epics. They are us.

Brooks, like a historical Lord of Misrule, moves these "ordinary" people from the periphery to the center of his epic. The wealthy, powerful, and privileged who traditionally occupy that narrative center are not displaced—they are still the ones with the power to make history, in Brooks' view; his scrappy heroes are just trying to survive it—but they *are* cut down to size.[13] "No man is a hero to his valet," and no "great man" of history is a hero to Brooks.

"Vulgarity" is abundant in *History of the World*, but it is rarely *just* deployed for the sake of an easy laugh. It is there to make Brooks' larger point. The scene of our newly bipedal hominid ancestors exploring what to do with their now-free hands works on multiple levels: as a sight gag, as an absurd juxtaposition with the portentous narration, and as a twitting of the deeply serious "Dawn of Man" sequence in *2001*. It also provides a cheeky comment on the well-worn anthropological observation that the shift from quadrupedal to bipedal locomotion was a watershed in human evolution. The "official" answers to "what can you do as a biped but not as a quadruped?" are "see further" and "use your now-free hands to make and use tools." Kubrick's hominids use their newly free hands to pick up a bone, which they use first as a tool and then as a weapon. Brooks' hominids—less concerned, in the moment, with the march of mankind than with their own pleasure—engage in displays of macho posturing, and then in self-gratification. Most of what we call history, Brooks suggests, is moments like this: people not trying to advance civilization but just trying to get through the day.[14]

The deeper levels of Brooks' superficially crude humor frequently involve imbalances of power. A vignette in the "Stone Age" segment, for example, shows a caveman (Sid Caesar) creating an elaborate, multi-colored image of a horse by daubing paint on a cave wall as his companions gesticulate vigorously and the narrator proclaims "the birth of art." Traditional historical epics would end the scene there, but Brooks presses on. "With the birth of the artist," the narrator continues, "came the inevitable afterbirth: the critic." The cave-artist looks up, excited and deferential, as a stranger joins the group. Stroking his beard, the critic contemplates the still-wet paint and expresses his opinion of the new-made masterpiece ... by urinating on it. Twenty minutes of screen time and several million years of history later, in Rome, Comicus (Brooks) and Josephus (Hines) are both condemned for ill-chosen words spoken to the powerful, but Empress Nympho (Madeline Kahn) uses directs double entendres to every man within earshot. To her aide, Bob, after she has been urged to add Josephus to her entourage: "Do I have any openings that this man might fit?" Josephus invites her to "say when" while pouring wine into her goblet: "Eight-thirty." To a besotted Marcus Vindictus, who asks, "what bait" to use to catch her love: "Ah, but the servant waits while [nodding at her husband, Emperor Nero] the *master* baits."

Crudeness is, in *History of the World*, almost invariably the province of the powerful and directed against the powerless. Comicus, standing in the unemployment office line, is asked his occupation by a clerk (Bea Arthur). When he replies, "Stand-up philosopher," she responds: "Oh, a *bullshit* artist!" When the Roman senators are asked, "Shall we continue to build palace after palace for the rich? Or shall we aspire to a more noble purpose and build decent housing for the poor?" they respond, in unison, "FUCK THE POOR!" In the French Revolution segment, royal advisor Count De Monet (Harvey Korman), takes delight in demonstrating his place in the hierarchy by urinating on the shoes of a lesser functionary. King Louis XVI commits multiple acts of casual cruelty: extorting sexual favors from the daughter of a condemned prisoner, using peasants as skeet-shooting targets, and ending a chess game played with human "pieces" by declaring: "Knight jumps queen! Bishop jumps queen! Pawns jump queen! Gangbang!" He punctuates each with a self-satisfied smirk and the line "It's good to be the king!"

"It's good to be the king" is, to judge by anecdotal evidence, the film's most-quoted line. It could even be described, sardonically, as the film's message. In Brooks' version of pre–Revolutionary France, it *is* good to be the king, at least for the moment. Wealth, power, and privilege—whether wielded by Louis, Torquemada, Nero, Nympho, or a Stone-Age art critic—means never having to say you're sorry, let alone having to fear for your body, your freedom, your reputation, or your life. The wealthy, powerful, and privileged are free to do as they please, knowing that someone *else*, not them, will wind up with a red-hot poker—or, as one helpful Roman citizen suggests, a live snake—shoved up their ass, with no Preparation H in sight.

That, in the end, is the deeper message of *History of the World, Part I*. The tidy, streamlined histories filled with well-behaved people doing high-minded things are—whether encountered on movie screens, pageant stages, or the pages of textbooks—the self-serving fantasies of the powerful and privileged. The reality of history is summed up in the chorus of an old music-hall ballad:

> It's the same the whole world over
> Isn't it a bleedin' shame?
> It's the rich what gets the pleasure,
> And the poor what gets the blame.

The best that the rest of us can do, Brooks suggests, is to live our lives, dodging and weaving as best we can, take our pleasures where we can find them, and have each other's backs.

Conclusion

Parody lies at the core of Mel Brooks' film and television work, but—beyond their basic, shared parodic nature—Brooks' contributions to the form have been wildly diverse. *Blazing Saddles* lampoons the entire Western genre, laying comedic waste to plot, character, and thematic tropes used by scores of filmmakers over hundreds of films, but *Young Frankenstein* parodies not the horror genre as a whole but a specific manifestation of it: the Universal Studios productions of 1932–1942. *High Anxiety* is a parody of Alfred Hitchcock thrillers wrapped around a lampoon of a specific Hitchcock film (*Spellbound*, 1945), the latter element presaging *Spaceballs* and Brooks' later, lesser single-film parodies such as *Robin Hood: Men in Tights* and *Dracula: Dead and Loving It*. Like the far more ambitious *Silent Movie*, however, *Spaceballs* also takes parodic aim at the movie business itself, breaking the fourth wall in order to do so. *Get Smart* is traditionally (and rightly) read as a parody of contemporary spy sagas like *The Man from U.N.C.L.E.* and the James Bond films, but its savage skewering of bureaucratic absurdities is also a takedown of earnest 1940s and '50s tales about government agents in gray flannel suits.

History of the World, Part I, though it premiered to decidedly mixed reviews, and was faulted—even by those critics who enjoyed it—for its crude humor, disorganized structure, and lack of a plot, is firmly part of that tradition. Even if it lacks the effortless assurance of *Blazing Saddles* or *Young Frankenstein*, it is a formidable work of parody and—of all Brooks' genre parodies—is second only to *Blazing Saddles* as social commentary. *History of the World* is a frontal assault on the pretensions of what passes,

206 אויסגעקליבן ווערק / Selected Works (1965–1991)

in Hollywood epics and the historical narratives in which they are rooted, for the history of the world ... an assault headlined, appropriately, by a Black man from Harlem and a short Jew from Brooklyn.

Notes

1. Barry Keith Grant's *Film Genre Reader IV* (Austin: University of Texas Press, 2012) can scarcely be bettered as a starting point.
2. For a discussion of one particularly iconic example, see Valerie Wee, "The Scream Trilogy, 'Hyperpostmodernism,' and the Late Nineties Teen Slasher Film," *Journal of Film and Video*, vol. 57, no. 3, Fall 2005, pp. 47–61.
3. See Cynthia J. Miller and A. Bowdoin Van Riper, editors, *The Laughing Dead: The Horror-Comedy Film from* Bride of Frankenstein *to* Zombieland (Lanham, MD: Rowman & Littlefield, 2016), xvi–xviii.
4. See John G. Cawelti, *Adventure, Mystery, and Romance: Formula Stories as Art and Popular Culture* (Chicago: University of Chicago Press, 1976), pp. 37–50.
5. On this point, see Suman Gupta, "On Mapping Genre: Literary Fiction/Genre Fiction and Globalization Processes," *Globalizing Literary Genres: Literature, History, Modernity*, edited by Jernej Habjan and Fabienne Imlinger (New York: Routledge, 2015), 213–227.
6. Trailers for the American release of the softcore pornography film *Emanuelle* (1974) appealed to mainstream audiences on precisely this level. They promised an "elegantly erotic" film that had "given millions who had never seen this kind of movie the courage to watch," and that "lets you feel good without feeling bad" (*Emanuelle* 1974 Theatrical Trailer, YouTube.com, https://www.youtube.com/watch?v=DsOXacenEk8).
7. Over the history of the Academy Awards, a solid third of the Best Picture winners have fit into the "historical epic" category.
8. On the historical epic as genre see, for example, Sheldon Hall and Steven Leonard, *Epics, Spectacles, and Blockbusters: A Hollywood History* (Detroit: Wayne State University Press, 2010), and Brian Taves, *The Romance of Adventure: The Genre of Historical Adventure Movies* (Jackson: University Press of Mississippi, 1993).
9. Brooks is staging a cartoonishly exaggerated version of a mid-century trope that—even in its time—was read as cartoonish and uncomplimentary. Awareness of that context mitigates the fact that the scene depicts assault and kidnapping and implies rape ... but not entirely.
10. In *Story of Mankind*, the narration is delivered onscreen by Ronald Colman and Vincent Price. In *How the West Was Won* and *The Bible*, it is delivered as voiceovers by Spencer Tracy and John Huston, respectively.
11. Huston, in *The Bible*, provides not only the narration, but the *literal* voice of God.
12. See Mark Harris, *Pictures at a Revolution: Five Movies and the Birth of the New Hollywood* (New York: Penguin, 2009).
13. The "new social history" that shook the foundations of the historical profession on the eve of Brooks' entry into filmmaking had a broadly similar agenda: To center (in 21st century parlance) the experiences of the 99 percent rather than the 1 percent in the narrative. Its practitioners have been accused, ever since, of iconoclasm for its own sake, and an irrational hatred of the "great men" and occasional "great women" around whom the traditional narrative centers.

For early statements of its purpose and goals, see: Werner Conze and Charles A. Wright, "Social History," *Journal of Social History*, vol. 1, no. 1, Autumn 1967, pp. 3–17; Eric J. Hobsbawm, "From Social History to the History of Society," *Daedalus*, vol. 100, no. 1, Winter 1971, pp. 20–45; and Laurence Vesey, "The 'New' Social History in the Context of American Historical Writing," *Reviews in American History*, vol. 7, no. 1, March 1979, pp. 1–12.

For an overview of the conservative backlash, and the resulting cultural upheaval, see (for example) Edward T. Linenthal and Tom Engelhardt, editors, *History Wars: The* Enola

Gay *and Other Battles for the American Past* (New York: Holt, 1996) and Gary B. Nash, Charlotte Crabtree, and Ross E. Dunn, *History on Trial: Culture Wars and the Teaching of the Past* (New York: Knopf, 1997).

14. It is, in fact, a short step from Brooks' masturbating hominids to the oft-floated observation that the first use for every new communication technology is the delivery of sexually explicit material. See, for example, Patchen Barss, *The Erotic Engine: How Pornography Has Powered Mass Communication from Gutenberg to Google* (Toronto: Doubleday Canada, 2010).

Filmography

Ben-Hur. Dir. William Wyler. Metro-Goldwyn-Mayer, 1959. DVD. Warner Bros. Home Video, 2013.
The Bible: In the Beginning. Dir. John Huston. Dino De Laurentiis, Cinematografica and Seven Arts Productions, 1966. DVD. Twentieth Century Fox, 2001.
Black Sunday. Dir. Mario Bava. Galatea-Jolly Film, 1960. DVD. Kino Lorder films, 2015.
Blazing Saddles: 30th Anniversary Special Edition. Dir. Mel Brooks. Crossbow Productions, 1974. DVD. Warner Bros. Home Video, 2007.
Chariots of Fire. Dir. Hugh Hudson. Allied Stars Ltd and Enigma Productions, 1981. DVD. Warner Bros. Home Video, 2011.
Cleopatra. Dir. Joseph L. Mankewicz. Twentieth Century Fox, 1963. DVD. Twentieth Century FoxHome Entertainment, 2013.
Dracula: Dead and Loving It. Dir. Mel Brooks. Gaumont, Brooksfilms, Castle Rock Entertainment, 1995.
Get Smart. Created by Mel Brooks and Buck Henry. Talent Associates and CBS Productions (Season 5). NBC, 1965–1969; CBS, 1969–1970.
High Anxiety. Dir. Mel Brooks. Twentieth Century Studios, 1977. DVD. Twentieth Century Fox Home Entertainment, 2006.
History of the World, Part I. Dir. Mel Brooks. Brooksfilms, 1981. DVD. Twentieth Century Fox, 2006.
How the West Was Won. Dirs. Henry Hathaway, John Ford and George Marshall. Metro-Goldwyn-Mayer, 1962. DVD. Warner Home Video, 2007.
Intolerance. Dir. D.W. Griffith. D.W. Griffith, 1916. DVD. Diaphana, 2010.
Life of Brian. Dir. Terry Jones. Handmade Films and Python Monty Pictures,1979. DVD. Sony Pictures Home Entertainment, 2008.
The Man from U.N.C.L.E. Created by Sam Rolfe and Norman Felton. NBC 1964 –1968.
The Music Man. Dir. Morton DaCosta. Warner Bros. Pictures, 1962. DVD. Warner Bros. Home Video, 2012.
One Million Years B.C. Dir. Don Chaffey. Hammer Films and Production Arts, 1966. DVD. Twentieth Century Fox Film Corporation, 2018.
The Pit and the Pendulum. Dir. Roger Corman. Alta Vista Productions, 1961. DVD. American International Pictures, 2001.
The Producers. Dir. Mel Brooks. Embassy Pictures, 1967. DVD. MGM (Video & DVD), 2003.
Quo Vadis. Dir. Mervyn LeRoy. Metro-Goldwyn-Mayer, 1951. DVD. Warner Home Video, 2011.
Robin Hood: Men in Tights. Dir. Mel Brooks. Brooksfilms and Gaumont, 1993. DVD. Twentieth Century Fox Home Entertainment, 2009.
Silent Movie. Dir. Mel Brooks. Crossbow Productions, 1976. DVD. Twentieth Century Fox Home Entertainment, 2006.
Spaceballs. Dir. Mel Brooks. Metro-Goldwyn-Mayer, Brooksfilms and Industrial Light and Magic, 1987. DVD. MGM, 2015.
Spellbound. Dir. Alfred Hitchcock. Selznick International Pictures and Vanguard Films. 1945. DVD. MGM (Video & DVD), 2008.

אויסגעקליבן ווערק / Selected Works (1965–1991)

The Story of Mankind. Dir. Irwin Allen. Cambridge Productions, 1957. DVD. Warner Archives, 2009.
The Ten Commandments. Dir. Cecil B. DeMille. Motion Picture Associates, 1956. DVD. Paramount Pictures Home Entertainment, 2017.
The Tower of London. Dir. Roger Corman. Admiral Pictures, 1962. DVD. MGM, 2006.
2001: A Space Odyssey. Dir. Stanley Kubrick. Stanley Kubrick Productions, 1968. DVD. Warner Home Video, 2015.
Witchfinder General. Dir. Michael Reeves. Tigon British Film Productions, 1968. DVD. MGM, 2007.
Young Frankenstein. Dir. Mel Brooks. Gruskoff/Venture Films, Crossbow Productions, Inc. and Jouer Limited, 1974. DVD. Twentieth Century Fox, 2014.

Works Cited

Barss, Patchen. *The Erotic Engine: How Pornography Has Powered Mass Communication fromGutenberg to Google*. Doubleday Canada, 2010.
Cawelti, John G. *Adventure, Mystery, and Romance: Formula Stories as Art and Popular-Culture*. University of Chicago Press, 1976.
Conze, Werner, and Charles A. Wright. "Social History." *Journal of Social History*, vol. 1, no. 1, Autumn 1967, pp. 3–17.
Grant, Barry Keith. *Film Genre Reader IV*. University of Texas Press, 2012.
Gupta, Suman. "On Mapping Genre: Literary Fiction/Genre Fiction and Globalization Processes." *Globalizing Literary Genres: Literature, History, Modernity*, edited by Jernej Habjan and Fabienne Imlinger, Routledge, 2015, pp. 213–227.
Hall, Sheldon, and Steven Leonard. *Epics, Spectacles, and Blockbusters: A Hollywood History*. Wayne State University Press, 2010.
Harris, Mark. *Pictures at a Revolution: Five Movies and the Birth of the New Hollywood*. Penguin, 2009.
Hobsbawm, Eric J. "From Social History to the History of Society." *Daedalus*, vol. 100, no. 1, Winter 1971, pp. 20–45.
Linenthal, Edward T., and Tom Engelhardt, eds. *History Wars: The* Enola Gay *and Other Battles for the American Past*. Holt, 1996.
Miller, Cynthia J., and A. Bowdoin Van Riper, eds. *The Laughing Dead: The Horror-Comedy Film from* Bride of Frankenstein *to* Zombieland. Rowman & Littlefield, 2016.
Nash, Gary B., Charlotte Crabtree, and Ross E. Dunn. *History on Trial: Culture Wars and the Teaching of the Past*. Knopf, 1997.
Taves, Brian. *The Romance of Adventure: The Genre of Historical Adventure Movies*. University Press of Mississippi, 1993.
Vesey, Laurence. "The 'New' Social History in the Context of American Historical Writing." *Reviews in American History*, vol. 7, no. 1, March 1979, pp. 1–12.
Wee, Valerie. "The *Scream* Trilogy, 'Hyperpostmodernism,' and the Late Nineties Teen Slasher Film." *Journal of Film and Video*, vol. 57, no. 3, Fall 2005, pp. 47–61.

Mel Brooks, THE Producer

David Lynch's The Elephant Man *(1980) and David Cronenberg's* The Fly *(1986)*

Jonathan Winchell

A titan in the world of comedy for over seventy-five years, Mel Brooks has been highly successful in multiple areas of comedy, from performing on stage in the Catskills at a young age; to writing on Sid Caesar's variety television show *Your Show of Shows*; to performing the hit 2000-Year-Old Man comedy albums with Carl Reiner; to writing, directing, producing, and acting in comedy films; to writing a smash Broadway musical. He is a rare EGOT, a person who has received an Emmy, a Grammy, an Oscar, and a Tony. It is fitting to describe his stature in the comedy world by quoting one of his most indelible lines from *History of the World: Part I*: "It's good to be the King." As successful as Brooks has been writing, directing, and acting across stage, television, and film, and perhaps because he is so synonymous with comedy, his work as a producer is often overlooked. As prolific and long as Brooks' career has been, he has directed only eleven films. He has produced or executive produced eighteen films, more than he has directed, and over half of them are ones he did not write or direct. Six of those films are not even comedies. Two of the most notable films Brooks produced were critically acclaimed, financially successful Oscar-nominated dramas from the 1980s with titles starting with "The" and followed by an animal name, directed by dark visionary auteurs named David. These films are David Lynch's *The Elephant Man* and David Cronenberg's *The Fly*.

Brooks began producing his own films in the late 1970s and started his own production company called Brooksfilms. The first film his company made was *Fatso* (1980), the first feature film his wife, Anne Bancroft, wrote and directed. The second film that Brooksfilms made and the first which Brooks produced under the company (executive produced, and uncredited) was David Lynch's *The Elephant Man*, which came out later that same year. Six years later, he produced (also uncredited) David Cronenberg's *The Fly* (1986). It may seem incongruous that the director of *The Producers* and *Blazing Saddles* would produce *The Elephant Man* and *The Fly*, films that differ in so many ways from his own directorial efforts. If one, however, considers Brooks' own films and taste more closely, it is not so unusual that he produced films so unlike his own. Brooks is a true auteur, and, like most true *cineastes*, one who has a broad range of taste in film, an artist who creates films pushing the boundaries of good taste and what is acceptable in society—be they broad comedies or dark dramas.

Brook begins his 2021 memoir *All About Me!* with a story about seeing a film but not a comedic one. The very first anecdote he tells relates to being five years old and viewing the 1931 film *Frankenstein* directed by James Whale. Born in 1926, Brooks saw the horror classic the year it was originally released. A true film fanatic, he starts his memoir speaking about the effect cinema had on him from a young age while also making sure the reader is aware that he knows Frankenstein was actually the doctor, not the monster. His older brother Bernie took him to see the film, and it frightened him so much that he wanted to sleep with the window closed, even though it would make the room very hot. Brooks told his mother, "No, we must keep it closed! Because if we keep it open, Frankenstein will come up the fire escape and grab me by the throat and kill me and eat me!" Immediately after this, Brooks interjects, "Even though it was the doctor who was named Frankenstein, all the kids called the monster Frankenstein because that was the title of the picture" (Brooks 3). Brooks writes in his memoir: "Even as a kid, I loved all movies, black and white, color, what have you" (Brooks 33). He continues, saying that all the children had favorite movie stars, and his were mainly cowboys. He writes about his love of Charlie Chaplin, Buster Keaton, whom his "soul adored" (Brooks 35), Laurel and Hardy, and The Marx Brothers, before mentioning films that also spoke to him. "Later in life," he says, "I could wax eloquently about masterpieces like Marcel Carné's *Les Enfants du Paradis*, Jean Renoir's *La Grande Illusion*, Vittorio De Sica's *The Bicycle Thief*, Akira Kurosawa's *Rashomon*, Orson Welles's *Citizen Kane*" (Brooks 33).

Some people have a narrow conception of what filmmakers' taste in cinema is and assume film directors only appreciate and respond to and perhaps even only watch films that are very similar to the works that they themselves direct. With that logic, Ingmar Bergman would like only somber, bleak, existential black-and-white dramas about man's place in the world. Stanley Kubrick would like only technically precise and emotionally distant films. David Lynch would like only dark, nightmarish, surreal motion pictures. Mel Brooks would like only outrageous comedies and spoofs. Like Brooks, people who are true film connoisseurs tend to watch a variety of films from many genres, countries, and eras. Greta Gerwig spoke in a *Vanity Fair* interview about her husband and fellow film director Noah Baumbach going to Ingmar Bergman's house in Sweden. She said, "We went to Sweden ... and the island where Bergman spent the last years of his life, and we went to his house.... And we were looking at all the VHS tapes, and you would think that they were all very highbrow, and we kept finding these VHSs of things we didn't think he'd have, like *Beverly Hills Cop*. And it was great. We were just imagining Bergman at 70 being, like, 'I think I'll watch, uh, ... *Anger Management* tonight.' And Noah said, 'It's so good to know that everyone's the same'" ("What Greta Gerwig"). In 1963, Stanley Kubrick submitted a list of his Top 10 films for a magazine titled *Cinema*. It included Charlie Chaplin's *City Lights* and the W.C. Fields comedy *The Bank Dick* (Wrigley). He also was (reportedly) a fan of the American television comedy series *Roseanne*, *Seinfeld*, and *The Simpsons* (Offman).

David Lynch loves certain films, but he himself has said on multiple occasions that he is not a *cineaste*. In a 2018 interview with *The Guardian*, he said, "I never was a movie buff. I like to make movies" (Carroll). However, in a video in which he was asked to name some of his favorite films, he lists, among others, Jacques Tati's *Monsieur Hulot's Holiday* and the W.C. Fields film *It's a Gift* ("David Lynch Favorites"). Filmgoers sometimes even mistake directors as only making one type of film. Ignorant Marvel fans like to lob insults online at Martin Scorsese for only making gangster films when, in reality, well over half of his films are not crime films (for example, *Alice Doesn't Live Here Anymore*, *The Last Temptation of Christ*, *Hugo*). Lynch *himself* directed only ten feature theatrical films, and two of them are rather straight-forward dramas based on the lives of real men. *The Elephant Man* is one of them, and the other, *The Straight Story*, is a G-rated Disney film about a man riding a lawnmower a few hundred miles across the Midwest to visit his ailing brother.

Mel Brooks has directed only comedy films, with a relatively small filmography (in comparison, his fellow *Your Show of Shows* writer Woody Allen has his fiftieth film as writer/director released in 2023). Although Brooks has not directed even a dozen films, his affection for classic Hollywood films and genres is evident through all of the films he directed, from the Western spoof *Blazing Saddles* to the Universal horror parody *Young Frankenstein* to the Alfred Hitchcock send-up *High Anxiety*. In fact, the last film he directed, *Dracula: Dead and Loving It*, was criticized by some are being too faithful to Bram Stoker's novel and previous film versions of it. Leonard Maltin wrote in his movie guide that the film "spends so much time retelling the familiar Transylvanian's story it forgets to be funny" (Maltin 382). Brooks is at his best when he is spoofing genres and films for which he has true affection, and the audience can tell. His attention to detail was so strong in *Young Frankenstein* that he shot the film in black and white and even used some of the props and sets from the original James Whale films (Brooks 238). The film is as funny as it is because Brooks re-created the horror classics so precisely.

Mel Brooks' passion for cinema and playing with genres can be seen in his work as a director, but his love for film is even more evident in the films in other genres he made as a producer. By the end of the 1970s, Brooks had directed six films. He wrote or co-wrote all of them, and he acted in four of them, being the lead in the last two: *Silent Movie* and *High Anxiety*. Brooks writes in his memoir *All About Me!*, "*High Anxiety* was actually the start of a new chapter in my career. Not only was I writing it with my co-writers, directing it, and starring in it, but for the first time I was also the producer. It was a natural outcome of overseeing my movies at every stage from script to screen" (Brooks 294).

Brooks hired Stuart Cornfeld, who had been his assistant producer on *High Anxiety*, to produce his wife Anne Bancroft's first feature film, *Fatso* (1980). "Cornfeld was a student at the AFI's producer's program, where he focused his energies on its directing workshop for women. Actress Anne Bancroft was a student there at the time, and Cornfeld produced a half-hour short for her" (Lynch and McKenna 140). *Fatso* became the first film of Brooks' new company Brooksfilms, which was an expansion of the short she had done. In his memoir, Brooks asks the question that he felt people would have had at the time: "Why Brooksfilms?" He answers, "Well, because I had a problem. If the name Mel Brooks was on a movie screen, the audience would expect to see a Mel Brooks comedy. It was Pavlovian! Ring the bell, and the dog salivates. Put the name Mel Brooks on the screen, and the audience is already laughing" (Brooks 295). One of the leading comedy writers, directors, and actors in Hollywood, Brooks was able to get an outrageously irreverent and racially explosive Western spoof, a black-and-white film, and a silent film all made at major Hollywood studios in the 1970s. But as wildly successful as Brooks was throughout the decade, he had a proven track record in only comedy. He was so synonymous with comedy, especially broad, hysterical ones, that he knew it would be difficult for audiences to accept any work that he put his name on that was not a comedy. As Brooks said, "What was helping me gain ascendance in comedy was also limiting me because the name Mel Brooks meant 'expect to laugh,' which constrained me as far as making films that were not meant to just make you laugh but to make you experience a whole range of thoughts and feelings" (Brooks 295).

When David Lynch was asked in an interview at the Bryn Mawr Film

Institute in 2014 why Mel Brooks tapped an independent filmmaker with his particular vision to direct a true-life Victorian drama with John Gielgud and Anthony Hopkins, he answered, "This is one of the great mysteries of life" ("David Lynch on beginning"). Lynch had only directed one feature film when the prospect of directing *The Elephant Man* came to him. That one feature was *Eraserhead*, a disturbing, avant-garde black-and-white horror film about a man who finds out that he has fathered a mutant baby. It is one of the weirdest films ever made, a challenging and dark work of experimental cinema. Lynch studied at the American Film Institute, and it took him five years to get the film made. He would raise some funds to shoot the film and would work until he ran out and had to go out and look for more. The film eventually became a cult hit and one of the key films in the midnight movie circuit, along with others such as Alejandro Jodorowsky's *El Topo* (1970), John Waters' *Pink Flamingos* (1972), and Jim Sharman's *The Rocky Horror Picture Show* (1975).

For the type of film it was, *Eraserhead* had great success, but it certainly was not a standard hit in the way Hollywood thinks of hits. Stuart Cornfeld, who was working for Mel Brooks at his newly formed company Brooksfilms, had seen *Eraserhead* and "absolutely loved it" and "was totally blown away by" it (Lynch and McKenna 140). He knew David Lynch had gone to the AFI, so he got his number and reached out to him to see what he was doing. They began having lunch once a week. At that point, in the late 1970s, Lynch was trying to get another film made, one titled *Ronnie Rocket*. It was about "a man who's three and a half feet tall, with a red pompadour, who runs on sixty-cycle alternating-current electricity" (Lynch and McKenna 161). Like the film that would eventually become his second feature, *The Elephant Man*, *Ronnie Rocket* dealt with themes of deformity and body differences. However, Cornfeld and Lynch could not find the financing for such an unusual and bizarre film. Lynch was poor at the time, doing small jobs to make some money, but mostly being supported by his wife. He eventually thought that he might try and direct a film he did not initially write. As Lynch recalls in the 2009 documentary *Great Directors*, he talked to Cornfeld one day and said, "'Stuart, I was just wondering if you knew of any scripts that I might be able to direct. And he said, 'I know of four scripts.' And he said, 'David, the first one is called The Elephant Man,' and a bomb went off in my head, and I said, 'That's it'" (*Great Directors*). The script, written by Christopher De Vore and Eric Bergren, was based on the true story of Joseph Merrick (John in the film), a man born with severe deformities in Victorian England in 1862. He was a circus "freak" and badly mistreated by his "owner" until he was brought in for an examination by Dr. Frederick Treves. Merrick was eventually welcomed into society before dying at age 27.

Lynch and Cornfeld went all around Hollywood trying to get the film made, but no studio expressed interest, because Lynch was told "no one wants to see a film about a monster like this" (*Great Directors*). Cornfeld, who was working for the newly formed Brooksfilms, persuaded Anne Bancroft to read the script for *The Elephant Man*, and she then got her husband Mel Brooks to read it. Brooks was "deeply moved by the story" and "wanted Brooksfilms to make it" (Brooks 297). Brooks was set with the screenwriters (Christopher De Vore and Eric Bergren), the producer (Jonathan Sanger), and the executive producer (Stuart Cornfeld), but he needed to find out about this man that Cornfeld spoke so highly of named David Lynch. Sanger told Brooks that he needed to see Lynch's first film *Eraserhead*. When Lynch heard about this, he said, "Well, it's been nice knowing you guys" (*Great Directors*). Lynch was certain that he was not going to get the job after Brooks screened his first feature film.

What person in Hollywood would see Lynch's only feature film at that point, a film as challenging and disturbing as any that has ever been made, and give that director a studio film, especially a moving historical drama set in Victorian England? The answer is Mel Brooks. There seem to be some discrepancies about exactly where Brooks saw *Eraserhead*, who was there, and when he first met Lynch. According to Brooks in his memoir, Cornfeld took him to the Nuart Theatre, "a small out-of-the-way movie house on Santa Monica Boulevard known for showing different films like John Waters's *Pink Flamingos* (1972) … because Stuart was bugging [Brooks] to see the work of this guy, a new director on the block called David Lynch, and his new film *Eraserhead* (1977)" (Brooks 298). However, in David Lynch's 2018 hybrid biography/autobiography *Room to Dream*, in which each chapter is broken into two parts, one biographical section written by Kristine McKenna and one written by Lynch based on his recollections, McKenna writes that, "accompanied by [Jonathan] Sanger, Brooks had a private screening of the film in the Darryl F. Zanuck Theater in a basement on the Twentieth Century–Fox lot while Lynch and Cornfeld waited outside" (Lynch and McKenna 142–143). Lynch himself recalls waiting "in the lobby outside this screening room" (Lynch and McKenna 162). In multiple interviews and in his book, Lynch relates his experience of nervously waiting outside the screening room for Brooks' reaction to *Eraserhead*. In the documentary *Great Directors*, Lynch says, "I was standing outside the room, the screening room, when the doors blew open, and Mel came racing toward me, and he embraced me, and said, 'You're a madman. I love you. You're in'" (*Great Directors*).

In his memoir, Brooks, however, claims that "[Lynch would] only meet at one place, a restaurant called Bob's Big Boy … way out in the Valley." He writes, "When I first saw him I thought, Am I meeting David

Lynch or Charles Lindbergh?" (Brooks 298). Also, in a video interview years earlier, Brooks claims that when Lynch walked into his office, he looked beyond him because he thought maybe he was a messenger. He said, "I expected to meet a young Max Reinhardt. I expected the guy to have, like Picasso, two eyes on one side of his nose. And here is a young Charles Lindbergh. He looked just like Charles Lindbergh" ("When Mel Met David"). Jonathan Sanger even claimed in an interview that at the screening where Brooks saw *Eraserhead*, "Stuart [Cornfeld] wasn't around, and David said, 'I'm not coming. I'm not coming to the screening.' He said, 'I'll send you the print, but I don't want to be there.' So I said, 'OK.' So I set a screening at 20th Century-Fox. They have a screening room. ... Empty screening room. Me. Mel." After the screening, which felt interminable to Sanger, who thought Brooks was going to physically whack him in the back of the head for suggesting Lynch, Sanger said that Brooks started to interpret the film. He said Brooks said, "'OK. I like this guy. I think he's really interesting and unusual. Let's meet him.' OK. I call up David" ("Why Mel Brooks"). It seems most likely that Brooks saw *Eraserhead* at the screening room at 20th Century-Fox, which both Sanger and Lynch recall, and that Lynch was waiting outside the room when Brooks came out with that warm burst of enthusiasm towards Lynch and told him he was in as the director of *The Elephant Man*.

As sharp as Brooks' memory is, especially for someone who is now 99, he is a raconteur, so the specifics of who met whom where and when should be taken with a grain of salt. Brooks clearly saw a gifted and unique young filmmaker and took a chance on him, something very few people in Hollywood would do after seeing a film like *Eraserhead*. Brooks not only executive produced the film, he also worked carefully on the script with Lynch and the other screenwriters. Cornfeld recalls, "David and Mel were the driving forces on the rewrite, and Mel had a lot of input on the script. ... Mel made important contributions to the script and he made the story more dramatic. It differs in the film from the way it actually happened, but Mel said, 'It doesn't matter what really took place; our concern is how this operates emotionally as a movie'" (Lynch and McKenna 143). As a raconteur Brooks continued to be more interested in telling a good story and capturing an emotional truth.

Although Brooks and Lynch may seem to be an unlikely pairing, the two have similar beliefs about filmmaking and vision. Brooks writes in his memoir: "I have worked with producers all my life. For the most part, I had great relationships with my producers. ... That certainly prepared me to be a producer myself because I knew every single issue and struggle a writer and a director had to go through to make a film. The challenge for me was to find and nurture talented filmmakers. At this point in my life, I knew real talent when I saw it. The second and most important challenge for me was to hold back. I was so used to managing every aspect of production, from the initial idea, the first time a pencil touched a piece of paper, all the way through to the final cut, what the audience got to see on the screen. I had to figure out a balance, how to help and manage the process, without suppressing anyone else's creative vision. And Brooksfilms was the answer. I helped where help was needed, and was hands off when I realized I might be interfering in the filmmaker's vision. When I first opened Brooksfilms, my motto, my mission statement was 'Give talented people room to express their vision'" (Brooks 295–96).

Lynch was once quoted in *The New York Times* as saying, "'I would rather not make a film than make one where I don't have final cut" (Woodward). Lynch technically did not have final cut on *The Elephant Man*, but Brooks supported him all the way. Lynch said, "There was no studio people telling Mel anything. From the very beginning, he let me make the film. I was protected" (Rodley 13). In an interview for the Criterion Collection Blu-ray and DVD release of the film, Lynch said, "Working with Mel was sort of close to heaven." He continued: "People see the humorous side of Mel, and a certain kind of humor, and those people who know him see this superintelligence and depth of caring and intelligence. He's a very special human being. He was so supportive of me. I didn't have, technically, final cut on *The Elephant Man*. It was my first, really, you know…. It wasn't a studio picture, really. It was a Brooksfilms picture. But Mel supported me from the beginning through some very tough times 'til the very end and gave me a break in life that was phenomenal" ("David Lynch, 2009"). In *Funny Man*, Patrick McGilligan writes about Brooks warding off the studio suits who wanted to change and cut parts of the film. Remembering comments by the Paramount executives about "not liking the beginning or the ending—'too oblique,'" Stuart Cornfeld remarks, "Brooks said, 'We showed you the cut … because we are involved in a business deal and we wanted you up to date on the progress of the product we're working on. Don't misconstrue that as soliciting the input of raging primitives!' Then he slammed down the phone. 'Mel at his best'" (McGilligan 441).

Another notable comparison that also links Brooks and Lynch is that they each directed one of the few black-and-white films distributed by a Hollywood studio in the era deemed "New Hollywood" (late 1960s to the early 1980s) that were highly successful, both financially and critically. Brooks' film was *Young Frankenstein*. Lynch's *The Elephant Man* was a box office hit, grossing $26 million in the United States ("The Elephant Man" Box Office Mojo) and was nominated for eight Academy Awards: Best Picture (Jonathan Sanger), Best Director (David Lynch), Best Actor in a Leading Role (John Hurt), Best Writing, Screenplay Based on Material from Another Medium (Christopher De Vore, Eric Bergren, Lynch), Best Art Direction-Set Decoration (Stuart Craig, Robert Cartwright, Hugh Scaife), Best Costume Design (Patricia Norris), Best Film Editing (Anne V. Coates), and Best Music, Original Score (John Morris). Although the film ended up winning no Oscars (*Ordinary People* won three of the awards in categories *The Elephant Man* was nominated in: Best Picture, Best Director, and Best Writing) (Oscars.org), the Victorian-era drama did win three BAFTA awards, including Best Film and Best Actor, and Lynch was nominated for Best Direction and Best Screenplay (BAFTA).

Ever since *The Elephant Man* came out in 1980, David Lynch has spoken highly of Mel Brooks and acknowledged how paramount he was in helping his career. Lynch had a Twitter account. The enigmatic auteur did not often send messages and, since December 8, 2022, did not tweet or retweet anything. However, he did tweet more than once celebrating the birthday of "the great Mel Brooks!!!" (Lynch, David [@DAVID_LYNCH], Dear Twitter Friends, It's a day late" and "Dear Twitter Friends, Happy Birthday").

In 2012, both Mel Brooks and David Lynch received honorary degrees from the American Film Institute at that year's commencement ceremony. In his comments, Lynch said, "I think about Mel Brooks many times during the year and especially around his birthday, which is June 28" ("David Lynch Receives"). He turned around asking for confirmation from the man himself, and Brooks said the date was correct. Film critic and journalist Pete Hammond covered the event and wrote about how Lynch, a man who is often elusive about his own work, was grateful and acknowledged how important Brooks was in his career. Hammond wrote, "For his part Lynch, a man of few words, kept his prepared remarks to a minimum generally talking about his fellow honoree." "If AFI put me on the map, Mel Brooks came along and put me on a beautiful mountaintop. He called me 'Jimmy Stewart from Mars' but he's the crazy one. He picked me after just one film to direct an Edwardian drama with John Hurt, Anthony Hopkins, Anne Bancroft, Sir John Gielgud and Dame Wendy Hiller. It was my good fortune that Mel had this insanity. I don't have any more speech" (Hammond).

The 1986 film *The Fly*, directed by David Cronenberg, is a remake of the 1958 film of the same name directed by Kurt Neumann and starring Vincent Price. That film was based on the short story of the same name by George Langelaan, which originally appeared in *Playboy* magazine. The first screenplay for the 1986 film was written by Charles Edward Pogue. Cronenberg is a Canadian screenwriter and director whose films up to that point were all science fiction or horror films, with the exception of the race car drama *Fast Company* (1979), yet another example of how even the output of distinctive auteurs can be hard to pin down. Cronenberg's two previous films before *The Fly* were *Videodrome* and *The Dead Zone*, both of which came out in 1983. Although both films were shot in Canada, in the United States *Videodrome* was distributed by Universal Pictures, and *The Dead Zone* was distributed by Paramount Pictures. Cronenberg was asked in a 1992 interview concerning his comments about Hollywood being "limiting" when he was still able to make exactly the films he wanted. He said, "But I haven't made my films within Hollywood. I flirt with it.... The closest I came was with *The Fly*, which was the only studio film I've done; it was a Mel Brooks, Brooksfilm[s] production, although it was already understood it was going to be a Fox picture" (Schwartz 87).

Cronenberg had gained some notable reception for his films, especially among genre fans, but there was still a disreputable quality to his work. Although intellectually stimulating to adventurous filmgoers, his films featured graphic violence, gore produced with ground-breaking special effects, and provocative sexual content. *Videodrome* was a box office failure, only making $2.1 million at the box office on its $5.9 million budget ("Videodrome," Box Office Mojo). *The Dead Zone*, although based on a Stephen King novel, was Cronenberg's least graphic horror film to date, and it was one of the director's most critically successful films to date and a modest box office success, grossing $20.7 million ("The Dead Zone," Box Office Mojo) on a $10 million budget ("The Dead Zone," AFI). Stuart Cornfeld approached Mel Brooks with the original script by Charles Edward Pogue, and he liked it but felt that it needed rewrites. "Producers Mel Brooks and Stuart Cornfeld wanted Cronenberg to direct the film from the beginning" (Baker), and they approached him early on, but he was attempting to make his own science fiction film based on a short story, Philip K. Dick's "We Can Remember It for You Wholesale," which Paul Verhoeven eventually ended up making as *Total Recall* (1990), so he passed on the opportunity. When the Dick adaptation fell apart, Cronenberg came back on *The Fly* "with one major concession. He was given the freedom to rewrite Pogue's script from the ground up" (Baker). One of the major differences between the original script and Cronenberg's rewrite was that the main character Seth Brundle was married in the first version. "Cronenberg's draft kept the bare bones of the film's overarching plot," and "he maintains to this day that without Pogue's foundation there would be no film," but Cronenberg infused his script with his unique interests in body horror and identity and made it his own.

Cronenberg was a more established director than David Lynch when he made *The Fly* (it was his eighth widely theatrically released film, tenth if one counts his underground features), but it was the cast that Mel Brooks helped Cronenberg fight for. In his memoir, Brooks remembers seeing "a brilliant actor Jeff Goldblum ... in *The Big Chill* (1983) and thought he was wonderful." However, Brooks wrote that Fox, the film's "distributor, said, 'No. Goldblum is good, but he's not a star. We need a star.'" Brooks responded, "No, we don't need a big star. We need the right guy for the role, and that guy is Jeff Goldblum." He said, "Finally, they gave in" (Brooks 352).

Because of the casting of Goldblum, he asked Brooks to screen test his then girlfriend for the female lead. Brooks recalls, "We tested her, and we loved her. Her name was Geena Davis. It was her first real starring role. She was marvelous in the part" (Brooks 352). Brooks came up with the idea of using an iconic line in the film as the major tagline when promoting the film. In one scene, Brundle has brought another young woman to his loft, and "when she's a little frightened by the explanation of his teleporting chamber, he calms her with, 'It's okay. Don't be afraid.' Geena steps out of the shadows where she has been hiding and says, 'No, be afraid. Be very afraid.'" Brooks, the savvy businessman, said, "The phrase jumped out at me and I thought it would be perfect for the lead line in our advertising campaign" (Brooks 352). *The Fly* was "Cronenberg's most lucrative release to date, grossing more than all of his previous films combined" (Marriott and Newman 253), making it "one of the biggest box-office hits the horror genre had in the 1980s—and it remains Cronenberg's best-known and most popular picture" (Mathijs 310). The film was also critically acclaimed, especially for a horror/science fiction film. Jeff Goldblum was nominated for Best Actor by the National Society of Film Critics, the National Board of Review named the film one of the Top Ten Films of the year, and the film even won an Academy Award for Best Make-Up (Chris Walas and Stephen Dupuis) ("The Fly: Awards").

The Elephant Man and *The Fly* are radically different from the films Brooks directed himself, yet a thematic line can be drawn between Brooks' crazed comedies, Lynch's moving Victorian drama and Cronenberg's grotesque sci-fi/horror romance. Like Lynch and Cronenberg, Brooks always questioned societal norms, pushing the boundaries of good taste and commenting on and twisting the rules of society. He also frequently incorporated deformed, disabled, or strange characters in order to comedically reveal the harsh ways in which society can treat outsiders. In *Blazing Saddles*, Mongo is a large, mentally slow man with great physical strength, but inwardly he is a soft-spoken innocent child who mutters poetic thoughts such as "Mongo only pawn in game of life." The townsfolk of Rock Ridge only see Mongo as a mongoloid (hence the name) and a brute, but once Sheriff Bart knows how to handle him, "Mongo ... has deep feelings for Sheriff Bart," much like *The Elephant Man*'s John Merrick, who becomes devoted to Dr. Treves when he is accepted by him. Generally, Cronenberg

אויסגעקליבן ווערק / Selected Works (1965–1991)

is known for his use of body horror and graphic violence and gore in his films, and *The Fly* features some of the most remarkable practical effects make-up in cinema history. After Seth Brundle inadvertently gets into the transporter pod with a fly, their DNA is combined, and Brundle's body starts to deteriorate with his skin rotting away, his teeth and fingernails falling out, and his digestive system causing him to vomit up his food as corrosive liquid. Cronenberg thought of the film as a commentary on aging while others in the mid-1980s saw the film as a parable on the AIDS epidemic. Whatever reading one takes away from the film, in it a brilliant man becomes ostracized from society and treated like a monster.

Brooks' own films present the human body in outrageous and provocative ways. In *Blazing Saddles*, Brooks was one of the first directors to feature the bodily function of flatulence in a major Hollywood motion picture when the cowboys sit around the campfire eating beans and breaking wind repeatedly and loudly. In *High Anxiety*, in a spoof of *The Birds*, Brooks had birds not pecking at his character but defecating on him as he fled. In *Dracula: Dead and Loving It*, his character Van Helsing gets Harker to drive a wooden stake through the heart of his lover, who is now a vampire, and an absurdly huge geyser of blood explodes from her coffin, drenching the forlorn male. Unlike Cronenberg, Brooks rarely depicted violence on screen, and when he did, it was for comedic effect. But at the same time, Brooks, like Cronenberg, liked to push the boundaries of taste and what could be depicted on screen. Mel Brooks, a majorly successful filmmaker and a serious artist at heart who passionately makes and supports cinema, produced two of the strongest and most successful films by the singular auteurs David Lynch and David Cronenberg and did not even put his name on the films to better support them. He is, to use a phrase he has often uttered, a *mensch*.

Filmography

Alice Doesn't Live Here Anymore. Dir. Martin Scorsese. Warner Bros., 1974. DVD. Warner Home Video, 2004.
Anger Management. Dir. Peter Segal. Columbia Pictures, Revolution Studios and Happy Madison Productions, 2003. DVD. Sony Pictures Home Entertainment, 2003.
The Bank Dick. Dirs. Edward F. Cline and Ralph Ceder. Universal Pictures, 1940. DVD. In *The W.C. Fields Comedy Collection: Volume 1*. Universal Studios Home Entertainment, 2013.
Beverly Hills Cop. Dir. Martin Brest. Don Simpson/Jerry Bruckheimer Films and Eddie Murphy Productions, 1984. DVD. Paramount Pictures Home Entertainment, 2018.
The Bicycle Thief. Dir. Vittorio De Sica. Produzione De Sica, 1948. DVD. Sony Pictures Home Entertainment, 2003.
The Big Chill. Dir. Lawrence Kasdan. Carson Productions, 1983. DVD. Sony Pictures Home Entertainment, 1999.

The Birds. Dir. Alfred Hitchcock. DVD. Alfred J. Hitchcock Productions, 1963. Universal Studios Home Entertainment, 2012.
Blazing Saddles: 30th Anniversary Special Edition. Dir. Mel Brooks. Crossbow Productions, 1974. DVD. Warner, 2004.
Citizen Kane. Dir. Orson Welles. RKO Radio Pictures and Mercury Productions. DVD. Warner Bros., 2016.
City Lights. Dir. Charlie Chaplin. United Artists, 1931. DVD. Video Service Corp., 2016.
The Dead Zone. Dir. David Cronenberg. Dino De Laurentiis Company, 1983. DVD. Warner Bros. Home Video, 2013.
Dracula: Dead and Loving It. Dir. Mel Brooks. Gaumont, Brooksfilms and Castle Rock Entertainment, 1995. Warner Bros. Home Video, 2008.
The Elephant Man. Dir. David Lynch. Brooksfilms, 1980. DVD. Video Service Corp., 2020.
Les Enfants du Paradis. Dir. Marcel Carné. Pathé Consortium Cinéma, 1945. DVD. Criterion, 2012.
Eraserhead. Dir. David Lynch. AFI Center for Advanced Studies, 1977. DVD. Criterion, 2014.
Fast Company. Dir. David Cronenberg. Admit One Presentations and Danton Films, 1979. DVD. Blue Underground, 2004.
Fatso. Dir. Anne Bancroft. Brooksfilms, 1980. DVD. Starz/Anchor Bay, 2006.
The Fly. Dir. David Cronenberg. Brooksfilms, 1986. DVD. 20th Century Fox Home Entertainment, 2005.
La Grande Illusion: Essential Art House. Dir. Jean Renoir. Réalisation d'Art Cinématographique, 1937. DVD. Criterion Collection, 2008.
High Anxiety. Dir. Mel Brooks. DVD. Twentieth Century Studios, 1977. Twentieth Century Fox Home Entertainment, 2006.
History of the World: Part I. Dir. Mel Brooks. Brooksfilms, 1981. DVD. 20th Century Fox, 2006.
Hugo. Dir. Martin Scorsese. GK Films and Infinitum Nihil, 2011. DVD. Paramount Pictures Home Entertainment, 2017.
It's a Gift. Dir. Norman Z. McLeod. Paramount Pictures, 1934. DVD. In *The W.C. Fields Comedy Collection: Volume 1.* Universal Studios Home Entertainment, 2013.
The Last Temptation of Christ. Dir. Martin Scorsese. Universal Pictures, Cineplex Odeon Films, Testament Productions, 1988. DVD. Universal Pictures, 2005.
Monsieur Hulot's Holiday. Dir. Jacques Tati. Cady Films, 1953. DVD. eOne Films, 2004.
Ordinary People. Dir. Robert Redford. Wildwood Enterprises, Inc., 1980. DVD. Paramount, 2017.
Pink Flamingos. Dir. John Waters. Dreamland, 1972. DVD. Warner Archives, 2017.
The Producers. Dir. Mel Brooks. Embassy Pictures, 1967. DVD. MGM (Video & DVD), 2002.
Rashomon. Dir. Akira Kurosawa. Daiei Film, 1950. DVD. Criterion, 2002.
The Rocky Horror Picture Show. Dir. Jim Sharman. Michael White Productions, 1975. DVD. 20th Century Studios, 2020.
Roseanne. Created by Roseanne Barr. ABC ,1988–1997.
Seinfeld. Created by Larry David and Jerry Seinfeld. NBC, 1989–1998.
Silent Movie. Dir. Mel Brooks. Crossbow Productions, 1976. DVD. Twentieth Century Fox Home Entertainment, 2006.
The Simpsons. Created by Matt Groening. Fox 1989–present.
The Straight Story. Dir. David Lynch. Asymmetrical Productions, Canal+, Film4 Productions and Le Studio Canal+, 1999. DVD. Walt Disney Video, 2000.
El Topo. Dir. Alejandro Jodorowsky. Producciones Panicas, 1970. DVD. Universal Music, 2021.
Total Recall. Dir. Paul Verhoeven. Carolco Pictures, 1990. DVD. Lionsgate Home Entertainment, 2020.
Videodrome. Dir. David Cronenberg. Filmplan International, Canadian Film Development Corporation, Famous Players and Guardian Trust Company, 1983. DVD. Universal Studios Home Entertainment, 2005.

אויסגעקליבן ווערק / Selected Works (1965–1991)

Young Frankenstein. Dir. Mel Brooks. Gruskoff/Venture Films, Crossbow Productions and Jouer Limited, 1974. DVD. Twentieth Century fox, 2014.
Your Show of Shows. Created by Sylvester L. Weaver, Jr. Max Liebman Productions. NBC, 1950–54.

Works Cited

BAFTA (British Academy of Film and Television Arts). "Year of Presentation: 1981." http://awards.bafta.org/explore?year=1981. Accessed 7 June 2023.
Baker, Chrishaun. "David Cronenberg's *The Fly* Is More Relevant Than Ever." *Inverse*, 18 Oct. 2022. https://www.inverse.com/culture/scifi-movies-hbo-max-october-2022-the-fly. Accessed 6 June 2023.
Brooks, Mel. *All About Me!* Ballantine, 2021.
Carroll, Rory. "David Lynch: 'You gotta be selfish. It's a terrible thing.'" *The Guardian*, 23 June 2018. https://www.theguardian.com/film/2018/jun/23/david-lynch-gotta-be-selfish-twinpeaks. Accessed 4 June 2023.
"David Lynch Favorites Movies and Film Makers." *YouTube*, uploaded by Diego Schonhals, 13 Oct. 2007. https://www.youtube.com/watch?v=G1s7EwOeowU.
"David Lynch on Beginning THE ELEPHANT MAN." [Video]. *YouTube*, uploaded by brynmawrfilm (Bryn Mawr Film Institute), 30 Sept. 2014.
"David Lynch Receives AFI Honorary Degree From Laura Dern." [Video]. *YouTube*, uploaded by American Film Institute, 27 May 2022. https://www.youtube.com/watch?v=_efRtSfN-M4.
"David Lynch, 2009." *The Elephant Man*, The Criterion Collection, 2020. Blu-ray.
"The Dead Zone." *AFI Catalog*. https://catalog.afi.com/Catalog/MovieDetails/57919. Accessed 6 June 2023.
"The Dead Zone." *Box Office Mojo*. https://www.boxofficemojo.com/title/tt0085407/?ref_=bo_se_r_1. Accessed 6 June 2023.
"The Elephant Man." *Box Office Mojo*. https://www.boxofficemojo.com/title/tt0080678/?ref_=bo_se_r_1. Accessed 7 June 2023.
"The Fly: Awards." *IMDb*. https://www.imdb.com/title/tt0091064/awards/?ref_=tt_awd. Accessed 7 June 2023.
Great Directors. Directed by Angela Ismailos, featuring David Lynch, Anisma Films, 2009.
Hammond, Pete. "Mel Brooks, David Lynch Receive Honorary Degrees At AFI Commencement." *Deadline*, 13 June 2012. https://deadline.com/2012/06/mel-brooksdavid-lynch-receive-honorary-degrees-at-afi-commencement-285991/. Accessed 4 June 2023.
Lynch, David [@DAVID_LYNCH]. "Dear Twitter Friends, Happy Birthday to the great Mel Brooks!!!" *Twitter*, 28 June 2019, https://twitter.com/DAVID_LYNCH/status/1144651707449655297.
Lynch, David [@DAVID_LYNCH]. "Dear Twitter Friends, It's a day late, but Happy Birthday to the great Mel Brooks!!!" *Twitter*, 29 June 2018, https://twitter.com/DAVID_LYNCH/status/1012742476052885504.
Lynch, David, and Kristine McKenna. *Room to Dream*. Random House, 2018.
Maltin, Leonard. *Leonard Maltin's 2015 Movie Guide: The Modern Era*. Plume, 2014.
Marriott, James, and Kim Newman. *Horror! 333 Films to Scare You to Death*. 2nd edition, Carlton Books, 2010.
Mathijs, Ernest. "The Fly." *101 Horror Movies You Must See Before You Die*, edited by Steven Jay Schneider, Quintessence, 2009.
McGilligan, Patrick. *Funny Man*. Harper, 2019.
Offman, Craig. "Kubrick Gets a Herr Piece." *Salon*, 7 July 1999. https://www.salon.com/1999/07/07/herr/. Accessed 5 June 2023.
Oscars.org. THE 53RD ACADEMY AWARDS | 1981. https://www.oscars.org/oscars/ceremonies/1981. Accessed 5 June 2023.
Rodley, Chris. "Some Weird Breeze of the Essence of This Beautiful Soul." Excerpts from

Lynch on Lynch in the Criterion Collection Blu-ray booklet of *The Elephant Man*. Farrar, Straus and Giroux, 2005.

Schwartz, David. *David Cronenberg Interviews*. University Press of Mississippi, 2021.

"Videodrome." Box Office Mojo. https://www.boxofficemojo.com/title/tt0086541/?ref_=bo_se_r_1. Accessed 7 June 2023.

"What Greta Gerwig Discovered in Ingmar Bergman's House Will Probably Surprise You." [Video]. YouTube, uploaded by Vanity Fair, 24 Jan. 2016. https://www.youtube.com/watch?v=uZT1VTQkx44.

"When Mel Met David." [Video]. YouTube, uploaded by tobykeeler, 22 May 2010. https://www.youtube.com/watch?v=BsmVEI6aVTo.

"Why Mel Brooks Hired David Lynch to Direct The Elephant Man." [Video]. YouTube, uploaded by Jog Road Productions, 5 Oct. 2015. https://www.youtube.com/watch?v=-vkndhiA0w.

Woodward, Richard B. "A Dark Lens on America." *The New York Times Magazine*, 14 January 1990. https://www.nytimes.com/1990/01/14/magazine/a-dark-lens-on-america.html. Accessed 6 June 2023.

Wrigley, Nick. "Stanley Kubrick, Cinephile." *British Film Institute*, 9 Mar. 2017. https://www2.bfi.org.uk/news-opinion/sight-sound-magazine/polls-surveys/stanleykubrick-cinephile. Accessed 6 June 2023.

A Jewish Future
The Diverse Diasporic Universe of Spaceballs *(1987)*

DAVID L. REZNIK

Unfortunately, I was just a tad too young to see Mel Brooks' *Spaceballs* during its initial theatrical release in 1987. However, as a Jewish boy born to immigrants from Russia who grew up in the WASP-y environs of early 1990s Orange County, California, I will never forget the impact the film had on me when renting it from the neighborhood video store. Not only was I tickled by Brooks' provocative mixture of genre (science fiction) and tone (farcical satire), but I was enthralled by the cinematic landscape Brooks had created, one filled with all sorts of Jewish personas I recognized. From garish families like those in the immigrant cohort to which my own family belonged to authoritarian wimps directly resonant to my own inner conflicts, the characters in *Spaceballs* felt like an identificatory breath of fresh air. And unlike so many other exemplars of "Jewish film," both at its time (for example, *Barton Fink*, *Schindler's List*, *Clueless*) and in the decades since (Reznik), *Spaceballs* is unique in both the range of its Jewish representations and, just as importantly, the temporality of its narrative: Brooks constructs a vision of the future in which Jews are neither non-existent nor peripheral but rather one in which Jewishness is at the center of an entire human universe. Hence, to me, *Spaceballs* is one of the most important works of Jewish cinema. Yet, scholarly accounts of *Spaceballs* have barely even mentioned its Jewishness. To be sure, academics have successfully analyzed the film across multiple dimensions: as a political parody (Castleberry and McMurry), as a form of myth mockery (Bonnstetter), and as a pedagogical lens for deconstructing postmodernity (Ott and Bonnstetter). Still, the existing literature on the film somehow lacks any comprehensive assessment of the diverse and seemingly ubiquitous representations of Jewish identity Brooks provides in his popular science fiction (sci-fi) spoof.

In this essay, I hope to remedy such oversight by unpacking and parsing the omnipresence and variety of *Spaceballs*' "Jews in space" (a set-up Brooks teases in his earlier film, *History of the World, Part I*). Throughout my analysis here, I emphasize the radicality of *Spaceballs*' setting (i.e., "once upon a time warp [...] in a galaxy very, very, very, very far away") for Jewish cinematic representation. I argue that the futurity Brooks makes visible in *Spaceballs* redeems a haunting absence of Jewry in the "out there's" and "tomorrows" of popular culture while simultaneously interrogating the trajectory of contemporary Jewish identity politics. For these reasons, I make the case for recognizing Brooks' film as an essential addition to the canon of Jewish cinema.

No Jews?

The scholarship on *Spaceballs*, though not as extensive as the literature for some of Mel Brooks' other films, is nevertheless quite theoretically rich. In Ott and Bonnstetter's article, *Spaceballs* is analyzed as an important postmodern text, a "cultural museum tour" of "parodic tourism" inviting audiences to participate actively in acquiring the symbolic resources necessary to successfully navigate the three logics of "PO": provocation, presumption, and provisionality. Rather than simply reproducing science fiction by focusing on its own constructed universe, *Spaceballs* is described as a "meta-science-fiction" film in which the "extraordinary object" of inquiry is the production of science fiction cinema itself (315). Ott and Bonnstetter argue that the film's ongoing popularity (and transcendental value) emerges out of its capacity to help viewers "manage semiotic excess, [...] confront fragmentation, and [...] address rapid cultural change" (324) in their increasingly unstable realities. Yet despite meticulous close reading of various characterizations and narrative elements in the film, the authors never mention Jewishness at all, even when thinking through the audience interactivity and intertextual allusions emphasized throughout *Spaceballs*.

Another important contribution to *Spaceballs* studies is Bonnstetter's solo-authored chapter. Here, she focuses on the film's use of parody to help audiences deconstruct problematic science fiction mythologies without replacing them with other pernicious ideologies. Through analysis of both semantic and syntactic elements in *Spaceballs*, Bonnstetter posits that the film reveals the social constructedness and generic limitations of three specific myths: the annihilation of humanity by an "alien Other," the epic hero's journey toward destiny, and the phallocentric/triangulated Oedipal conflict. While engaging in its work of critique, *Spaceballs* neither punishes nor destroys the mythologies it deconstructs, instead opting to pleasurably emphasize the myths' arbitrariness and contingencies. Bonnstetter applauds this generosity as an exemplar of the productiveness of parody over satire for the purposes of audience engagement and persuasion. However, though Jewish identity politics receive an explicit mention in the chapter, Bonnstetter limits this discussion to the "Druish" people (198), leaving out other constellations of characters (including the Spaceballs themselves) and other narrative components that are available for similar analysis.

A recently published chapter by Castleberry and McMurry offers a third robustly academic treatment of *Spaceballs*. In this piece, the film is contextualized within Mel Brooks' *oeuvre*, while also being celebrated for its comprehensive commentary on branded commodity culture as well as a new concept the authors develop: franchise fascism. This multidimensional idea, embodied most clearly by *Spaceballs*' parodic target, *Star Wars*, includes several dimensions, including "nostalgic commodity acquisitions toward global media monopolization," "'might makes right' fascistic ideology," "entitled fan communities," and "increasingly interconnected imperial narratives" created "under homogenous producing and directing stylistics" (100). While the co-authors expand the number of Jewish characterizations in the film to include two smaller roles (Dot Matrix and Yogurt), the film is otherwise left unexamined for its identity politics, instead focusing the discussion almost exclusively on the "critical funhouse mirror" *Spaceballs* holds up to a seemingly de-racialized "Yuppie capitalism and American consumerism" (101).

Hence, while there are clearly references to Jewishness in *Spaceballs*, the film has not as yet been treated by the available scholarly literature as a Jewish film per se. This is not altogether surprising, given historical accounts of Jewish-authored science fiction as well as American Jewish film. For example, Batya Weinbaum writes about the outsized role Jewish authors played in early U.S. sci-fi; she describes an ambivalence surrounding Jewish identity in many of these works, as they often feature "the presentation of Jewish themes, of themes that affect and concern Jews, [while] disguising the makers (the author's name, the character's name)" (186). Nevertheless, she argues that the genre of early U.S. sci-fi should be understood as a "structure of communication" among Jewish immigrants to help make sense of a new, strange, and even "alien" environment in which they now found themselves (180). Importantly, Weinbaum invokes Bakhtin's concepts of "trangredience" and "outsideness" to suggest readers learn how to read Jewish sci-fi by "looking at cameos [and] examining the down-played background rather than [...] the presented frame" (181). This is a more nuanced approach than that taken by another scholar, Lavie

Tidhar, who insists there are "no Jews" in these sci-fi worlds, even while conceding that Jewish characters may be coded or in disguise.

The question of coding also features prominently in discussions of Jewish identity in U.S. cinema writ large. A recent *New York Times* feature by Esther Zuckerman exemplifies the hand-wringing consternation in attempting to construct a canon of American Jewish film. Admitting that the exercise itself "provokes more questions than it provides answers," Zuckerman ultimately lands on "movies that are explicitly Jewish, ones that acknowledge and depict their characters' backgrounds and traditions, while placing them in the context of the American landscape." It is important to note, however, that Zuckerman deems Mel Brooks' oeuvre as marginal at best, and, at worst, outside of such a canon. This is because, though Brooks' humor is "specifically Jewish," the "subject matter" is considered not to be; though Jewishness is part of Brooks' "identity onscreen" and "shtick," Zuckerman still dismisses his Jewish filmic representations as "ancillary to the plot."

Such critical conundrums are instructive, as they reveal fundamental questions about American Jewish identity politics in U.S. cinema. As I describe in my book, *New Jews?*, a "postracial" mindset within much of American society has constructed Jews as "just another bunch of 'white folks'" (viii). Such a metanarrative conveniently sidesteps the most important historical dynamic involved in American Jewish identity: the persistent dialectic of antisemitism and assimilation. To re-center this tension, my book argues that American Jewry onscreen should be understood as always already identified/identifiable through historically sedimented, socially legible markers of ethno-racialization, regardless of whether there are any explicit Jewish identifications made in a film itself. Such a hermeneutic includes analysis of characters' physiognomic embodiments as well as other racialized behavioral "signifiers," even if identity is otherwise only vaguely inferred (167). I am thus interested not only in cinematic Jews per se but also Jewish portrayals (167), in order to proactively excavate the deep structures of racialization embedded within a movie rather than passively accepting the unreliable narration of that filmic text.

Through this shift in identificatory analysis, it becomes possible to recognize just how profoundly Jewish a movie like *Spaceballs* really is. I disagree with Tidhar that Mel Brooks "promised us something we never really saw," since *Spaceballs* is in fact the "Jews in … *spaaaace!*'" that Brooks previewed in his *History of the World, Part I*. What is more, *Spaceballs* features an exceptionally diverse tapestry of Jewish diasporic identity onscreen, and in the sections to follow, I delve into three specific constellations of Jewish characterizations portrayed in the film: the protagonist Druish royal family, a satire of American Jewish assimilatory fantasies;

the imperial Spaceballs antagonists, a rebuke of Jews perpetrating their own historical persecution; and Yogurt, a critique of Zionism set in an Oz-like desert planet. Brooks' varying depictions of Jewish diasporic identity in *Spaceballs* thus constitute a cinematic universe of Jewish futurity that is missing from the canon of otherwise ostensibly Jewish film. In fact, together they form a comprehensive interrogation of the most salient questions facing Jewish identity politics today.

"Funny, she doesn't look Druish"

From the opening title card sequence, modeled after the *Star Wars* opening title card sequence in its font and upward scroll before a starry space backdrop, Brooks makes clear the side in *Spaceballs* that the audience is meant to root for: the "peace-loving" Planet Druidia, whose "every breath of air" is sought after by their "evil" neighbors, Planet Spaceball. As the scroll concludes, viewers are told that Druidia's Princess Vespa is to be married that day, though "danger lurks in the stars above." Brooks' first shot of Planet Druidia reveals a Disney-meets-Tolkien landscape, as majestic castle-like structures are set amidst an immaculate backdrop of snowcapped mountains, evergreen trees, and turquoise water.

Once the film zooms into the actual wedding proceedings, however, there is a decided shift in our sense of these protagonists. Never mind the perfunctory crosses, a priest-looking officiant, or King Roland's cartoon-like medieval regal adornment; the scene is more like a goyish fairy-tale fantasy of a profoundly Gentile-assimilated American Jewish family. Note, for instance, the name of the venue for Vespa's nuptials, "First Intergalactic Temple (Reformed)," a nod to the unoffensively suburban synagogues that have increasingly lined middle-class Jewish enclaves across the United States over the past century. Likewise, the planet's inhabitants are referred to as "Druish" rather than Druids, a running joke throughout the film in its obvious rhyming reference to Jewish.

In fact, by scratching the surface of several Druish characterizations, one finds a bountiful well of even more subtle Jewish identity markers. For instance, King Roland and the gold-plated android he has watching over his daughter, Vespa ("Dot Matrix," a *Star Wars* C-3PO stand-in) form an overbearing tag team that harkens to the "meddling matriarch" stereotype I detail in *New Jews?*. This trope, emerging out of diasporic Jewish family dynamics, is distinguished by overprotective and codependent "excesses of nurturance" (Prell 75), and is most notable both in Roland's materialistic pampering of Vespa as well as Dot's micromanaging surveillance of her. The former includes the "million space bucks" Roland is willing to pay for Vespa's rescue as well as the "brand-new white Mercedes 2001 SEL Limited Edition" spaceship, complete with a "moon roof" and "all-leather interior," that he bought for her. In an aside, to help reinforce Roland's Jewishness, Brooks adds that the king got "a good deal" on the spaceship by leveraging his cousin, "Prince Murray," who owns "a dealership in the Valley" (another explicit reference to American Jewish demography, specifically an enclave in the Los Angeles metropolitan area). And Dot, voiced by American Jewish comedy icon, Joan Rivers, spends the entire film hovering over Vespa's every move, whether sacrificing her own wellbeing to provide Vespa with umbrella shade in the hot desert sun or mobilizing (per a "virgin alarm") to jealously safeguard Vespa's sexual chastity.

Vespa herself embodies another relevant cinematic stereotype: the Jewish American princess. For starters, her appearance is scrutinized vis-à-vis racialized narratives about Jewish physiognomy, as evidenced by the incredulity expressed in the title line of this section. Furthermore, when Vespa is captured by the Spaceballs, it is revealed that she had a nose job as a "Sweet 16 present" by her father, with a profile photo of her pre-surgery visage featuring an absurdly hook nose meant to caricature the most insidious antisemitic myths about Jewish appearance. At the same time, Vespa is obsessively attached to her luxury goods and personal hygiene as well as psychically drawn to "no object of desire other than the self" (Prell 80). Throughout the film, Brooks hyperbolizes Vespa's materialism and vanity, including jokes about her love affair with her designer "matched luggage," her inability to live without her "industrial strength hair-dryer," and her ubiquitous wedding gown costuming. Per the socio-historical foundations of the Jewish American princess cinematic trope (Prell 84), Vespa is thus reflective of American Jewish upward mobility into the middle-class commodity fetishism and consumerist over-indulgence of late capitalism in the United States.

Importantly, this Druish trio at the center of *Spaceballs* can be read as a cautionary tale by Brooks regarding the discontents of American Jewish familial assimilation. While sweet in his disposition, Roland is farcically ineffectual; examples include his ridiculous passcode of "1-2-3-4-5" used to protect his entire planet's air supply as well as his clearly erroneous choice of groom for Vespa's arranged marriage (Prince Valium, performed by 1980's queer icon, Jim J. Bullock). Dot too is portrayed as decidedly old-fashioned in her sexual mores and desperate codependency. But Vespa is arguably the biggest disappointment of the three. She demonstrates autonomy through heroic acts of valiance (like shooting down several Spaceball foot soldiers single-handedly) and displays a less materialistic code of ethics through her attraction to a character who seemingly refuses her father's money (Lone Star); however, Vespa ultimately foregoes a potentially more independent existential trajectory by marrying Lone Star in the film's closing scene once it is revealed that he is, in fact, a prince (with the added assumption that the two will thus still live off their royal assets).

While Brooks humors *Spaceballs*' audiences with his usage of familiar stereotypes, he simultaneously asks larger, more unsettling questions about the cooptation of the American Jewish family's political imagination. Is a "Druish" (i.e., American Jewish) future possible if it remains wedded to fantasies of medieval Europe? Can Roland, a proxy for the American Jewish patriarch, really buy his way into acceptance and admiration? What does Dot, an American Jewish meddling matriarch cyborg, dream of once Vespa is no longer her infantilized preoccupation? And how truly fulfilling can a royal life be for an American Jewish princess like Vespa? Through his satire of 1980's American Jewish domestic drama in *Spaceballs*, Brooks urges American Jewish identity politics to seek salvation beyond Gentile-inspired middle-class suburban satisfactions.

"I see your Schwartz is as big as mine"

The antagonists in *Spaceballs* are, according to the opening title card sequence, "a ruthless race of beings" called Spaceballs who have "foolishly squandered their precious atmosphere" on Planet Spaceball. The film's narrative conflict involves a plot hatched by a trio of Spaceball "evil leaders" (President Skroob, played by Mel Brooks; Dark Helmet, played by Rick Moranis; and Colonel Sandurz, played by George Wyner) to steal Planet Druidia's air by whatever means necessary, including kidnapping Vespa. Like the introduction of Planet Druidia, Brooks uses audiovisual cues to help audiences recognize the Spaceballs as a pastiche of familiar sources: the space ship they ride in is accompanied by *Jaws*-like theme music; their costuming combines elements of both Nazi uniforms and the Galactic Empire outfits from *Star Wars*; and their architecture, insignia, and titles directly refer to the U.S. government (for example, the headquarters of Spaceball City is a replica of the Capitol building; the Spaceballs seal is a blown-up version of a dime with Skroob profiled like FDR; and the Spaceballs ship transforms into a Statue of Liberty facsimile called "Mega Maid").

And like the Druish characters, Brooks codes the Spaceball leaders as Jewish. Firstly, Brooks cast three Jewish screen actors, including himself, to perform these roles despite the indirect connection to Aryan ethnonationalism. Additionally, Brooks plays the Spaceballs as a mash-up of two other well-worn stereotypes in American Jewish cinema that I have analyzed in *New Jews?*: the neurotic nebbish and scheming scumbag. The first of these tropes, historically rooted in the "*schlemiel*" of Yiddish theater, is a "physically undesirable, romantically ineffectual, and sexually impotent male" whose haplessness and profound insecurity often lead to calamitous mishaps (Reznik 4); these roles are frequently cast to highlight certain antisemitic myths about Jewish men, whether physical stereotypes like "large pronounced noses, eyeglasses, dark and/or curly hair, frailty, [and] short stature" (Reznik 4), or behavioral ones like "sexual over-aggressiveness" and/or "an exaggerated penchant for lusting after Gentile women" (Reznik 4–5).

Every neurotic nebbish aspect listed above is embodied in Moranis' performance of Dark Helmet. Indeed, almost all of the entire comedic basis for Dark Helmet's characterization is how explicitly emasculated an inversion he is of the hypermasculine Darth Vader from *Star Wars*. For example, a physical gag repeated throughout the film is how oversized Helmet's headgear appears relative to his petite stature, a direct contrast to the massively framed, barrel-chested Vader. Helmet's physical incongruity is further highlighted when he is shown searching for Vespa on a desert planet wearing a ridiculously large safari version of a helmet; just to see out of this unwieldy headpiece, Helmet must open a small door in the front of it.

The Jewish-coded humor about Helmet's bodily features is further reinforced by Brooks' jokes about Helmet's psychosexual proclivities. Starting with an absurdly extended panning of the Spaceball warship's phallic size, virtually every scene featuring Dark Helmet has him either castrating other characters or preoccupied with his own genitality. Such anxiety reaches its climax in the literal swordfight duel that Dark Helmet has with Lone Star, the narrative context for the line that serves as the title of this section. The most jarring neurotic nebbish behavior exhibited by Dark Helmet, though, is him secretively playing out a perverse scene with action figure dolls of him, Vespa, and Lone Star, a barely disguised enaction of the Oedipal triangle with sexualized violence included.

Two other Spaceballs (Skroob and Dr. Schlotkin, the plastic surgeon brought in to rework Princess Vespa's nose) display elements of the neurotic nebbish as well. Both are distinctly diminutive in physical stature, especially relative to the objects of their libidinal desire—the "Doublemint twins" of chewing gum advertising fame in the case of the former and an Amazonian nurse for the latter. It is important to note that these women are intentionally cast to represent Gentile standards of beauty; both Skroob and Schlotkin are caught in compromising sexual trysts with these shiksa love interests, emphasizing a powerlessness over such lust. To leave no doubt over the Jewishness of these neurotic nebbishes, Brooks inserts a Yiddish-tinged double entendre joke, as Dark Helmet advises Schlotkin (in Skroob's presence) to "go back to the golf course and work on your putts."

Spaceballs also features filmic portrayals of the scheming scumbag stereotype related to Jewish diasporic identity. Equally borne out of historical European antisemitism, the notion that Jews engage in "conspiratorial designs for societal domination through political deceit and commercial miserliness" (Reznik 6) is reflected in characterizations of "slimy social climber[s]" (Bronner 144) whose "self-interest and personal profit" supersede all other moral/ethical imperatives (Reznik 6). While Brooks uses neurotic nebbish traits to help identify the Spaceball leadership as Jewish, it is in his depiction of them as scheming scumbags seeking to conquer the universe that he offers a powerful critique of political assimilation by the Jewish diaspora, particularly in the United States.

To help establish this point, it is important to first note that the Spaceballs are clearly intended to represent historical Fascism. This is made obvious by their aforementioned clothing/symbols as well as other clues (for instance, their *Lebensraum*-like murderous designs to expropriate a neighboring planet's air supply, Skroob's Hitler-adjacent mustache, the Spaceball salute that combines a Nazi arm motion with an "up yours" gesticulation, etc.). However, Brooks also seeks to complicate what would otherwise be an overly facile association between the Spaceballs and the Third Reich. For starters, there is the confounding factor of the U.S. governmental motifs described above.

But there are also subtler hints as well. Take, as an example, Dark Helmet's quizzical response when a Spaceball foot soldier addresses him with an SS-like "Jawohl"; the confused/concerned look registering on Helmet's face indicates a sudden recognition that he, a Jewish neurotic nebbish, is in over his (oversized) helmet by attempting to mimic the same historical regime that sought to exterminate him. Also, Germanic foot soldier-aside, the rank-and-file crew of the Spaceballs ship is racially diverse, including a cameo appearance made by the *Police Academy* franchise's Michael Winslow as a Black American radar technician providing his usual variety of voiced sound effects. Brooks thus leaves viewers with the impression that the Spaceballs are actually more analogous to a futuristic Jewish-led American space empire than a simple proxy for Nazi Germany.

A famous scene helps to solidify this provocative perspective on the film. In it, Colonel Sandurz explains to Dark Helmet an innovative cinematic technology that the Spaceballs have developed to monetize both past and future earnings through the present moment. This "now, now" sequence, in which the simultaneity of active filming/VHS recording is painstakingly articulated, has already been read as a glimpse into postmodern capitalism (Ott and Bonnstetter). When the characters involved are identified as Jewish, however, it can also be understood as a reflexive joke Brooks is making about the long-standing antisemitic paranoia over perceived Jewish control of mass media: here are two Jewish-coded leaders of an "evil" "race of beings" engaged in a farcical back-and-forth over not only their ownership of movie distribution but the nature of time itself.

While such reflexive humor in the Spaceball characterizations does offer levity to help disarm the malice of antisemitic stereotypes, I believe Brooks is also engaging in a quite serious critique of the logical ends of Jewish assimilation—this time not only aimed at the consumerism of the American Jewish family, but at the Jewish diaspora as political citizenry vis-à-vis nationalist imperial ambitions. Given increasing Jewish involvement in contemporary neoconservatism (Friedman), Brooks uses his Spaceball neurotic nebbishes/scheming scumbags to deliver a warning about the perils of Jewish alignment with phallocentric fascism. These characters' hapless ridiculousness satirizes the otherwise seductive promise of militarized conquest and domination with an over-identification with empire that might otherwise tempt the Jewish diaspora. To drive home this important proposition, Brooks creates an additional layer of characterization to address the global geopolitical issue at the heart of contemporary Jewish identity politics: the question of Zionism for Jews worldwide, which is the topic of the next section.

"Merchandising, merchandising"

Arguably the least ambiguously Jewish character in *Spaceballs* is Yogurt, the straight-from-the-shtetl, Yiddish-accented, Mel Brooks–performed parody of Yoda from *Star Wars*. Yogurt is clearly intended to serve as a throwback to early 20th-century Jewish diasporic comedy, with a "bupkis" here and a "Schwartz" there. And while Yogurt provides plenty of wholesome humor, a deeper examination of the real-world resonances with his onscreen portrayal reveals Brooks' subtle critique of Zionism, the geopolitical project of a Jewish ethnonational state in historic Palestine. In questioning the wisdom of the state of Israel, Brooks knows he is creating a sandstorm among the Jewish diaspora, so the textual clues he leaves are relatively obscure and subliminally operant.

One must begin with the Shakespearean "green world" inversion that Brooks devises as Yogurt's setting. Vespa and Dot (now aboard a Winnebago spaceship with Gentile-coded Lone Star and his "mawg" sidekick, Barf) crash-land on a desert planet featuring nothing but sand dunes and scorching sunshine. While there are homage-related reasons why Brooks chooses such a location (for instance, the parallel to Tatooine, the *Star Wars* desert planet; the inclusion of the *Lawrence of Arabia* theme as score, etc.), it does not entirely explain why Yogurt would be based there, especially as Yoda is found on Dagobah, a lush planet filled with swamps and forests, not Tatooine. The logic for this adaptive decision is made clearer by the introduction of the Dinks, a tribe of munchkin-like minions who rescue the heat-exhausted *Spaceballs* protagonists; harkening to *The Wizard of Oz*, the Dinks lead their guests to their diminutive ruler, Yogurt, a guru who dwells within an imposing fire-breathing shrine statue of himself to inspire fear in all those in its presence.

At this point, the social structure of this planet comes into sharper focus—an Oz-like figure with an ambiguously similar physique to the native populace (short stature, shimmering skin, etc.) and grandiose self-importance harnesses technologies of terror to attain autocratic dominion over a seemingly deserted landscape. This narrative set-up bears more than a striking resemblance to post–Zionist historical accounts of the founding of Israel (Pappe). An additional parallel includes the spiritual veneer for an otherwise nakedly political-economic project: while Yogurt announces that he is "the keeper of a greater magic" (for example, the Schwartz), a moment later he admits that the *raison d'être* for his cave temple is really "merchandising." A la the title of this section, Yogurt repeatedly admits that his venture is quite simply a profiteering outpost for intergalactic capitalism, explaining that his gift shop of *Spaceballs*-branded tchotchkes is "where the real money from the movie is made." Indeed, upon bidding farewell to his guests, Yogurt seamlessly mixes religious idiom with the cash nexus: "God willing, we'll all meet again in *Spaceballs 2: The Search for More Money*!" In short, a supposedly divinely inspired movement is less about resurrecting a "land of milk and honey," and more of an imperially-backed extension of global commerce.

Not to be overlooked is one final seemingly insignificant detail within Yogurt's *Spaceballs* cameo. While Vespa and her Druish people are announced as the film's protagonists, they are joined by Lone Star, a Goy-ish character on a hero's journey whose persona mimics a rugged cowboy-like individualism. During the party's encounter with Yogurt, it is noteworthy that Yogurt selects only Lone Star as a pupil to receive "the Schwartz"—the Dinks have clearly never been granted access to such power, and Vespa et al. are equally disregarded. While there is narrative rationale for this screenwriting choice, Brooks' decision to feature onscreen an exclusive/preferential relationship between overt characterizations of Zionism and Gentile Americanness, respectively, is not without its socio-historical precedent; one wonders if this cinematic alliance is not analogous to Israel's steadfast loyalty to the West, even at the expense of its non–Jewish, neighboring, and own peoples.

To summarize, the preceding three sections have highlighted Jewish characterizations throughout *Spaceballs*. Not only does Brooks encode nearly all of the major roles in the film with Jewish stereotypes as identity markers, but he utilizes these constellations of characters to facilitate a number of critical reflections among Jewish diasporic audiences. To match the organization of the sections, the scale of these interrogations increases with each constellation; starting with American Jewish families' assimilation to Gentile cultural norms, including consumerism and middle-class suburban life, Brooks' film expands out into broader issues like Jewish diasporic allegiance to imperialist nationalist projects and culminates with the most fundamental geopolitical question of all: Zionism and its discontents. Hence, not only is *Spaceballs* a work of Jewish cinema, but I argue that it represents a soul-searching introspection about some of the most important identity politics-related dynamics in contemporary Jewish life.

"When will then be now?"

Returning to the main argument of this essay, what allows Brooks to engage in such a sweeping analysis and critique of Jewish diasporic identity politics is his chutzpah in constructing a futuristic universe in which Jewishness is not only centered but almost ubiquitous. This is not as simple an undertaking as it may appear, as Brooks would have had to overcome a heavily-sedimented legacy of Jewish identity being defined by a temporality of the past. Dara Horn meticulously explores this phenomenon in her *People Love Dead Jews*, highlighting how Jewishness in modern culture has almost unanimously been represented as a historical relic plumbed for its trite present-day lessons. Through such tropes, Jews become a "people whose sole attribute was that they had been murdered, and whose murders served a clear purpose, which was to teach us something. Jews were people who, for moral and educational purposes, were supposed to dead" (xiv). Horn ultimately claims that this "obsession with dead Jews" has even become "necessary […] to so many people's unarticulated concept of civilization […and] themselves" (xix). Even Brooks' oeuvre parallels Horn's assertion, as many of his own films featuring Jewish themes had a temporality rooted in the past, including the aforementioned *History of the World, Part I* (for which a Brooks-produced sequel will be released soon as a streaming television series).

In *Spaceballs*, though, Brooks blows right through the past, launching his Jewish characterizations with "ludicrous speed" into a temporal "galaxy very, very, very, very far away." Not only does such a project transcend the "dead Jews" trap Horn describes, as well as the pattern established by almost all of Brooks' works, but it actually serves as an ideal setting to interrogate the Jewish diasporic present. To support this claim, I conclude this essay with an application of sociologist Avery Gordon's conceptualizations of "haunting" and "futurity" to *Spaceballs*. Projecting specters of contemporary Jewish identity politics into a temporality of the not as-yet, Brooks offers an inspiring plea for a happier ending than is possible by staying the course of the status quo.

In her renowned monograph, *Ghostly Matters*, Gordon describes "haunting" as "an animated state in which a repressed or unresolved social violence is making itself known" (xvi). Haunting also involves the appearance of real "ghosts" (i.e., not invisible apparitions) demanding attention (xvi) and representing spectral "reminders of lingering trouble" (xix). As Gordon puts it in one of her articles on the topic, haunting serves as a notification that "what's been suppressed or concealed is very much alive and present" (2). Not surprisingly, Gordon emphasizes throughout her theorizing that those groups who have historically suffered at the hands of "abusive systems of power" are those who are disproportionately prone to being haunted (xvi).

Along with ghostly appearances and attentional demands, haunting is characterized by "an altered experience of being in time, the way we separate the past, the present, and the future" (xvi). Gordon explains that haunting "jams up" the process of the present seamlessly becoming the future, creating a "socio-political-psychological state" that challenges those being haunted with what she calls a "something-to-be-done" (2-3). Put differently, haunting creates a "critical analytic moment" that announces "a contest over the future" (3), one in which there is an invitation to act differently than simply continuing the status quo. There is a "certain retrospective urgency" to the something-to-be-done, as it begs for recognition of the possibility for an emergent rather than fatalistic futurity; Gordon quotes Marcuse to articulate that haunting offers up "historic alternatives" that could have been, were already needed/wanted before, and can now be (3).

Leveraging Gordon's ideas, *Spaceballs* can be read as the ultimate filmic haunting of the modern Jewish diaspora. Brooks offers audiences a spectral vision of the Jewish future—one in which the distant tomorrow reveals problematic ends to current trajectories of Jewish identarian/ideological assimilation and imperial/international ambition and thus serves as a ghostly reminder of a something-to-be-done differently from this day forward. What superficially reads as an otherwise joyous and light-hearted space opera filled with extraordinarily diverse Jewish characterizations also features stark moments revealing the loss and suffering of a historical antisemitism that has not yet been redeemed. Brooks thus complicates any self-satisfaction Jewish audiences experience watching such a film that reflects themselves, as elements of the repressed past that have been displaced in the present are rendered quite visible as symbols of a tragical, regretful future.

Returning to the example of the stunned realization written on Helmet's face when his foot soldier salutes him in Nazi-like fashion, Brooks' *Spaceballs* creates viscerally painful recognitions for Jewish audiences that Gordon would describe as haunting. Or take Yogurt's comedic but also sardonically bittersweet revelation that his temple mount in the desert serves as an outlet for multinational corporate profiteering. And remember Princess Vespa's explicitly articulated dreams of independence from a vapid consumerism and overbearing domesticity that are ultimately short-circuited by the denouement of yet another marriage to a (Gentile) prince. To be clear, *Spaceballs'* varying and multidimensional portrayals of Jewish identities, especially given their futurity, are obviously inspiring and wonderful. But I argue that Brooks' real genius here is leaving his Jewish characters something different/else to be desired. It is the socio-political-psychological deficit of *Spaceballs'* then, a haunting call to action for diasporic Jews living in whatever "now, now" they find themselves in, that I want to claim as the film's greatest legacy.

Filmography

Barton Fink. Dir. Joel Coen. Circle Films, 1991. DVD. Kl Studio Classics, 2017.
Clueless. Dir. Amy Heckerling. Paramount Pictures, 1995. DVD. Paramount Pictures Home Entertainment, 2017.
History of the World, Part I. Dir. Mel Brooks. Brooksfilms, 1981. DVD. Twentieth Century Fox, 2006.
Jaws. Dir. Steven Spielberg. Zanuck/Brown Company and Universal Pictures, 1975. DVD. Universal Studios Home Entertainment, 2012.
Lawrence of Arabia. Dir. David Lean. Horizon Pictures, 1962. DVD. Sony Pictures Home Entertainment, 2002.
Police Academy. Dir. Hugh Wilson. The Ladd Company, 1984. DVD. Warner Home Video, 2003.
Schindler's List. Dir. Steven Spielberg. Amblin Entertainment and Universal Pictures, 1993. DVD. Universal Pictures Home Entertainment, 2018.
Spaceballs. Dir. Mel Brooks. Metro-Goldwyn-Mayer, Brooksfilms and Industrial Light and Magic, 1987. DVD. MGM, 2015.
Star Wars. Dir. George Lucas. 20th Century Fox, 1977.
The Wizard of Oz. Dir. Victor Fleming. Metro-Goldwyn-Mayer, 1939. DVD. Warner Bros. Home Video, 2013.

Works Cited

Bonnstetter, Beth E. "Of Structures, Stories, and *Spaceballs*: Parody as Criticism of Genre Film and Myth." *Sith, Slayers, Stargates, + Cyborgs: Modern Mythology in the New Millennium*, edited by David Whitt and John Perlich, Peter Lang, 2008, pp. 190–210.

Bronner, Stephen Eric. *A Rumor About the Jews: Reflections on Antisemitism and the Protocols of the Learned Elders of Zion*. St. Martin's Press, 2000.
Castleberry, Garret L., and William S. McMurry. "*Spaceballs* as Mel Brooks's Parodic Prophecy of Franchise Fascism." *The Political Mel Brooks*, edited by Samuel Boerboom and Beth E. Bonnstetter, Lexington Books, 2019, 87–107.
Friedman, Murray. *The Neoconservative Revolution: Jewish Intellectuals and the Shaping of Public Policy*. Cambridge University Press, 2005.
Gordon, Avery F. *Ghostly Matters: Haunting and the Sociological Imagination*. University of Minnesota Press, 2008.
———. "Some Thoughts on Haunting and Futurity." *Borderlands*, vol. 10, no. 2, 1995, pp. 1–21.
Horn, Dara. *People Love Dead Jews: Reports from a Haunted Present*. W.W. Norton, 2021.
Ott, Brian L., and Beth Bonnstetter. "'We're at Now, Now': *Spaceballs* as Parodic Tourism." *Southern Communication Journal*, vol. 72, no. 4, October–December 2007, pp. 309–327.
Pappe, Ilan. *The Ethnic Cleansing of Palestine*. Simon & Schuster, 2007.
Prell, Riv-Ellen. "Why Jewish Princesses Don't Sweat: Desire and Consumption in Postwar American Jewish Culture." *Too Jewish? Challenging Traditional Identities*, edited by Norman L. Kleeblatt, Rutgers University Press, 1996, pp. 74–92.
Reznik, David L. *New Jews? Race and American Jewish Identity in 21st-Century Film*. Routledge, 2012.
Tidhar, Lavie. "Jews in Space: On the Unsung History of Jewish Writers and the Birth of Science Fiction." *Literary Hub*, June 14, 2021. https://lithub.com/jews-in-space-on-the-unsung-history-of-jewish-writers-and-the-birth-of-science-fiction/. Accessed 15 June 2022.
Weinbaum, Batya. "Early U.S. Sci Fi: Post-Nationalist Exploration for Jews in Outer Space?" *Studies in American Jewish Literature (1981-)*, vol. 24, *ReVisioning American Jewish Literature: Yesterday and Today and Tomorrow*, 2005, pp. 180–201.
Zuckerman, Esther. "Contemplating a Canon of Jewish American Films." *The New York Times*, December 16, 2022. https://www.nytimes.com/2022/12/16/movies/jewish-american-films.html. Accessed 17 December 2022.

The Rich Get Richer
Life Stinks *(1991)*

CYNTHIA J. MILLER

Introduction

There is little doubt that Mel Brooks is one of the undisputed masters of American comedy. With an entertainment career spanning over seven decades, he has left an unmistakable stamp of bawdy humor on both television and motion pictures. But there is another side to Brooks—one that is sentimental, philosophical, and reflective—and it was that side of Brooks that gave rise to *Life Stinks*, a Brooksian comedy with a message that, for some, life really does stink.

In over thirty years since its release, the film—one of his lesser-known works about life on the streets—has generated discussion about class, economics, and whether a compassionate project, crafted by an artist known for irreverent sendups, can sink beneath the weight of its own sincerity. The film, reported to have been inspired, in part, by Brooks' personal moment of awakening about homelessness, shifts uneasily between humor and pain as he spins a tale of riches-to-rags while attempting to remain true to both his creative style and one of life's harshest realities.

This essay takes an in-depth look at the complex interplay between the two, considering the impact of their merging on the film's portrayals and perceptions of homelessness as well as on its delivery of Brooks' trademark humor. If indeed, life is "just a bunch of moments," as Lesley Anne Warren's character Molly tells Brooks' Goddard Bolt, how then is the film framing life on the margins? Do those "moments" level the terrain between the haves and the have-nots by virtue of their seemingly random nature? Do they humanize a population that is often made monstrous as a result of social and economic conditions? Or do they diminish the realities of the homeless, affirming that, as Molly says, "even without money, life is good"?

Life Stinks, *but Only for Some*

The context through which these questions emerge is Los Angeles, a city known for dramatic economic inequalities. The film opens with establishing shots of traffic on the L.A. freeway, tracking a spotless white Rolls Royce limousine as it makes its way through the city. In the background, a stock report plays on the vehicle's radio, setting the context: stocks are declining, new unemployment claims have risen 45,000, with 3.5 million collecting benefits. Gold, however, is up, and just as that announcement is made, the limo, now on local surface roads, speeds carelessly through a series of large, trash-infused puddles, drenching the homeless men sleeping on the sidewalk. As one of the men exclaims "Aw, shit," the title credits appear: *Life Stinks*.

The limo carries none other than the film's lead character, mogul Goddard Bolt (Mel Brooks), owner of Bolt Enterprises, whose stock, the radio report advises, is up $6 amidst a sea of declines in manufacturing, utilities, and elsewhere, thanks to breaking news that Bolt intends to purchase a blighted section of downtown real estate currently inhabited by the poor. As the scene shifts to the high rise that houses Bolt's office, evidence rapidly mounts that he is egotistical, unethical, and sees nothing wrong with making his fortune walking on those lacking his power and privilege—indigenous people, the elderly, and of course, the poor. (To drive the point home, he literally steps on the hand of a service worker polishing the floor as he walks through the building's lobby.) He reveals to his ineffectual legal staff that he intends to purchase the downtown tract adjacent to one he already owns, displacing countless impoverished individuals, to build his dream—"the ultimate achievement of my life"—the sleek, futuristic Bolt Center, only to find out that his rival, Vance Crasswell (Jeffrey Tambor) has already purchased the property and has his own plans for redevelopment. When negotiating fails, Crasswell tricks Bolt into agreeing to a bet to determine the fate of the property. The wager? Whether or not Bolt can survive 30 days, destitute, in the slums. The prize: The winner takes the whole tract of land. There are conditions: first, he must begin his ordeal penniless—no cash, no credit cards; second, he must wear a tracker that will activate if he leaves the perimeter of the slum for more than 30 seconds; third, he must never reveal his true identity. He shaves his trademark moustache, rends his clothes, and is tossed out of his limo into the slums. The storyline, as Brooks observes, is thus quite simple:

> Two billionaires, both vying for the same slum property in L.A. that could be developed into a multimillion-dollar area, make a bet.... Goddard Bolt bets that he can survive without a penny in his pocket for thirty days in that same slum property. And if he can do it, his rival will have to sign over his half of

the property to Goddard. It was a daring and foolish bet, but his billionaire's ego told him that he could do it. And so begins a series of adventures in which Goddard Bolt learns the hard truth about what being poor and homeless really entails [373].

During Bolt's odyssey on the streets, many of those truths are taught to him by a cast of downtrodden characters who walk a fine line between representation and stereotype; each helping him craft a life in L.A.'s Skid Row. Early in his journey, he has a chance encounter with Sailor (Howard Morris) when the unwitting homeless man urinates on a box covering the sleeping Bolt. As the two share a more formal introduction, Sailor bestows a street identity on his new friend, dubbing him "Pepto," when he sees that the Pepto Bismol logo has transferred from the box to Bolt's forehead. "Don't rub it off—it's nice! It's a nice name 'Pepto'! I'm 'Sailor.' Everybody calls me 'Sailor' 'cause I was nearly in the Navy." With this, Bolt's transformation has begun.

Soon after, a hungry and foundering Bolt is set upon by a pair of muggers who steal his shoes. They are sent running by a feisty Molly (Leslie Ann Warren), who alternately aids and menaces the desperate man, gifting him replacement shoes that are "close enough" in size (as he wisely stifles his objection to their color). She agrees to guide him to the mission that provides meals for the needy but cautions: "I saved your life, I saved your feet—this is your last help." As the film continues, however, romance blossoms between the two, providing a catalyst for what Brooks casts as Bolt's final transformation into a kinder, more compassionate billionaire.

Bolt settles uneasily into the homeless community with Molly, Sailor,

Sailor (Howard Morris, left) gives billionaire Goddard Bolt (Mel Brooks) a new name, "Pepto," in *Life Stinks* (1991).

and their friend Fumes (Teddy Wilson). During the course of the film's narrative, the characters' lives are all infused with the sorts of stereotyping that accompany poverty—alcoholism, drug trafficking and abuse, mental illness—and are the antitheses of Bolt, who was born into money and never looked back. When Fumes displays an enthusiastic appreciation for the mission's stew, after dousing it with the contents of a bottle in a crumpled brown paper bag: "Mmm, mmm.... Man, oh man ... stewed stew!! You get it?? Stewed stew!!" the others laugh, but the billionaire-turned-bum looks on with disgust. At every turn, however, as the film peels away the trappings provided by power and privilege, Bolt lags behind his compatriots in empathy, loyalty, strength of character, and even simple manners. Slowly, though, his outlook begins to shift. He develops a fondness for his Skid Row street-mates, falls in love with Molly and, like Dickens' Scrooge after the trials of his ghostly visitors, reconnects with his own humanity. When his thirty days are over, he celebrates and expresses his gratitude to the Almighty, saying, "Thank you, God! I'm sorry I didn't believe in you when I was rich!"

Having won the bet, Bolt attempts to reclaim his identity and resume his former life, only to find that Crasswell has bribed his lawyers to declare him incompetent and then seized control of the coveted downtown property that launched the ill-fated wager. Bolt and his homeless friends crash the televised groundbreaking ceremony for Crasswell's new development and wreak havoc partying with its high-class guests. In a final showdown that pays comic homage to classic *kaiju* films, the two financial titans battle it out in hydraulic excavators that lumber and groan like prehistoric giants. After toppling his rival's machine, a victorious Bolt dangles Crasswell in the air with the giant earthmover's grapple until he confesses to his shady dealings on national television. At the tale's end, Bolt regains his affluent life, his corporation, the property *and* gets the girl. He turns the long-sought downtown property into a zone to aid the destitute, where they can live, get educated, and find jobs. The white limo that opened the film, now decorated for his wedding to Molly, picks the pair up outside the little Skid Row church where the ceremony was performed. Before getting in, however, Molly rushes to the back of the vehicle, gathers up dozens of cans tied to the bumper, and tosses them into the back seat, reminding Bolt, "You may not know this, but these cans are worth a lot of money!" Bolt laughs in gentle amusement and replies, "Get in that car!"

Problematizing Homelessness

In his autobiography *All About Me*, Brooks asserts that "comedy has the most to say about the human condition because if you laugh, you can get by. You can survive when things are bad if you have a sense of humor" (380). In many ways *Life Stinks* was his visualization of that theory: amidst poverty, violence, disease, and homelessness, the film's denizens of Skid Row still laugh and joke, create "homes" and friendships, wax philosophical, fall in love, and even find their "happily ever afters." There are ample moments of humor throughout the film, as Brooks attempts to mitigate the harsh realities of life on the streets with his own brand of slapstick comedy. Body humor and poverty humor both flow easily from the characters as the narrative unfolds. Brooks' film is not alone in this rosier vision of homelessness: another 1991 release, *The Fisher King*, directed by Terry Gilliam and starring Robin William, offers a darkly comic narrative with an equally mythic happy ending, as does the even lighter *Curly Sue*, also screened in 1991 and directed by John Hughes and starring James Belushi. Released within months of each other, the films all offer humor-infused, empathetic views of the humanity of homeless men and women, yet at the same time suggest that through a combination of perseverance, a good heart, and the benevolence of those more fortunate, the lives of homeless people can be turned around.

But for members of the homeless community, lived reality carries a harsher tone. As an embedded community, homeless individuals reside in sites of multiple injustices. They are generally the most disadvantaged of the extremely poor (Rossi). Whether living on the streets by choice, or due to soaring housing costs, low wages, inadequate healthcare, or ever-tightening limits on public assistance programs, homeless people are generally bracketed apart from the wider community's concerns for social justice and quality of life. In fact, many relate feelings of being an integral part of the general population's perceived injustices, seen as part of the community's problems, rather than members of the community needing solutions (Miller). As anthropologist Joanne Passaro explains, Americans have a cultural tendency to place blame on the homeless (in particular, men), and to see them as shouldering the sole responsibility for their circumstances—as having failed in the performance of their designated social roles. This perception of "unworthiness" eases the complicated feelings and difficult questions that confront society about homelessness and allows homeless individuals and the injustices they face to be dismissed. They typically fall well outside the realm of consideration on issues ranging from inflation and affordable housing to personal safety and health care and are, instead, additions to any list of ills plaguing the wider community.

In her examination of how poverty and homelessness are framed in Brooks' film, Melissa Boehm argues that one of the significant flaws of *Life Stinks* is its failure to problematize capitalism (111). This is particularly relevant in that a constellation of factors, chiefly, poverty and the lack of affordable housing, are seen as key elements in the continually rising number of homeless in American cities. While housing is not considered affordable if its cost exceeds more than thirty percent of a renter's income, the average cost of a one-bedroom apartment in L.A. at the time of the film's production was $642/month (*Los Angeles Almanac*). During this same period, the minimum wage was $3.80/hour, which meant a monthly income of just $658.66 before taxes, making a one-bedroom apartment dramatically out of reach for unskilled full-time workers. The National Low Income Housing Coalition agrees, indicating that nearly forty percent of low-income renters at the time were fully employed (Pitkoff n.p.). Dollars and cents alone, then, place affordable housing (rather than personal failings) at the top of the list for causes of homelessness.

Despite this, extreme poverty is linked in complex ways with Passaro's notion of "unworthiness" in the generalized image of homelessness within communities. Commonly reported stereotypes of homelessness are most often of people loitering outside shelters, panhandling on corners and in bus stations, and sleeping on park benches; and since the people who live on the streets—the unsheltered homeless—are the most visible, they tend to be the most closely associated with homelessness. As writer and activist Steve Vanderstaay explains:

> Homeless people on the street are also the most feared and least identified with: people who die ignominious deaths in trash compactors, who freeze outside the doors of hospitals, and who have been burned alive while sleeping on park benches. They are the most hated of homeless people; loathed for their destitution, their apparent inability to provide for themselves, and for the conflicting array of emotions they evoke in passersby [4].

Bolt learns quickly what all this means as he is unable to secure shelter or food and finds himself treated like a pariah, lurching, as Thomas Christie observes, from one indignity to another (Christie 263). Many of the individuals he encounters, like Sailor, Fumes, and the other inhabitants of Brooks' Skid Row, also remain unsheltered, facing severe social and environmental conditions, as a result of one of the most significant injustices facing the homeless community: the shelter system. There is an ever-growing shortage of beds in city shelters, and while the Los Angeles' shelters housed over four thousand individuals during the time of the film's production, three quarters as many individuals were still on the streets due to shortages of beds (*Los Angeles Almanac*). Many homeless individuals also find remaining on the streets preferable to conditions in city shelters, where they experience not only overcrowding in underfunded facilities, but also paternalism, infantilization, and resources that function, sadly, more like band-aids than solutions. We see Brooks' characters largely reject the outreach system in the film, except for meals. Only in desperation, when a raging storm washes out their makeshift sleeping quarters, do they turn to the mission for help—only to find its doors locked, in a power play by the wealthy Crasswell to thwart Bolt and force them all out of the area.

Neoliberalism Meets Recession

Brooks observes that "the country was going through some hard economic times in 1991," when the *Life Stinks* was released, but the social and economic struggles marking the beginning of the decade had taken root long before (373). The film's present day is merely a snapshot of thirty days in a long and complex progression. The activism and upheaval of the 1960s and '70s cast a long shadow over the 1980s, as debilitating recession yielded to the promise of prosperity, and the pendulum of collective consciousness swung sharply from rights, equality, and opportunity to unfettered economic growth and upward mobility. Little remained unaffected as late-capitalism shifted to an information economy, and conflicts abounded: The youth counterculture of the '60s gave way to young urban professionalism, characterized by high expectations and little experience; second-wave feminism propelled women into a workplace where glass ceilings were still firmly in place; the faces of both policy and sentiment turned sharply away from social welfare, even as increasing numbers of Americans fell into need; and post-recession fears for national well-being, combined with late-twentieth-century rejection of traditional lifeways, led to mistrust and marginalization of immigrants in spite of the increasing diversity of the nation's population.[1]

In the two-plus years (and six drafts) that Brooks claims that it took before *Life Stinks* was ready for production, the United States found itself in the throes of postwar recession, savings and loan collapse, the Persian Gulf crisis, and massive job cutbacks (Whitty n.p.). The recession affected every major industry group, with construction—prominently featured in the film as the beneficiary (and agent) of strong capitalism—and manufacturing hit the hardest. Personal consumption spending plummeted, and total employment fell by 1.1 million in less than a year (Singleton 15). For L.A., the site of the film's troubled tale, the period from the late 1980s into the early '90s saw a full-scale affordable housing crisis. The number of shelter beds quadrupled and estimates of the city's homeless population ranged as high as 59,000 people, giving rise to numerous "tent cities" and other makeshift dwellings like those sheltering Bolt's compatriots on the streets (Sheeley 45–47). This constellation of economic forces and social attitudes both resulted from and, in turn, caused, rapid social change that echoed throughout the remainder of the 20th century as neoliberalism held sway in the Reagan years.

Following David Harvey, we may think of neoliberalism as "the elevation of capitalism, as a mode of production, into an ethic, a set of political imperatives, and a cultural logic" (Thompson 23). It is a project to "strengthen, restore, or in some cases constitute anew" the power of the economic elites (Thompson 23), earmarked by those transactions actively supported by large, impersonal financial institutions: privatization, accumulation by dispossession, and the association of freedom with the power of the consumer (Primrose 6). Under neoliberalism, "capital" (following Marx) represents more than merely economic variables—it is a process that shapes and influences goals, values, ethics, and relationships—it is "an ethic in itself, acting as a guide to all human action" (Thompson 23). Brooks' Bolt and Tambor's Crasswell stand as embodiments of neoliberal ideologies and practices, even though Crasswell, himself, was raised in poverty. At the film's outset it is clear that the two billionaires follow a shared—and self-perpetuating—cultural logic whereby the rich get richer.

Those notions are, of course, privileged in capitalist systems; they have no limits or ceilings, but rest on what Anthony Giddens terms "ontological security"—a sense of order and continuity, of routine, based on frameworks of meaning that provide a stable sense of self. As Gullette argues, the security underpinning individual conceptions of progress and success are achieved by various means:

> Some acquire this security by agency, some by luck, some by inheritance. Some conceive progress in masculinist metaphors of overcoming less fit adversaries or cruising directly on time's arrow. Some envision it through a version (relevant to their class, race, gender, ableness) of the life-course narrative called "the American Dream" [Guillette 18].

This dream—the belief in the attainment of success—is the glue that informs the construction of the film's narrative world and, also, its social critique. Embedded in that dream is the promotion of unfettered free market activity that defined Reaganomics, where "survival of the fittest" determined success and prosperity. The true question raised by the film is whether or not Bolt, whose very essence seems to be encoded with neoliberalism, is capable of meaningful, fundamental change. Hope for his genuine transformation in the world of the film would also signal hope for the transformation of all he symbolizes in the world of the audience.

The "Deserving" Homeless

The logic of 1990s romantic comedy says, "Why, yes! Of course!" Bolt has walked a mile in the tattered shoes of the underclass and has had an awakening—an infusion of social responsibility—and is now prepared to use his power and privilege to better the conditions of all those around him, with the understanding that, paraphrasing Hubert Humphrey, society is only as strong as its weakest members.[2] How else could a sympathetic figure like Molly, who has already lost everything—her career, her husband, her mental health, and even her meager belongings—fall in love with him? Lived reality, of course, says otherwise; and so, I argue, does the reality of the film, despite its "happily ever after" ending.

Brooks has argued that *Life Stinks* is a "testament to the enduring human spirit," intended to both raise awareness and humanize the poor and homeless on the big screen (380). His inspiration was drawn, as he relates, from a moment of awakening. The details shift a bit through various retellings, but it all started when his car developed engine trouble. "Your car has all of these tubes in it, and when they suck, it goes. And when they don't suck, it doesn't go, and my hoses weren't sucking that day" (Ebert). Taking an unfamiliar exit off the freeway in L.A., he was shocked at finding himself in the middle of greater poverty than he realized existed in the United States:

> There was all this steam emanating from under the hood. I pull into a garage, I don't know where I am. When the steam clears away I think, "Oh, my God, am I in Calcutta? Where am I?" If truth be told, I couldn't believe it. I didn't know anything like that existed.... It bowled me over [Ebert].

As he explained to film critic Roger Ebert, he walked around looking for a phone and could not believe his eyes at the numbers of men and women living on the streets there. He met a woman named Molly (the inspiration for Leslie Ann Warren's character) who told him about her failed marriage and subsequent inability to meet the rising costs of rent. When she could no longer make ends meet, she then moved into a transient hotel but, soon after, transitioned to living on the streets because they were cleaner and safer (Ebert). Months later, this experience would germinate into the idea for a depression-era comedy crafted to address the economic and social issues of the day while also offering lighthearted laughs, a la *My Man Godfrey* (1936) or *Sullivan's Travels* (1941). Through the film, Brooks hoped to explore three things: "What happened to society? What happened to brotherly love? What happened to caring about your fellow human beings?" (373). But in this, he faced challenges: "You can't put something up there that's too depressing. That's a waste of everybody's time. It's got to be funny and entertaining" (McDonald n.p.). As Robert Alan Crick offers, "if the material is played too gently, nobody laughs; come on too strong, risk charges of blatant insensitivity" (169). Brooks mused to Ebert:

> People should have a place to lay down their heads at night, and our society is too cheapskate to give them one. If you made a movie about the homeless,

maybe nobody would come. But if you make the movie about a megalomaniac goofball, and put him in the middle of the homeless and call it a comedy, maybe somebody will come to see it [Ebert].

The line between using visual humor to problematize poverty and creating laughs at the expense of the poor can be too easily crossed, though, and this admixture ultimately did not sit well with many audiences and critics. Crick chides that "*Life Stinks* is Dickens' *Oliver Twist* magnified; not one Oliver gets adopted, but scores of them, rescued from the gutter by Fagin-turned-philanthropist Goddard Bolt" (178). Marjorie Baumgarten of the *Austin Chronicle* laments, "The problem with *Life Stinks* is that it's got its heart in the right place but not a whole lot else," while Stan James from *The Advertiser* cautions that Brooks' "brassy style of humor is hardly suitable for a satire of the appalling poverty of a section of Los Angeles street people who live out of paper bags and sleep in cardboard boxes—if they are lucky" (n.p.).

What most critics and viewers seem not to recognize is that all of these things are true—there is no black-and-white about *Life Stinks*. Brooks created a film that was at once sentimental and insensitive; that eroded some stereotypes and reinforced others; that challenged audiences to think and then distracted them. We laugh and cry, both at *and* with Bolt and his disenfranchised compatriots, just as we watch with disdain as the film's rich lay their plans for gentrification that exclude the poor and homeless while supporting those visions in communities in lived reality. There is no question that the film's poor are its protagonists and its wealthy (along with those who support them, like Bolt's legal team) are self-serving, underhanded, and lacking in any sort of moral character—and the urge to identify with both sides of the rich/poor divide leaves audiences feeling uneasy.

Melissa Boehm points out that the film does important work in its departures from the typical framing of poverty and homelessness at the time of its release. Most of the individuals Bolt encounters living on the streets are white—the harmful stereotype of the African American welfare queen so prevalent at the time is nowhere to be found, nor is that of her drug-dealing, violent male counterpart—and Brooks' homeless characters are never blamed for their own plights, but rather, are framed as casualties of socioeconomics (Boehm 128). Bolt's initial discomfort with the poor he encounters fades into gentle fondness as he begins to actually *see* them and hear their stories; they become human ... individuals ... and so much more than their collective status as "the homeless." When the sickly Sailor dies from exposure on a stormy night, Bolt genuinely grieves and eulogizes the old man before scattering his ashes, attesting that while his friend may have been perpetually filthy, "his heart was always good and clean." (The touching moment is cut short by Brooksian comedy, of course, when a gust of wind blows the ashes back on Bolt and his friends.)[3]

Conclusion

What we also see is a narrative that is far more insidious: An affluent man temporarily enters the world of the poor and homeless believing that he can survive by brains, determination and fortitude, knowing that comfort and resources await him at the end of his trial, and ultimately he is proven correct. Even though the residents of Skid Row possess the "local knowledge" that provide him with food and shelter, Bolt never loses his air of power and privilege, until he is swindled by Crasswell, betrayed by his own advisors, and left truly penniless—then the façade falls. Even so, when he discovers his rival's plan to create Crasswell City, he attempts to rally his destitute companions to take action, stop being victimized by the wealthy, and reclaim their homes:

> No! No more running! They forced me to live in the crap ... and now they want to take the crap away? No! ... Don't give up! This is America! Every person has a right to have a place to live! Come! Join me! Let's fight for our rights! Let's take our homes back! Follow me! If we run now, we'll always be running....

That is the voice of power and privilege; of a man who is used to being heard. His poor and homeless compatriots, however, are accustomed to invisibility. They *know* that their words and actions hold no sway, and so they continue to leave until Molly reaches them on another, more practical, level, yelling, "Free food!" In the blink of an eye, bedlam ensues, as the well-to-do and the down-and-out come face-to-face. The wealthy attendees are aghast as the unkempt poor gleefully help themselves to food and drink, start conversations, and even flirt a little.

Once the chaos of this final clash of the classes has stilled and Bolt's life is again firmly under control, we learn that he plans to turn his newly acquired property into an area to benefit the slum's current residents, complete with low-cost housing, a clinic, and a park—a grand gesture that suggests a "happily ever after" for the film's destitute characters. But what it also suggests is that their community has been aided by an affluent benefactor, reinforcing the notion that power and privilege have ultimately saved the day.

So, apparently, does love, which, here at the end of the film, provides a more intimate means for Bolt to lift Molly out of poverty—by marrying her. Having once been a professional dancer ("I didn't just have a job, I had a career!"), she held a social status closer to Bolt's, so the gap between the two feels somehow bridgeable. He falls in love with her feisty combination of grit and grace, and she appears to see a wayward soul in need of her kind heart and grassroots practicality. They marry in a small Skid Row church where Bolt once expressed his amazement that anyone could find happiness in the midst of poverty. Now, however, happy and surrounded by the characters who brought the area to life during the course of the film, it seems as though the billionaire may have found the ability to relate to and, perhaps, remain connected to both worlds.

The camera shifts from the newlyweds to the white Rolls Royce that waits for them. It remains a symbol of Bolt's elevated status in the downtrodden neighborhood. As the newlyweds climb in and the limo drives away, we see that it has a new "vanity" license plate that reads "PEPTO." An optimistic reading of the scene is that Bolt is paying homage to his street identity and has incorporated its lessons into his return to affluence. An alternate and, perhaps, more realistic reading suggests that the billionaire's time on the streets—like any other challenge met and bested—has been "accessorized" and relegated to a similar status as a "26.2" decal or an "I Survived Mt. Everest" bumper sticker. Brooks leaves that bit for audiences to decide.

Notes

1. See, for example, Hainmueller and Hopkins.
2. "The moral test of government is how that government treats those who are in the dawn of life, the children; those who are in the twilight of life, the elderly; those who are in the shadows of life, the sick, the needy and the handicapped"—Senator Hubert H. Humphrey, remarks at the dedication of the Hubert H. Humphrey Building, November 1, 1977.
3. In his autobiography, Brooks relates that this scene was inspired by a true event.

Filmography

Curly Sue. Dir. John Hughes. Hughes Entertainment, 1991. DVD. Warner Archives, 2016.
The Fisher King. Dir. Terry Gilliam. Hill/Obst Productions, 1991. DVD. Sony Pictures Home Entertainment, 2001.
Life Stinks. Dir. Mel Brooks. Brooksfilms, 1991. DVD. MGM, 2006.
My Man Godfrey. Dir. Gregory La Cava. Universal Pictures, 1936. DVD. Criterion, 2002.
Sullivan's Travels. Dir. Preston Sturges. Paramount Pictures, 1941. DVD. Criterion, 2002.

Works Cited

Baumgarten, Marjorie. "Life Stinks." *The Austin Chronicle*. August 2, 1991. http://www.rottentomatoes.com/click/movie-1036157/reviews.php?critic=all&sortby=default&page=1&rid=25324.

Boehm, Melissa. "The Framing of Poverty in Mel Brooks's *Life Stinks*: A Content and Textual Analysis." *The Political Mel Brooks*. Eds. Samuel Boerboom and Beth E. Bonnstetter. Lanham, MD: Lexington Books, 2019, pp. 109–133.
Brooks, Mel. *All About Me! My Remarkable Life in Show Business*. New York: Ballantine, 2021.
Christie, Thomas A. *Mel Brooks: Genius and Loving It!* Kent: Crescent Moon, 2015.
Crick, Robert Alan. *The Big Screen Comedies of Mel Brooks*. Jefferson, NC: McFarland, 2002.
Ebert, Roger. "Taking the Off-Ramp to Reality." https://www.rogerebert.com/roger-ebert/taking-the-off-ramp-to-reality.
Giddens, Anthony. *Modernity and Self-Identity*. Stanford: Stanford University Press, 1991.
Guillette, Margaret M. *Aged by Culture*. Chicago: University of Chicago Press, 2004.
Hainmueller, Jens, and Daniel J. Hopkins. "Public Attitudes Toward Immigration." *Annual Review of Political Science* 17 (2014): 225–249.
Humphrey, Hubert H. *Congressional Record* 123:37287. November 4, 1977.
James, Stan. "Mel Lifts the Lid, but the Message Is Lost." *The Advertiser*, October 12, 1991.
Los Angeles Almanac, http://www.laalmanac.com/economy/ec40.php.
McDonald, Dan. "The Message in Mel's Jokes." *The Advertiser*, October 10, 1991.
Miller, Cynthia J. "Memories from the Margins: Stories and Images of Urban Homelessness." *Linguaculture. International Journal of the Iasi Linguaculture Centre for (Inter)cultural and (Inter)lingual Research*. Ed. Iulia Andreea Milica. Iasi, Romania: Alexandru Ioan Cuza University Press, 2012, pp. 77–91.
Passaro, Joanne. *The Unequal Homeless: Men on the Streets, Women in Their Place*. New York: Routledge, 1996.
Pitkoff, Winton, et al. "Out of Reach 2003: America's Housing Wage Climbs." National Low Income Housing Coalition, 2003. http://www.nlihc.org/oor2003.
Primrose, David. "Contesting Capitalism in the Light of the Crisis: A Conversation with David Harvey." *Journal of Australian Political Economy* 71 (December 2013): 5–25.
Rossi, Peter. *Down and Out in America*. Chicago: University of Chicago Press, 1989.
Sheeley, Kirsten Moore, et al. "The Making of a Crisis: The History of Homelessness in Los Angeles." Luskin Center for History and Policy, 2021. https://luskincenter.history.ucla.edu/wp-content/uploads/sites/66/2021/01/LCHP-The-Making-of-A-Crisis-Report.pdf.
Singleton, Christopher. "Industry Employment and the 1990–91 Recession." *Monthly Labour Review* (July 1993): 15–25.
Thompson, Michael. "The World According to David Harvey." *Dissent: A Journal of Politics and Ideas* (2005): 22–27.
Vanderstaay, Steven. *Street Lives*. Philadelphia: New Society, 1992.
Whittey, Stephen. "Does Life Stink? Ask Mel Brooks" *Deseret News*, August 20, 1991. https://deseretnews.com/article/178948/DOES-LIFE-STINK-ASK-MEL-BROOKS.html.

Afterword

Jeremy Dauber

Mel Brooks is, among much else, a poet of rage. Think of the wondrous fits of Zero Mostel in *The Producers*; Gene Wilder's undignified reactions to early failed experiments on *Young Frankenstein*; even, for that matter, the simmering resentment of *The Critic*. So Brooks, and the students of his work gathered together here in this remarkable collection of essays, will understand how my reaction, in reading through these essays, was that of near-incandescent fury.

You see, I've written about Mel Brooks on several occasions, first in a more wide-ranging history of Jewish comedy, and then, very recently, devoting a whole book to his "Jewish biography," as the series advertising has it. And if I had been able to read these essays *then*, *while* I was writing, the books would have been *so radically improved*.

By these scholars' wide-ranging familiarity with Brooks' influences, cinematic and otherwise. By their acute and sophisticated insights into Brooks' works themselves, both what we see and what lay behind the scenes. By their judicious application of some of the most sophisticated theoretical and conceptual taxonomies to help illuminate—while not smothering—Brooks' achievements, and that's not an easy line to walk, let me tell you. And by the verve and style with which they carry it off, which is absolutely infectious.

Or would have been.

If I hadn't already written the books, sent them off to press, gotten them back, and put them on my shelf.

Where they now stare at me reproachfully, begging in vain to be updated with insights and inspirations gleamed from this collection of wonderful scholarship.

I'm telling you. I'm *furious*.

A Bibliography on Mel Brooks

Camille McCutcheon

The following selective, representative bibliography of resources contains books, book chapters, and journal, magazine, and newspaper articles on Mel Brooks. Also included are interviews of Brooks on YouTube and reviews of major biographies on him, his memoir, television series that he co-created, and films that he directed.

Books

Alexander, Lisa Doris. *Expanding the Black Film Canon: Race and Genre Across Six Decades*. UP of Kansas, 2019.
Apatow, Judd. *Sick in the Head: Conversations about Life and Comedy*. Random House, 2015.
Austerlitz, Saul. *Another Fine Mess: A History of American Film Comedy*. Chicago Review Press, 2010.
Banks, Miranda J. *The Writers: A History of American Screenwriters and Their Guild*. Rutgers UP, 2015.
Berger, Arthur Asa. *Jewish Jesters: A Study in American Popular Comedy*. Hampton Press, 2001.
Bianculli, David. *The Platinum Age of Television: From* I Love Lucy *to* The Walking Dead, *How TV Became Terrific*. Doubleday, 2016.
Boerboom, Samuel, and Beth E. Bonnstetter, editors. *The Political Mel Brooks*. Lexington Books, 2019.
Britton, Wesley A. *Spy Television*. Praeger, 2004.
Brooks, Mel. *All About Me! My Remarkable Life in Show Business*. Ballantine Books, 2021.
_____. *Young Frankenstein: A Mel Brooks Book: The Story of the Making of the Film*. With Rebecca Keegan, Black Dog & Leventhal, 2016.
Brooks, Mel, and Carl Reiner. *"The 2,000 Year Old Man" in the Year 2,000: The Book*. Cliff Street Books, 1997.
Brooks, Mel, and Thomas Meehan. *The Producers*. Hyperion, 2001.
Crick, Robert Alan. *The Big Screen Comedies of Mel Brooks*. McFarland, 2002.
Daniel, Douglass K. *Anne Bancroft: A Life*. UP of Kentucky, 2017.
Dauber, Jeremy. *Jewish Comedy: A Serious History*. W.W. Norton, 2017.
_____. *Mel Brooks: Disobedient Jew*. Yale UP, 2023.
De Forest, Sloan. *The Essential Directors: The Art and Impact of Cinema's Most Influential Filmmakers*. Running Press, 2021.
Desser, David, and Lester D. Friedman. *American-Jewish Filmmakers: Traditions and Trends*. U of Illinois P, 1993.

Dreifus, Claudia. *Interview*. Seven Stories Press, 1999.
Dubowsky, Jack Curtis. *Intersecting Film, Music, and Queerness*. Palgrave Macmillan, 2016.
Dunne, Michael. *METAPOP: Self-Referentiality in Contemporary American Popular Culture*. UP of Mississippi, 1992.
Eichenbaum, Rose. *The Director Within: Storytellers of Stage and Screen*. Edited by Aron Hirt-Manheimer, Wesleyan UP, 2014.
Feldman, Marty. *EYE Marty: My Life in Words and Pictures*. Coronet, 2015.
Garr, Teri. *Speedbumps: Flooring It Through Hollywood*. With Henriette Mantel, Penguin, 2005.
Gehring, Wes D. *Parody as Film Genre: "Never Give a Saga an Even Break."* Greenwood Press, 1999.
Glut, Donald F. *The Frankenstein Archive: Essays on the Monster, the Myth, the Movies, and More*. McFarland, 2002.
Golson, G. Barry, editor. *The Playboy Interview*. Wideview Books, 1981.
Harvey, Karen J. *Sid Caesar and Your Show of Shows: The Birth of the Television Sketch Comedy Series*. McFarland, 2021.
Hecht, Stuart Joel. *Transposing Broadway: Jews, Assimilation, and the American Musical*. Palgrave Macmillan, 2011.
Hischak, Thomas S. *Boy Loses Girl: Broadway's Librettists*. Scarecrow Press, 2002.
Holtzman, William. *Seesaw, a Dual Biography of Anne Bancroft and Mel Brooks*. Doubleday, 1979.
Homan, Sidney, and Hernan Vera. *Hitler in the Movies: Finding Der Führer on Film*. Fairleigh Dickinson UP, 2016.
Joslin, Lyndon W. *Count Dracula Goes to the Movies: Stoker's Novel Adapted*. 3rd ed., McFarland, 2017.
Kackman, Michael. *Citizen Spy: Television, Espionage, and Cold War Culture*. U of Minnesota P, 2005.
Kawin, Bruce F. *Horror and the Horror Film*. Anthem Press, 2012.
Leachman, Cloris. *Cloris: My Autobiography*. With George Englund, Kensington Books, 2009.
Levinson, Barry. *Levinson on Levinson*. Edited by David Thompson, Faber & Faber, 1992.
Limon, John. *Stand-Up Comedy in Theory, or, Abjection in America*. Duke UP, 2000.
Madison, William V. *Madeline Kahn: Being the Music, a Life*. UP of Mississippi, 2015.
Maltin, Leonard. *Starstruck: My Unlikely Road to Hollywood*. GoodKnight Books, 2021.
Mast, Gerald. *The Comic Mind: Comedy and the Movies*. 2nd ed., U of Chicago P, 1979.
McGilligan, Patrick. *Funny Man: Mel Brooks*. Harper, 2019.
Nachman, Gerald. *Seriously Funny: The Rebel Comedians of the 1950s and 1960s*. Pantheon Books, 2003.
Parish, James Robert. *It's Good To Be The King: The Seriously Funny Life of Mel Brooks*. Wiley, 2007.
Pinsky, Mark I. *The Gospel According to The Simpsons*. 2nd ed., Westminster John Knox Press, 2007.
Reiner, Carl. *I Remember Me*. AuthorHouse, 2013.
Ross, Robert. *Marty Feldman: The Biography of a Comedy Legend*. Titan Books, 2011.
Sacks, Mike. *Poking a Dead Frog: Conversations with Today's Top Comedy Writers*. Penguin Books, 2014.
Saunders, John. *The Film Genre Book*. Auteur, 2009.
Sherman, Dale. *Mel Brooks FAQ: All That's Left to Know about the Outrageous Genius of Comedy*. Applause Theatre & Cinema Books, 2018.
Steinberg, David. *Inside Comedy: The Soul, Wit, and Bite of Comedy and Comedians of the Last Five Decades*. Alfred A. Knopf, 2021.
Symons, Alex. *Mel Brooks in the Cultural Industries: Survival and Prolonged Adaptation*. Edinburgh UP, 2012.
Tueth, Michael. *Reeling With Laughter: American Film Comedies: From Anarchy to Mockumentary*. Scarecrow Press, 2012.

Wilder, Gene. *Kiss Me Like a Stranger: My Search for Love and Art*. St. Martin's Press, 2005.
Wisse, Ruth R. *No Joke: Making Jewish Humor*. Princeton UP, 2013.
Yacowar, Maurice. *Method in Madness: The Comic Art of Mel Brooks*. St. Martin's Press, 1981.

Book Chapters

Bonnstetter, Beth E. "Of Structures, Stories, and *Spaceballs*: Parody as Criticism of Genre Film and Myth." *Sith, Slayers, Stargates, and Cyborgs: Modern Mythology in the New Millennium*, edited by David Whitt and John Perlich, Peter Lang, 2008, pp. 190–210.
Brooks, Mel. "Mel Brooks Meets Joseph Heller." *Conversations with Joseph Heller*, edited by Adam J. Sorkin, UP of Mississippi, 1996, pp. 201–09.
Dokou, Christina. "Springtime for Defaults: *The Producers* as the Ruin of History and the Triumph of Hystery." *Ruins in the Literary and Cultural Imagination*, edited by Efterpi Mitsi, et al., Palgrave Macmillan, 2019, pp. 199–212.
Edney, Kathryn. "Actors Act. Directors Direct. Producers…Produce? Mel Brooks's *The Producers* and the Creation of an Archetype." *The Palgrave Handbook of Musical Theatre Producers*, edited by Laura MacDonald and William A. Everett, Palgrave Macmillan, 2017, pp. 11–17.
Jaen, Rafael, and Robert I. Lublin. "Fashioning *Frankenstein* in Film: Brides of Frankenstein." *Fashioning Horror: Dressing to Kill on Screen and in Literature*, edited by Julia Petrov and Gudrun D. Whitehead, Bloomsbury Academic, 2017, pp. 65–82.
Jenkins, Henry. "Mel Brooks, Vulgar Modernism, and Comic Remediation." *A Companion to Film Comedy*, edited by Andrew Horton and Joanna E. Rapf, Wiley-Blackwell, 2013, pp. 151–71.
Knapp, Raymond. "The Straight Bookends to Camp's Gay Golden Age From Gilbert and Sullivan to Roger Vadim and Mel Brooks." *Music & Camp*, edited by Christopher Moore and Philip Purvis, Wesleyan UP, 2018, pp. 200–219.
Knight, Stephen. "*Robin Hood: Men In Tights*: Fitting the Tradition Snugly." *Robin Hood: An Anthology of Scholarship and Criticism*, edited by Stephen Knight, D.S. Brewer, 1999, pp. 461–67.
LaGrandeur, Kevin. "*Frankenstein*, Young and Old: An Interview with Mel Brooks." *Frankenstein: How a Monster Became an Icon, the Science and Enduring Allure of Mary Shelley's Creation*, edited by Sidney Perkowitz and Eddy von Mueller, Pegasus Books, 2018, pp. 84–104.
Latchaw, Joan, and David Peterson. "Tragicomedy and Zikkaron in Mel Brooks's *To Be Or Not To Be*." *Jews and Humor*, edited by Leonard J. Greenspoon, Purdue UP, 2011, pp. 195–210.
Lederer, Peter Scott. "Mel Brooks's Subversive Cabaret: *The Producers* (1968)." *Jewish Radicalisms: Historical Perspectives on a Phenomenon of Global Modernity*, edited by Frank Jacob and Sebastian Kunze, Walter de Gruyter, 2020, pp. 361–90.
McKeague, Matthew. "The Comedy of Terrors: A Humor Theory Analysis of Mel Brooks's *Dracula: Dead and Loving It*." *Spoofing the Vampire: Essays on Bloodsucking Comedy*, edited by Simon Bacon, McFarland, 2022, pp. 34–45.
Mulcahy, Robert. "Chasing the Wealth: The Americanization of Il'f and Petrov's *The Twelve Chairs*." *Border Crossing: Russian Literature into Film*, edited by Alexander Burry and Frederick H. White, Edinburgh UP, 2016, pp. 188–201.
Pinsker, Sanford. "Mel Brooks and the Cinema of Exhaustion." *From Hester Street to Hollywood: The Jewish-American Stage and Screen*, edited by Sarah Blacher Cohen, Indiana UP, 1983, pp. 245–56.
Van Riper, A. Bowdoin. "Spy Versus Reality: *Get Smart*, Satire, and Absurdity." *The 25 Sitcoms That Changed Television: Turning Points in American Culture*, edited by Laura Westengard and Aaron Barlow, Praeger, 2018, pp. 54–67.
Wyse, Bruce. "'The Human Senses Are Insurmountable Barriers': Deformity, Sympathy, and Monster Love in Three Variations on *Frankenstein*." *Global Frankenstein*, edited

by Carol Margaret Davison and Marie Mulvey-Roberts, Palgrave Macmillan, 2018, pp. 75–90.

Journal Articles

Antelyes, Peter. "'Haim Afen Range': The Jewish Indian and the Redface Western." *MELUS: The Journal of the Society for the Study of Multi-Ethnic Literature of the United States*, vol. 34, no. 3, Fall 2009, pp. 15–42.
Atlas, Jacoba, and Mel Brooks. "New Hollywood: Mel Brooks Interview." *Film Comment*, vol. 11, no. 2, Mar.-Apr. 1975, pp. 54–7.
Bonnstetter, Beth E. "Mel Brooks Meets Kenneth Burke (and Mikhail Bakhtin): Comedy and Burlesque in Satiric Film." *Journal of Film & Video*, vol. 63, no. 1, Spring 2011, pp. 18–31.
Brennan, Matthew C. "Mary Shelley's Cinematic Progeny: The Fidelity of *Young Frankenstein*." *South Carolina Review*, vol. 48, no. 1, Fall 2015, pp. 195–202.
Cameron, S. Brooke, and Suyin Olguin. "A Very Victorian Feast: Food and the Importance of Consumption in Modern Adaptations of *Dracula*." *Journal of Dracula Studies*, vol. 15, 2013, pp. 65–92.
Cawelti, John G. "The Gunfighter and the Hard-Boiled Dick: Some Ruminations on American Fantasies of Heroism." *American Studies*, vol. 16, no. 2, 1975, pp. 49–64.
Elliot, Mark. "*Spaceballs*: The Special Effects." *Cinefex*, no. 31, Aug. 1987, pp. 4–25.
Fermaglich, Kirsten. "Mel Brooks's *The Producers*: Tracing American Jewish Culture through Comedy, 1967–2007." *American Studies*, vol. 48, no. 4, Winter 2007, pp. 59–87.
Greely, Henry T. "*Frankenstein* and Modern Bioscience: Which Story Should We Heed?" *Huntington Library Quarterly: Studies in English and American History and Literature*, vol. 83, no. 4, Winter 2020, pp. 799–821.
Greenberg, Jonathan. "Springtime for *Ulysses*." *PMLA: Publications of the Modern Language Association of America*, vol. 136, no. 5, Oct. 2021, pp. 728–45.
Gubar, Susan. "Racial Camp in *The Producers* and *Bamboozled*." *Film Quarterly*, vol. 60, no. 2, Winter 2006–2007, pp. 26–37.
Heffernan, James A.W. "Looking at the Monster: *Frankenstein* and Film." *Critical Inquiry*, vol. 24, no. 1, Autumn 1997, pp. 133–58.
Hug, Bill. "*Blazing Saddles* as Postmodern Ethnic Carnival." *Studies in Popular Culture*, vol. 36, no. 1, Fall 2013, pp. 63–81.
Jenkins, Tricia. "Feminism, Nationalism, and the 1960s' Slender Spies: A Look at *Get Smart* and *The Girl from U.N.C.L.E.*" *Journal of Popular Film & Television*, vol. 43, no. 1, Jan.-Mar. 2015, pp. 14–27.
Liakos, Panos, and Ioannis Papadimitriou. "Parodying the Monsters…and Loving It!" *Journal of Dracula Studies*, vol. 23, 2021, pp. 55–75.
McDonald, Paul. "'They're Trying to Kill Me': Jewish American Humor and the War against Pop Culture." *Studies in Popular Culture*, vol. 28, no. 3, Apr. 2006, pp. 19–33.
Merwin, Ted. "Jew-Face: Non-Jews Playing Jews on the American Stage." *Cultural & Social History*, vol. 4, no. 2, 2007, pp. 215–33.
Moshin, Jamie. "On the Big Screen, but Stuck in the Closet: What Mel Brooks's *The Producers* Says About Modern American Jewish Identity and Communicating the Holocaust." *Journal of the Northwest Communication Association*, vol. 35, Spring 2006, pp. 22–45.
Phillips, W.D., and Isabel Pinedo. "Gilligan and Captain Kirk Have More in Common Than You Think: 1960s Camp TV as an Alternative Genealogy for Cult TV." *The Journal of Popular Television*, vol. 6, no. 1, Mar. 2018, pp. 19–40.
Potgieter, Zelda. "From Freud to Funny Music in Films: The Case of *Blazing Saddles*." *Communicatio: South African Journal for Communication Theory & Research*, vol. 39, no. 3, 2013, pp. 344–61.
Schiff, Ellen. "Sinners, Scandals, Scoundrels, and Scamps on the American Jewish Stage." *American Jewish History*, vol. 91, no. 1, Mar. 2003, pp. 83–96.
Sebesta, Judith. "From Celluloid to Stage: The 'Movical,' *The Producers*, and the Postmodern." *Theatre Annual*, vol. 56, 2003, pp. 97–112.

Magazine and Newspaper Articles

Arnold, Gary. "Inside Mel Brooks: A Complex Funnyman." *Boston Globe*, 5 Mar. 1978, pp. A8+.
Brooks, Mel. "Springtime for the Music Man in Me." *New York Times*, 15 Apr. 2001, pp. AR1+.
_____. "The World According to Mel Brooks." *New York Times*, 7 June 1981, pp. D1+.
Champlin, Charles. "Mel Brooks Is Finally Taken Seriously." *Los Angeles Times*, 29 Dec. 1974, pp. L1+.
Chozick, Amy. "Mel Brooks: 'The 2,000 Year Old Man,' at 85." *Wall Street Journal*, 12 Aug. 2011, p. D5.
Christiansen, Richard. "It's a Classic Case of Chutzpah." *Los Angeles Times*, 11 Feb. 2001, pp. G8+.
Cohn, Al. "Mel Brooks: 'The Laugh Is the Answer': The LI Interview." *Newsday*, 21 July 1974, pp. E12+.
Crews, Chip. "The Producer: Nearly 78, Mel Brooks Still Has a Song in His Heart, A Skip in His Step and a Monster Hit on His Hands." *Washington Post*, 27 June 2004, pp. N1+.
Gelmis, Joseph. "But Seriously Folks, Mel Brooks Is One of the Brightest People You're Gonna Run Into In Your Life: Just Ask Him." *Newsday*, 21 Jan. 1971, p. 3A.
Gorov, Linda. "Mel Brooks Politically Incorrect." *Moment Magazine*, Nov./Dec. 2010, pp. 27-31.
Gostin, Nicki, and Cathleen McGuigan. "The Pride of *Frankenstein*." *Newsweek*, 12 Nov. 2007, pp. 72-4.
Hoberman, J. "When the Nazis Became Nudniks." *New York Times*, 15 Apr. 2001, pp. AR13+.
McKinnon, George. "'I Happen To Be Sensational—That's My Problem': Now a Filmmaker, Brooks Can't Get Serious." *Boston Globe*, 22 Nov. 1970, pp. A25-26.
Mitchell, Lisa. "…And Please Love Melvin Brooks!" *Saturday Evening Post*, May/June 1978, pp. 63+.
Noland, Eric. "The Many Faces of Mel." *Emmy*, Jan. 2013, pp. 60-3.
Schaap, Dick. "A Man Who Makes Us Laugh: What You Should Know about Mel Brooks's Humor." *Boston Globe*, 22 Jan. 1984, pp. SMA16+.
Siskel, Gene. "Mel Brooks: He's Worth a Million…Laughs, That Is." *Chicago Tribune*, 1 Aug. 1976, pp. E2+.
_____. "Mel Brooks Is Funnier Than Ever, If He Does Say So Himself—And He Does." *Chicago Tribune*, 27 Feb. 1983, pp. D8+.
_____. "No Kidding, Mel Brooks Is a Serious Filmmaker." *Chicago Tribune*, 6 Nov. 1977, pp. E2+.
_____. "Stars Go Pell-Mel for *Silent Movie*." *Chicago Tribune*, 2 Aug. 1976, p. D4.
Unger, Arthur. "Chat with a Comedy Sensation: Mel Brooks, Writer/Director." *Christian Science Monitor*, 8 Sept. 1975, p. 20.
"Way Off Broadway." *Film Review*, Jan. 2006, pp. 70-3.

Interviews on YouTube

Allen, Steve. *Interview with Mel Brooks*. [Video]. (1968, April 1). YouTube. https://www.youtube.com/watch?v=e189RZfnWDc
Carson, Johnny. *Interview with Mel Brooks*. [Video]. (1975, February 13). YouTube. https://www.youtube.com/watch?v=WYuv-8SjjPg
_____. *Interview with Mel Brooks*. [Video]. (1983, December 15). YouTube. https://www.youtube.com/watch?v=M5zo_woibvI
_____. *Interview with Mel Brooks*. [Video]. (1992, May 19). YouTube. https://www.youtube.com/watch?v=vMmNm1CiSGE
Cavett, Dick. *Interview with Mel Brooks*. [Video]. (1970, April 6). YouTube. https://www.youtube.com/watch?v=QUd___tPbRE

_____. Interview with Robert Altman, Peter Bogdanovich, Mel Brooks, and Frank Capra. [Video]. (1972, January 21). YouTube. https://www.youtube.com/watch?v=7yCQ_ko28IQ
Denton, Andrew. Interview with Mel Brooks. [Video]. (2004, April 19). YouTube. https://www.youtube.com/watch?v=bV4aLwQTblI
King, Larry. Interview with Mel Brooks, Carl Reiner, and Sid Caesar. [Video]. (1995, October). YouTube. https://www.youtube.com/watch?v=fsEFfH0nytU
Rose, Charlie. Interview with Mel Brooks and Carl Reiner. [Video]. (1997, October 9). YouTube. https://www.youtube.com/watch?v=ovKJbf5dWBg
Wogan, Terry. Interview with Mel Brooks. [Video]. (1984, February 18). YouTube. https://www.youtube.com/watch?v=WuzAm70xLJ8
Wolsgaard-Iversen, Henrik. *Interview with Mel Brooks*. [Video]. (1978, September 2). YouTube. https://www.youtube.com/watch?v=OxZw16Ol41A

Reviews of Brooks' Memoir and Biographies

Mel Brooks' *All About Me! My Remarkable Life in Show Business* **(Ballantine Books, 2021)**
  Jacobs, Alexandra. "A Legend of Comedy Looks Back in Laughter." *New York Times*, 2 Dec. 2021, p. C7.
  Ryan, Patrick. "Brooks's Best Stories Aren't All about Him." *USA Today*, 2 Dec. 2021, p. D3.
William Holtzman's *Seesaw, a Dual Biography of Anne Bancroft and Mel Brooks* **(Doubleday, 1979)**
  Bandler, Michael J. "Likeable Unlikely Couple." *Christian Science Monitor*, 19 Sept. 1979, p. 18.
  Hershman, Marcie. "Short Takes." *Boston Globe*, 2 Sept 1979, p. A7.
  Kristiana, Gregory. "Brooks & Bancroft: Teaming for Laughs." *Los Angeles Times*, 23 Sept. 1979, p. N34.
James Robert Parish's *It's Good To Be The King: The Seriously Funny Life of Mel Brooks* **(Wiley, 2007)**
  Brown, Liz. "Funny as All Get-Out: Mel Brooks Made a Buck Off Hitler." *New York Times*, 3 June 2007, p. G49.
  Pomerantz, Earl. "*It's Good To Be The King: The Seriously Funny Life of Mel Brooks*." *Television Quarterly*, vol. 38, no. 3/4, Spring/Summer 2007, pp. 62–4.
Patrick McGilligan's *Funny Man: Mel Brooks* **(Harper, 2019)**
  Gimbel, Steven. "A Comedian's Seriously Bad Behavior." *Philadelphia Inquirer*, 7 Apr. 2019, p. K18.
  Itzkoff, Dave. "Ham on Wry." *New York Times*, 2 June 2019, p. A12.
  Kosner, Edward. "Anything for a Laugh." *Wall Street Journal*, 16 Mar. 2019, p. C12.
  O'Neill, Brian. "Blazing Satirist! Unauthorized Biography of Mel Brooks No Laughing Matter." *Pittsburgh Post-Gazette*, 26 May 2019, p. E5.
  Sandlin, Michael. "*Funny Man: Mel Brooks*." *Cineaste*, vol. 45, no. 1, Winter 2019, pp 68–9.

*Reviews of Television Series and Films**
In chronological order

Television Series Co-Created by Mel Brooks

Get Smart (NBC, 1965–1970)
  "Get Smart." *Variety*, 22 Sept. 1965, p. 44.
  Gould, Jack. "TV and Radio: New Programs Reviewed." *New York Times*, 18 Sept. 1965, pp. SUA10:2+.
When Things Were Rotten (ABC, 1975)
  Adler, Dick. "*When Things Were Rotten*." *Los Angeles Times*, 10 Sept. 1975, p. G22.

O'Connor, John J. "Brooks and Robin Hood: Peasants Liven *When Things Were Rotten.*" *New York Times*, 10 Sept. 1975, p. 88.
"*When Things Were Rotten.*" *Variety*, 17 Sept. 1975, p. 47.

The Nutt House (NBC, 1989)
"*The Nutt House.*" *Variety*, 27 Sept. 1989, p. 76.
Rosenberg, Howard. "Lions, Tigers and Crises—Oh, My." *Los Angeles Times*, 20 Sept. 1989, pp. E1+.

Films Directed by Mel Brooks

The Producers (1967)
Adler, Renata. "Screen: *The Producers* at Fine Arts." *New York Times*, 19 Mar. 1968, p. 38.
Champlin, Charles. "Zero Mostel Stars in Comedy *The Producers*." *Los Angeles Times*, 29 Mar. 1968, pp. C1+.
"*The Producers.*" *Variety*, 6 Dec. 1967, p. 6.

The Twelve Chairs (1970)
Canby, Vincent. "Mel Broods on Prowl in Soviet: *12 Chairs*, a Comedy, at Tower East." *New York Times*, 29 Oct. 1970, p. 58.
Champlin, Charles. "*Twelve Chairs* Opens Run." *Los Angeles Times*, 29 Oct. 1970, p. D12.

Blazing Saddles (1974)
"*Blazing Saddles.*" *Variety* 13 Feb. 1974, p. 18.
Canby, Vincent. "*Blazing Saddles*, a Western in Burlesque." *New York Times*, 8 Feb. 1974, p. 21.
Champlin, Charles. "Was the West Ever Like This?" *Los Angeles Times*, 7 Feb. 1974, pp. D1+.
Golden, Daniel. "*Blazing Saddles*: Heading 'Em Off at the Cliché." *Jump Cut: A Review of Contemporary Media*, no. 3, Sept.-Oct. 1974, pp. 3–4.

Young Frankenstein (1974)
Canby, Vincent. "*Young Frankenstein* a Monster Riot." *New York Times*, 16 Dec. 1974, p. 48.
Champlin, Charles. "Portrait of a Young Monster." *Los Angeles Times*, 18 Dec. 1974, pp. F1+.
Hess, Judith W. "*Young Frankenstein*: Some Things Just Aren't Funny." *Jump Cut: A Review of Contemporary Media*, no. 6, Mar.-Apr. 1975, p. 12.
"*Young Frankenstein.*" *Sight & Sound*, vol. 44, Spring 1975, pp. 125–6.
"*Young Frankenstein.*" *Variety*, 18 Dec. 1974, pp. 13+.

Silent Movie (1976)
Canby, Vincent. "*Silent Movie* With Golden Subtitles." *New York Times*, 1 July 1976, p. 22.
Champlin, Charles. "The Fine, Flaky Flow of Silent Brooks." *Los Angeles Times*, 27 June 1976, pp. M1+.
"Film Guide." *Cineaste*, vol. 7, no. 3, Fall 1976, p. 52.
"*Silent Movie.*" *Variety*, 23 June 1976, p. 16.

High Anxiety (1977)
Canby, Vincent. "Mel Brooks in *High Anxiety.*" *New York Times*, 26 Dec. 1977, p. 30.
Champlin, Charles. "Mel Brooks's *High Anxiety.*" *Los Angeles Times*, 23 Dec. 1977, p. G1.
"*High Anxiety.*" *Variety*, 21 Dec. 1977, p. 20.

History of the World: Part I (1981)
Benson, Sheila. "Brooks's *History*: The Formula Turns Sour." *Los Angeles Times*, 11 June 1981, pp. H1+.
"*History of the World: Part I.*" *Variety*, 10 June 1981, pp. 18+.
Maslin, Janet. "Brooks's *History of the World*: From Time Immemorial." *New York Times*, 12 June 1981, p. C14.

Spaceballs (1987)
Maslin, Janet. "Film: *Spaceballs*, A Mel Brooks Comedy." *New York Times*, 24 June 1987, p. C23.

Milne, Tom. "*Spaceballs.*" *Monthly Film Bulletin*, vol. 54, Dec. 1987, pp. 377–8.
"*Spaceballs.*" *Variety*, 24 June 1987, p. 12.
Sutton, Martin. "*Spaceballs.*" *Films & Filming*, no. 399, Dec. 1987, pp. 31–2.
Wilmington, Michael. "*Spaceballs* Stuck In Its Shtick." *Los Angeles Times*, 25 June 1987, pp. G1+.

Life Stinks (1991)
Brown, Geoff. "*Life Stinks.*" *Sight & Sound*, Oct. 1991, p. 52.
Ferguson, Ken. "*Life Stinks.*" *Film Monthly*, vol. 3, Oct. 1991, p. 19.
"*Life Stinks.*" *Variety*, 27 May 1991, p. 80.
Maslin, Janet. "Mel Brooks, From Riches To Rags To Humility." *New York Times*, 26 July 1991, p. C19.
Wilmington, Michael. "Brooks Takes Risks in an Uneven *Life Stinks.*" *Los Angeles Times*, 26 July 1991, p. F8.

Robin Hood: Men In Tights (1993)
Canby, Vincent. "Mel Brooks Aims His Comedic Barbs at Robin Hood et al." *New York Times*, 28 July 1993, pp. C13+.
Grant, Edmond. "*Robin Hood: Men In Tights.*" *Films in Review*, vol. 44, Oct. 1993, pp. 338–9.
Klady, Leonard. "*Robin Hood: Men In Tights.*" *Variety*, 9 Aug. 1993, p. 35.
Macnab, Geoffrey. "*Robin Hood: Men In Tights.*" *Sight & Sound*, Jan. 1994, pp. 51–2.
Rainer, Peter. "*Men In Tights*: A See-Through Laugh." *Los Angeles Times*, 28 July 1993, p. F5.

Dracula: Dead And Loving It (1995)
Kronke, David. "Brooks's *Dracula* Parody: Dead or Undead?" *Los Angles Times*, 22 Dec. 1995, p. F4.
Leydon, Joe. "*Dracula: Dead And Loving It.*" *Variety*, 18 Dec. 1995, p. 67.
Maslin, Janet. "Giving New Fangs to an Old Vampire." *New York Times*, 22 Dec. 1995, p. C35.

About the Contributors

Nathan **Abrams** is a professor of film studies at Bangor University, UK. He is the founding co-editor of *Jewish Film and New Media: An International Journal.* He is the author and editor of many books and articles, including most recently *Kubrick: An Odyssey* (with Robert P. Kolker; Pegasus, 2024).

Ralph **Beliveau** is the area head for creative media production and professional writing at Gaylord College and affiliate faculty in both film and media studies and women and gender studies at the University of Oklahoma. He has written about women in horror, documentary rhetoric, African American noir, Richard Matheson, Shirley Jackson, and Paolo Freire and media literacy, among other topics.

Matthew **Cipa** teaches and researches in film and television studies, aesthetics, and cultural studies at the University of Queensland, Brisbane, and at the Queensland University of Technology, Brisbane. He is the author of *Is Harpo Free? and Other Questions of the Metaphysical Screen* (SUNY Press, 2024).

Jeremy **Dauber** is the Atran Professor of Yiddish Language, Literature and Culture and, for a decade, he directed the Institute of Israel and Jewish Studies at Columbia University, where he also teaches in the American studies program. His most recent books are *American Comics: A History* (W.W. Norton, 2022) and *Mel Brooks: Disobedient Jew* (Yale UP, 2023).

Thomas **Grochowski** is a professor and chair of English at St. Joseph's University, New York. He has published essays on the Marx Brothers, Woody Allen, *Sex and the City,* and recently, on *The Last Waltz* and *I'm Not There.* He is on the editorial board of *Literature/Film Quarterly* and the *Journal of Film and Video.*

Peter Scott **Lederer** is a lecturer in English at Rotherham College in South Yorkshire, England. His areas of expertise include post–Holocaust literature, dark Jewish humor, New Hollywood, and 1960s and 1970s American counterculture. Recent publications have focused on Mike Nichols's *The Graduate* (1967) and Jewish humor in the stories of of Sholem Aleichem, Franz Kafka, Philip Roth, and Ephraim Kishon.

Chris **Lindvall** is an MFA-certified filmmaker and screenwriter from Los Angeles, California. He first worked at Disney where he wore many hats, writing for a Star Wars video game, filming bumpers for Marvel, all while penning jokes for the Muppets to speak in their show at Disneyland.

Terry **Lindvall** has occupied the C.S. Lewis Chair of Communication and Christian Thought at Virginia Welseyan College since 2006. He received his Ph.D. from the University of Southern California and his MDiv from Fuller Theological Seminary. He was a visiting professor at Duke University School of Divinity and the Walter Mason Fellow in Religious Studies at the College of William and Mary.

Michael **Lipiner** is a Ph.D. candidate in film studies at Bangor University in Wales. He created the ongoing film studies program at Bayside High School in conjunction with St. John's University in New York City. His publications are on the topic of American cinema.

Douglas C. **MacLeod**, Jr., is an assistant professor at SUNY Cobleskill where he teaches intercultural communication, script writing, visual media, cinema, mass media, and composition and literature courses. A widely-published inter-disciplinarian, he has presented on various subjects at conferences, including *The Twilight Zone*, Alfred Hitchcock, *Marathon Man*, empathy in the Digital Age, stand-up comedy as a tool for composition writers, and Oliver Stone.

Sue **Matheson** is a professor of English at the University College of the North in Manitoba, Canada. She teaches American literature, Canadian literature, and film and popular culture. Her many interests in film, culture, and literature may be found in more than sixty essays published in a wide range of books and scholarly journals.

Camille **McCutcheon** is the coordinator of collection management for the University of South Carolina Upstate Library and is library liaison for education, physical education, exercise science. She earned a joint master's degree in English and library and information science from USC, and she holds a certificate of advanced graduate study in library and information science.

Cynthia J. **Miller** is a cultural anthropologist specializing in visual media. She teaches in the Marlboro Institute for Liberal Arts at Emerson College and is the editor or co-editor of twenty scholarly volumes, including the recently published *Journeys Into Terror: Essays from the Cinematic Intersection of Travel and Horror* (McFarland, 2023), as well as the author of dozens of articles in journals and edited scholarly volumes.

Frances **Pheasant-Kelly** is a reader in screen studies and director of the Centre for Film, Media, Discourse and Culture at the University of Wolverhampton. Her research centers on American cinema, especially in relation to abject space, the Western, fantasy and 9/11. She is also interested in trauma, medical humanities and the connections between science and visual culture.

Murray **Pomerance** is an independent scholar living in Canada and adjunct professor in the School of Media and Communication at RMIT University, Australia. He is the author of many books, including *A Silence from Hitchcock* (State University of New York Press, 2023), *Color It True: Impressions of Cinema* (Bloomsbury Academic, 2022), and *A Voyage with Hitchcock* (State University of New York Press, 2021).

David L. **Reznik** is a senior professional lecturer in the Department of Sociology at American University in Washington, D.C. His scholarship is at the nexus of critical social theory, intersectional identity politics, and current popular culture. He has published on a variety of topics, including White working-class masculinity in high-profile murder trials, utopian visions among independent Hollywood filmmakers, and queer comradeship in contemporary prestige television.

Kerry **Soper**, a professor in the Department of Comparative Arts and Letters at Brigham Young University, writes about the history of comedy and satire in comic strips, television, film, and other popular media. His books include *Gary Larson and The Far Side* (University Press of Mississippi, 2019) and *We Go Pogo: Walt Kelly, Politics, and American Satire* (University Press of Mississippi, 2012).

A. Bowdoin **Van Riper** is a historian who works for the Martha's Vineyard Museum as a researcher, reference librarian, journal editor, and public historian. He is interested in the intersections of science and technology with society and culture. An award-winning editor, he is also the author of more than thirty articles and five monographs on a wide range of subjects.

Jonathan **Winchell** earned his B.A. at the University of South Carolina in film and media studies, and his M.A. at New York University in cinema studies. He lives in Stillwater, Oklahoma, and is pursuing a Ph.D. in English with an emphasis in screen studies at Oklahoma State University.

Index

Abbott and Costello Meet Frankenstein (1948) 132
absorption 147, 155–157
absurd 21, 22, 25, 32, 68, 69, 114, 121, 124, 126n6, 195, 199–201, 203, 205, 220, 229, 231
adaptation 9, 14n3, 57, 100, 102, 132, 134, 135, 138, 159, 160, 162–164, 166, 167, 170, 218; micro-adaptation 165, 166, 170
Admiral Broadway Revue (television series) 2, 14n7, 127n8
Advise and Consent (1962) 196
Agent 99 57, 67, 68
Alfred Hitchcock Presents (television series) 178
Alice Doesn't Live Here Anymore (1974) 211
Alice in Wonderland (2010) 165
Allen, Woody 6, 14n7, 34n1, 40, 46, 104, 211
allusion 46, 47, 78, 82, 119, 140, 164, 166, 167, 169, 225
American Character 117, 118
American Dream 2, 125
anagnorisis 124
anarchy 6, 110, 194
anachronism 9, 47, 109, 124
Anger Management (2003) 211
anti-hero 4, 20
anti-Semitism 18, 32, 72, 74, 81, 227, 232, 236; *see also* racism
Aristophanes 50, 113
assimilation 18, 13, 77, 154, 227, 228, 232, 233, 235, 236
amateur 6, 46, 181
auteur 5, 10, 56, 60, 63–66, 69, 70, 186, 290, 210, 217, 218, 220
The Avengers (television series) 65

Bancroft, Anne 6, 24, 38, 40, 79, 146, 154, 209, 212, 214, 217
The Bank Dick (1940) 211

Barry Lyndon (1975) 72
Barthes, Roland 155
Barton Fink (1991) 224
Baudrillard, Jean 118, 120–123, 125
Ben-Hur (1959) 196, 200
Beverly Hills Cop (1984) 211
The Bible: In the Beginning (1966) 198, 201
The Bicycle Thief (1948) 3, 113, 210
The Big Chill (1983) 219
bigotry 7, 39, 49, 202
The Birds (1963) 12, 47, 178, 189–191, 220
black comedy 11, 72, 83, 84; *see also* irony
Black Sunday (1960) 200
Blazing Saddles (1974) 3–6, 10, 11, 14n5, 14n6, 24, 29, 30, 42–44, 46, 48, 49, 56, 61, 70, 84n1, 96, 102, 108–127, 147, 159–162, 168, 169, 186, 194, 198, 205, 210, 211, 219, 220
Blow-Up (1966) 167
Bonanza (television series) 119, 120
Bond Girl 58, 65, 68
Bond, James 4, 10, 41, 58, 60, 65–67, 70, 205
Borscht Belt 2, 14n11, 20, 27, 34n1, 40, 88
Brecht, Bertolt 19, 125, 127n10
bricolage 119, 120
Bride of Frankenstein (1935) 81, 131–133, 136, 139, 142–144
Broadway 4, 8, 10, 12, 14n6, 26, 29, 33, 42, 77, 83, 87–89, 91–94, 102, 114, 160, 161, 164, 199, 209
Brooks, Mel; army 12, 74; auteur 5, 9, 10, 56, 60, 63–66, 69, 70, 186, 209, 210; Broadway 2, 4, 10, 12, 26, 28, 33, 92, 209; brother 01, 74, 210; childhood 1, 60; cabaret 9, 10, 21, 22, 25–29, 32, 42, 119; father 1, 24, 38; Hollywood 1–5, 8, 9, 14n6, 22, 24, 26, 43, 61, 112, 211, 212, 215, 216, 220; Hollywood star 6, 14n6; mother 1, 7, 24, 38, 60, 210; television 4, 5, 9–13, 20, 39–41, 56, 60, 63–65, 72, 96, 103, 106, 108, 152, 161, 205, 209, 239

265

266 Index

Brooksfilms 12, 121, 209, 213, 214, 216
Buffy the Vampire Slayer (1992) 164
Burke's Law (television series) 65
burlesque 4, 8, 40–42, 48, 111, 133

cabaret 9, 10, 18–34, 42, 114, 119; Weimar cabaret 18, 22, 23, 26, 29–31
Cabaret (1972) 27, 28, 114, 119
Caesar, Sid 2, 4, 6, 13n2, 14n7, 34n1, 40, 63, 64, 76, 113, 114, 126n6, 127n13, 146, 160, 161, 199, 203, 209
Caesar's Hour (television series) 13n2, 114
Caesar's writers 14n7, 113, 114
Call Northside 777 (1948) 167
camp 10, 27, 78, 117
Candid Camera (television series) 102
The Candid Microphone (television series) 102
capitalism 7, 9, 234, 243, 245, 246
caricature 25, 27, 30, 31, 41, 92, 229; *see also* irony
carnivalesque 62, 65, 110, 115, 117
Carson, Johnny 1, 8
Catch-22 (book) 102
Chagall, Marc 109, 125
Chariots of Fire (1981) 196
chutzpah 39, 108, 235; *see also* Yiddish
Citizen Kane (1941) 210
City Lights (1931) 211
Clueless (1995) 224
The Cobweb (1955) 167
comedy 2–13, 14n6, 18–20, 23, 25, 31, 33, 34, 38–40, 42, 43, 45, 48, 50, 60–62, 64, 67–69, 76, 80, 82, 84, 84n1, 88–90, 94, 96, 99–103, 108–111, 118, 119, 123, 125, 126, 131, 133, 135, 140, 144, 146–148, 150–152, 155, 157, 159, 161, 162, 167, 178, 180, 181, 183, 189, 191, 198, 209, 211, 212, 229, 233, 239, 242, 243, 246–249, 252
comic frenzy 120, 124
commedia dell'arte 111, 117, 121, 123
concentration camp 30, 31, 79, 90, 91
consumerism 226, 233, 236
counterculture 3, 18, 244
cowboy 43, 47, 48, 108, 109, 114–116, 121, 122, 124, 126n2, 127n18, 210, 220, 234
Cowboy Code 116, 118
The Critic (1963) 104, 111, 147–150, 153, 156, 157, 252
Cronenberg, David 190, 217–220
The Curse of Frankenstein (1957) 81
Curly Sue (1991) 243

Dali, Salvador 11, 111–112, 125, 190
Dead Souls (book) 6, 113
The Dead Zone (1983) 218

Der blaue Engel (1930) 19, 29, 30, 42, 114, 119
Der ewige Jude (1940) 30
Destry Rides Again (1939) 30, 42, 114
Dial M for Murder (1954) 166
Dietrich, Marlene 23, 28, 42
dolly zoom 181
Dostoyevsky, Fyodor 46, 99, 113
Dr. Strangelove or: How I Learned to Stop Worrying and Love the Bomb (1964) 73–83, 84n1
Dracula (1931) 135, 142
Dracula (1958) 135
Dracula: Dead and Loving It (1995) 102, 162, 205, 211, 220

Eisenstein, Sergei 156, 183, 188–189
El Dorado (1966) 118, 120
El Topo (1970) 213
The Elephant Man (1980) 12, 209–211, 213, 217, 219
Emanuelle (1974) 206n6
émigré 73, 74, 83
Les Enfants du Paradis (1945) 210
epic 9, 12, 112, 125, 132, 194, 196, 198, 199, 201–203, 206n7, 206n8, 225
Eraserhead (1977) 213–215
Evil Dead 2 (1987) 195
expressionism 11, 131, 136, 137, 144, 186, 187

fascism 7, 78, 226, 232, 233
Fast Company (1979) 211
Fear and Desire (1953) 72
feminism 58, 68, 245
femininity 58, 67
femme fatale 140, 181
Fiddler on the Roof (1964) 32, 92
film noir 131, 139, 140, 181
The Fisher King (1991) 243
The Fly (1986) 12, 209, 210, 217–220
folklore 11, 81, 83, 100
fool 21, 23, 39, 56, 62, 66–68, 80, 111, 115, 117, 126, 230, 241
foolishness 14n4, 62, 67
fourth wall 2, 43, 124, 139, 199, 205
Frankenstein (1931) 81, 131–134, 138, 139, 142, 144, 210
A Frenchman in Lincoln's America (book) 8
Frenzy (1972) 159, 166, 190
Full Metal Jacket (1987) 73
A Funny Thing Happened on the Way to the Forum (1966) 92

gag 13, 20, 40, 41, 43, 69, 70, 109, 110, 124, 125, 147, 160, 198, 199, 203, 231

Index 267

genocide 11, 74, 83
genre film 56, 60, 61, 198
Gentile 3, 4, 8, 18, 19, 21, 23, 24, 28, 30, 31, 34, 45, 61, 66, 228, 230, 231, 233–235, 237
Get Smart (television series) 4, 5, 10, 14n8, 41, 56–70, 96, 102, 108, 126n1
The Godfather (1970) 102
Gogol, Nikolai 6, 11, 113, 125
Gold Diggers of 1933 (1933) 26
Goldfinger (1964) 57–59, 65, 70
golem 11, 80, 83
The Golem: How He Came Into the World (1920) 81
Grand Hotel (1932) 96
La Grande Illusion (1937) 210
grotesque 9, 11, 28, 51, 62, 89, 113, 114, 116, 122, 123, 125, 200, 211
Gunfight at the O.K. Corral (1957) 127cf
Gunsmoke (television series) 120

Hellzapoppin' (1941) 119
Henry, Buck 4, 41, 63, 64, 66, 69
hero 1, 13, 19, 48, 58, 59, 61, 62, 65, 66, 68, 73, 79, 89, 100, 116, 160, 165, 170, 198, 200, 202, 203, 225, 234
High Anxiety (1977) 11–12, 14n6, 26, 27, 34, 42, 43, 47, 48, 102, 147, 159–174, 178–190, 205, 211, 212, 220
High Noon (1952) 118, 120, 127n16
History of the World, Part I (1981) 6, 12, 14n6, 162, 194–206, 225, 227, 235
History of the World, Part II (2023) 6
Hitchcock, Alfred 47, 146, 159–165, 169–172, 174, 175n1, 178–181, 184–191
Hitler 22, 23, 25–27, 30, 31, 33, 34, 72–80, 82, 83, 87–94, 123, 197, 232
Hollywood 1–6, 8–11, 14n6, 18–19, 21–24, 26, 43, 56, 60, 61, 66, 67, 70, 81, 102, 105, 112, 114, 120, 122, 124, 125, 131, 147, 159, 162, 170, 187, 194, 196, 201, 202, 206, 211–215, 218
Holocaust 10, 11, 21, 22, 24, 72–74, 77, 79, 80, 83, 84, 88, 91, 94
homage 132–139, 143, 144
homosexual 33, 26, 28–29, 33, 78, 79, 122
Honey West (television series) 65
Honey I Shrunk the Kids (1989) 165
horror 7, 30, 43, 47, 73, 83, 88, 90, 91, 97, 102, 131–136, 139, 147, 159, 173, 180, 196, 200, 205, 210–213, 217–220
How the West Was Won (1962) 198, 201, 206n10
Hugo (2011) 211
humor 8, 10, 18, 21, 22, 25, 27, 72, 89, 93, 106, 143, 151, 160, 205, 216, 233
Hutcheon, Linda 60, 133, 159

hypermasculinity 28, 231; *see also* masculinity

I Spy (television series) 65
identity 3, 13, 14, 18, 58, 59, 62, 64, 68, 76, 77, 80, 103, 174, 218, 232, 233, 236, 240–242, 250; *see also* Jewish identity
idiocy 62, 90
improvise 45, 65, 74, 105, 161, 180
innuendo 11, 22, 75, 131, 142, 144
irony 6, 45, 68, 88, 121, 133, 156; *see also* black comedy; caricature; lampoon; paradox; parody; satire; spoof
intertextuality 11, 50, 63, 132–136, 139, 141, 144, 164, 167, 225
Intolerance (1916) 196
It's a Gift (1934) 211

Jewish diaspora 232, 233, 236
Jewish identity 10, 19, 21, 22, 38, 61, 62, 160, 224–228, 230, 233, 235
Jewishness 10, 12, 22, 28, 34, 62, 72, 76, 79, 224–227, 229, 231, 235
Jewish filmmakers 19, 84, 160
Jules and Jim (1962) 188
juxtaposition 26, 105, 113, 116, 119, 124, 126, 201, 203

Kafka, Franz 22, 23
Kahn, Madeline 29, 30, 42, 115, 126n4, 127n12
King Lear 39
Kubrick, Stanley 10–11, 72–81, 83–84, 84n1, 201, 203, 210, 211

Lacan, Jacques 59–61
Laemmle, Carl 9, 39
lampoon 12, 41, 43, 56, 59, 65, 70, 78, 115, 117, 194, 200, 205; *see also* irony
Land of the Pharaohs (1955) 194
The Last Temptation of Christ (1988) 211
Le Petomane, William J. 116
Life of Brian (1979) 198
The Lodger (1927) 171, 172
Life Stinks (1991) 10, 12, 239–250
Lolita (1962) 73–81
Lynch, David 12, 209–220

MacGuffin 189–191
Mad About You (television series) 161
Madame Curie (1943) 196
The Man from U.N.C.L.E. (television series) 65, 205
The Man Who Knew Too Much (1956) 170
Man Without a Star (1955) 127n16
Marnie (1964) 175n1
Marx, Groucho 62, 64, 140, 197

268 Index

masculinity 26, 58; *see also* hypermasculinity
melting pot 8, 14n10, 152
mensch 106, 220
Merrick, Joseph 213
The Metamorphosis (book) 21
A Midsummer Night's Dream (play) 195
Million Dollar Mermaid (1952) 27
mise-en-scène 11, 92, 131, 132, 135, 136, 139, 140, 144
Moby Dick (book) 40, 126n6
Molière 113
monster 88, 90, 93, 135, 214, 220; Frankenstein's monster 4, 28, 42, 81–83, 136–138, 143, 144, 191, 210
Monsieur Hulot's Holiday (1953) 211
montage 184–189
monster 4, 28, 42, 81–83, 88, 91, 93, 135–138, 143, 144, 191, 210, 214, 220
Mostel, Zero 22, 31–32, 34n1, 87, 88, 92, 252
Mr. Flip (1909) 123
The Music Man (1962) 199
musical 10, 14cf, 21, 23, 24, 26, 27, 33, 34, 40, 42, 43, 60, 76, 78, 79, 87–89, 93, 106, 114, 122, 131, 134, 139, 140, 161, 188, 189, 191, 199, 209
My Man Godfrey (1936) 247

nebbish 67, 76, 80, 84, 231–233; *see also* Yiddish
New York City 1, 3, 5, 7, 8, 12, 31, 39, 46, 72, 73, 102, 104, 108, 111, 112, 141, 143
North by Northwest (1959) 12, 164–166, 172, 174, 178, 185, 190, 191
Notorious (1946) 166, 172
The Nutt House (television series) 161

Olympia (1938) 30
Once Upon a Time in the West (1968) 119
One Flew Over the Cuckoo's Nest (1975) 167, 169
One Million Years B.C. (1966) 200
Open City (1945) 3, 113
opera 24, 29, 42, 102, 155, 196, 236
Ordinary People (1980) 217
Other 82, 84, 225
Otherness 19, 44

pantomime 4, 19, 31, 198
paradox 6, 7, 50, 114; *see also* irony
parody 3, 4 , 8, 11, 12, 19, 26–28, 39, 41–49, 56, 57, 59–60, 61, 63, 64, 67, 70, 72, 78, 82, 97, 102, 111, 113, 114, 119, 127n12, 132–137, 141–144, 147, 151, 159, 160, 162, 164, 165, 167, 168, 178, 181, 187, 189–191, 194, 198, 201, 205, 211, 224–226, 233; *see also* irony

pastiche 8, 10, 12, 39, 50, 119, 132–133, 156, 164, 162, 174, 187, 189, 230
Paths of Glory (1957) 72, 79
picaresque 10, 103, 104, 106
picaro 103, 106; *see also* trickster
Picasso 43, 111, 113, 122, 215
Picnic at Hanging Rock (1975) 196
Pickens, Slim 84n1
Pink Flamingos (1972) 213, 214
The Pit and the Pendulum (1961) 200
A Place in the Sun (1950) 91
The Producers (1967) 5, 6, 9–11, 14cf, 20–22, 24, 25–28, 31–34, 73, 76, 78, 82, 84n2, 87–96, 102, 104, 110, 112–114, 160, 161, 164, 202, 210, 252
Psycho (1960) 12, 162, 168, 169, 174, 178, 186, 188–191
The Prisoner of Zenda (1952) 200
punchline 89, 169
pun 33, 199
pure cinema 12, 178–180, 183, 185–189, 191
Pushkin, Aleksandr 113
Puzo, Mario 102

Quo Vadis (1951) 194, 200

Rabelais 8, 9, 43, 48, 51, 115, 123
racism 10, 39, 49, 61, 62, 64, 11, 125, 127n17; *see also* anti-Semitism
Rashomon (1950) 210
Rawhide (television series) 119, 120
Rear Window (1954) 12, 171, 173, 174, 178, 188–190
Rebecca (1940) 133, 140, 166
Reiner, Carl 7, 14n7, 40, 41, 64, 96, 102, 113, 126n6, 153, 161, 209
Robin Hood: Men in Tights (1993) 9, 102, 162, 205
The Rocky Horror Picture Show (1975) 28, 213
Rio Bravo (1959) 118
Romeo + Juliet (1996) 164
Ronnie Rocket (unfinished film) 213
Roseanne (television series) 211

Saboteur (1942) 169
Sartor Resartus (book) 2
satire 2, 3, 6, 10, 11, 22, 25, 31, 48, 69, 70, 74, 83, 91, 97–101, 103, 104, 112–115, 125, 133, 224, 226, 227, 230, 248; *see also* irony
schlemiel 67, 76, 84, 231
Schindler's List (1993) 224
schmuck 83
schtick 45, 48, 69, 92, 101
science fiction 102, 167, 196, 217–219, 224–226
Seinfeld (television series) 211

Index

self-reflection 156, 187
Shadow of a Doubt (1943) 178
Shane (1953) 127n13
The Short Night (unfinished film) 159
The Sick Humor of Lenny Bruce (album) 25
sign 80, 102, 121, 123, 124, 142, 170, 198, 201
signifier 131, 152, 237
silent film 101, 147, 149, 151, 153, 154, 155, 157, 159, 171, 188, 212
Silent Movie (1975) 5, 6, 11, 14n6, 97, 102, 146–157, 159, 162, 186, 205, 212
The Simpsons (television series) 211
simulacra 120–122, 124
simulation 121
Sinatra, Frank 42, 161, 162
Singin' in the Rain (1952) 199
Smart, Maxwell 57, 66–69
Son of Frankenstein (1939) 142
Sontag, Susan 27, 117
Spaceballs (1987) 12, 14n6, 46, 47, 89, 102, 162, 163, 167–169, 205, 224, 237
Spartacus (1960) 73, 78, 84
spectacle 18, 20, 26–28, 30, 34, 48, 57–60, 115, 138, 187, 194
spoof 4, 41, 47, 48, 56, 69, 114, 127, 160, 200, 210–212, 220, 224; *see also* irony
Springtime for Hitler (fictional musical) 10, 22, 26–28, 33, 42, 76, 78, 79, 87–89, 91, 92, 94, 202
Stage Fright (1950) 127n12
star 1, 6, 14n6, 32, 33, 115, 119, 146, 147, 152–155, 157, 197, 210, 219
Star Wars (franchise) 8, 45, 100, 167, 226, 228, 230–234
stereotypes 9, 18–20, 28, 30, 32, 34, 49, 61, 62, 80, 118, 121, 228–233, 241, 244, 248
The Story of Mankind (1957) 196, 197, 201, 206n10
Strangers on a Train (1951) 12, 178, 180, 181, 184, 185, 187, 189, 191
Sullivan's Travels (1941) 247
surrealist 111–112, 119, 125, 190
surreality 11, 119, 120, 123, 125, 126n6
Suspicion (1941) 166

A Tale of Two Cities (1935) 200
Teufelsdröckh, Diogenes 2
"Tex X" (film treatment) 5, 108
theater 8, 22, 24, 27, 29, 60, 62, 75, 78–82, 88, 92–94, 105, 109, 112, 124, 138, 139, 153, 160, 162, 230
theatricality 11, 117, 147, 155–157
Third Reich 21, 232
The 39 Steps (1935) 166
The Three Musketeers (1948) 194, 200

3:10 to Yuma (1957) 127n16
The Threepenny Opera (1928) 19, 24, 29
To Be or Not to Be (1983) 24, 28, 34, 73, 76, 78–80
Tolkin, Mel 14n7, 113, 126n6
Tolstoy, Leo 5, 113
The Tonight Show (television series) 1, 8
Top Hat (1935) 119
The Tower of London (1962) 200
The Treasure of the Sierra Madre (1948) 118
trickster 62, 67, 68, 100; *see also picaro*
Triumph des Willens (1935) 30
The Trouble with Harry (1955) 178
tumler 12, 14n11, 40
The Twelve Chairs (1970) 2, 5, 8, 10, 14cf, 25, 46, 96–106, 111, 113
2001: A Space Odyssey (1968) 84, 200, 201
The 2000-Year-Old Man (album) 7, 12, 38, 41, 153, 161

v-effeckt 114, 127cf
Vertigo (1958) 12, 165, 166, 170, 178, 179, 181, 182, 185, 189–191
Videodrome (1983) 218
vulgarity 5–6, 43, 48, 49, 51, 62, 74, 105, 106, 109, 114, 115, 203

Wayne, John 3, 112
Western 3, 4, 7, 41–43, 57, 58, 60, 61, 84n1, 97, 102, 110, 111, 114–126, 127n18, 139, 140, 147, 159, 160, 168, 196, 205, 211, 212
Westworld (1973) 120
What We Do in the Shadows (2014) 195
When Things Were Rotten (television series) 161
The Wide World of Sports (television series) 119
Wilder, Gene 28, 44, 46, 87, 88, 93, 127, 132, 135, 140, 141, 252
wit 39, 69, 100, 178, 183
Witchfinder General (1968) 200
The Wizard of Oz (1939) 123, 165, 167, 169, 234
Wogan, Terry 2
Woman of the Year (1949) 91
The World of Salvador Dalí (book) 112
World War II 2, 12, 25, 72–74, 77, 79, 80, 91, 93, 103, 112, 172, 196

Yiddish 7, 14n4, 23, 25, 28, 29, 33, 93, 105, 127n11, 231, 232, 233; *chutzpah; mensch; nebbish; schlemiel; schmuck; schtick*
Young Frankenstein (1974) 4, 6, 7, 10, 11, 14n6, 28, 42–44, 47, 56, 70, 81–83, 96, 102, 131–144, 147, 159–162, 186, 191, 194, 205, 211, 212, 216, 252

Your Show of Shows (television series) 3, 4, 12, 13n2, 14n7, 40, 64, 76, 96, 111, 113, 114, 126–127n6, 127n7, 161, 163, 209, 211

zani 74, 88, 111–113
Zionism 228, 232, 234, 235
Zukor, Adolph 9

www.ingramcontent.com/pod-product-compliance
Ingram Content Group UK Ltd.
Pitfield, Milton Keynes, MK11 3LW, UK
UKHW041937210426
5322IPUK00016B/234